GOERING

GOERING

The Rise and Fall of the
Notorious Nazi Leader

ROGER MANVELL
AND HEINRICH FRAENKEL

FRONTLINE BOOKS, LONDON   SKYHORSE PUBLISHING, NEW YORK

Skyhorse Publishing books may be purchased in bulk at special discounts for sales promotion, corporate gifts, fund-raising, or educational purposes. Special editions can also be created to specifications. For details, contact the Special Sales Department, Skyhorse Publishing, 307 West 36th Street, 11th Floor, New York, NY 10018 or info@skyhorsepublishing.com.

www.skyhorsepublishing.com

This edition published in 2011 by Frontline Books, an imprint of Pen & Sword Books Limited, 47 Church Street, Barnsley, S. Yorkshire, S70 2AS. For more information on Frontline books, please visit www.frontline-books.com, email info@frontline-books.com, or write to us at the above address.

Skyhorse edition: ISBN 978-1-61608-109-6
Frontline edition: ISBN 978-1-84832-600-2

10 9 8 7 6 5 4

Library of Congress Cataloging-in-Publication Data

Manvell, Roger, 1909-1987.
 Goering : the rise and fall of the notorious Nazi leader / Roger Manvell and Heinrich Fraenkel.
    p. cm.
 Originally published: New York : Simon and Schuster, 1962.
 Includes bibliographical references and index.
 ISBN 978-1-61608-109-6 (pbk. : alk. paper)
 1. Göring, Hermann, 1893-1946. 2. Nazis--Biography. 3. Politicians--Germany--
Biography. 4. Generals--Germany--Biography. 5. Germany. Heer--Officers--Biography.
6. Germany. Luftwaffe--Officers--Biography. 7. Hitler, Adolf, 1889-1945--Friends and
associates. 8. Germany--History--1918-1933--Biography. 9. Germany--History--1933-
1945--Biography. I. Fraenkel, Heinrich, 1897-1986, joint author. II. Title. III. Title: Göring.
 DD247.G67M3 2011
 943.086092--dc22
 [B]
                            2010041075

A CIP data record for this title is available from the British Library.

Printed in the United States of America

CONTENTS

INTRODUCTION

HERMANN GOERING *took poison in his cell on the night of October 15, 1946, little more than an hour before he was due to be led to the scaffold erected in the gymnasium at Nuremberg jail. He died by his own hand to demonstrate that he was still master of his destiny, the last Napoleon of the Nazi regime which he had defended with such energy and skill before the International Military Tribunal that eventually condemned him to death by hanging. His guilt, according to the wording of his sentence, was "unique in its enormity."*

Neither Heinrich Fraenkel nor I really understood Goering when we began the research for this biography. We had read a great deal about him in the many histories of the Third Reich, in which he seems to figure like some inanimate giant waiting to be brought to life beside the extraordinary and closely observed character of his master, Hitler. Attempts to solve the enigma of this ace pilot of the First World War who became an exile and a deranged drug addict, this man whom Hitler did not want to take back into the Nazi movement but who became the second ranking Nazi in the Reich, were made a few years after the Second World War in the short but useful biographies written by Butler and Young and by Frischauer. But since then a great deal of new evidence has become available, some published, some still unpublished, which we studied alongside the fresh and often startling testimony given us by men and women who, in various capacities, had known Goering well and who felt themselves free to talk more explicitly now than they had done in the past, or to speak now for the first time. Many of them revealed new and important facts.

At first, the more we discovered about Goering the deeper the mystery of his character became. At one moment we were dealing with the simple, devoted husband, the man kneeling to pray with an overflow of emotion in the little private chapel in Stockholm belonging to the family of his Swedish wife Carin, and at the next

*we were faced with the evidence of the heartless organizer of slave
labor, extortion and starvation in the countries occupied by the
Reich. The initiator of some of the fairest and most humane game
laws in Europe also put his name to the decrees setting up concentration camps in which, he admitted, brutality must inevitably take
place. These things were perhaps understandable in the strange
dichotomy of the Nazi mentality to which by now we, along no
doubt with most of our readers, have become accustomed. But how
could one reconcile the childish, epicene vanity of the man who,
while entertaining guests at his mansion called Carinhall, would
keep disappearing to change into various kinds of fancy clothes,
and who would display jewels of enormous size upon his person,
with the brilliant, astute and courageous man who was ready to
outface the prosecutors at Nuremberg and even at times get the
better of them, though he had one of the worst cases in history to
defend?*

*In the fat, ungainly body of this man of brutal humor and vul-
gar self-display there existed also a man of genuine knowledge and
some taste in art, a man who appreciated books and read widely, a
man who enjoyed for several years the company of diplomats and
aristocrats and charmed them into recording many tributes to him
both as host and as negotiator. Such men as Halifax and Henderson
of Britain, François-Poncet of France, Sumner Welles of America
and Dahlerus of Sweden all stated that they were, at the time of
meeting him, convinced of his sincerity and of his probable goodwill. Both of Goering's wives were devoted to him, as he was to
them.*

*No account we had met of Goering explained these and other
contradictions in his nature. Heinrich Fraenkel spent over eighteen
months in research traveling in Germany, meeting people who had
known Goering in his public and in his private life. He found Goering's widow, Frau Emmy Goering, still convinced of his greatness
and of his devotion to Germany, and still resenting bitterly the way
in which he was finally treated by Hitler. However, from the men
who had to associate with him in public life Fraenkel gained a more
critical account of Goering's opportunism—men such as Franz von
Papen, for instance, or Hjalmar Schacht. Senior officers and aides*

of Goering in the Luftwaffe, notably Karl Bodenschatz, Erhard Milch, Adolf Galland and Bernd von Brauchitsch, gave Fraenkel another picture, that of the commander who became more ruthless and arbitrary with his subordinates as he became more abject in the face of Hitler's obsessions. That Goering grew inordinately afraid of Hitler during the last years of the war is now certain, just as it is evident that he retired as much as he possibly could from the devastation and disappointments of a losing struggle in order to enjoy the remaining fruits of luxury and indulge his preoccupation with the art and the treasures he had gathered at Carinhall—the mansion that became the symbol of his pride and success and was in its form and structure as eccentric as William Randolph Hearst's San Simeon.

Still the explanation of Goering's strange mixture of charm and ferocity, devotion and ruthlessness, physical courage and moral cowardice, urge for power and abjectness before Hitler, remained to be found. Was his ill-health, the glandular trouble that caused his excessive weight, a cause of his inconsistencies? Fraenkel studied the details of his personal habits with the men who had in one way or another tended him, and in particular with Robert Kropp, his valet from 1933 until his imprisonment in Mondorf in 1945.

Then late in the period of research a chance remark let out in conversation revealed the truth about Goering's drug addiction, resolving all the rumors current in Germany during his lifetime. The addiction that Goering first acquired in 1923, when morphine was prescribed to ease the pain from the poisoned wounds he sustained during the unsuccessful putsch in Munich, was never finally cured. Like certain other flyers in the First World War, he came under the care and observation of the celebrated Professor Kahle of Cologne, a specialist in drug addiction. This fact was confirmed by the staff of the Kahle sanatorium, which Fraenkel visited and where he was given details of the drastic cure which Kahle administered periodically whenever the toxic elements had to be removed from Goering's system.

Among the symptoms of morphine addiction described by the Kahle Institute were great excitement of the nervous system, excessive activity of certain glands, outpourings of vital energy, and ab-

normal vanity. This went a long way toward explaining the ex-
tremes of behavior so often described by those who knew Goering.

At the same time I met in Stockholm one of the specialists who
observed Goering during the worst period of his addiction, in 1925,
when his violence made him dangerous and his confinement in
Langbro sanatorium became necessary. He assured me that Goe-
ring's mental capacities were quite unimpaired, that his derange-
ment was caused entirely by the excessive quantity of morphine he
could no longer prevent himself from taking.

Our contacts then led us back to several men and women who
had known Goering as a child, the most important of whom were
Fräulein Erna and Fräulein Fanny Graf and the eminent physicist
Professor Hans Thirring, who gave us the account of the significant
relationship between Goering's mother and his Jewish godfather,
the Ritter von Epenstein, as a result of which he was for many years
brought up in the castle of Veldenstein, where the Goering family
were invited to live so long as they enjoyed this arbitrary and un-
pleasant man's favor. Goering always referred to this castle as if
it had belonged to his father, but Heinrich Ernst Goering in fact
lived there only on sufferance and in the end the family were turned
out by Epenstein and went to live in Munich in comparative pov-
erty. Later Goering was not only to inherit Veldenstein from Epen-
stein's widow but to own a mansion that far outshone in splendor
the provincial grandeurs of his youth.

These, and certain other facts, began to make the unique charac-
ter of Goering more credible; the violence of his motives and the
extravagance and opportunism of his behavior could now be under-
stood more clearly. The excesses of his vanity were at any rate to
some extent the product of his bodily condition. But even his ene-
mies were prepared to allow his ability as a negotiator, and the
late Lord Birkett, whom we consulted about Goering's behavior at
Nuremberg, noted at the time of the trial "how Goering had from
the start managed to dominate the proceedings." "No one," wrote
Lord Birkett in his private notes, "appears to have been quite pre-
pared for his immense ability and knowledge, and his thorough
mastery and understanding of every detail of the captured docu-
ments. . . . Suave, shrewd, adroit, capable, resourceful, he quickly

saw the elements of the situation, and, as his confidence grew, his mastery became more apparent."

For the first time the full range of evidence covering Goering's character and career has been sifted, and what has come to light has made Goering a much more remarkable, complex, fascinating and human person than has probably been generally realized. He was not simply the swashbuckling representative of the common man that most people accepted him as being, the genial but ruthless political gangster who somehow managed to make the Nazis seem socially acceptable to the diplomats. He was, in fact, far more than this; he was shrewd and intelligent, capable of grasping and controlling a wide range of affairs when he cared to take the trouble to do so. But because of his weakness of character and lack of moral courage he was often, especially in his later years, stupidly greedy for power, vain to the point of megalomania, an emotional child who suffered from delusions of grandeur and a chronic inability to stomach unpleasant facts or the consequences of his own failure. In the face of Germany's collapse he continued to extend his fabulous Carinhall, and his greatest single achievement at the close of his career did not lie in politics or economics or warfare, but in the vast collection of works of art which he amassed with all the shrewdness, ruthlessness and calculating vision that had characterized his initial service to Hitler.

In this book we have concentrated on telling the story of Goering's life and his career as a leader in the Nazi Party and later as Hitler's deputy in the Third Reich. The history of the period as a whole has, of course, been told many times, and notably by Dr. Alan Bullock, William L. Shirer and Professor Trevor-Roper, and it was no part of our purpose to repeat what has already been investigated so thoroughly, except in such summary form as to make Goering's thoughts and actions clear.

In a review of our previous biography of Goebbels, Professor Trevor-Roper, after a generous commendation of the work we had done, asked whether such men as Goebbels deserved to have time spent in research about their lives. We believe that, quite apart from the need to know as nearly as possible why historical events developed in the way they did, facts about the characters and ca-

reers of men who have been influential cannot fail to be of value
and interest. Nazism was not merely a factor in the immediate
past; it was a manifestation of a part of human nature, and it may
recur at any time and in any place. It is doing so now in parts of
Africa. For this reason alone it is always salutary to understand how
men like Goebbels and Goering came to power, and how they behaved once they had achieved it. They are not alone in history, nor
have we any reason to suppose that they will be the last of their
kind to bring suffering to the people who allow such men to rule
them.

We would like to acknowledge our indebtedness to the many
people who have helped us to understand Goering and have given
us facts about him. These include, in addition to Frau Emmy
Goering and those of Goering's friends and associates whom we
have already mentioned, other members of his family, Frau Goering's legal adviser Dr. Justus Koch and Professor Hans Thirring.
Among the art experts who served Goering we consulted especially
Dr. Bruno Lohse, Goering's personal adviser in Paris, and Fräulein
Gisela Limberger, his librarian, who had special charge of his art
collection. I am also grateful to Christopher Hibbert, the biographer
of Mussolini, and to Denis Richards, historian of the R.A.F., for
their help. The books and archives at the Wiener Library in London, at the Institut für Zeitgeschichte in Munich, at the American
Document Center in Berlin, at the Deutsches Staatsarchiv in Potsdam, and at the Rijksinstituut voor Oorlog Documentatie, Amsterdam were most generously placed at our disposal; at the Wiener
Library we received special help from Dr. L. Kahn, Mrs. Ilse Wolf
and Mrs. G. Deak, at the Institut from Dr. Hoch and Dr. Graml, at
the Deutsches Staatsarchiv from Professor Helmut Loetzke, and at
the Rijksinstituut from Dr. de Jong and Dr. van der Leeuw. Others
who have helped us greatly with background material are Dr. Ernst
Hanfstaengl and Dr. Hans Streck. In Stockholm we are grateful in
particular to Dr. Vilhelm Scharp, Dr. Uno Lindgren, Miss Maud
Ekman and Miss Inger Reimers. Finally, we would like to thank
Mrs. M. H. Peters, who undertook with skill and patience the
formidable task of typing a particularly difficult manuscript.

R. M.

Goering's father and mother, the former Minister Resident
Heinrich Ernst Goering and Frau Franziska Goering

The Ritter von Epenstein, Goering's godfather

Mauterndorf Castle

Carin

Goering as a young officer in *1918*

The principal room at Carinhall, shortly after Goering acquired the property

Goering at the Reichstag Fire trial, 1933

Hitler and Goering with Roehm (center) before the Roehm purge

Goering as an archer

Goering at a shoot

Goering with his daughter Edda

Frau Emmy Goering with Goering (in Luftwaffe uniform) at the theater

Goering in full-dress uniform, holding his Reich
Marshal's baton

Goering discusses the Four-Year Plan with
Hitler

Goering leaving the Italian **Royal Palace during a** visit to Italy, wearing the fur-lined motoring **coat that** Ciano remarked upon

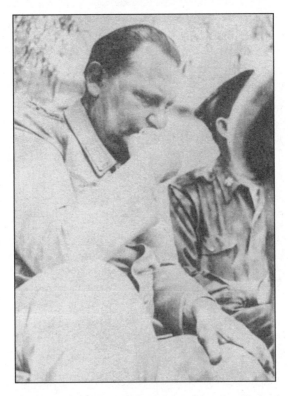

Goering shortly **after his capture** by the United States Army

I

Pour le Mérite

Hᴇʀᴍᴀɴɴ Wɪʟʜᴇʟᴍ Gᴏᴇʀɪɴɢ was born in the Marienbad sanatorium at Rosenheim in Bavaria on January 12, 1893, the second son of the German consul-general in Haiti by his second marriage. After only six weeks his mother left him in Germany and hurried back to her husband; she was not to see her child again for three years. By this time he was already proving to be a willful and difficult boy.

In 1885 his father, Heinrich Ernst Goering, a former cavalry officer and now a member of the German consular service, had made a second marriage at the age of forty-five to Franziska Tiefenbrunn, a Bavarian girl of modest birth. He had already had five children by his former wife. His new marriage had taken place in London, where Goering had been sent by Bismarck to study British methods of colonial administration before being put in charge of the harsh and difficult territory of German Southwest Africa. His studies lasted for a few months only, and he left for Africa with his bride. His title was Minister-Resident for Southwest Africa, and he did his work well, treating the African chiefs with tact and diplomacy. Within five years he had made the area safe for German trade, and he was, in this sense, the founder of the colony. While there he had won the friendship of Cecil Rhodes, and he had also become the friend of a Dr. Hermann Epenstein. On his return to Germany, he volunteered for another post overseas and was appointed consul general in Haiti.

By the time Hermann was conceived, Franziska, who needed

all the toughness of her Austrian and Bavarian blood to lead this
life of constant movement and rough, violent living, had already
borne three children, Karl, Olga and Paula. Shortly before the birth
of this fourth child she left Haiti and traveled home alone. When
she returned to Haiti she left the six-week-old baby in Fürth, Bavaria, in the hands of a friend of the family, Frau Graf, whose daughters became his playmates and remember him today as a handsome,
headstrong boy.

When the child was three years old his father returned to Germany to face retirement. Hermann Goering's earliest recollection
was of expressing his resentment toward his mother by hitting her
in the face with his fists when she tried to embrace him after her
prolonged absence. She was deeply upset.[1]

The family were reunited in Berlin and lived for the next five
years in the Fregestrasse in Friedenau, a quiet residential suburb of
the capital. From this time Hermann's childish ambition was to
become an officer in the German Army, and at the age of five his
father gave him a hussar's uniform. Later he liked to recall how as
a very small boy he would ask the family servant to bring him the
swords and caps belonging to his father's military guests so that he
could admire them while he lay in bed at night.

Epenstein, Heinrich Goering's friend in Africa, and, as it proved,
the particular friend of his wife Franziska, had also finally settled in
Germany. In contrast to Heinrich Goering, who had comparatively
little money apart from his State pension on which to bring up his
young family of five children, Epenstein was a very rich bachelor.
He could afford to indulge his whims, among which was to let
Hermann, together with his brothers and sisters, become his
godchildren.

A domineering man, Epenstein was punctilious in his demands
and insistent on receiving a proper degree of respect. He would lose
his temper if his guests were so much as a minute late for meals. He
was small, dark and fat, obsessed by the sense of class, though his
father had been no more than an Army surgeon in Berlin. He liked
to pretend he was the son of a court surgeon, and he acquired his
title of Ritter von Epenstein by donations presented in the right
quarters. His lifelong friend was a Dr. Thirring, whose two sons
were later to be among his many godchildren; one of them, Professor Hans Thirring, was to become a distinguished physicist.

Epenstein remained a bachelor, traveling a great deal and enjoying life. He practiced little as a doctor, though he attended Franziska in Africa when she bore her first child. When he decided to settle, it was Dr. Thirring who found him the castle of Mauterndorf in Austria, not far from the border with Bavaria. Epenstein spent a great deal of money on the restoration and furnishing of this castle, re-creating in it the heavy and pompous atmosphere of German medievalism that so stirred the young imagination of his godchild Hermann. After Heinrich Goering had returned to Germany Epenstein bought a second and smaller castle called Veldenstein, fifteen miles from Nuremberg; he offered this new property, which was a house built onto the ruins of an ancient Franconian fortress of the eleventh century, to the Goering family as a home. Here Herman Goering was finally settled with his elder brother, his two sisters and his younger brother, Albert.

Veldenstein always appeared to him to be the family seat. While the world of his father represented Prussia with its militarist etiquette, its rigorous uniforms, its pompous parades and its memories of Bismarck, the rich world of his godfather represented medieval Germany. Its romantic castles gave him his first vision of medieval splendor in the magnificent scenery of the Bavarian mountains and excited in him a desire for feudal power that he was never to lose. He was already headstrong and spoiled, dominating his elder brother and sisters and displaying his aggressive instincts at the first sign of any opposition or restraint. He lived out of doors as much as he could, his eyes on the dark slopes of conifers stretching up to the Alps that even as a child he longed to climb.

It was at Veldenstein that Franziska, Goering's mother, lived as Epenstein's mistress. Her elderly and complacent husband had to accept this situation on humiliating terms. Epenstein kept the finest bedroom in the establishment for himself, while Franziska slept in a hardly less well-appointed room situated conveniently close by. Heinrich Goering was not admitted to this part of the house; he had to sleep on the ground floor. When the family visited Epenstein at Mauterndorf, Hermann's father was lodged in a house that stood apart from the castle. He was content, or pretended to be so, with the dignity left him in the title of Minister-Resident that had gone with his colonial governorship. (His son was later to refer to him always as "the Minister *President*.") In his old age he found some remaining comfort in drinking and skittles, and he exercised little or no control over his second family of young children. Franziska was to remain Epenstein's mistress for some fifteen years; it was perhaps ironic that the relationship should finally break down just before Heinrich Goering's death.

Nominally Epenstein was a Christian, having been baptized in childhood. But he was of Jewish family and appearance, and his name appeared in the *"Semi-Gotha"* of the time, a volume in which all titled families of Jewish descent were listed. He was a man who liked to be regarded as the benefactor of numerous children, who were all encouraged to address him as Pate or Godfather. Not only the five children of the Goering family enjoyed this privilege, but the two sons of Dr. Thirring as well. He would write long letters to his friends on how to educate their sons, how to marry off their daughters and how to invest their money.

It is not difficult to see the effect of this situation on Hermann Goering as a child. His father became a nonentity living on the memories of his past service to Germany; his godfather provided the symbol of power and of possessions to which he was instinctively drawn, though he must at a comparatively early age have begun to resent the situation in which Epenstein had involved his mother.

In the authorized biography written by Gritzbach and published when Goering was in power, it was asserted that as a child he would set his dog on the local Jews to show off his innate racial integrity; but this was one of the Nazi legends which most of the leaders imposed on their biographers. Hermann, however, was willful enough and spoiled enough to do exactly what he wanted. In place of discipline and authority he found only indulgence, since the relationship of his parents had no basis of affection or respect. He was his father's favorite and he knew it. On one occasion before he could read, he stole a telegram addressed to his father while he was out and then offered it to him already opened on his return. *"Ich bin doch Papas Liebling!"* he used to say. "I'm Daddy's darling!"

From the beginning, Hermann was set against attending school. He failed at his first school, in Fürth, to which he was sent in 1900 at the age of seven, boarding with one of the masters. He was wild and difficult to control, ordering his companions about in his eagerness to play at soldiers. At home, like other boys, he marshaled his lead soldiers, but he added to the drama of his games by piling up rugs in order to make mountains for his maneuvers, and by using mirrors to increase the dimensions of his forces. Stories of the Boer

War were current at the time, and the natural sympathies of the Germans for a whole generation to come lay with the Boers and not with the British. His father gave him a Boer uniform with khaki shorts and a broad-brimmed hat, and he wore them with pride when he was away from school, calling himself General of the Boers. The boys dreaded him as a great fighter.

At the age of eleven he was sent to a boarding school at Ansbach, which his father chose at random from an alphabetic list. From the first he hated it; the discipline was strict and the food bad. Already he was learning to love good food, and the *Rindfleisch* provided every day revolted him. He organized a strike among the boys. Then he sent his bedding home in a neatly packed parcel and a few hours later arrived at Veldenstein, having sold a violin for ten marks to pay for his fare. He was told he must go back, but he refused so stubbornly that his parents gave way. According to his own account later, when he had reached the stage at which he could bear the restrictions and the discipline at Ansbach no longer, he had taken to his bed and defied both teachers and doctors to get him up again until he obtained their consent to let him go. Once he was back at Veldenstein, he believed the success of his defiance was a sign of his natural heroism, the birthright of a child whose ancestors had, as his father had always told him, played a part in the greatness of German history. He knew well enough by now that Michael Christian Goering, his great-great-grandfather, had been *Commissarius Loci*, a sort of economic gauleiter, for Frederick the Great of Prussia. Goering was to remember this ancestor with pride when he himself became *Commissarius* for all of Nazi Germany.

Meanwhile, the only leadership he could exercise was over the children around him. Later, in his maturity, he would laugh at his recollections of hitting the heads of any boys who challenged his authority. He claimed that he first of all defended and then besieged the castle of Veldenstein, urging on his friends to show their prowess and courage as he scaled the walls at the risk of his life. The ruined castle inspired his romantic imagination. When he was eight years old, he looked at the surrounding countryside from the castle tower and had a vision of Roman chariots with plumed warriors passing through the valley below. He ran to tell his mother and sister, but they only laughed at him. It was this spectacular aspect of history that appealed to him; he was enthralled by the Teutonic legends, such as the Nibelungen saga, and by the heroes of German history, such as Charlemagne and Frederick the Great. His only interest in books was to provide his imagination with the images of chivalry. Later he was to have a fictitious genealogical table constructed which linked his family directly with Frederick the Great, Charlemagne and Saint Elizabeth of Thuringia, and he spent time impressing these legends about himself on the psychiatrists whose duty it was to study him in the cells of Nuremberg jail.

During the school holidays, young Goering's blood was roused by the sight of the mountains, and while still a boy he became a skilled climber. Knowing almost nothing, he persuaded his brother-in-law and a friend to take him up the twelve-thousand-foot peak of the Grossglockner. He insisted that they try the ascent by the more difficult route from the northwest. They started to climb at dawn, cutting their way up foothold by foothold until the morning sun warmed their faces on the first summit of the Teufelshorn. They now had to pass along a sharp ridge which led up to the peak of the Grossglockner. Roped together, they edged their way along with a drop on one side of twenty-five hundred feet and on the other of three thousand feet over the glacier of the Glockner-Kars. They reached the peak, but during the descent the boy nearly lost his life. Attempting a feat beyond his skill, he would have slipped to his death far below if his brother-in-law had not interposed his own body and caught him as he fell.

At fifteen, when he was climbing one of the needles in the Mont Blanc chain, he is said to have dislocated his shoulder during the action of swinging his body up into a cleft, and then, after readjusting the arm himself, continued his climb in spite of the pain.[2] He seemed utterly fearless, and the stories grew of his disregard of danger. There was the occasion when, in the Austrian Alps, he encountered an avalanche. He was so struck by the spectacle of crashing rocks and boulders of snow that he was unaware of the panic among those who were with him. At another time, he was in a boat with some friends when they began to drift toward a waterfall. Goering's recollection is that he told them to stop being fools—if they were to die, that was nothing to get excited about. Goering's belief, which remained in adult life, was that nothing could happen to harm him. He was, quite literally, insensitive to physical danger.

Legends or not, these are the heroic tales which surrounded his youth and encouraged his indiscipline and lack of self-control.[3] There is, however, no question of his physical courage and endurance in his early youth, and it justified his father and Epenstein in sending him at the age of twelve to a military academy, the Cadet School at Karlsruhe in Baden. There, they felt, he should meet his match in discipline. And there, not so strangely, he at last found a school that he considered fit for heroes to work in. His sister Paula and the Graf sisters, who were some three years older than Hermann, attended a finishing school which was also at Karlsruhe. One day, when he was about fifteen, he was invited to lunch by the headmistress, Fräulein Grüber, to visit his sister and their friends. He arrived looking erect and smart in his uniform, and presented the headmistress with a large bouquet of lilac, clicking his heels and kissing her hand. The girls were most impressed until they found later that when he took them out to a *Konditorei* he had no money left to pay for the cakes they ate.

At the age of sixteen, Goering went to the military training college at Lichterfelde, close to Berlin. The social life at this academy was in keeping with his tastes; he enjoyed himself at night in what he was later to insist was the most exclusive of the *Kadettenkorps*, to which he naturally belonged, and in the daytime he responded to the clique discipline and the uniform-wearing, which had excited his childhood imaginings. He did well and left the academy with the highest distinction, and in March 1912 he was commissioned in the Prinz Wilhelm Regiment, the 112th Infantry, the headquarters of which were at Mulhouse. His age was nineteen. Goering assumed his status as a commissioned officer with conventional pride. "If war breaks out, you can be sure I'll give a good account of myself and live up to the name of Goering," he told his family and friends when they assembled to admire him in his new uniform.

It was in the following year, 1913, that the Goerings finally broke with Epenstein and had to leave Veldenstein. The relationship between Epenstein and Franziska had worn itself out, and tedious quarrels had been developing with the old man. The situation grew impossible, and Heinrich Goering was forced to move his family to Munich. Almost immediately afterward he died, and there was an imposing funeral in Munich at the Waldfriedhof. Goering fought hard to control himself, but suddenly burst into tears and wept openly as he stood in his officer's uniform beside his father's grave.

At Mulhouse he had settled down to the routine of an Army life still embedded in the traditions of Frederick the Great, but he spent in mountaineering every moment he could free himself from his duties. His best friend was a fellow officer, Lieutenant Bruno Loerzer, with whom he was to keep in contact all his life. Both he and Loerzer were still based at Mulhouse when war was declared in August 1914. Mulhouse was a border garrison town in German Alsace barely a mile or so from the frontier with France, and Goering's regiment was immediately withdrawn and restationed behind the Rhine. His first chance for adventure came when the platoon of which he had charge was sent to reconnoiter the enemy positions. French advance parties were already penetrating into German territory and had occupied Mulhouse. Lieutenant Goering and his men crossed the Rhine toward Mulhouse in an armored train. Goering soon forgot the limitations of his orders when he heard from the excited civilians that the French were in occupation of the town hall. He went straight there and, finding the French no longer in possession of the building, tore down the posters they had put up declaring that the city was under French martial law, and then continued his pursuit of the invaders. Eventually, having exchanged fire with the French, Goering returned to base with four French dragoon horses as a token of his initiative in action.

The following day the possession of Mulhouse was more seriously contested. Once more, Lieutenant Goering enjoyed his own individual skirmishing. He equipped his platoon with bicycles, and at dawn this seven-man patrol pedaled along the familiar road to the town that had once been their base. Their first encounters with the French outposts were a little too successful, and with courage bursting in their hearts they rushed on through the suburbs until they had passed under the railway bridges, which were in fact held by French, and cycled into the heart of the city, where the enemy was in full occupation. Once there, Goering was quick to commandeer a horse. He intended capturing the French General Paul Pau by charging suddenly into the midst of the men surrounding him, catching him up across his saddle and then galloping back to the German lines. But the plan misfired—one of his men lost his nerve and let off his rifle. Goering and his platoon swung their bicycles round and, feet whirling on the pedals, fled furiously back to headquarters, where they arrived breathless but unharmed. Goering never got over that lost chance to make a spectacular start to his war. But another task was immediately assigned him, and he found himself that afternoon high up in the church tower of Ill-zach, with the French entering the village streets below. The platoon escaped with some French prisoners.

Goering became an experienced junior officer, and in the campaigns that followed all he finally suffered was an attack of rheumatism resulting from the damp of trench warfare. He was sent to hospital in Freiburg. Meanwhile, his friend Lieutenant Bruno Loerzer had been seconded to an air training school in the same town, and his stories filled the invalid with envy. Goering soon felt well enough to visit the flying school, though certainly not sufficiently recovered to go back to the damp trenches. He applied for an official transfer, which was immediately turned down. But Goering was not discouraged. When Loerzer finished his training, he was accompanied in the sky by a new observer. Goering had arranged for his own transfer and risked the consequences. He was, in effect, pardoned when a military court sentenced him to three weeks' confinement to barracks. The sentence was never carried out, however, because, through the nebulous organization of the Air Force, by the time it was imposed Loerzer and Goering had become attached as a team to the 25th Field Air Detachment of Crown Prince Friedrich Wilhelm's Fifth Army—though it seems that they had to steal a plane in order to qualify.

Reconnaissance was their principal duty. Goering, photographing and sketching the enemy positions and gun emplacements, was in his element. His skill and accuracy became famous. Based now on Stenay, in northeastern France, he photographed the chain of forts surrounding Verdun. With Loerzer flying low, he strafed men on the ground with his pistol. They would fly over enemy positions, guiding and directing the bombardment by the guns. The Crown Prince invested both Goering and Loerzer with the Iron Cross, first class, for their work. The task of photographing from these primitive planes was extremely difficult and dangerous, and Goering had to lean right out of the cockpit, bracing his mountaineer's legs against the opposite side of his seat, for the underwing of the plane prevented a direct view to the ground below. He would stretch out from the plane, holding the heavy camera and exposing plate after plate with the lens pointed vertically downward.

This was Goering's occupation during the spring of 1915. Soon he was learning Morse in order to send messages down to base. His first message to a battery commander below is reported to have been "You can stop firing; you won't hit the bloody target anyhow!" The observation was not even put into code. Another exploit occurred on the occasion of a French air raid on the Crown Prince's headquarters at Stenay, which coincided with a visit to her husband by the Crown Princess Cecilie. The raid was effective, and Goering and Loerzer set out alone and without orders to avenge the Crown Princess's honor. Goering shot up a French plane with his pistol and dropped his small but effective bombs (called "airmen's mice") on the sheds of the French airdrome. It was this raid that was said to have inspired him with the idea of carrying an improvised machine gun on the plane. He was the first German airman to do so.

When better German aircraft came into service, in particular the Aviatik, Goering felt an urge to pilot his own plane. There is no doubt he had enjoyed the exercise of his skill as an observer, and also the special control it gave him over the work of officers of superior status to his own. He knew that they depended on him for guidance as he flew above their heads, assessing the position like a general in command and signaling his "instructions" to the ground. He and Loerzer attended staff conferences which would normally have been closed to such junior men—but their advice was sought and the photographs they had taken needed their expert interpretation. In this way Goering became known to Crown Prince Friedrich Wilhelm himself. It did not take Goering long to realize that the future of the war for him lay in the air, and that it was necessary for him to become a pilot. He went back to the flying school at Freiburg, where he gained his wings in record time and boasted that he never crashed a machine. In October 1915 he became a *Jagdflieger*, a "pursuit flyer," or fighter pilot. Goering and Loerzer were members of Jagdstaffel 5, a section of the new armada of twin-engine fighter planes which Germany was putting into the air on the western front.

The British had just introduced the huge Handley-Page bomber to meet the rapidly evolving strategy in air warfare. One misty November day the new pilot saw a black giant flying ahead in the clouds, and without thought he plunged in to secure a closer view and, if possible, wing the aircraft with his machine guns. He was alone; he had taken no heed, as his fellow pilots had done, of the fact that there were British fighters in the vicinity. Goering moved in close, marveling at the great machine with guns set in its tail as well as amidships. He put one gunner out of action and then another, for the maneuverability of his aircraft was far greater than that of the Handley-Page. He set one of its engines on fire. Then suddenly he was being strafed by a descending swarm of Sopwith fighters, who turned and twisted about him. His engine was hit and his tank was holed; then he was wounded and his senses began to leave him as his machine stalled and faltered. With fuel pouring into the cockpit, he did what he could to control the plane, which was falling now toward the enemy lines and would soon be in range of the machine-gun fire from the ground. The fighters had gone, but his plane was spinning down through mist and cloud. It was the machine-gun fire from below that shook him into action. He put the plane's nose up and hedge-hopped back into German territory with what was left of his fuel and crash-landed into the cemetery of a church that was being used as a hospital. He was operated upon for a serious wound in the hip from which he might easily have bled to death had expert care not been immediately available. They counted sixty bullet holes in the fuselage of his plane.

Goering was immobilized for the greater part of a year. While he was convalescing he had his first recorded love affair, with a girl named Marianne Mauser, the beautiful daughter of a well-to-do farmer near Mauterndorf. Her parents were undistinguished, but even so they did not permit the young couple to reach the point of an engagement. Herr Mauser regarded the matter shrewdly: a flyer might be a romantic figure, but his expectation of life, unfortunately, was short.

While Goering slowly recovered, the new concept of the "air ace" was being created on the battlefronts. The fighter pilot who faced death in a deadly duel of wits with men as skilled in endurance as himself, and who flew high above the mud and degradation of earthbound warfare, became a new hero whose photograph stole the publicity. The names of Richthofen and Udet became admired alike by the Germans and the Allies, because their exploits or those of their comrades made exciting news. Loerzer was appointed commandant of Field Squadron 26, based at Mulhouse, where Goering joined him again on his discharge from hospital in 1916. In Aachen one bright day, Loerzer saved Goering's life when he was being set upon by three French fighters; once more he only just made the ground with a machine punctured by bullets, its undercarriage in fragments. But Goering had done the same for Loerzer on a previous occasion. This was the quick-witted war of the air, with its own comradeship based on a mutual trust in skill.

By 1917, Goering's reputation as a fighter pilot was fully established. In addition to the Iron Cross, he was to be awarded the Zaehring Lion with swords, the Karl Friedrich Order and the Hohenzollern Medal with swords, third class, all prior to his final award, Pour le Mérite. In May he was put in command of Squadron 27, which needed an improvement in morale. Goering was now responsible for both administration and strategy; he had to show inspiring leadership. He set about the immediate strengthening of the squadron, working day and night to ensure efficiency first on the ground and then in the air. In the summer the two squadrons, 26 and 27, were operating alongside each other, flying from the same airdrome on the Flanders front—at Iseghem, near Ypres. The air attacks on the Allies were now built up into a major offensive; Goering's squadron in particular had to help in the protection of the other planes, attracting enemy fire away from them. The Allies, meanwhile, were redoubling their efforts in the air, and the Germans countered by forming specially large composite squadrons, called *Jagdgeschwader* (pursuit squadrons), equaling four of the others; the first of these was commanded by Manfred von Richthofen. Goering and Loerzer were among those whose squadrons were merged to create the third of these major formations.

As the final great offensive of March 1918 developed, Goering was recognized as an outstanding officer whose leadership had an invigorating effect on men whose morale was flagging. He was moved to any area where difficulty of this kind was being experienced. Life in the air was brief and hazardous. After April, when Richthofen was killed in action, his promotion was rapid. One morning in May, when Goering was in the cockpit ready to take off on a mission, his adjutant came running toward the aircraft waving a paper. Against the roar of the engines he shouted that the Emperor had awarded him the Pour le Mérite. The decoration was the highest that could be given; it was awarded not for some single action of outstanding bravery but for continuous courage in action.[4]

Captain Reinhardt, a celebrated pilot, had been chosen to succeed Richthofen as squadron commander. One day in May he too was killed, while testing a new plane in which Goering himself had just flown. It was then, on July 7, that Goering was chosen to command Richthofen's famous squadron, now gravely depleted. On July 14, the day he assumed his command, the men of the squadron went on parade to meet him. Karl Bodenschatz in his book *Jagd in Flanders Himmel* remarks how tough he looked. "You could see this," he says, "in his movements and the way he spoke." Lieutenant von Wedel introduced him to the men, and Goering replied in a "strangely insistent tone of voice," the words informal and unprepared. He said it was a special honor to be made commandant of such a unit as this, and he spoke of the men who had died in order to make the fame and spirit of the squadron what it was, a spirit they would all need to remember in the grave days ahead. Then Lieutenant Bodenschatz, as adjutant, gave Goering the Richthofen emblem, the walking stick made for Germany's most famous flyer by a craftsman called Holzapfel, who had so pleased Richthofen by his gesture that he had kept the stick with him to the day he died. Reinhardt had possessed it for only four weeks.

On July 17 Goering dispatched his first official report, in which he wrote:

The British single-seaters are giving as good an account of themselves as ever, but the French fighters rarely penetrate beyond the front line; they usually avoid serious encounters. On the other hand, the French two-seaters usually appear in close formation, pushing home their bombing attacks ruthlessly and from low level. For this they usually employ twin-engined Coudrons whose armor is proof against our ammunition. I myself, attacking a Coudron at close distance on 15.7.18, wasted almost my entire ammunition; the Coudron simply flew on, completely ignoring me. Those well-armed and well-armored machines should be attacked by antiaircraft guns. Flying in close formation they offer good targets for our flak . . . Many [of our] pilots have to take to the air up to five times a day. In the long run, neither the men nor the engines can stand up to such strain. . . . Lack of direct telephone communication between squadron and fighter groups adds to our difficulties. Imperative to have new telephone lines completed.

On the following day Goering himself secured his twenty-second Allied aircraft, a Spad which he shot down early in the morning. He reported briefly:

At 8:15 A.M. I attacked several Spads. One of them I forced down and, after some spiraling, shot down. It fell into the woods of Bandry.

This was Goering's final personal victory. In spite of the urgency of the times he went on leave ("well-deserved," says Bodenschatz) on July 26, leaving Lieutenant Lothar von Richthofen, Manfred's brother, in charge of the squadron. He did not return until August 22.

The *Geschwader*, claims Bodenschatz, shot down some five hundred Allied planes during the nine months of its existence, but by the end of September the numbers of officers and men were much reduced: fifty-three officers, including medical and administrative staff, and 473 N.C.O.s and men. The weather was bad. "The features of Lieutenant Goering are getting harder," noted Bodenschatz. But the end of the war was in sight. On the ground the German armies were in retreat, and as summer turned to autumn the British Air Force shot down many of Goering's pilots.

In November, during the last days of the war, the weather was bad and the news grew worse. Rumors circulated that the Kaiser was abdicating, that there was unrest in Berlin, that the Navy was in a state of mutiny; it was said even that soldiers were firing at their officers. On November 9 Goering called his officers together and urged them to be as loyal to each other during these difficult days as they had been in action, and to fight to the last.

The period November 7 to 9 was one of growing disorder. Goering's reports as recorded by Bodenschatz show this clearly. On November 7 there was heavy fighting east of the Meuse, and the Allied advance forced Goering to withdraw his men and equipment to an airdrome west of Tellancourt, where the ground conditions were bad for take-off and landing. The rainy weather prevented flying, and Goering's reports are brief and formal.

November 8. Settling down at Tellancourt airdrome. Drizzle; deep cloud.

November 9. Weather unfavorable. Nothing much happened. Preparing for retreat.

During the three days November 9, 10 and 11 Goering received many contradictory instructions from an irresolute high command. The whole atmosphere of capitulation was hateful to a man of his temperament who had so recently won the supreme award and whose squadron, in spite of bitter losses and half-trained replacements, had been responsible for great acts of courage and considerable successes in the air until they were grounded so unaccountably (as indeed it seemed to this young commander of twenty-five, whose photograph was by now on sale to the German public as a war hero). Varying instructions came in: he was to surrender his planes to the Americans, he was to take his machines and armament to Darmstadt.

On November 10 the weather still made flying impossible, and the agony of waiting dragged on.

November 10. By order of the commander, Fifth Army Air Force, aircraft flying to Darmstadt, the more valuable equipment to be sent on by road transport . . . two columns of eight trucks each. Tents and some useless machines and equipment left at Tellancourt. Men moved partly by truck and partly on foot to be entrained. Food supplies were adequate.

Then, on November 11, the official news of the armistice arrived, and the evacuation was halted. Bodenschatz writes of the strange silence that closed on the countryside. Goering called his men together and told them he would never surrender to the Allies; he would continue with the evacuation to Darmstadt. Bodenschatz was put in charge of the trucks, and the pilots took to the air in spite of the arrival of a staff officer with orders that the squadron should put their planes at the disposal of the French in Strasbourg. Goering at first refused bluntly; if this had to be done, he said, then someone else could do it. In the end, a few machines were flown to Strasbourg, but their pilots crash-landed them as a final act of defiance against the enemy.

In the confusion, some of Goering's pilots mistook their route to Darmstadt and landed at Mannheim, which was one of the places where soldiers' and workers' councils, in active revolt against what authority remained, had taken charge of the airport. On landing, the pilots were disarmed and sent on to Darmstadt by road. When they arrived with the report of what had happened, Goering was furious. He put the entire squadron into the air again and flew the short distance to Mannheim, where, while the officers deprived of their arms landed, Goering and the rest of his pilots circled over the airdrome. The officers on the ground presented the soldiers' and workers' council with an ultimatum that unless the stolen arms were returned to them at once and they were allowed to take off with them unmolested, their commandant, Lieutenant Goering, would machine-gun the airdrome. The pilots were hastily given back their arms, and they rejoined the squadron in the air. Goering then led the flight back to Darmstadt and ordered those who could to crash-land their planes.

Goering's final record on the day of armistice is a formal tribute to his squadron.

November 11. Armistice. Squadron flight in bad weather to Darmstadt. Mist. Since its establishment the Geschwader has shot down 644 enemy planes. Death by enemy action reached 56 officers and noncommissioned pilots, 6 men. Wounded 52 officers and noncommissioned pilots, 7 men.

HERMANN GOERING,
Lieutenant O.C. Geschwader.

Goering was demobilized, with the honorary rank of captain, in the old Bavarian town of Aschaffenburg, some thirty miles from Frankfurt. There, it seems, he stayed, at the villa of the managing director of the Buntpapier A.G., a firm of paper manufacturers, and the actual disbanding of the *Geschwader* took place in the courtyard of the firm's premises where the officers' luggage was stowed before being sent on to their homes. Goering and his officers spent most of their time in the Stiftskeller, the best restaurant and drinking place in the town. They were determined to keep together as long as they could. On November 19 Goering finally said goodbye, and he discovered his gifts as a speaker in a speech he made at the Stiftskeller. He spoke of the history and the achievements of the famous Richthofen squadron, of the bitter times that Germany must now endure, and of the disgraceful behavior of the German people in their attitude to those who had, as officers, sacrificed themselves for their country. He was outraged by the revolt of soldiers against authority, and by the support the soldiers' councils were receiving in many parts of Germany. "The new fight for freedom, principles, morals and the Fatherland has begun," he said. "We have a long and difficult way to go, but the truth will be our light. We must be proud of this truth and of what we have done.

We must think of this. Our time will come again." He gave the toast to the Richthofen *Geschwader*; solemnly they drank, then smashed their glasses.

Outside, crowds of civilians and ex-soldiers gathered in the streets to insult the officers, who, they were now led to think, had betrayed Germany and sacrificed the lives of their men in order to win for themselves decorations of the kind the Emperor had bestowed on Goering. The story goes that Goering was set on in the street and that with difficulty he prevented the mob from stripping the medals from his breast. He stayed in Aschaffenburg until early December, and then, without gratuity or pension, he went to Munich, where his mother was living. It was plain to him that he must make his own way in the world.

In Munich he was at first very fortunate. During the war he had given generous treatment to a prisoner of war, Captain Frank Beaumont, a pilot in the Royal Flying Corps, who had made a forced landing in a damaged plane after destroying two German fighters in the air. It was part of Goering's creed to admire a good enemy, and he did his best to keep Captain Beaumont from being taken over by the Army; he had talked to him at length about the profession of flying, about which they were both enthusiasts. Goering now discovered that Captain Beaumont, who spoke German fluently, was stationed in Munich with the responsibility of preparing the way for the breaking up of the German Air Force. Together with Ernst Udet, Goering presented himself and was made welcome. Indeed, for some weeks, until Munich became politically too warm for Goering to stay, Captain Beaumont acted as host to Goering and Udet and repaid past kindness with a generosity that enabled the two young men to live with ease whilst deciding what it was best for them to do.[5] Meanwhile, his unofficial engagement to Fräulein Mauser was forgotten. Herr Mauser wrote to Goering, "What have you got now to offer my daughter?" Goering telegraphed back, "Nothing."

During these immediate postwar weeks, Goering found himself in a new and alien world. He was a Prussian officer whose only background was his military training and the sense of caste inspired by his father, and the traditions represented by his early life in the castles of the south. Now he was an unemployed man of twenty-five in search of work. Politically Germany had collapsed into a form of mob rule, owing to the weakness of the hastily established government set up to formulate some kind of peace treaty. In Munich the throne of Bavaria had collapsed and a republic had been proclaimed on November 8, a few days before the armistice. Wilhelm II, the Emperor of Germany, had fled to Holland, and General Ludendorff, Chief of the General Staff, had also disappeared. The German working class had turned on the men they felt to be responsible for the war, and the soldiers who remained in uniform regarded their officers as traitors. A Socialist revolution had been proclaimed officially in Berlin and in a number of other German cities.

The officers, meanwhile, banded themselves together to defend their caste. They organized the so-called *Freikorps*—"free corps" of volunteers—in an effort to keep the German Army in being. In December Goering attended an officers' rally in the Berlin Philharmonic Hall at which the new Prussian Minister of War, General Walter Reinhardt, spoke, urging the packed audience to support the new government and obey its order that officers should discard the traditional insignia of their rank and replace their epaulets with stripes on their jacket sleeves. The General himself wore his three stripes; his epaulets and his medals were gone.

As Reinhardt was about to dismiss the meeting, Goering stood up in the body of the hall. He was wearing his full uniform, with his silver epaulets and the stars of his new rank of captain, and with the Pour le Mérite prominent among his medals and decorations. He stepped onto the platform, saying, "I beg your pardon, sir." The large gathering of officers fell silent. Goering had discovered his ability as a speaker in Aschaffenburg; now, as one of the more famous of Germany's young officers, he was forced to say what he felt. He began:

I had guessed, sir, that you, as Minister of War, would put in an appearance here today. But I had hoped to see a black band on your sleeve that would symbolize your deep regret for the outrage you are proposing to inflict on us. Instead of that black band you are wearing blue stripes on your arm. I think, sir, it would have been more appropriate for you to wear red stripes!

The officers broke into applause, but Goering held up his hand for silence and went on speaking.

We officers did our duty for four long years . . . and we risked our bodies for the Fatherland. Now we come home—and how do they treat us? They spit on us and deprive us of what we gloried in wearing. And this I can tell you, that the people are not to blame for such conduct. The people were our comrades—the comrades of each of us, irrespective of social conditions, for four weary years of war . . . Those alone are to blame who have goaded on the people—those men who stabbed our glorious Army in the back and who thought of nothing but of attaining power and of enriching themselves at the expense of the people. And therefore I implore you to cherish hatred—a profound, abiding hatred of those animals who have outraged the German people. . . . But the day will come when we will drive them away out of our Germany. Prepare for that day. Arm yourselves for that day. Work for that day.[6]

Then Goering left the hall, refusing to serve any longer in an Army that was ready to obey the degrading orders of a republican government.

He wanted only one thing now, to turn his back on the disgrace of Germany. His chance came through the German aircraft industry, which was unaccountably still in business. Goering knew the aircraft manufacturers, since he had often, as an air ace, visited their works and tested their machines. He undertook now to demonstrate the Fokker F7 at an aeronautical display in Copenhagen, and in return for doing this he was presented with the aircraft to keep as his personal property. He flew the machine to Kastrop airport and there gave flying demonstrations to the crowds. He performed aerobatics and gave people brief flights for fifty crowns a trip. In this way he made sufficient money and lived well in a hotel. His brilliant war record, which was a liability at home, was a social advantage in Denmark. He remained in that country for the greater part of the year 1919, living as gay a life as his earnings allowed, and the women enjoyed his company. He flew by day and flirted by night.

Goering's behavior in Denmark was not always exemplary, but he was good-looking and unattached, a useful and attractive man to make up a hostess's table. One hostess, however, suffered badly from his lack of manners and self-control on the day the terms of the Treaty of Versailles were published, when at a dinner party at which there were twenty or more guests present, he shouted, "One day we will come back to write another treaty!" Eventually he made life impossible for himself socially in Denmark, and a married woman with whom he was in love did everything she could to influence him to leave the country for Sweden.[7]

Goering was ambitious to obtain an official position in flying. Aerobatics might test his courage and please the crowds, but this way of life was scarcely the right one for a soldier and a would-be gentleman. He heard that a civil airline was to be established in Sweden, and in 1920, after some preliminary approaches, he was successful in obtaining a position as pilot for Svensk-Lufttrafik. Before this, however, after a period during which his plane was out of action because of damage to the undercarriage, he earned a living with demonstration flights and aerobatics near Stockholm. (Goering favored the legend which had grown up that his plane was the one he had piloted as commander of the Richthofen squadron; the publicity was good for business.) He was also making some money as agent in Stockholm for the Heinicken parachute, which opened automatically when a pilot baled out.

Goering, as a pilot of long experience, was frequently engaged to fly businessmen and other travelers on private flights. One of these private trips was to become important in his life. On a winter afternoon in 1920 Count Eric von Rosen, a well-known and adventurous explorer, came to the airdrome and asked to be flown on the short journey to his estate at Rockelstad on Lake Baven, near Sparreholm. It was snowing, and it seemed to him that flight, though extremely hazardous, was the quickest way of getting home. He liked the idea of the adventure of flying through snow, if there was a pilot brave enough to take the risk. Goering was quite willing to make the journey in the hour or two of daylight that was left. After losing their way as the plane lurched and dipped over trees and hills, they eventually landed on the ice of Lake Baven near Rockelstad Castle. Count von Rosen was very airsick. It was too late for Goering to return, and he accepted Rosen's and his wife's invitation to stay the night at the castle.

Here, once more, was a home that Goering could treat with respect. The medieval atmosphere recalled the castles of his youth in Germany. He ran his eyes over the armor, the hunting trophies and the relics of exploration, the paintings that showed the taste and traditions of an ancient family. There was the gesticulating carcass of a great bear which the Count had killed with a spear in the true

Viking manner. After a bath and a warm drink the frozen flyers felt life restored to them beside a huge log fire.

As Goering stood in front of the blazing logs, he must have noticed the swastika inset in the ironwork surrounding the fireplace. Probably it was the first time he had seen the emblem.[8] Opposite the fireplace stood the great staircase that led down into the hall. Goering looked up, and at once his attention was held by the sight of a woman who was coming down the stairs toward him; he thought her very beautiful. The Count introduced her as his wife's sister, the Baroness Carin von Kantzow, who was staying with them at the castle.

Goering was twenty-seven. During the evening as he watched this tall woman, five years older than himself, he began to fall in love with her. To have come down out of the snow-filled sky and found this magnificent castle beside the frozen lake was in itself romantic enough. And now in the warmth and comfort, with the hot drink stirring his blood, the sensation of romantic love grew in him, a love quite unlike the gay adventures and small affairs of the cities. Carin's eldest sister, the Countess von Wilamowitz-Moellendorff, in her biography of Carin, claims that Goering experienced love at first sight. He and the family stayed up half the night, singing German and Swedish folk songs to the accompaniment of Count von Rosen's guitar.

Carin von Kantzow was a maternal and very domesticated woman; she was sentimental, unhappy, estranged from her husband, and ready to respond to the kind of idealized love that Goering was prepared to offer her. She was not strong in health. There was no question, in the circumstances, of any other form of love than one based on romantic devotion, for Carin was closely looked after by her sister and her brother-in-law, as well as by her parents, and she had an eight-year-old son, Thomas, whom she loved dearly. Her husband, Nils von Kantzow, to whom she had been married for ten years, was an Army officer and the former Swedish military attaché in Paris.

By the time Goering was able to leave the castle, he had asked Carin to meet him in Stockholm. It was arranged that he should visit her at her parents' home. Her father, Baron Karl von Fock, was, like her husband, an officer in the Swedish Army; her mother, the Baroness Huldini Beamish-Fock, was an Englishwoman whose family lived in Ireland and whose father had served in the Cold-

stream Guards. Her sister Fanny had been married to a German
officer, Count Richard von Wilamowitz-Moellendorff, who was
killed in the war. Carin's sympathies were entirely with Germany
as it was symbolized by her brother-in-law and now by the handsome German war hero who, she began to realize, was deeply in
love with her.

Carin was by nature and upbringing sentimentally religious. Her
mother maintained a special Christian sisterhood which was cen-
tered in her house. This sisterhood, called the Edelweiss Society, had
been originated by Carin's grandmother, Mrs. Beamish, who had
settled in Sweden when she was widowed. Mrs. Beamish had died
on Christmas Day, 1895, and her daughter, the Baroness, had promised her that she would maintain the society in the same spirit.

The Edelweiss Society had its own chapel, a small building in the
little walled garden behind the family home in Greve-Ture-Gatan.
The chapel, like the society, still survives, with the present Countess
von Rosen as its sister superior. Its meetings were, and still are, confined to weekdays, when the members meet for prayer and music.
The chapel can hold only a very few people. It is bright and cheerful with the sunlight streaming through its windows; its floors are
beautifully carpeted and it is furnished with antique pieces. Four
prie-dieu stand before the miniature chancel with its altar. Outside
is a walled garden with religious statuary. This chapel was later to
have terrible memories for Goering, but now it seemed to him,
under Carin's influence, like a revelation of spiritual peace and
beauty.

The small chapel in the garden and the sisterhood bound together through prayer under the emblem of a flower were to some
extent influenced by the florid mysticism fashionable at the close
of the nineteenth century—the mysticism which affected many
poets of that time, and most of all the Irishman W. B. Yeats. One
of the sisters, Princess Marie Elisabeth zu Wied, published in 1937
a book deriving from this faith and called *The Inner Life*. It is dedi-
cated to "Hermann Göring, in friendship and gratitude."[9]

Goering, impressionable, lonely and in love with Carin, was
drawn into the cult of the Edelweiss Chapel. He wrote a sentimental
letter to the Baroness, in imperfect Swedish:

I should like to thank you from my heart for the beautiful moment
which I was allowed to spend in the Edelweiss Chapel. You have no idea

how I felt in this wonderful atmosphere. It was so quiet, so lovely, that I forgot all the earthly noise, all worries, and felt as if in another world. I closed my eyes and absorbed the clean, celestial atmosphere which filled the whole room. I was like a swimmer resting on a lonely island to gather new strength before he throws himself once more into the raging stream of life. I thanked God, and sent up warm prayers.

The uncertain life of a pilot had less appeal now for Goering. He wanted to marry Carin and return to Germany. But there were many obstacles, among them his lack of a settled job and the unfavorable attitude of Carin and her family to the idea of a divorce. He decided he must go back and educate himself in preparation for work other than flying or soldiering. Early in the summer of 1921, he left Carin in Sweden and returned to Munich, where his mother still lived. There he enrolled at the age of twenty-eight as a student at the university, reading political science. Carin meanwhile visited Frau Goering in Munich and, as a result, finally decided to ask her husband for a divorce. Nils von Kantzow behaved with the greatest generosity and gave his wife money along with her freedom. This enabled Goering and Carin to marry and set up a home in Germany. The wedding took place in Munich on February 3, 1922. The Goerings' first home was a hunting lodge at Hochkreuth in the Bavarian Alps, near Bayrischzell, some fifty miles from Munich, and it was there that they spent their honeymoon.

Both husband and wife were ardent nationalists. Goering needed little persuasion either at the university, where he was a desultory student, or elsewhere to express himself violently against the Weimar Republic and to attend nationalist meetings at which the government was vilified. There was also the Treaty of Versailles, which rankled in his mind as a national disgrace. Germany since the war had passed through a period of crisis, revolution and economic collapse, all due to the vindictive hatred of her enemies and the weakness and treachery of her own government. So thought Goering.

The period during which Goering had been flying in Scandinavia was that in which Adolf Hitler had been developing his Nazi Party, the N.S.D.A.P. (Nationalsozialistische Deutsche Arbeiterpartei— National Socialist German Workers' Party). By 1922, when Goering met him for the first time, Hitler had established the S.A. (Sturmabteilung), his force of storm troopers, who were used as hall guards at his political meetings and to provoke disturbances at the meetings of other parties. His base was Munich. The Bavarian state government was tolerant and weak; it should have taken action to disband these troublemakers as the old postwar *Freikorps* were disbanded. But the attacks made by the storm troopers on the Communists were not unwelcome to the Bavarian government; pitched battles were regular occurrences in the streets. No one living in Munich could be unaware of Hitler by 1922.

During Goering's defense at the Nuremberg trial he was to give this account of how he and Hitler met in the autumn of that year.[10]

One day, on a Sunday in November or October of 1922, the demand for the extradition of our military leaders was again placed in the foreground on the occasion of a protest demonstration in Munich. I went to this protest demonstration as a spectator, without having any connection with it. Various speakers from parties and organizations spoke there. At the end Hitler too was called for. I had heard his name briefly mentioned once before and wanted to hear what he had to say. He declined to speak, and it was pure coincidence that I stood nearby and heard the reasons for his refusal. . . . He considered it senseless to launch protests with no weight behind them. This made a deep impression on me; I was of the same opinion.

I inquired and found that . . . he held a meeting every Monday evening. I went there, and Hitler spoke about that demonstration, about Versailles . . . and the repudiation of that treaty. He said that . . . a protest is successful only if backed by power to give it weight. As long as Germany had not become strong, this kind of thing was to no purpose. The conviction was spoken word for word as if from my own soul.

On one of the following days I went to the business office of the N.S.D.A.P. . . . I just wanted to speak to him at first to see if I could assist him in any way. He received me at once and after I had introduced myself he said it was an extraordinary turn of fate that we should meet. We spoke at once about the things which were close to our hearts—the defeat of our Fatherland . . . , Versailles. I told him that I myself, to the fullest extent, and all I was and possessed were completely at his disposal for this, in my opinion, most essential and decisive matter: the fight against the Treaty of Versailles.

Hitler spoke at length about his program and then offered Goering a position in the Nazi Party.

He had long been on the lookout for a leader who had distinguished himself in some way in the last war . . . so that he would have the necessary authority. . . . Now it seemed to him a stroke of luck that I in particular, the last commander of the Richthofen squadron, should place myself at his disposal. I told him that it would not be so very pleasant for me to have a leading office from the very beginning, since it might appear that I had come merely because of this position. We finally reached an agreement: For one or two months I was to remain officially in the background, and take over the leadership only after that, but actually I was to make my influence felt immediately. I agreed to this, and in that way I joined forces with Adolf Hitler.

So Goering, well pleased with himself, joined the Nazi Party and at the age of twenty-nine assumed once more what he most desired, the command of men.

II

Failure and Exile

Fᴏʀ Gᴏᴇʀɪɴɢ the command of the storm troopers, which at his own suggestion he did not formally assume for two months, became an absorbing task. As he put it himself: "At first it was important to weld the S.A. into a stable organization, to discipline it, and to make of it a completely reliable unit which had to carry out the orders which I or Adolf Hitler should give it . . . I strove from the beginning to bring into the S.A. those members of the party who were young and idealistic enough to devote their free time and their entire energies to it. . . . In the second place, I tried to find recruits among laborers."[1] These men were needed for organized street fighting and as an offensive force at Hitler's political meetings. Goering was the ideal man to raise morale. As Hitler himself put it, recalling this early association: "I liked him. I made him the head of my S.A. He is the only one of its heads that ran the S.A. properly. I gave him a disheveled rabble. In a very short time he had organized a division of eleven thousand men."[2]

From the very beginning of their extraordinary relationship, Hitler, the corporal in the raincoat, exercised supreme power over Goering, the famous commandant of the Richthofen squadron. Hitler was not of good birth, nor had he had a good education; for years he had lived in destitution, unable to solve the elementary problem of making a bare living. In the Army, where he was a *Meldegänger*, or officer's runner, he had gained one stripe and no more. But now he was obsessed with the need for political power, and his gift for argument and agitation had made him the accepted master of

Goering. They seemed a most unlikely pair, but each had the perception to recognize the advantages the other could bring him. Goering offered Hitler the services of an officer and a gentleman of fortune; Hitler offered Goering the chance to become an active revolutionary and to shake a bloody fist with the cry, "To hell with Versailles!"

Goering brought Carin down from the mountains to Munich, and they set up a new home in the suburb of Obermenzing. They furnished the little house as best they could, and soon it became a meeting place for the more permanent members of the new party. Carin met Hitler and attended the first big Marsfeld parade, on January 28, 1923. She liked Hitler, who knew how to charm women, and soon the Goerings were offering their hospitality to the Leader and his friends, such as Rudolf Hess, who had also been a pilot in the Air Force, Alfred Rosenberg, the so-called philosopher, a Baltic German from Riga who had fled to Germany at the time of the Russian Revolution after living in Moscow and had become a virulent anti-Communist, and Captain Ernst Roehm, a professional soldier aged thirty-six, who still held an Army commission; although not by birth a member of the officer caste, Roehm had during the war become known to General Ludendorff, the last Chief of Staff of the German Army. Apart from Rosenberg, these men were militarists who made suitable company for Goering even if they scarcely seemed so for his aristocratic wife.

Roehm, in particular, was useful because of the wide variety of friends he had in Army circles, and he had done much to increase the number of volunteers for the S.A. In fact, he saw in the S.A. the nucleus of a secret army which would eventually replace the Reichswehr, the defense forces of the Republic, which consisted mainly of the Army and which the Versailles Treaty had supposedly limited to 100,000 men. This thick-necked homosexual was an able man who regarded Goering more as a rival than as an ally. But Hitler, already practicing his future policy of divide and rule, recognized that Goering would be a useful brake on the unruly energies of Roehm, to whom he gave the high-sounding title of chief of staff, while Goering was the actual commandant of the S.A.

Carin, the former baroness of gentle upbringing and mystical outlook, must have regarded with a strange kind of awe these men who tramped in and out of her house and talked themselves hoarse, after the companions she had known during her sheltered life in

Stockholm. But Hermann was evidently in his element, and greatly
helped by his wife's Swedish bank account. Carin was determined
that her husband should serve to the best of his ability the country
that was now hers as well as his. Above all, she, like her husband,
accepted Hitler's genius without question, and she listened to the
endless discussions in which the behavior of the new democracy
represented by the Weimar Republic and the treatment of Germany by the Allies after the defeat were invariably denounced,
along with the Jews and the Communists, who were regarded as the
powerful promoters of Germany's disgrace and suffering.

   To show their seriousness of mind, both Hess and Goering went
to the University of Munich and attended, according to Ernst Hanfstaengl, who first met them at this period, a course of lectures on
the German war of liberation against Napoleon, delivered by the
historian Karl Alexander von Müller.[3] Hanfstaengl, who found Goering amusing company though "a complete *condottiere*, the pure
soldier of fortune," says that he also had a humorous contempt for
the provincial Bavarians by whom at this time Hitler was surrounded; he tried to assert his birth by wearing a monocle. Hitler
apparently returned the compliment when Goering was not there
by making fun of the uxorious "darlings" with which Carin was
always addressing her husband. Yet Hanfstaengl found Goering
attractive and intelligent, with "a much broader fund of common
sense than the other Nazis."

   The S.A. was one of the many semimilitary refuges for the displaced soldiers of the postwar years. Many of them had originally
joined the *Freikorps* movement, which was deliberately tolerated
by the Allies after the formal dissolution of the Imperial Army, because of fear of the Communist strength in Germany and the revolutionary fervor of the Soviet Union. The *Freikorps* movement was
the answer of the right to the left both inside and outside Germany;
it was organized regionally on a private basis and financed by the
wealthy to oppose the left-wing government. Nevertheless, the *Freikorps* men had soon become undisciplined freebooters, out of favor
with both the Allies and the Weimar Republic. They formed ideal
recruits for the Nazis, who were themselves freebooters. To Hitler
the *Freikorps* had always acted as an inspiration; according to Gerald Reitlinger, he took over from them the swastika banner, the
brown shirt and what became the Hitler salute. He also took over
Roehm, who had been a *Freikorps* leader after the war.

When eventually in 1921 the Allies enforced the disarming of the *Freikorps*, Hitler immediately turned what was in effect his own particular *Freikorps* movement into a "sports" organization; later he renamed it the Sturmabteilung, or S.A., which, as we have seen, is what it was already called when Goering took over its command. While Roehm wanted to link the Sturmabteilung with the "Black Reichswehr," the undercover supplementary army secretly supported by the Weimar Republic, Hitler wanted to retain the S.A. for himself to act as a bodyguard and a propagandist force for the development of political agitation through violence directed against the Weimar Republic and left-wing Germany. For this reason alone, Goering was from Hitler's point of view a more suitable commander of the S.A. than Roehm.

Throughout 1923 Goering worked on the reorganization of the S.A., which rapidly grew in numbers until even the right-wing Bavarian government became alarmed. Hitler, though still an amateur in revolution, knew that at this stage of complication and chaos in German politics he was not strong enough to lead a rebellion on a national scale; he needed allies who shared his views sufficiently to work with him and whom he could eventually seek to dominate by the force of his own personality. For this reason, 1923 was for him a year of strenuous and mostly abortive negotiation, in which Goering was closely involved, while at the same time the S.A. was being disciplined and drilled in military style in the woods on the outskirts of Munich. The Bavarian government, always uncertain of its relations with Hitler, was nevertheless in the latter part of 1923 itself in open rebellion against the government in Berlin. In this situation lay Hitler's hope of the amalgamation of forces which would unseat the national government and bring him personally to some form of power on the crest of a revolutionary wave originating from Bavaria.

In January Hitler succeeded in persuading the Bavarian authorities to permit him to hold a rally of some five thousand storm troopers in Munich. At this mass meeting he spoke against the central government in an attempt to show his followers that the party's bid for political power in Germany was far more important than training to fight the French in the Ruhr. Opposed to any association with the Army, Hitler was also aware that to succeed he must ally himself with kindred nationalist movements and so swell the strength of his forces. This he managed to do in February with the help of Roehm. In the spring he began his attempts, without success, to persuade General Otto von Lossow, the Army commandant in Bavaria, to march with him on Berlin after the manner of Mussolini. In April Goering occupied the offices of the Nazi Party newspaper, the daily *Völkischer Beobachter*, in order to prevent the arrest of Dietrich Eckart, the disreputable writer who edited the paper for Hitler. This act was a further challenge to authority.

On May 1 Hitler made a fatal error. He had planned a major demonstration for this traditional day when the Munich Socialists held their rally; he had expected to receive the support of Lossow, but this support, asked for at the last moment, was resolutely refused. This put him in a most embarrassing situation, since, if he caused the disturbance that he intended, both the Army and the police would be forced to attack instead of support the storm troopers, who had already been ordered to assemble in full strength bearing all the illegal arms they possessed. Hitler himself, still anxious about what to do, met Goering and other prominent colleagues and associates at the Oberwiesenfeld paradeground, where thousands of men were waiting for orders. He, Goering and the rest wore their decorations; both Goering and Hitler aimed to look fierce and formidable in their steel helmets. Roehm, in his turn, exceeded himself by bluffing the regular Army into surrendering arms to the storm troopers. This was too much for General von Lossow. He summoned Roehm, who was still a regular officer, and told him he must return the arms at once. He then sent Roehm under escort to the paradeground with an ultimatum that the storm troopers must not march or cause any further disturbance. Hitler knew he was defeated, accepted the fact against the angry advice of the others and, in front of all his men, capitulated to Lossow, without whose support he knew there could be no successful outcome to large-scale violence. Eventually he returned to his Berchtesgaden home to replan the future, and for some weeks he took little part in the discussions that followed in Munich. He spent most of the summer in the mountains.

The discussions, with or without Hitler present, took place endlessly in the party offices, in the homes of the leaders, more particularly in Goering's house in Obermenzing, and at the Bratwurstglöckle tavern near the Frauenkirche, in the center of Munich. Here Goering and Roehm, Heines, the homosexual friend of Roehm and a convicted murderer, Anton Drexler, one of the founders of the Nazi Party, Eckart and Rosenberg, the so-called intellectuals of the group, and Ernst Hanfstaengl, the wealthy representative of Munich culture, would variously sit together in the evening at a regular table, drinking their beer and discussing their politics in loud, uncompromising voices. Often Carin would join them as their principal woman companion, and occasionally Julius Streicher would come over from Nuremberg to add his particular contribution of foulmouthed anti-Semitism. When Hitler was in Munich he would join them, though it seems he preferred to visit Obermenzing and the quieter comforts provided by Carin. It was she who put new heart into both Hitler and her husband in the dark days that followed the defeat of May 1.

By the autumn, Hitler and Goering were once more on General von Lossow's doorstep urging him to join with them in the common cause against the central government. Meanwhile, in August, Gustav Stresemann had become Chancellor in Berlin, and on September 27, alarmed by the insurrection that now seemed inevitable in Bavaria, he proclaimed martial law throughout Germany. Three weeks prior to this, on September 2, Hitler had strengthened his consolidation of nationalist forces at a mass meeting held in Nuremberg, at which his speech against the central government had been loudly cheered; General Ludendorff had also consented to appear in support of the movement. Quite apart from the Nazis and their Bavarian associates, unrest had been growing since January, when the French had occupied the Ruhr in order to enforce the delivery of the reparations promised them in the Treaty of Versailles. The *Freikorps* movement had gone into a phase of passive resistance to harass the invader, and, encouraged by this, the Black Reichswehr, the illegal supplementary corps of the regular Reichswehr, had shown itself ready to lead a revolt against the government in Berlin. This Black Reichswehr, under Major Buchrucker, numbered some twenty thousand men and had been tolerated in the past because it guarded the eastern frontier of Germany against the Poles. But now this illegal force had ugly associations with the secret society known as the Feme, which practiced a medieval tradition of brutality and atrocities, and, like the militaristic movements in Bavaria, it was a growing threat to the security of the central government in Berlin.

It was Stresemann's objective to end the passive resistance in the

Ruhr, to save Germany from anarchy and to come to terms with the Allies; the Bavarian government, on the other hand, was opposed to any form of concession to the Allies. Meanwhile inflation had gripped the German economy, and the mark, already fallen to over seven thousand to the dollar in January, had declined into astronomical figures by November.

Goering during this period had been trying, on behalf of Hitler, to persuade General von Lossow, as commander of the Bavarian Military District, to break his formal allegiance to Berlin and march with the S.A. and its associates to unseat the Stresemann government, which by the winter had come to regard Bavaria as the chief center of rebellion in Germany and so was prepared to bring force to bear to suppress any likely outbreak. Mussolini had provided them all with a splendid demonstration of what could be done when he had staged his March on Rome in October of the previous year. Hitler's uneasy attempts at alliance with the Bavarian government could not, however, be developed to the point of action, and Hitler decided to force the issue with his own immediate associates. While he was deciding what action to take, a political meeting was announced by Gustav von Kahr, the new State Commissioner and virtual dictator of Bavaria. This was due to take place on November 8, 1923, and Hitler was deeply suspicious that Kahr, whom he did not trust, would on his personal initiative announce Bavarian independence and so steal the thunder of the Nazis. This Hitler determined should not happen, and he ordered Goering to get the storm troopers ready for action. Goering hurried to take up his duties from the bedside of Carin, who had had pneumonia and was still feverish. To add to his worries, his mother had recently died. He kissed Carin and told her he might be very late and that she was not to worry. Then he rushed to join Hitler and assemble the storm troopers.

The public meeting called by Kahr was held in the vast auditorium of the Bürgerbräukeller, a tavern in the suburbs that could accommodate an audience of three thousand people. Kahr took the platform with the Premier of Bavaria, Dr. von Knilling, General von Lossow and other ministers of state. Kahr spoke to his audience as they sat drinking from their great mugs of beer; he spoke of the need for a new German Army to inherit the glory of that which was lost. For the audience this was familiar stuff, and they were settling down to steady drinking when suddenly they heard a man's voice shouting and the sound of pistol fire. Hitler, looking odd in an ill-fitting morning coat, was standing on a table pointing his pistol at the ceiling. Beside him were Hess and Goering and the Leader's bodyguard, a wrestler called Graf. They pushed forward to the platform, where Kahr stood, shocked like his audience by this savage intrusion.

Hitler strode in front of him and shouted, "The national revolution has begun. The building is occupied by six hundred armed men. No one may leave the hall." The beer drinkers saw that a machine gun was posted at the main entrance. Hitler bluffed the audience into believing that the governments of both Bavaria and the Reich were overthrown, and that the Army and the police had joined the ranks of the swastika. Then at pistol point he removed the ministers from the platform for a conference in another room. Goering was left in charge.

The audience recovered from the shock and began to talk. Goering could see that they were not satisfied, so he decided to address the meeting himself, speaking from the platform.

"There is nothing to fear," he shouted. "We are your friends. You've no reason to grumble—you've got your beer!" A new government was formed, he added, indicating the room where Hitler, gun in hand, was feverishly bluffing the three ministers to join with him in a government to be formed with General Ludendorff. Ludendorff in fact knew nothing of this, though at that moment he was being brought by Hitler's emissaries to the beer hall.

The ministers, uncertain what to do with Hitler, who was in a desperate state of excitement, parried his demands. The situation was tense because Ludendorff was expected at any moment, and the huge audience could not be kept under duress for an indefinite time. Hitler had to act. Without further discussion he rushed back onto the platform, announcing to the astonished audience that a new national government was in process of being formed with the collaboration of the ministers outside. He announced that he would be in control of the policy of the national government and that General Ludendorff would lead the new national army which would march forthwith on Berlin. The audience, believing that Hitler was indeed in a powerful association with men whom they trusted as much as they trusted anyone, began to raise a cheer. Then Ludendorff arrived. Although he was furious at the surprise that had been sprung on him, he let his presence appear to give support to what was happening. Hitler, deliriously happy, swore vengeance on the "November criminals" of 1918 and claimed that a new, strong, free, splendid Germany was being born. "Tomorrow," he shouted, "will either see a new national government or it will see us dead! I shall win tomorrow, or I shall be a dead man." And, like an actor in a melodrama, he pressed the pistol to his head.

The problem, as the audience poured out, was to decide what should be done with the ministers. Hitler had to leave them in the charge of Ludendorff, while he went to settle a street battle that he heard was breaking out between the storm troopers and a detachment of regular troops. When at length he returned he found that the ministers, after giving their word of honor to Ludendorff to stand by what was agreed, had been allowed to leave. There was great confusion of thought as to what action should now be taken. Meanwhile Kahr, threatened by telephone with action from Berlin, took what steps he could to retaliate. At dawn hundreds of printed proclamations renouncing any agreement with Hitler and dissolving the Nazi Party were posted throughout Munich. Kahr then transferred the state government to Regensburg. It was clear to all that the armed forces of the state had not been bluffed into joining Hitler's revolution and that the original government was still in power.

As soon as there was a moment to spare, Goering asked Hanfstaengl to telephone Carin and tell her not to worry if he did not get home that night; then he gave him a letter to post addressed to her. He was deeply worried about her, though reassured to some extent by the fact that her sister Fanny was there to help look after her. Then he turned his attention once more to the uncertainties of the night's action.

Hitler, Goering and Roehm were learning by experience that revolution could not be staged in so quick, so careless or so melodramatic a manner. Only Roehm had taken decisive action and occupied the military headquarters in Munich, where he stayed with his men. Hitler visited them during the night to discuss the situation. Hess, meanwhile, was busy taking hostages, who included two ministers of the Bavarian government. It was Ludendorff who proposed a solution to the dilemma of what should be done. He suggested an action based, as he pointedly said, on his personal reputation. He did not think that the armed forces or the police would fire on him, and he proposed that on the following morning,

November 9, he should march at the head of the storm troopers with Hitler beside him and that they should take over the center of Munich. Hitler, with no other plan left in his head, agreed reluctantly.

Accordingly, near eleven on the morning of this bleak November day the march began. Hitler, Ludendorff, Goering and Hess, together with certain others of the Nazi leaders, put themselves at the head of a body of some three thousand storm troopers, only some of whom were armed. They left the grounds of the Bürgerbräukeller and proceeded along the road toward the center of the city. The swastika flag was held high above them, and a truck carrying storm troopers with machine guns moved along near the front of the column. Hitler flourished his pistol as he marched. Goering, who expected trouble, saw to it that a number of hostages under guard were taken along with them, in case their presence might prove useful.

The Nazi marchers had to cross the Ludwig Bridge over the river Isar before they could reach the heart of the city. Here a detachment of armed police was posted to oppose them and Ludendorff halted the march. It was Goering who took action. Walking forward alone, grim and tough in his black leather coat, with the Pour le Mérite suspended from his neck, he saluted the officer in charge of the police and told him that they held hostages, including certain ministers, who would be shot if the march was opposed by force. The police officer, uncertain what to do, eventually decided to allow them through. The storm troopers triumphantly snatched the weapons from the hands of the police. The first victory was theirs.

They marched slowly across the river and entered the Zweibrückenstrasse, going in the direction that led to the Marienplatz, where the Town Hall was situated, rather over a mile from their starting point back over the river. At the Marienplatz they were joined by Julius Streicher, who was anxious not to be left out of the historic procession and had come up from Nuremberg in order to see what was happening.

By now it was after midday, and the march continued. Ludendorff was still in the front, and beside him his adjutant, Hans Streck. On Ludendorff's left walked Hitler, his arm for some strange reason linked with that of Scheubner-Richter, another of his close associates. Graf, Hitler's bodyguard, strode with Goering a pace or two in front of Hitler, on the left. Their objective was the War

Ministry, almost a mile away, in the Schoenfeldstrasse; there Roehm and his men were still in occupation from the previous night, though besieged by a detachment of regular soldiers. To reach the Ministry the Nazi leaders had to take the storm troopers down a narrow street on the right of the Marienplatz called first the Dienerstrasse and then the Residenzstrasse. They went forward and were urged to sing as they marched, but they were soon to meet their main obstacle. The end of this long street was blocked by armed police. The Nazi singing died down, and the march came to a stop.

This time it was Graf who stepped forward with the challenge. "Don't shoot!" he cried. "His Excellency General Ludendorff is coming!"

Hitler, standing behind him, shouted, "Surrender! Surrender!"

Then, from one side or the other, shooting began. Ludendorff, oblivious of the danger, strode forward and walked unharmed through the ranks of the police; he pushed them aside with the arrogance of past authority, though he was dressed as a civilian. But he went forward alone toward the open square beyond. Behind him Scheubner-Richter, with whom Hitler stood arm in arm, fell dying to the ground, and Hitler, stumbling or seeking cover from the bullets, fell heavily and dislocated his shoulder. Unnerved by the confusion and the pain, he fled in a car that was following the procession. At the same time, Hess also escaped. But Goering fell in the street, badly shot in the groin, and the blood began to flow from his wound. According to her own account, Carin's sister Fanny followed the procession and saw something of what had happened. She took the news to Carin.

Their principal leaders either escaped, arrested or wounded, the Nazi procession rapidly disintegrated. Those at the back of the column had heard the exchange of shots and then had seen the men ahead of them running back. Ludendorff, whom no one had thought to follow, was placed under arrest; Roehm and his men surrendered. Goering was carried by storm troopers into a nearby house, which happened to belong to a Jewish furniture dealer named Ballin, whose wife, Ilse, dressed Goering's wounds as best she could with a towel. She and her sister took charge of him in the house until darkness, when he was sent secretly to the clinic of a friend, Professor von Ach.[4] The professor informed Carin at once where Goering was. According to Fanny, Carin seems to have had a premonition at the moment Goering fell. Even though she was ill, she dressed and went at once to the hospital. There she learned that Goering's injuries were serious. She also heard that there was a warrant out for his arrest, issued by Lossow. Goering begged her to find some way to save him from capture. Fanny describes her sitting by the bedside holding her husband's hand, calmly and quietly working out what was the best thing to do, never taking her eyes off him for a single moment.

At the risk of his life, she arranged for friends to come from Garmisch, near the Austrian border, and drive him the seventy miles from Munich to their home, where he lay weak and ill and bitter. Carin knew that Hitler had been arrested on November 11 in Uffing, where the Hanfstaengl family had been taking care of him. But she was preoccupied with her own troubles. In a letter written to her mother on November 30, she described her husband's condition.

Hermann is in a terrible state. His leg hurts so much he can hardly bear it. Four days ago almost all the wounds that had healed broke out again and there is a horrible amount of pus in the leg still. He was X-rayed and they discovered a mass of fragments of shot as well as the dirt from the street buried in his thigh muscles. They operated on him with an anesthetic, and for the past three days he's been very feverish. His mind seems to wander; sometimes he even cries, and sometimes he dreams of street fighting. All the time he is suffering indescribable pain. His whole leg is fitted with little rubber tubes to draw out the pus. He is so kind, so patient, so good, but deep in his heart he is desperately unhappy.

Carin realized that her husband's presence was becoming known, and that she must attempt to get him away to the safety of Austria. She was unsuccessful. He was arrested and was placed under guard at the hospital in Garmisch, where he became the subject of friendly demonstrations during which the police were threatened with violence. Goering gave his word of honor to the police that he would not attempt a further escape, but Carin was determined he should do so, although his passport had been confiscated. With the help of friends and of sympathizers among the police, he was taken straight from his bed by car to the border and smuggled out of Germany, using a false passport. The men who took him posed as members of the police who were under orders to remove him.[5]

His injuries had not yet received proper care, and he was taken to a hospital in Innsbruck. There the wounds were reopened and X-rayed, and he was operated upon. Fever followed, and great pain, and the doctors prescribed morphine; according to Hanfstaengl, who had also escaped to Innsbruck, he had two injections a day.

Carin, in a letter written to her mother on December 8, reveals what both she and Goering were suffering.

I'm sitting here by my beloved Hermann's sickbed. I've got to watch him suffer in body and soul—and there's hardly anything I can do to help him. You know how awful that feels. His wound is just all pus, all over his thigh. He bites the pillow because it hurts him so much, and he moans all the time. You can imagine how this eats into my heart. It's exactly a month since they shot at him, and in spite of being dosed with morphine every day, his pain stays just as bad as ever. I left the hotel and moved here into the hospital a fortnight ago. I feel so much better to be with him all the time. Spies watch over our villa in Munich; our letters are being confiscated; our bank accounts are blocked, and our car has been taken away. . . . They tell me a warrant has been issued for my arrest, too.

Goering was kept in hospital until December 24, when he was released, though he still had to use crutches.

Meanwhile, the Nazi underground in Austria was at work, and, with the help of the maid and the gardener at Obermenzing, they began to smuggle in clothes and other necessities that would help the Goerings in their exile. By now the streets of Munich were covered with posters bearing Goering's photograph and announcing that he was a wanted man.

In Austria there were many Nazi sympathizers who came to Goering's help. They sent a Christmas tree to the Tiroler Hof, the hotel owned by another sympathizer where Goering spent Christmas with Carin. While Goering was still in hospital he had been visited by Kurt Ludecke, one of the senior party members, to whom he gave a vivid account of the Munich putsch. Goering asked Ludecke to represent him at a Nazi convention which was to be held in Salzburg. Hitler's lawyer came to see him on New Year's Eve, and the Tiroler Hof gave them a party. Hitler's sister Paula was also a constant visitor. Carin had caught a feverish chill over Christmas, and the reaction to the strain under which she had been put made her illness worse. Goering kept himself going with morphine. By February 3, their wedding anniversary, Carin was somewhat better, and Goering managed to give her a portable typewriter, which delighted her and encouraged her to write more letters home.

Goering's first assignment after his recovery was an invitation to speak to a group of nationalists at Innsbruck, but by February he was taken up with the organization of the party in Austria, following instructions received from Hitler, who was now in prison awaiting trial. Hitler refused to let Goering return, as he had offered to do, to stand trial alongside his Leader. He preferred him to gather the party together in Vienna, holding meetings, taking up collections and working with Austrian Nazis such as Walter Riehl. The Goerings continued to live at the Tiroler Hof, occasionally managing to pay their way, but their money and property in Munich had been impounded by the Bavarian authorities.

The trial in Munich of the leaders of the putsch began on February 26, and in April the news of the outcome reached Innsbruck: Ludendorff was acquitted, Hitler and the others, either in the dock or in exile, were declared guilty, and Hitler was to serve a five-year sentence in Landsberg fortress, though it was thought that his sentence was unlikely to last much more than six months. The trial had been a "soft" one, with Hitler acting aggressively throughout, his words filling the German press. Hess voluntarily returned from Austria to be his faithful companion in prison. In the fortress Hitler lived well, like some kind of guest; he spent the time in the composition of *Mein Kampf*. Goering appealed for an amnesty, but failed to achieve it. This was all the more galling because the Nazis did well in the April elections in Bavaria and were for the first time entitled to take seats in the Reichstag. Had Goering been allowed to return to Germany, Hitler might have been prepared to let him represent the party as a Reichstag deputy. Carin ventured back to Munich to try to free their property so that it could be sold to relieve their financial plight; she was unsuccessful. But on April 15 she visited Hitler at Landsberg and received from him a personal photograph inscribed, "To the honored wife of my S.A. commander."

However poor they were, the Goerings apparently chose not to show it. According to Hanfstaengl, they lived ostentatiously at their hotel and caused a great deal of resentment among the other exiles who had no means of support. Goering, apparently, had little conscience over money; he borrowed freely without attempting to pay back, as Hanfstaengl found out to his cost.

Meanwhile, the authorities in Vienna were troubled about the disturbances Goering's presence was causing in Austria. He and Carin were politely requested to leave. Goering's leg was painful and Carin felt ill, but it seemed best to accept this further stage of exile with good grace. With the help of the manager of the Tiroler Hof they moved at the end of April for a brief stay at the Hotel Britannia in Venice; the managers were friends and the Goerings received privileged treatment. Carin went on sending sentimental letters to her mother. While she rested, Goering forgot his politics and became a student of art. He found the galleries inspiring and in these days of sight-seeing laid the foundations of his future interest in the treasures of art. In May they went through Florence and Siena to Rome, where they were to stay until the spring of 1925.

In Rome Goering met Mussolini, whom he admired for having achieved in Italy what Hitler had just failed to do in Germany. He wanted to study fascism as well as art while he was there. He achieved an audience with Mussolini through his friend Prince Philipp von Hessen, who was in Rome paying court to Princess Mafalda, the King of Italy's daughter, whom he was subsequently to marry. Goering told Mussolini the story of Hitler and the abortive rising in Munich, and Mussolini expressed some interest in meeting Hitler once he was released from prison.

Hitler had been released from Landsberg on December 20, 1924, but he made no contact with Goering. He was too concerned by the disruption in the party during his absence to do anything but gather the reins of power once more into his hands. Meanwhile, Rosenberg had used his period of authority while Hitler was away to strike Goering's name off the party register.

The Goerings had other worries. Carin's mother was ill, and Carin wanted to be with her. Their depleted finances during this year of enforced idleness made life in Rome impossibly difficult; they were forced to live on the charity of friends and relations, and their pride suffered. Eventually, the money was got together for the long journey north. They traveled to Sweden through Austria, Czechoslovakia, Poland and the Free City of Danzig, where Goering did not fail to note that he stood on what he felt should be

German territory. In Stockholm, he and his wife went to live in a modest flat in Odengarten.

Goering was thirty-two now, a sick man described by his doctor as having a body like an elderly woman, fat, pale and white. Carin, though happy to be home in Sweden, now succumbed to her illness; her heart was weak and she was developing epileptic tendencies. For eighteen months she had had to watch the gradual deterioration of her beloved husband as the morphine which he had first used to cure the pain caused by his wounds had finally mastered him. Goering became a morphine addict, and the sight of him shocked Carin's family; they had known him previously only as the enthusiastic young pilot who four years ago had been Carin's devoted lover; now he was unemployed and a charge on their family, injecting himself daily with morphine to keep despair at bay. He and Carin were spending the money realized by the sale of the house in Obermenzing, which had now been permitted.

By the summer he was showing the worst symptoms of morphine addiction. Outbreaks of violence made him dangerous, and Carin, sick herself, was forced to let the doctors take full responsibility for him. She wanted her only child, Thomas, now aged thirteen, to come and live with her, but von Kantzow, her former husband, who had treated her with such generosity, opposed this firmly. When Goering was taken from her to the Aspudden hospital for observation, she was involved in a lawsuit to claim possession of her son. Von Kantzow disputed this successfully with a doctor's certificate which declared that, since Goering was the victim of morphinism and Carin was suffering from epilepsy, neither could be regarded as fit to look after the boy.[6] Goering, in fact, was finally certified as a dangerous drug addict, and police sanction was obtained to confine him to the Langbro asylum on September 1, 1925, after he had violently attacked a nurse who had refused to supply him with morphine. He was taken under police escort to Langbro and placed in the violent ward. From there he was eventually released by a psychiatrist who managed to persuade him to be co-operative and face the suffering that inevitably occurs during the initial period of abstention from the drug.

Goering was now under direct psychiatric observation, and it is of some interest to compare the recollections of his Swedish doctor with the records kept by the American prison psychiatrists who watched over him twenty years later at Nuremberg jail. Even as early as 1925 he was discovered to be of weak character, a man who used bravado to cover a fundamental lack of moral courage. He was regarded by the Swedish doctor as an hysteric, unstable in his personality, sentimental yet callous, a violent man prompted by fear. Like many men capable of great acts of physical courage which verge quite often on desperation, he lacked the finer kind of courage in the conduct of his life which was needed when serious difficulties overcame him.[7]

He left Langbro after some three months, but had to return when he found that he could not maintain abstinence from the drug. When at length he entered the normal world again, he felt in better health and better spirits. Although his interest in Germany was reviving, he was still unable to return there, and in fact was not to do so until a political amnesty was proclaimed by the newly elected President von Hindenburg in the autumn of 1927.

III

Fulfillment

GOERING RETURNED to Germany eagerly. He went alone, for Carin was ill and needed treatment. He came back both to find work that would enable him to earn a proper living and to renew his contact with Hitler, whom he went to see in Munich. Hanfstaengl was the only member of the Nazi circle who seemed genuinely pleased to see him. He judged him to be "fatter, more businesslike and materialistic and concerned chiefly with the Babbitt aim of life."

Hitler was preoccupied with the problem of rebuilding the Nazi Party as a political force in the State. He was determined now to win power by constitutional means. Since the day he last saw Goering lying wounded in the street while he himself was being hustled away from the violence and the failure, a great deal had happened. He had been in jail; he had written *Mein Kampf*—that farrago of ignorance, prejudice and occasional astuteness which passed for his philosophy; and he had returned to Munich to revise his strategy for uprooting the government and achieving power. The party had fought two elections in 1924 and was represented in the Reichstag by fourteen members; they were to face another election campaign in 1928. Goering's former position as head of the S.A. was occupied by von Pfeffer, and Hitler at this stage was not willing to displace him and take back the penniless captain. Hitler was very conscious of money; he needed men who could keep themselves. What mattered most was attracting money into the party, not paying money out. Goering needed payment, and Hitler therefore did not receive

him with any show of warmth; he was always deeply suspicious of
a professional soldier, and Goering had not made himself popular
with the rest of Hitler's associates, who told their Leader that Goering had often criticized him during his exile in Austria and Italy
and that he was using the party for his own purely personal ends.
This was to some extent true; for Goering, a seat in the Reichstag
would have increased immeasurably his status as a business agent
and go-between. Hitler eventually compromised. It was agreed
Goering should go back to Berlin and make his fortune, keeping in
touch with the party.

Even though money was scarce, Hitler was by no means impoverished. The Nazi press was gaining ground. There were steady
profits coming in from the innumerable mass meetings, to which a
small entrance fee was always charged. There were gifts from
wealthy sympathizers. Hitler had an income; his tax records survive
and prove that he was learning how to argue about expenses with
the tax inspectors.

Goering gradually established himself during the winter months
as a business agent in the aircraft industry. He was in touch with
Erhard Milch, a senior executive in Lufthansa, which enjoyed a
monopoly in German civil aviation. He acted as an agent in Berlin
for the Bavarian Motor Works, which made aviation engines, and
for the firm of Heinkel. He was also agent for the Swedish Tornblad
parachute, and he worked from a small office in the Gaisbergstrasse,
which he shared with Victor Siebel, who was later to become an
aircraft manufacturer.[1] Heiden claims that the Bavarian Motor
Works had been bought by Camillo Castiglioni, an Italian Jew
from Trieste, who paid Goering generously to act as his representative, but that Goering achieved little for him. Heiden describes
Goering as tireless in work and in the social round, turning night
into day, working by candlelight in his flat, in front of him a picture
of Napoleon, behind him a medieval sword.[2]

In Berlin he was joined by Paul Koerner, another ex-officer, who
became his partner. He began also to work upon his old social contacts, such as Bruno Loerzer and Prince Philipp von Hessen.

Early in 1928 Goering apparently decided to put pressure on
Hitler. The elections were approaching in the spring, and he went
to Munich to fight for the recognition he felt that he deserved.
Together with Hanfstaengl, he walked in the snow to Hitler's flat
in the Thierschstrasse. Goering did not want to go in alone, but

Hanfstaengl refused to accompany him. Later he gathered that Goering had lost his temper, but won his point; Hitler consented that he should be regarded as a Nazi candidate for the Reichstag.[3] Hanfstaengl says that he often heard Hitler express fears that Goering would fail to be of any use to the party; however, he copied Hitler's style and delivery on the platform with remarkable effect.

Goering was by now reasonably established and was anxious to mix business with politics. He was particularly useful in Berlin, where the Nazis' main strength so far was among the working class, thanks to the seemingly radical influence of the brilliant young agitator Joseph Goebbels and of the party's "left-wing" leaders Otto and Gregor Strasser. Hitler wanted the ultimate power that he knew would come only from combining the votes of the proletariat with the money, influence and pressures of the industrialists. Goering, the soldier and the gentleman, knew how to behave in such company; Hitler was still embarrassed in society, uneasy when dressed in formal clothes that never seemed to fit his body, unhappy in his failure to make small talk with the kind of people with whom he had never mixed socially. While Goebbels, whom he had appointed party gauleiter for Berlin, fought on Hitler's behalf in the streets, Goering was expected and required to conquer the executive suite and the drawing room.

By May, on the eve of the elections, Goering felt sufficiently confident to write to Carin to come and join him in Berlin. It was a joyful reunion after months of separation, though he had managed to visit her in Stockholm at Christmas. He took her to his flat at 16 Berchtesgadenerstrasse.

Goering took his place on many platforms, even alongside the radical Goebbels. He discussed politics endlessly with Koerner and the other party members; evidently he began to neglect business and he became short of funds, for Carin records how they had to have hurried meals in cheap restaurants, even sharing a bowl of pea soup with Koerner. The old talking points, Versailles, Bolshevism, the Jews, reparations, the evils of a Social Democrat government, were thrashed out endlessly in voices that sounded like the cracking of whips.

The Nazis made a poor enough showing at the elections on May 20. They polled 810,000 votes, while the Social Democrats won over nine million. The Nazis were entitled to only twelve of the 491 seats in the Reichstag. Goering and Goebbels filled two of these seats on behalf of the party. As Goebbels put it, contemptuously: "I am not a member of the Reichstag. I am . . . the possessor of immunity and . . . a free railway pass."[4] Members of the Reichstag could not be prohibited by the authorities from speaking at political meetings, as both Goebbels and Hitler had been in the past; Hitler, in fact, was still forbidden to speak at public meetings in Berlin. Goering, less cynical than his colleague, was delighted at his election. He was elected as from Bavaria, says Hanfstaengl, and when the latter saw him off to Berlin from the station in Munich Goering wore a Bavarian mountaineer's hat with an edelweiss token and a huge brush; his "enormously fat" body was covered by a "showy great aviation overcoat made of leather" and he was happily waving his free first-class railway ticket. Among those who sent Goering their congratulations when he assumed his seat in the Reichstag was former Crown Prince Friedrich Wilhelm, who wrote: "Your extraordinary talent and your ability as a speaker, as well as your physical strength, should prove useful for your new position as a representative of the people in the Reichstag." Brawls in the Reichstag were only too frequent, when strength of speech had to be supplemented by strength of body.

Carin described for her mother in a letter dated June 14 the great day when Hermann took seat number 54 in the Reichstag.

With us everything is fine, and I think it's *colossally* interesting. Yesterday the Reichstag was opened, and naturally I was there, too. Hermann has a very good seat beside General von Epp of Bavaria; the two of them are on their own at a table in front. They got these good seats only because the number had to be increased anyway. And a good thing, too. It was quite uncanny to see the *Rotgardisten*; they've come up in the Reichstag in a quite unheard-of way, and they throw their weight about *colossally*. They were all in their uniforms adorned with the star of David—that is, the Soviet star, it's quite the same thing—red armbands, etc. Young mostly, and rearing for a fight. And some of them absolutely criminal types. How many in all these parties, except Hitler's, are Jews! . . . Hermann will be having a frightful lot to do, no doubt at all. Even now I see him only occasionally. But all his free time he spends with me. At least we are trying to eat together, but we hardly ever have a meal alone. . . . On Saturday or Monday we fly to Zurich. Hermann is invited to give a few lectures, and besides that he hopes to arrange some demonstrations of the Tornblad parachute. There have been so many parachute accidents recently (with other parachutes), and now Hermann would like to show what the Tornblad can do.

In the autumn of 1928 Carin mentions that their financial position was so far improved that they could rent a modern flat of five rooms at 7 Badenschestrasse and fill it with some of their original furniture, which they had fortunately managed to recover. Goering was now receiving a regular income amounting to some $125 a month as a Reichstag deputy, in addition to the money that came his way through business and through payments made him by Lufthansa. Fritz Thyssen, the industrialist, says that he also helped Goering during this period.

Hermann Goering I came to know in the following manner. One day the son of one of the directors of my coal-mining companies, a certain Herr Tengelmann, came to me. "Listen to me," he said, "there exists in Berlin a Herr Goering. He is trying very hard to do some good for the German people, but he is finding little encouragement on the part of German industrialists. Wouldn't you like to make his acquaintance?" In consequence of this suggestion I met Goering in due course. He lived in a very small apartment in these days, and he was anxious to enlarge it in order to cut a better figure. I paid the cost of this improvement.

At that time Goering seemed a most agreeable person. In political matters he was very sensible. I also came to know his first wife, Carin, who was a Swedish Countess by birth. She was an exceedingly charming woman and showed no signs of the mental derangement which clouded her life before she died. Goering idolized her, and she was the only woman who was able to guide him—as though he were a young man.[5]

It was decided that Goering's special interest in the Reichstag should be communications, which included aviation. The task the deputies set themselves was to harry the government on every point they could find. When there was a debate on the decline in efficiency of the state railways, Goering was virulent in his attack:

The real and only cause of this intolerable state of affairs is the exploitation of the German Reich Railway by the Dawes Plan and by reparations. All the parties in the Assembly must admit this today, but all these parties are equally responsible for the existing state of affairs. Now that is the core of the evil. The Reich Railway, formerly the pride of Germany, probably the best railway in the world, the loyal servant of the people and of all their economic needs, is regarded today just as something to be plundered and exploited by our enemies. My party has clearly and unequivocally emphasized this fact from the outset. When we come to power we will put an end to this intolerable state of affairs and restore the free German Reich Railway to the free German people![6]

Conscious of his debt to Lufthansa, he demanded during a debate in the Reichstag on the air estimates in June 1929, that the civil airline be voted more money because, as Heiden records it, German aviation had a "great patriotic task" to fulfill, namely, to act as a screen for German rearmament in the air. "Why is there no Air Minister?" he demanded.

Why are we economizing on these things when our duty to the nation demands the opposite? Why are individual members, and also the committee, harping on anonymous reports which only serve to destroy confidence in the German air arm? We airmen, whenever it has been required of us, have fought in the open, and we shall do so again. I hope, gentlemen, that you will decide to approach this matter in the same spirit of candor so that the difficulties which are confronting the German air arm may be eliminated.

He ended: "Save the air arm. If you don't you will live to regret it." He was constantly to urge the increase of subsidy for the air throughout his career as Reichstag deputy, encouraged always by the air service and the aircraft industry.

Goering now was called the "salon Nazi," the "ambassador of Hitler." Carin's letters to her mother during the next three years, at the end of which her health finally gave way under the strain of being Goering's wife, read like a social gazette. The Hohenzollerns were already being drawn into the party net; the Crown Prince was a friend in the background, but his brother August Wilhelm (whose nickname was Auwi), joined the party in 1930 and became a Nazi speaker on the platform alongside Goering, and his brother Eitel Friedrich was also interested in National Socialism. The Prince and Princess zu Wied had become constant guests at the flat in the Badenschestrasse and were on very intimate terms with the Goerings. "Princess zu Wied's cook will help in the kitchen," writes Carin, anxiously planning to give a picturesque

Swedish meal in the peasant style with the help of her friends and of her devoted maid Cilli; the guests were to include Thyssen, Hjalmar Schacht and Hitler. "Our house is so full of politicians that I would be driven mad if it were not so fascinating!" says Carin in a whirl. The widening circle included industrialists, officials from the embassies (whom Goering had met initially through business) and a range of aristocrats, all of whom for one reason or another were watching the progress of the party in the hope that it might one day offer protection for their business or personal interests.

Other guests mentioned in Carin's letters home include Prince Henckel-Donnersmark, a wealthy Silesian industrialist and land-owner, and Baron Koskull of the Swedish legation, as well as several other members of the aristocracy. On Christmas Eve, 1930, Goebbels brought "charming, personal gifts," and they all sang carols after eating cold meat and fruit; Thomas von Kantzow was there and sang carols in Swedish with his mother. Goebbels also came for lunch on Christmas Day, when Prince August Wilhelm arrived, bringing white lilies and a camel's-hair blanket as gifts. Later, in 1931, the Goerings were invited to Doorn to spend a week with the ex-Kaiser, who, according to Hanfstaengl, another close friend of Auwi, was sufficiently interested in the Nazis to write to Hitler at this time and informally appoint Auwi his representative with the party.[7] The Hanfstaengls' house in Munich became one of those social meeting places so useful to Hitler during the early years of discussion and organization, and Hanfstaengl records that it was here, on February 24, 1930, that Goering managed to prevent Hitler's delivering a funeral oration over the body of the disreputable Horst Wessel, who had been killed in a tavern brawl the day before —a propaganda move which Goebbels was anxious to achieve. Goering represented a moderating influence in this debate, and his victory over Goebbels was a sign that by now he had overcome Hitler's suspicion of him.

But before the industrialists were finally persuaded to support Hitler, the party had to deal with the dissension in its own ranks between the "left" and the "right" and fight the bitter election campaign in the summer of 1930. The command of the S.A. (now estimated as over 100,000 men, and therefore exceeding the figure permitted for the Reichswehr) was still in the hands of Pfeffer; this command Goering coveted. The S.A. was composed mainly of unemployed men with a taste for demonstration and violence; they were the more or less conscious representatives of the "dispossessed" in Germany. Hitler, Goering and Goebbels watched their growing force with a wary eye; it needed a strong hand to control it. Otto Strasser, editor of the *Berliner Arbeiterzeitung*, was, as he had always been, a radical, and his pseudorevolutionary articles supporting strikes and industrial unrest became increasingly embarrassing to Hitler and the right wing of the party, now that they were pledged to win power the legal way and persuade the industrialists to support them. In June 1930 Hitler and Otto Strasser met in Berlin, but reached no agreement. Hitler returned south to Munich and ordered Goebbels, as Gauleiter of Berlin and director of party propaganda, to expel Strasser from the party. Strasser answered him by founding his own nationalist movement, the Black Front.

This expulsion of the man who seemed the champion of the dispossessed angered the S.A., whose lawless behavior was regarded with grave suspicion by the industrialists with whom Goering was associating. The party offices in Berlin were stormed by the S.A. in September, the very month of the elections, and Hitler himself had to come to Berlin to rescue Goebbels from his impossible situation. He used his remarkable powers of persuasion and his prestige as leader of the party to quiet the hooligans and promise them paradise. He made himself their commander, and later, on January 1, 1931, he appointed Roehm, whom he had summoned back from a job as military instructor in Bolivia, as chief of staff. It was to be a bitter moment for Goering, but, as events were soon to show, he was far better placed where he was.

Goering, meanwhile, like all the Nazi leaders, was speaking at every possible public meeting that Goebbels could organize through the party representatives in Germany. The election slogan was "Germany awake!" Carin often traveled with her husband, her health suffering in the ceaseless rush from place to place. Her letters reveal the almost intolerable strain of this last year of her active life with Goering. During the summer of 1930 she collapsed and had to retire to a nursing home at Kreuth in Bavaria. Whenever he could, Goering, accompanied by his stepson Thomas, would visit her on weekends. In August she was just well enough to attend the party rally at Nuremberg with her husband, but once more the strain proved too severe and she returned to the nursing home for further treatment.

The elections were held on September 14. The result was an outstanding victory for the Nazis and a most significant step forward in their campaign for power. They polled nearly six and a half million votes, which entitled them to 107 Reichstag seats. Overnight they leaped from the lower depths of German political intrigue to the vantage point of the second largest party in the Reichstag. Now they could negotiate from strength, exploiting at every opportunity the weakness and vacillation of the democratic government in Germany.

The whole Western world was moving into a period of financial strain which was to sap its strength and weaken its moral resistance to corruption. These were the black years. The Wall Street collapse had come in the autumn of 1929. Stresemann, the only statesman of vision, resource and staying power that the successive democratic governments had produced, was dead. Field Marshal von Hindenburg, aged and obstinate, was President. Brüning, of the Catholic Center Party, honest and well-meaning, had tried to rule as Chancellor without the Reichstag, by obtaining emergency powers, and he had failed. The result had been the election which swept the Nazis onto the doorstep of power.

Hitler was now more than ever convinced that the right way to achieve his ambition was the legal and constitutional way. Goering completely accepted this policy. After a Law for the Protection of the Republic had been passed in March 1930, as an attempt to suppress the growing public disorder, Goering said, "We are fighting against this State and the present system because we want to destroy it utterly—but in a legal manner" to satisfy "the long-eared plain-clothes men. Before we had the Law for the Protection of the Republic we said we hated this State; under this law we say we love it—and still everyone knows what we mean!"[8] When three saboteurs had been charged by the Minister of Defense with spreading Nazi doctrines in the Army, Hitler himself had appeared before the Supreme Court in Leipzig as a witness for the defense; there he had made his celebrated statement that the time would come when the German national revolution would take place by constitutional means and that then, still by constitutional means, "we will form the State in the manner which we consider to be the right one." This was on September 25, eleven days after the results of the election.

So the Nazis continued to play a shrewd double game to entice both the workers and the industrialists into their political net.

On October 14 Goering was a co-signatory with Goebbels, Gregor Strasser and other Nazi deputies of a motion due to go before the chamber which recommended the confiscation of "the entire property of the banking and Bourse magnates . . . for the benefit of the German people without compensation," and that "all large banks, including the so-called Reichsbank," should "become the property of the State without delay."[9] Hitler was furious and the motion was withdrawn. Only two months later, in December, Stauss, a member of the board of the Deutsche Bank, was inviting Hjalmar Schacht, who had resigned from his position as president of the Reichsbank the previous March, to dinner in order to meet Deputy Hermann Goering. The latter impressed Schacht as "a pleasant, urbane companion" without "anything that might have been described as an irreconcilable or intolerable political radicalism."[10]

Goering was quick to invite Schacht to a dinner party where he might meet Hitler himself. This was on January 5, 1931; Fritz Thyssen and Goebbels were also present. Schacht remarked on the comfort and good taste of Goering's "pleasant middle-class home." There was, he found, no ostentation. He thought Frau Goering most winning and kindly; she gave him "an essentially simple meal" and then retired to lie on a sofa and listen to the conversation. Hitler did not arrive until after dinner, wearing his dark trousers and the brown jacket which was the uniform of the party. He was evidently anxious to reassure the former president of the Reichsbank; Schacht studied him carefully and thought him natural, unassuming and unpretentious. He noticed how Goebbels and Goering retired and left matters to Hitler, who monopolized the conversation. Schacht was impressed with Hitler's reasonableness and moderation, though at the same time he was stirred by Hitler's "absolute conviction of the rightness of his outlook and his determination to translate this outlook into practical action."

Schacht claims that, as a result of this meeting, he tried to convince Brüning that he should form a coalition government in order to use the Nazis' strength while at the same time moderating their policy, but that his suggestion was turned aside. Such suggestions were typical of the futile intrigues of a weak and vacillating democracy before the oncoming tide of the Nazis, who, though they controlled only eighteen per cent of the electorate, faced a divided front that still thought of government in terms of minor tactical advantages gained by one person over another. This may succeed when most men seeking or possessing office are honest and desire to serve the general welfare of a stable community. But in the Germany of 1930, with three million unemployed and the daily occurrence of street battles promoted by the Nazis against their chosen opponents, the Communists, such tactics were political suicide.

Hitler would have accepted no such form of restrictive coalition. He had more important work to do: to convince the bankers and the industrialists that the Nazis were their only hope of securing a stable, right-wing government, and that they should invest heavily in the party funds. William L. Shirer has listed certain heads of industry who decided that Hitler was their man. Walther Funk, editor of one of the leading financial newspapers, had joined the Nazi Party at the instigation of the industrialists controlling the mines in the Rhineland; they needed a spokesman who could influence Hitler in favor of private enterprise. Others were the banker Baron Kurt von Schroeder, Georg von Schnitzler of I. G. Farben, and the piano manufacturer Carl Bechstein, who was an early supporter of Hitler. Thyssen was already in the fold and Schacht well on the way. Shirer estimates that between 1930 and 1933 a substantial section of German industry was financing the Nazi Party to the extent of many millions of marks a year. In August 1931 Hitler was able to give Goering a large Mercedes; later he was to observe how erratic a driver Goering was, swinging his car over onto the wrong side of the road and sounding his horn continuously to warn approaching traffic who was coming.[11]

But 1931 was to become for Goering a year of personal suffering. At a party the previous Christmas Carin had fainted while the family were singing the carol "Stille Nacht." In the spring she was desperately ill again and overheard the doctor tell her husband that she would never recover; she managed to rally, however, and hold on to life for a few more months.

In spite of his anxiety over Carin's health, Goering had to face new and difficult tasks in the effort to defeat Brüning, who still commanded a majority of votes in the Reichstag. In May Hitler sent him to Italy on a mission to the Vatican. Hitler realized that Brüning received much of his support from the Catholic areas of Germany, such as the Rhineland and Bavaria, and that the party was held by the Catholics to be the advocate of paganism. Although Goering was a Protestant, he was regarded as the man in Hitler's immediate circle with the greatest flair for religion; he was also a skilled talker. When Goering reached Rome, he met Cardinal Pacelli, then Secretary of State in the Vatican but later to become Pope Pius XII. The visit caused much speculation in the press; after his return, Goering made it clear in an interview with the *Nationalzeitung* that he had not seen the Pope, as the journals of the left had claimed; then he added, "I pointed out . . . that the party unequivocally supported the constitution of positive Christianity, and I also uncompromisingly expressed the Führer's demand that the Catholic Church should not meddle in the internal affairs of the German people."[12]

Before this mission to Rome, Goering had on February 3 helped lead the march out of the Reichstag which the Nazis and certain other right-wing parties had organized in protest against the Brüning government. The Nazis were not to resume their seats until the following September, when they returned in order to try other tactics in the effort to compel Brüning to resign. This organized withdrawal of the party led to contact being established between General Kurt von Schleicher, representing the Army, and Roehm, representing the Nazi Party and the S.A. Schleicher's name in German means "intriguer," and this was to be the nature of his activity in his dealings with the Nazis. Schleicher had the ear of President von Hindenburg and had become the political agent of both the Army and the Ministry of Defense; he had even been instrumental in influencing Hindenburg to appoint Brüning Chancellor in 1930. The balance of power standing in opposition to Hitler at the beginning of 1931 was at best uneasy and unstable. Hindenburg was in his eighty-fourth year, his mind hopelessly prejudiced in favor of the deposed monarchy and the political importance of the Army; the Reichstag itself was weakened by too many minority parties seeking petty advantages over each other.

Brüning was trying to see a way through Germany's difficulties by emergency decrees which proved in the end to be ineffective. Schleicher favored an authoritarian government independent of the Nazis but dependent on the support of the Army. When the Nazis won their astonishing victory at the polls in September 1930, Schleicher changed the basis of his calculations. It might indeed be necessary in the light of these recent events to include the Nazis in his scheme for establishing a coalition which would impose its rule on Germany and bypass the stupid men in the Reichstag.

Goering, meanwhile, was very conscious of Roehm's increasing intrusion into a diplomatic field that he regarded as his own. It has been claimed that he was instrumental in bringing about the celebrated but abortive meeting between Hitler and Hindenburg on October 10, and that he prepared the ground by meeting Hindenburg privately in advance. The weight of the evidence seems, however, to favor the explanation that it was Schleicher himself who won this concession unwillingly from the President, and that Roehm initiated the idea. Roehm, however, lost whatever prestige he might have gained from this maneuver when Hindenburg refused on any account to meet a man whom he knew to be a pederast. The "Bohemian corporal," as the President called Hitler, must be suitably accompanied, and Goering, Reichstag deputy and former Army officer with a Pour le Mérite to his credit, was the man the President preferred.

The summons to the President came at a difficult time. For Hitler it was an inopportune moment for so important a meeting. His niece Geli Raubal had just killed herself with her uncle's pistol; although she had been twenty years younger than Hitler, he had been obsessed by love for her and had exercised over her a pathological despotism that is the only known or reasonable explanation for her suicide. Hanfstaengl's views on Hitler's pathological relationship with his niece are of some interest. He maintains that Geli, who, like her mother, was completely dependent upon Hitler, was used by him either to satisfy his peculiar sexual tastes or to rouse him from his probable impotence. Hanfstaengl claims to have seen some pornographic drawings of Geli made by Hitler which the Führer refused to have destroyed after her death, when they vanished, to reappear as a means for blackmail. The scandal surrounding her death soon reached the press; but Gürtner, the Bavarian Minister of Justice, was persuaded to overlook the obvious need for an inquest; the body was sent for burial to Vienna, where Himmler and Roehm represented Hitler. Goering apparently was quite prepared to accept a wholly romantic interpretation of Geli's death and said later in Hitler's presence that he thought what had happened to her was the result of an accident, not suicide. Whereupon, says Hanfstaengl, Hitler fell weeping on Goering's shoulder, crying, "Now I know who is my real friend." "Pure opportunism on Goering's part," comments Hanfstaengl. Like Goering, however, after his wife's death, Hitler kept a portrait of Geli, a sculptured bust, in a form of shrine surrounded by flowers.

The shock of Geli's death caused an emotional crisis in Hitler's life from which he never fully recovered. He retired to Tegernsee, Bavaria, in a state of collapse. When the news reached him that Hindenburg would at last see him along with Goering, he simply asked where Goering was. In Sweden, the answer was, watching by the bedside of his wife.

Carin was dying; her heart was worn out. In the early summer she had been in a nursing home in Silesia; later she had seemed to recover sufficiently to enjoy a motor tour in the new Mercedes. But on September 25 had come the news that her mother was dead. Carin collapsed in a faint; when eventually she regained consciousness she murmured, "I believed so much I would follow Mama . . ." She insisted that Goering should take her to Stockholm for the funeral. So weak was her condition that they arrived only after the funeral was over. Carin herself had only a few days left to live.

Goering loved his wife, but he had made life much too hard for her. She had lived quite selflessly for him and for the political cause she had in her foolish enthusiasm adopted because it was his. When Hitler's telegram arrived asking Goering to return at once to meet Hindenburg, Carin made her last gesture of self-sacrifice. Goering knelt by her bedside while she begged him to leave her and go back to Germany. Finally he agreed to go. They were never to see each other again.

The meeting for which Goering so unwillingly returned took place on October 10. No record has been preserved of what was said. An official statement published the same day read: "The President of the Reich today received Herr Adolf Hitler and Captain Hermann Goering, member of the Reichstag, and obtained from them a detailed account of the aims of the National Socialist movement. This was followed by a discussion of internal and external political questions."

The meeting was naturally the subject of much speculation. Hitler is said to have been nervous and to have talked too much, and Hindenburg, it was reported, told Schleicher that all Hitler would ever be fit for was Minister of Posts. Hitler and Goering left immediately after the interview for a nationalist rally in Bad Harzburg at which Brüning's government was yet again to be denounced by a strong contingent from the right-wing parties and many outstanding representatives among the industrialists. Hitler behaved perfunctorily and eventually withdrew from the rally because he personally was outshone by the leaders from the other parties. This unsuccessful affair was followed by a vast rally of the S.A. and the S.S. (the Schutzstaffel, elite guards) at Brunswick on October 17, at which Hitler stood for a parade that it was claimed lasted six hours and certainly restored his sense of power. Goering was back in Berlin organizing a further onslaught upon Brüning, who on October 13 had announced yet another reconstituted government to the Reichstag. On October 16 a motion of no confidence was defeated only by the narrow margin of twenty-five votes. Then on October 17, at four o'clock in the morning, Carin died.

As her sister Fanny describes the last hours of Carin's life, she was calm and her eyes seemed to show that she was happy, but she could not sleep; she talked to the night nurse about her husband and her son Thomas, and then she prayed for them both, her eyes opening wide as if she saw some vision. When the time came she died without pain.

Goering, distraught by sorrow, traveled to Stockholm accompanied by his brother Karl and his friend Koerner. He found his wife's body lying surrounded by flowers in the Edelweiss Chapel in the garden behind the house. He knelt beside her alone, overcome by grief and remorse that he had not been with her when she died. On her birthday, October 21, her body was carried away in a white coffin covered with pink roses and taken to Lövoe, near Drottningholm, for interment in the Fock family vault.

Goering went straight back to Germany after the funeral. He went to live at the Kaiserhof hotel, which was Hitler's headquarters in Berlin. The only way for him to overcome his sorrow was to devote himself entirely to the service of Hitler. This was no problem; the next fifteen months were to be among the busiest in his life.

The political calendar for 1932 was a full one. In March and April came the two successive presidential elections, followed immediately by the state elections. In May Brüning was forced to resign and in June Franz von Papen, an acquaintance of Goering, became Chancellor. In July followed the Reichstag elections, with an increased vote for the Nazis. In August came the refusal by

Hindenburg to make Hitler Chancellor, followed by the mobiliza-
tion of the S.A. and the declaration of martial law by Papen. In
September occurred the notorious affair of the tussel between Papen
and Goering over the dissolution of the Reichstag. In November
Papen resigned and the fresh elections brought a loss of two million
votes for the Nazis; in December Schleicher was made Chancellor.
Then followed the final negotiations which led to the downfall of
Schleicher and, through the intrigues of Papen, the offer of the
Chancellorship to Hitler on January 30, 1933.

The whole of this arduous campaign was planned and fought
from Hitler's headquarters at the Kaiserhof and, often enough,
from Goebbels' flat, where the inner circle of leaders would meet
and talk through the night. In their official diaries and biographies,
both Goebbels and Goering laid claim to considerable personal
initiative in this period of critical struggle. Both were close to the
Führer; both needed his reflected glory as their reward. Goebbels
had just married; his wife, Magda Quandt, like Carin a divorced
woman, had considerable means and was devoted to Hitler, whom
it was even thought at one stage she might marry. Goering had to
watch the Führer, who had been so fond of Carin, spending his
midnight hours in the company of a rival's family. Goering moved
to another flat, in the Kaiserdamm, and resumed the restless life of
a bachelor. When he was in Munich he was, like Hitler, a frequent
visitor in the Hanfstaengls' house. He missed deeply the domestic
atmosphere which Carin had created for him, and he must to some
extent have been aware that he was not liked by the other party
leaders. Hitler admired him within limits; he was impressed by his
capacities as a speaker and, above all, by his social connections.
"Give him a full belly and he really goes for them," said Hitler to
Hanfstaengl.

The first problem was to make Hitler decide to stand for the
presidential election. Hitler had refused point blank to support
Brüning's proposal that Hindenburg's term of office as President
should be extended without resort to elections, which, Brüning
maintained, would disturb the nation still further during this period of economic and political distress. But when the presidential
elections became inevitable, Hitler hesitated for weeks on end
before finally consenting that his name should go forward in opposition to the formidable candidacy of Hindenburg. Goebbels acknowledges that Goering was a "valuable help" to Hitler at this

time, a rare tribute from so self-centered a man. It was not, however, until February 22 that Hitler finally made up his mind and
permitted a public statement to be made of his intention to stand
for election. The whole machinery of Nazi propaganda immediately accelerated into action, and Goering, like the other Nazi
speakers, toured the country, speaking at an endless succession of
meetings.

Nazi speechmaking was rabble-rousing by voice and gesture, a
form of mime with a political purpose. What was regarded as Goering's greatest speech in support of Hitler, delivered in a rally at
the Berlin Sports Stadium, was in fact nothing but an empty fanfare of words, without one fact stated, one argument reasoned; yet,
proclaimed by Goering's powerful voice, it had a dynamic effect on
the audience of Nazis who looked on election speeches as a spectacle embellished by Goebbels' music and banners and armed by
Roehm's troops of marching men. These great organized shows,
with their sinister backing of violence in the streets, were the form
of pressure brought to bear on the German people to force through
the vote that would place ultimate power in Hitler's ready hands.
Goering submerged himself in the book of words which all of them
knew by heart and spoke without thinking, while the loudspeakers
echoed round the upturned faces of an audience dazed by noise.

German men and women! Only a short time parts us from the hour
which will be the hour of destiny for the German nation. The German
people shall themselves decide whether German history can begin
again or whether German history shall be forever—finished! It comes!—
the day which will speak its iron yes or no: whether the catastrophe,
whether the breakdown of November 1918, whether the want of the
last thirteen years shall lead completely to chaos or breakdown into
Bolshevism, or whether the new rise of Germany begins, allowing the
German people once again to carry on the glorious history of their fore-
fathers.

The German people themselves, whom I love with my deepest soul,
with all the feelings of my heart, will judge for themselves the system
which places them in dishonorable bondage, of internal and external
slavery. The protests of the suffering German people will be a tremendous scream against their torture, a torture which they have endured,
mentally and physically, for thirteen weary long years. The people rise!
They will be free again—internally and externally. We National Social-

ists have for years been the open accusers in the name of the people. We accuse the system! We accuse the parties which created the system. We accuse the men who represent it. We have shaken the people into an awakening. We have taken care that the German people cannot again be put to slumber with the narcotic of new, betraying promises, which always brought ill luck. We have labored for years and years to create a new nation, and heaven will bless this tremendous work and those who are doing it, from the lowest S.A. man up to our Leader, because God will not allow slavery.[13]

"Goering speaks well," noted Goebbels in his diary that night.

On March 13, the day of balloting in the presidential election, Hitler lost, but the loss was by no means catastrophic. Hitler polled more than eleven million votes as against a little over eighteen and a half million cast for Hindenburg. Allowing for the other candidates (Thaelmann, the Communist, polled about five million), Hindenburg just failed to win the necessary absolute majority required by the constitution, making a run-off election necessary. The Nazi offices were raided by the Prussian police on March 17, and the raids proved to Brüning's satisfaction that if Hitler had won the Presidency the S.A. would have been mobilized to stage an immediate coup d'état. On March 19, Goering called a press conference for the foreign correspondents at the Kaiserhof. He was very affable. He had brought them together, he explained, to assert once more the party's desire to proceed with absolute legality in all matters.

It was most commendable of us [he said] to concentrate three hundred and fifty thousand storm troopers in their own quarters on election day. By so doing we prevented bloodshed. As for the allegation of the police that we Nazis were preparing to surround Berlin, the whole idea is absurd. We are surely entitled to take our own measures for the evacuation from the city of our women and children so as to protect them from injury by government mobs, and that, in fact, is what we did. Why, heaven help us, we have so many former officers in our ranks that if we really wanted to stage a rising we could set about it in quite a different manner, I assure you, gentlemen.[14]

In the second balloting, that of April 10, Hindenburg just managed to gain his absolute majority in spite of the fact that Hitler increased his poll by a further two million votes. On April 13 an

emergency decree was issued prohibiting the S.A. and the S.S., and
also the Nazis' special flying corps, which Goebbels found useful
for transporting speakers from place to place, and which Goering
strongly favored because in it lay the seeds of a future Air Force.
Hitler, for once, exercised diplomatic patience at this seeming dissolution of his private army. By the beginning of May Hindenburg
had forced General Wilhelm Groener, Minister of Defense and of
the Interior, to extend the ban to all paramilitary organizations, including the Army's favorite, the right-wing veterans' organization
the Stahlhelm. Then the Nazis felt the time had come to act. On
May 9 Goering launched his anger against Groener across the floor
of the Reichstag:

Do not believe that by removing his brown shirt you can take away
the spirit from the S.A. man. When other parties often change their
policies, even as their shirt, here spirit and policy remain the same in
spite of prohibition and terror. Faithfulness and comradeship, which to
many of you have become phantoms, like your oath, are for us fundamental to the union of German men, who stand united for their country
and for their people. Therefore, it is natural that today, after the conclusive judgment of the Cabinet, we voice our suspicions. A government
which, internally, externally, and in political economy, has lost every
battle, can no longer ask for confidence. It is always so in history. When
a general has lost a battle he has to go. Troops are not there to bleed to
death for a general, and a people does not exist in order that a government which is not in the position to master the situation shall ruin it.
And so we declare today that the Cabinet no longer enjoys the trust of
the people; the people are clamoring for new men! We turn to all who
want to help to work for the rebuilding of Germany. . . . We will fulfill our historic mission to reconcile all classes and to make it clear to all
that the question of the nation's destiny has to be placed above the petty
questions of everyday life, and that the classes, confessions, and profes-
sions have to bow down to the problem of the destiny of the German
nation. . . . The Brüning Cabinet must go. It must go in order that
Germany can live.[15]

When he was greeted by shouts and whistling from the left,
Goering cried, "I think, gentlemen, that you specialize in high
treason!" Groener was forced to resign, betrayed behind his back

by Schleicher, who was now shifting his loyalty to Hitler. Schleicher
had told Hindenburg that Groener no longer enjoyed the confidence of the Army. Hindenburg coldly asked Brüning to resign;
Schleicher, in league with the Nazis, had prevailed. The S.A. and
the S.S. remained intact, but Hitler kept them temporarily out of
uniform and off the streets in marching formation. Hitler himself
stayed away from Berlin, concentrating on the next election. Goering remained in touch with Schleicher.

Brüning, the "monkish ascetic," as Goering called him, formally
resigned on May 30. Hindenburg at once summoned Hitler to
Berlin; Goering went with him to see the President, who informed
them, without inviting them to sit down, that he was appointing
Papen as Chancellor. Hitler said he was prepared to support him,
but the immediate price Papen had to pay was lifting the ban on
the S.A. on June 15.

Immediately a wave of murderous street battles between Nazis
and Communists began in many German cities. Hitler calculated
that Papen could never command the confidence of the Reichstag
and that another election, in which he could seek still further to
improve the party's position, would have to be fought. There was
some discussion that Hitler might be Papen's Vice-Chancellor. "I
remember that I told Herr von Papen," said Goering at Nuremberg
fourteen years later, "that Hitler could become any number of
things, but never a 'Vice.' Whatever he was to become, he would
naturally have to be in the highest position."[16] So on June 1 Papen
became Chancellor; he dissolved the Reichstag, and once more
new elections were announced, for July 31. So great were the disturbances during July that Papen dissolved the Prussian state
government and made himself Reich Commissioner for Prussia.

Eighteen months later Goering recalled, with the blatant sim-
plifications of a self-professed fanatic, his feelings at this time.
Above everything, he claimed, came his devotion to Hitler, the
sum of whose virtues he describes as "something mystical, inex-
pressible, almost incomprehensible . . . We love Adolf Hitler
because we believe deeply that God has sent him to us to save
Germany . . ." To Hitler he offers his "unbending . . . unques-
tioning loyalty"; in return he receives "unqualified confidence."
"His authority is a matter of course," writes Goering, "just like
King Arthur's authority at the Round Table! The great error of the
previous system of liberalism was to imagine that the people wanted

to govern themselves, to lead themselves. No, the people want to be led and to be governed . . . The party could well fight in opposition within the parliamentary system, but it would have been impossible for Adolf Hitler to govern in a democratic, parliamentary way."[17]

In the election, the Nazis increased their hold on the country by more than doubling their vote. They now had 230 seats. Nevertheless, Hindenburg refused to give the chancellorship to Hitler. At the meeting between them on the afternoon of August 13, Hitler, who was again accompanied by Goering, refused the demand made by Hindenburg that he should co-operate in a coalition government. Hindenburg, then eighty-four, was too contemptuous of his guests to offer them seats; he stood all the while in front of Hitler in an effort to command him. But it was useless. Hitler and Goering were determined to destroy Papen's government, and for that matter the government of any other minister who stood between Hitler and the chancellorship. They knew they were now almost in power. Goering stood and listened as the old man, leaning on his stick, "gravely exhorted Herr Hitler to conduct the opposition on behalf of the Nazi Party in a chivalrous manner."

The new Reichstag met on August 30, 1932. Goering was put forward as its president by the Nazis in alliance with the Center Party and the Bavarian People's Party and was elected.[18] In his first speech as president of the Reichstag he made a further attack on Papen:

I promise that I shall fulfil the duties of my office impartially, justly, and in accordance with the existing rules of the house. I shall show due regard for the regulations and for the dignity of this house. But I must make it perfectly plain that I shall be equally vigilant in taking care that the honor and dignity of the German people are not assailed in this house. The glorious record of the German people will always find in me a ready champion. I proclaim to the whole German people that this session has clearly proved that the new Reichstag has a large working majority and is capable of conducting the affairs of state without the government having need for recourse to emergency measures. The fact that we have a national Cabinet inspires me with the hope that I shall be able to discharge my duty as president of the Reichstag, and that the honor of the people, the safety of the nation and the freedom of the Fatherland will be the chief guiding stars of all my actions.[19]

Goering's election to the presidency of the Reichstag was a great personal triumph for the man who only five years previously had been an exile with neither place nor prospects in Germany, and who only seven years before had been confined in a strait-jacket at Langbro. In spite of his new office, Goering never ceased his direct negotiations for his political master. Like Goebbels and Roehm, he became a member of the Herrenklub, the most exclusive meeting place in Berlin, and there he could work upon the susceptibilities of the Junkers, the senior men in the Army and the German industrialists. All this success came as the result of what Goering termed "the tactics of legality." He was, however, a close observer neither of parliamentary procedure nor of chivalry on the day the Reichstag first assembled under his presidency. This was September 12, the day on which, as Goering points out, "that famous scene occurred in which Herr von Papen wished to dissolve the Reichstag, but I, as president of the Reichstag, sought to prevent his doing so."

Papen had adopted the unusual course of obtaining a decree from the President dissolving the Reichstag before it met. This he was determined to use the moment it suited him, though not at the first session. Initially he wanted to put forward his government's program in a prepared speech. He knew that the Communists were ready to launch a vote of censure on his government the moment the session opened, but he was depending in turn on a prearranged objection to this vote being taken that was due to be raised by one of the Nationalist Party deputies. This would have left him free to proceed. When in fact no deputy opposed the Communist vote of censure, the Reichstag adjourned at the request of the Nazi deputy Wilhelm Frick. During this recess Papen hastily sent for his decree of dissolution while Hitler discussed the situation with the principal Nazi deputies in Goering's residence, the Reichstag President's Palace, which was situated just opposite the Reichstag. The Nazi conspirators decided that the quickest way to defeat Papen was to spring the surprise on the Reichstag of supporting the Communists in their vote of censure. Papen would scarcely be expecting this.

The deputies trooped back into the chamber, and Papen reappeared carrying the red dispatch box which everyone knew was the symbol of the decree of dissolution. But Goering, his head deliberately turned away from Papen, asked the Reichstag to record its vote on the Communists' motion of censure. Papen immediately rose and demanded attention, waving the decree of dissolution, which, once read, would rid him of control by the Reichstag so long as he remained Chancellor. Goering, grinning broadly as if he were conducting a successful raid, took no notice whatsoever. Papen strode up to him and thrust the decree under his nose. Goering still took no notice of him, intent on recording the vote. Papen secured only thirty-two votes; 513 deputies voted against him. Then and only then did Goering glance down with a show of interest at the decree lying in front of him. He even read it out. Then he declared it invalid because it bore the signature of a Chancellor who was now no longer in office.

Papen in his memoirs describes his view of what happened.

The house became a scene of complete disorder. The session resolved itself into a shooting match, and amidst the tumult Goering refused to recognize my right to speak. He turned ostentatiously to the left side of the house and pretended not to hear me. Instead he shouted, "As no objections have come from the floor to the Communist proposal, I intend to proceed with the division." There was no other solution but for me to march over to the presidential platform, slap the dissolution order on Goering's desk, and walk out of the Reichstag with the members of the Cabinet, to the accompaniment of a positive howl of derision.

In his book *Germany Reborn* Goering describes this mockery of parliamentary procedure with a cynical delight.

It was seemingly just playing with words, a race with the second hand of the watch; it was ultimately of no importance how and where he handed me the President's writ; what was important was that we resisted it with all our strength . . . The von Papen Cabinet retired and the Reichstag continued to sit. I knew that to go on sitting was only a pretense, but that too was unimportant . . . the impossibility of continuing to play the parliamentary game was clearly demonstrated to the people.

In his evidence at Nuremberg in 1946, Goering was equally frank. He said, "It was a matter of indifference to me by what means I brought our party to power. If by means of parliamentary negotiations, very good; if through appointment by the Reich President, all the better." The President, however, did not approve of Goering's parliamentary game, and the Reichstag was dissolved.[20]

The next round of elections was announced for November 6. Meanwhile Papen continued in office by presidential decree. The Nazis had to some extent overplayed their hand. They lost over two million votes at the elections and the number of their deputies dropped from 230 to 196. Many people had ceased altogether to trust them, and they were short of money. Their tactics during the past few months and their attitude to both the President and his Chancellor did not please the industrialists on whom they still had mainly to rely for financial support. Also, the number of unemployed, on whose discontent the Nazis depended for their votes, had appreciably decreased; it can be said that the genuine peak of the Nazi vote in Germany was attained when the unemployment figure was at its height, in July 1932. Time was running out.

The battle between Hindenburg and Hitler and the conspiracy behind it began immediately after the elections and lasted throughout the final tragic weeks of Germany's tortured freedom. The decadent form of German democracy gradually petered out of existence, although Hitler was now supported by only 33.1 per cent of the total electorate, a fall of 4.2 per cent since the elections in July. The *éminence grise* behind Hindenburg was still Schleicher. On November 17 Papen resigned on his advice. According to Heiden, Goering was in Rome, sitting beside Mussolini at a banquet given in honor of the guests attending the European Congress of the Academy of Science, when news was brought to him of Papen's defeat. Having assured Mussolini that fascism was now about to triumph in Germany, he flew back to Berlin in time to make the necessary arrangements with the President's State Secretary, Otto Meissner, for a meeting between Hitler and Hindenburg. On November 19 Hitler met the President, and again on the twenty-first. Nothing came of it. Hitler was determined to be Chancellor, and Hindenburg would not allow this unless he could secure majority support in the Reichstag, which was now impossible.

The next stage came when Schleicher secured the chancellorship for himself. The Nazi leaders were divided as to whether they should or should not co-operate with him. They met on December 1 at Weimar, and again on December 5 at the Kaiserhof, to discuss the matter; Gregor Strasser, never really Hitler's man, had been in direct touch with Schleicher and was, in fact, secretly ready to lead a faction of the party deputies into Schleicher's trap in exchange for receiving the office of Vice-Chancellor. Goering, Goebbels and

Hitler were utterly opposed to any compromise. Goering was left, aided possibly by Roehm and Frick, to negotiate with Schleicher along the line determined at the final conference. According to Heiden, Goering had already been instructed to approach Schleicher on December 3 to ask for the office of Premier of Prussia and had been told there was support among the center parties only for Strasser to become State Premier.

When the new Reichstag met on December 6, Goering was re-elected president. He did all he could to bring the assembly into ridicule, and he told it bluntly that its life would be a short one. When he had sat down, the Reichstag continued with its business while Goering stared at the deputies through binoculars, comparing the faces that he did not know with a file of photographs on his desk. In particular, he stared at the men he suspected of complicity with Strasser, and at Strasser himself. Two days later Strasser quarreled violently with Hitler and then wrote him a celebrated letter of recrimination, resigned from the party and left for the south. Hitler, aware his future was in the balance, threatened to shoot himself if the party deserted him, while Goering threatened to break the neck of every follower of Strasser.

On January 4, 1933, Hitler had what he gathered was to be a secret meeting with Papen at the house of the banker Schroeder, at which some form of future collaboration was discussed. Meanwhile Schleicher in courting the unions was losing the support of the industrialists, whom he then proceeded to blackmail. Strasser had returned from Rome, and it was known that he was actively conspiring with Schleicher to become his Vice-Chancellor. The party leaders were now gathered in the minute state of Lippe, where Goebbels was concentrating on a special-election campaign for the propaganda value a victory there would have in the eyes of the nation as a whole. "At midnight Goering also came," wrote Goebbels on January 13 in his published diary of the period. "Strasser is the eternal subject of our discussion . . . The Berlin press say he is going to be appointed Vice-Chancellor." And the next day Goebbels spent the afternoon with Goering "discussing our worries."

Goebbels was right about the importance of the Lippe election as propaganda. After the Nazis had won a sufficiently decisive victory at the polls in this dimunitive state, the tide began to turn back in their direction. Strasser did not enter the Cabinet; the men behind Hindenburg, weary of the stalemate, decided at last to turn to Hitler. On January 22, the President's son Oskar and the State Secretary Meissner met secretly with Hitler, Goering and Frick. They met at the house of Joachim von Ribbentrop, a member of the Nazi Party who makes his historical debut here because he happened to be known to Papen. Goering arrived here from Dresden, where he had made a speech against Hitler's joining the present government. Hitler set out, apparently, to impress the President's son and succeeded.

Papen's scheme to turn the tables on Schleicher was beginning to work. The President refused to allow the Chancellor, who was unable to win sufficient support in the Reichstag, to establish a military dictatorship in place of parliamentary government. On January 28 Schleicher resigned, leaving the field open to his rivals. Hitler, aware that the chancellorship was about to fall to his stubborn siege as his rivals crumbled before him, became, according to Goebbels, "very quiet." The final negotiations were left to Papen, who was, of course, in touch with Goering. The same day, according to Papen, Hitler was told the President wanted him to form a Cabinet "within the terms of the constitution," which meant a Cabinet commanding a majority in the Reichstag. Hitler refused; he was willing to form a presidential Cabinet—a Cabinet independent of Reichstag support—incorporating men from other parties, but he demanded first that he be made Chancellor and Reich Commissioner for Prussia and that a member of his party (he meant Goering) be Minister of the Interior both for the Reich and for the key state of Prussia. Early the following morning Hitler and Goering called again early to propose that Frick be made Reich Minister of the Interior and Goering Interior Minister for Prussia. Papen replied that he, as Vice-Chancellor, would be appointed Reich Commissioner for Prussia, and Hitler accepted this "with a bad grace." He then left Papen to discuss the matter with the President. After all, Papen and his associates thought, they would outnumber the Nazis in the Cabinet four to one and so keep them in order.

On January 29, wrote Goebbels,

in the afternoon, whilst we are having coffee with the Leader, Goering suddenly comes in and reports . . . the Führer is to be appointed Chancellor tomorrow. . . . This is surely Goering's happiest hour. . . . He has diplomatically and cleverly prepared the ground for the

Leader in nerve-racking negotiations for months . . . This upright soldier with the heart of a child . . . confronts the Leader and brings him the greatest piece of news of his life!

But this was not quite the end of the intrigues, as Papen recalls in his memoirs.

Schleicher, in the meantime, found another card to play. He sent one of his private emissaries, von Alvensleben, to Goering, who immediately hurried over to me with the news. Schleicher had sent a message that my real intention was to deceive the Nazis, and that they would do very much better to combine with Schleicher, who only wished to retain the post of Minister of Defense. Alvensleben had indicated that means could be found to neutralize Hindenburg. Schleicher had apparently even gone so far as to suggest that if the "old gentleman" should prove difficult, he, Schleicher, would mobilize the Potsdam garrison. Goering told me that he and Hitler had returned a flat negative to the plan and had immediately told Meissner and Oskar von Hindenburg.[21]

To forestall such a move as this by Schleicher, the President hastily ordered General Werner von Blomberg, who was attending a conference in Geneva, to return on the next train. At the station he was met independently both by Oskar von Hindenburg and by a staff officer who had directions to take him to the Ministry of Defense. Blomberg chose to go to the President, and was told he would be Minister of Defense in Hitler's Cabinet.

As the members of the new Cabinet were walking across the garden that joined Papen's Chancellery to the President's Palace, where they were to be received by Hindenburg, Hitler was still truculent about the limitations that, he claimed, were being placed upon his powers. He threatened the Cabinet with new elections, which, he said, would soon confirm the majority he at present lacked in the Reichstag. A quarrel began at once, and Hindenburg became impatient at being kept waiting. At last it was decided to ask him to decree the dissolution of the Reichstag, and the Nazis, accompanied by their unhappy associates, entered the President's room to be sworn in.

Goering has described the tension of this period.

From January 20th on I was, as political delegate, in constant touch with Herr von Papen, with Secretary of State Meissner, with the leader of the Steel Helmets [Stahlhelm], Seldte, and with the leader of the German Nationalists, Hugenberg, and was discussing with them future developments. . . . At last an agreement was reached . . . I had, as Hitler's representative, often in the past year gone back and forth between the Kaiserhof and the Wilhelmstrasse, and I shall never forget the moment when I hurried out to my car and could be the first to tell the expectant crowds: "Hitler has become Chancellor!"[22]

The tactics of legality had won. "How gloriously," wrote Goering, "had the aged Field Marshal been used as an instrument of God."

IV

Conquest of the State

At half past two in the afternoon, Goering received the press in his palace. He was overcome by the emotions of victory, and he beamed at the foreign journalists who gathered anxiously about him. They were conscious of the changing atmosphere in the streets outside, which were filled with triumphant Nazis. Goering felt a need to ease the tension, and he turned the reception into a social occasion. It grew dark quickly in the winter afternoon; the "Horst Wessel Song," sung by the men who knew their Leader was master at last of the Reich Chancellery, began to sound menacing in the ears of the majority of Germans who had nothing to celebrate.

It was night when Hitler, with Goering by his side, held his first Cabinet meeting. The duennas of democracy, Vice-Chancellor von Papen, Baron Konstantin von Neurath, Minister of Foreign Affairs, Count Lutz Schwerin von Krosigk, Minister of Finance, and Hindenburg's special man General von Blomberg, Minister of Defense and head of the Reichswehr, believed in the blindness of their innocence that they were there to maintain due modesty of behavior now that the untried Nazis held the reins of power. Facing them and their lesser colleagues were Hitler, Goering and Frick, three Nazis to nine old-time politicians. Outside they could hear the crowds singing "Deutschland über Alles." The Nazis were invading the streets of every city in Germany.

But Hitler had not obtained from Hindenburg a presidential Cabinet, and his government could, therefore, fall at any time the Reichstag voted it out of office. The alternative facing the Nazis

was either to offer concessions to the Catholic Center Party, in
order to gain its support, or to persuade the Cabinet, the majority
of whose members belonged to other parties, to agree to fresh elections in which, they must realize, the Nazis could bring every kind
of pressure to bear on the public to ensure a decisive majority for
themselves in the Reichstag. Hitler and Goering, their eyes on the
wary men sitting opposite, were trying to make the present situation
seem so impossible that their colleagues could do nothing else but
agree to the dissolution of the Reichstag.

Meanwhile, a few hours had to be spared for rejoicing before
these indelicate negotiations were renewed. Drums were beating,
echoing in the distance from the Brandenburg Gate. In the Tiergarten the S.A. and the S.S. were assembling to gather torches filled
with fuel for the night's festivity. The people stood waiting along
the Wilhelmstrasse and in the Wilhelmplatz for the procession to
come. Then, with bands playing, the brown ranks began to march
in a flare path of torches while Hindenburg, the helpless President,
stood at his window watching the homage paid to Hitler, who stood
rigid with outstretched arm on the balcony of the Chancellery
nearby. "For the first time the German people in demonstration
is being broadcast," wrote Goebbels in his diary, and Goering
roared his enthusiasm through the microphone installed in the
Chancellery:

"January 30, 1933, will be recorded in German history as the day
when the nation was restored to glory once more, as the day when a new
nation arose and swept aside all the anguish, pain and shame of the last
fourteen years . . . There stands the renowned Field Marshal of the
World War, and by his side the young Führer of Germany, who is about
to lead the people and the Reich to a new and better era. May the German people herald this day as joyfully as it is heralded by the hundreds
of thousands in front of these windows who are inspired by a new faith
. . . that the future will bring us what we fought for in vain for a long
time—bread and work for our fellow men, and freedom and glory for the
nation."[1]

On this night of celebrations Goering's mind was already occupied with the opportunities ahead. In Hitler's Cabinet he was
Minister without Portfolio, Minister of the Interior for Prussia
and Reich Commissioner of Aviation. The first office made him

Hitler's plenipotentiary, ambassador, paladin (to use what was to become his favorite term); the second office, though technically under Papen's supervision, gave him unique power over the police in what was by far the most important state in Germany; and the third recognized that he would soon have an immediate, special duty to develop an Air Force in the Reich. He also remained president of the Reichstag, which was dissolved the following morning, when Hitler finally reported to his Cabinet that there was no chance of agreement between the Nazis and the Center Party. The new elections were announced for one month ahead, on March 5; meanwhile the new Cabinet was to stay in office. "It was understood by all of us that as soon as we had once come into power we must keep that power under all circumstances," said Goering in his evidence at Nuremberg. "We did not want to leave this any longer to chance, elections and parliamentary majorities. . . . In order to consolidate this power now, it was necessary to reorganize the political relationships of power."

Hitler and Goering still kept the masks of legality held firmly in front of their faces at Cabinet meetings, according to both Schwerin von Krosigk and Papen. "The concept 'illegal' should perhaps be clarified," Goering was to explain later to his judges. "If I aim at a revolution, then it is an illegal action for the state then in existence. If I am successful, then it becomes a fact and thereby legal." Goering's procedure was therefore to use his new position as Minister of the Interior for Prussia as the principal channel through which to consolidate the Nazi hold on both the elected and the permanent officials, not only in Prussia itself but in all the provincial states.

According to Gritzbach, his official biographer, Goering all but lived in the Prussian government office for the next two months; he took his meals in the building and worked all through the night. On the first day he assembled the staff of the Prussian civil service and addressed them "as the representatives of the new patriotic spirit that has arisen." He reminded them that his own father had once been a senior civil servant. Then he put aside the charm with which he had deliberately opened the meeting and told them their first duty was to eradicate any taint of Communism which might exist among them. Those who felt they could not work with him were invited to resign at once.[2]

While Goebbels set out during February to achieve what he called "a masterpiece of propaganda" to ensure sweeping victories at the polls on March 5, Goering was careful not to consult Papen, his senior as Reich Commissioner for Prussia, who was engaged in the election campaign; instead he began quickly and ruthlessly to take over control of the Prussian civil service and police. The Prussian Parliament was dissolved against its will on February 4. Men whom Goering could not trust had been or were being blacklisted; they were then dismissed, suspended, ordered or induced to resign, and their places given to Nazis. "Goering is cleaning out the Augean stables . . . Names of great importance yesterday fade away to nothing today," scribbled Goebbels with delight on February 15. "To begin with," wrote Goering in his *Germany Reborn*, the following year, "it seemed to me of the first importance to get the weapon of the police firmly into my own hands. Here it was that I made the first sweeping changes. Out of thirty-two police chiefs I removed twenty-two. Hundreds of inspectors and thousands of police sergeants followed in the course of the next month. New men were brought in, and in every case these men came from the great reservoir of the storm troopers and guards." Batons and rubber truncheons, which were in Goering's view undignified, were replaced by revolvers.

The importance of this administrative revolution, carried out during the single month of February while everyone was occupied with the election campaign, cannot be overestimated. It put the law directly into Hitler's hands. In a series of manifestoes and decrees of ruthless audacity, Goering openly revealed what he was doing and enabled the Nazis to conduct their campaign against the other parties as if protecting the nation against criminal subversion. The Prussian Ministry of the Interior in fact controlled the greater part of Germany; the powers of the Reich Ministry of the Interior were purely nominal. Goering's manifestoes on behalf of the police force that he was so rapidly strengthening and reshaping in his own image read like a declaration of war on all forms of opposition. These were the tactics of legality—once, that is, the law was in your hands. Hitler, as Chancellor, gave Goering full powers. And Papen, the Vice-Chancellor and Reich Commissioner for Prussia, when he reflected later on this period of disintegration, seemed able to say only, "My own fundamental error was to underrate the dynamic power which had awakened the national and social instincts of the masses."[3] He had no party behind him, only the ear of the ancient President. "I see," he wrote, "that there were many times when I should have invoked the President's authority." The other ministers, including Blomberg, turned aside and left these tiresome affairs to Hitler's energetic administration. Papen claims he was often in dispute with Goering over his highhanded methods and once even suggested that he ought to resign. Goering turned on him violently and cried, "You will only get me out of this room flat on my back!" Sir Horace Rumbold, the British ambassador, reported to London on March 1 about Goering's activities: "In a recent private conversation with Baron Neurath, the latter described Goering to me as a 'dreadful man,' whom Herr von Papen was quite unable to control. Goering is regarded as the real Fascist in the Hitler Party . . ."[4]

On February 17, after two and a half weeks spent on dossiers, dismissals and appointments, Goering published this manifesto:

I do not think it necessary to point out that the police must in all circumstances avoid even the appearance of a hostile attitude toward, or even the impression of any persecution of, the national associations and parties. I expect rather from all the police authorities that they will create and maintain the best understanding with the above-mentioned organizations, in the ranks of which the most important forces of political reconstruction are to be found. Moreover, every kind of activity for national purposes and national propaganda is to be thoroughly supported. On the other hand, the activities of organizations hostile to the State are to be checked by the strongest measures. With Communist terrorism and raids there must be no trifling, and, when necessary, revolvers must be used without regard to consequences. Police officers who fire their revolvers in the execution of their duty will be protected by me without regard to the consequences of using their weapons. But officers who fail, out of mistaken regard for consequences, must expect disciplinary action to be taken against them. The protection of the national populace, who are continually cramped in their activities, demands the strictest application of the legal regulations governing prohibited demonstrations, prohibited meetings, plunderings, incitements to high treason, mass strikes, revolts, press offenses, and all other punishable offenses of the disturbers of law and order. No officer should lose sight of the fact that failure to adopt a measure is more heinous than the making of mistakes in its application. I hope and expect that all officers will feel at one with me in our common purpose of saving our Fatherland from threatened calamity by the strengthening and consolidation of all our national forces.

Goering reinforced this point in the notorious speech he made soon afterward at Dortmund.

In the future there will be only one man who will wield power and bear responsibility in Prussia—that is, myself. Whoever does his duty in the service of the State, who obeys my orders and ruthlessly makes use of his revolver when attacked, is assured of my protection. Whoever, on the other hand, plays the coward, will have to reckon on being thrown out by me at the earliest possible moment. A bullet fired from the barrel of a police pistol is my bullet. If you say that is murder then I am the murderer. . . . I know two sorts of law because I know two sorts of men: those who are with us and those who are against us.[5]

All Communist meetings had been banned early in February; now any attempt by the Communists to organize their political campaign in public (they had in the election the previous November commanded some six million votes, and they held 101 seats in the Reichstag) could now be opposed by the police legally with force of arms. Their press had been forbidden further publication; the ban was followed by the suppression of the Socialist press and of any journal that had had the courage to print what it thought about the Nazis. The S.A., unopposed by their new allies the police, broke up the rallies and meetings even of the Social Democrats and the Catholic Center Party. Speakers were beaten up, among them the Catholic trade-unionist Stegerwald. Fifty-one anti-Nazis died during February in this last melancholy stand made against Hitler's absolute dictatorship.

On February 22 Goering strengthened the police still further by creating an auxiliary force from the S.A., the S.S. and Hugenberg's Stahlhelm. The wording of the decree was another example of the new legality:

The demands made on the existing police force, which cannot be adequately increased at the present juncture, are often beyond its power; by the present necessity of utilizing them outside of their places of service, police officers are often removed from their proper field of activity at inopportune times. In consequence, the voluntary support of suitable helpers to be used as auxiliary police officers in case of emergency can no longer be dispensed with.[6]

These men, fifty thousand strong, armed and wearing their old party uniforms but with a white armband added to show their new official status, terrorized the population wherever they went. They could get on and off public transport as they liked, traveling without payment. They drew only three marks daily as a wage, but few shopkeepers or waiters dared refuse them what they demanded.

Goering made increasing use of the services of Rudolf Diels, a handsome but sinister young official in the political department of the Prussian police whom he had met in 1932 and who had proved very willing to supply information to the president of the Reichstag. Diels had married a cousin of Goering's called Ilse. The information he had previously given Goering from the police dossiers was open now for the Minister's official inspection; Diels, promoted to head of the political department, became a person on whom his master depended to help him in the compilation of his blacklists. He was a violent anti-Communist, and Goering looked to him to keep his desk stacked with the secret dossiers of the left-wing conspirators who he believed existed not only throughout the state but inside the Prussian Interior Ministry itself. Diels became his man.

In the ministry there existed a special department controlling the political police. This department Goering reorganized the moment he took charge of the ministry. Again he made no secret of what he was doing. Only a year later he wrote for publication in Britain:

I have created, on my own initiative, the Secret State Police Department. This is the instrument which is so much feared by the enemies of the State and which is chiefly responsible for the fact that in Germany and Prussia there is no question of a Marxist or Communist danger. . . . The achievement of Diels and his men will always remain one of the glories of the first year of German recovery. . . . We had to proceed against these enemies of the State with complete ruthlessness . . . And so the concentration camps were set up, to which we had sent first of all thousands of officials of the Communist and Social Democratic

Parties. It was only natural that in the beginning excesses were committed. It was natural that here and there beatings took place. . . . But
if we consider the greatness of the occasion . . .[7]

This was the beginnings of the Gestapo, which was not to become an officially named and recognized organization until April
26, after Goering had replaced Papen as Reich Commissioner for
Prussia. But the work of organizing these men began under Diels
at Goering's urgent instigation, and the excesses they committed
were a "natural" outcome of "the greatness of the occasion."

On February 24 Goering's men raided the Communist Party's
headquarters in the Karl Liebknecht House. Although by now most
of its leaders either had been arrested or had fled, Goering's men
found Communist propaganda in the cellars, or "catacombs," as
Goering called them. A few days later, after the Reichstag had been
fired, Goering, as we shall see, was to claim that documents had
also been found in the "catacombs" proving the Communists were
planning insurrection and the assassination of the principal members of the Cabinet. In fact all that the cellars contained was stocks
of Communist pamphlets, and Goering was never to reveal this
so-called documentary evidence. Nevertheless, arrest and suppression followed with renewed venom.

On the night of February 27, between the hours of eight o'clock
and ten, an extraordinary sequence of events took place. Aderman,
the night porter at Goering's Reichstag President's Palace, came on
duty at eight and took his place in the porter's lodge in the hallway.
At seven minutes past eight a porter on duty in the Reichstag
locked the southern entrance, while between 8:15 and 8:30 Ernst
Torgler, the Communist parliamentary leader, left the building
with some colleagues and went to Aschinger's restaurant, some ten
minutes' walk away. At the same time, around 8:20, Schultz, a
lamplighter, walked through the session chamber and observed that
all was quiet. About half an hour later Otto, a postman, passed
between the door of the restaurant in the Reichstag and the entrance to the session chamber; there was no sound.

Ten minutes later, at about 9:05, a student called Flöter was
passing the building when he saw a man with a burning brand on
the balcony of a first-floor window of the Reichstag; he immediately
found a policeman and gave the alarm. At approximately the same
time Thaler, a typesetter who was also passing, saw a man climbing

through the restaurant window, and he almost immediately joined a police sergeant, Buwert, who had already been warned by another unidentified civilian. Along with Thaler, Buwert began to investigate. They saw lights moving behind the ground-floor windows; Buwert fired his revolver at the lights, which immediately disappeared. All this happened within a few minutes, and the first fire alarm was received at a local fire station at 9:14.

Three minutes later Police Lieutenant Lateit arrived at the Reichstag with a posse of men from the Brandenburger Tor police station. The first fire engine arrived at 9:21, at the same time that Lateit, who was now inside the building, saw a small fire burning near the Reichstag president's chair in the session chamber. He was joined by the house inspector two minutes later; by now new fires were burning among the seating. At 9:24 Fire Captain Klotz arrived to find, not flames in the session chamber, but a thick haze accompanied by tremendous heat, and at 9:27 there was a tremendous explosion under the glass roof of the session chamber, and great flames leaped up. At the same time, a half-naked man was arrested in the Bismarck Hall, a large room at the rear. He was covered with grime and sweat. This was Marinus van der Lubbe, a young Dutchman.

It was about 9:35 when Goering arrived in his car. Weber, the commander of his bodyguard, was now searching the tunnel that connected the Reichstag President's Palace with the Reichstag; he found nothing untoward.

Goering had been working in his office at the Prussian Ministry of the Interior on Unter den Linden, a short distance away, when he was told of the fire; he had thrust on his trench coat and had been driven to the burning building. By now the Reichstag was bursting with flames, and large crowds were gathering. Douglas Reed, correspondent of the *Times* of London, was driving in his car along the snow-covered Tiergarten when he saw fire leaping from the cupola of the building. His arrival coincided with that of Goering, whom he saw rushing into the building through the deputies' entrance. There Goering found a newspaperman telephoning his office. He flung him out, but Reed himself followed Goering's party inside and saw the session chamber in a mass of flames before he too was thrust back. As he put it, the Reichstag was like "a block of stone in which tunnels have been bored and wooden cubes inlet, the tunnels being the lobbies and corridors and the cubes the timber-panelled session-chamber" and other halls and rooms. While the main stone structure could not be destroyed, the wood-paneled halls burned furiously, and the session chamber was "cut out of the building by the fire as neatly as a stone from a peach."

Goering claimed that he had heard the word "arson" spoken by one of the crowd as he got out of his car, and that a veil had fallen from his eyes. "It never even occurred to me that the Reichstag might have been set alight; I thought the fire had been caused by carelessness . . . In this moment I knew that the Communist Party was the culprit." Papen had been dining with Hindenburg at the Herrenklub when he was warned of the fire, and he had sent the President home by car before hurrying himself to the scene. He found Goering, surrounded by members of his staff, furiously directing the fire fighting. "This is a Communist crime against the new government!" Goering shouted to Papen.

Hitler also arrived late upon the scene. He had gone to have dinner in Goebbels' apartment at nine, and the party was already enjoying music when Hanfstaengl telephoned with the news of the fire. Goebbels and Hitler thought this was one of Hanfstaengl's bad jokes, but the message was soon confirmed, and they hurried to the Reichstag. "Clambering over thick fire hoses we reach the great lobby by entrance number two. Goering meets us on the way . . . There is no doubt that Communism has made a last attempt to cause disorder by means of fire and terror," wrote Goebbels. Hitler, standing in the stench of the ruined building, cried, "This is a signal [*Fanal*] from heaven." As the night passed the fire died back before the streams of water poured from the firemen's hoses, and soot, carried by the wind, gradually settled like a blight upon the snow.

Already the rumor was spreading that the Nazis were themselves responsible for the fire. Whatever the degree of Goering's personal connection (and there is still no direct evidence whatsoever to prove that he was implicated), there is no doubt that he became actively involved the moment the fire was reported to him. His torch was brandished furiously against the Communists, who were proclaimed once more the proven enemies of the State. The following day, February 28, Hitler induced Hindenburg to sign a decree suspending all civil liberties in the cause of "the protection of the people and the State." The fire that Hitler had called "a signal from heaven" had certainly served to shake the President. The decree was specifically directed against the Communists and "their acts of violence," and it widened the application of the death sentence. It was only now, at a Cabinet meeting held on March 2, that Goering chose to refer to a Pharus map and, according to Papen, documents planning the assassination of the ministers, all of which, he said, had been found during the raid four days previously on the Communist headquarters, though why this map and these documents had not been produced immediately was not explained.[8] At the time, Papen saw no reason to doubt their authenticity; their circulation among the ministers was promised but never fulfilled. Thousands more people were arrested; whether they were Communists or merely anti-Nazis no longer mattered. The warrants had been prepared some days before the Reichstag fire.

Goering, of course, was well aware of the suspicion directed against him; he even referred to it at the Cabinet meeting on March 2. It seems fair to say that he did not take the accusations much to heart. He had no further use for the Reichstag or the office of its president; the other offices he now held gave him far greater powers. For the Nazis the Reichstag, both as a center for the remnants of democratic government and as a building of state, was obsolete; even the election due in one week was intended to be a certificate of death from natural causes. The following year Goering wrote: "If I am further accused of having myself set fire to the Reichstag in order to get the Communists into my hands, I can only say that the idea is ridiculous and grotesque. I did not need any special event to enable me to proceed against the Communists . . . The firing of the Reichstag did not, as a matter of fact, at all fit in with my plans . . ."[9] According to his mood, he could be ironic about it: "I knew people would probably say that, dressed in a red toga and holding a lyre in my hand, I looked on at the fire and played while the Reichstag was burning," or joke about it, as he did at a lunch in 1942 in the presence of General Franz Halder, who later recalled that "Goering interrupted the conversation and shouted: 'The only one who really knows about the Reichstag is I, because I set it on fire!' With that he slapped his thigh with the flat of his hand." At the Nuremberg trial and during his interrogations Goering more solemnly denied any responsibility for the fire; he said to General William J. Donovan, head of the United States Office of Strategic Services, "You must at least be convinced that with death staring me in the face, I have no need to resort to lies.

I give you my word that I had nothing whatever to do with the Reichstag fire." Schwerin von Krosigk, when he was a fellow prisoner of the Americans at Mondorf, asked Goering with a smile, "Tell me the truth, now. Did you really burn the Reichstag?" Goering merely shrugged his shoulders and replied, "My dear chap, I'd be proud even now to have done it. But I just didn't." He said much the same thing to Papen during their captivity together. Sir Horace Rumbold, the British ambassador, had also gone to see the fire; in his report to London on March 1 he wrote, "I find that there is a feeling by many level-headed people that this act of vandalism may have been inspired by Nazi elements, but not by the leaders of the Nazi Party."[10]

The origin of the Reichstag fire was not fully investigated during the Nuremberg trial, and it has been left an open question to what degree the pathological incendiarist van der Lubbe, who was only twenty-four, was a dupe of the Nazis and how far he was acting in his own right. Gradually suspicion consolidated round Karl Ernst, the S.A. leader in Berlin, who, it was claimed, led a party of storm troopers through the passage connecting the Reichstag President's Palace with the Reichstag itself and there rendered various sections of the building immediately inflammable by spraying the woodwork with gasoline and self-igniting chemicals. Seven months later, when the Reichstag fire trial was about to start, Ernst, after drinking heavily at a storm trooper celebration in Berlin, told a Dutch Nazi who had questioned him about his implication with the fire, "If I said yes, I did it, I'd be a bloody fool; if I said no, I'd be a bloody liar!"[11] Hans Bernd Gisevius, who was on the staff of the Prussian Ministry of the Interior in 1933, remains the principal protagonist in the case against Goebbels and Goering and their agent Ernst. Diels, who defected from the Nazis, swore that Goering "knew exactly how the fire was to be started" and ordered him to prepare in advance a list of men to be arrested immediately after the fire. But Diels, at best a sorry witness, has also said, "From a few weeks after the fire until 1945, I was convinced that the Nazis had started it. Now I have changed my mind."[12]

The arrests ordered by Goering were left to Diels and his police, together with their reinforcements from among the S.A. Ernst Torgler, the leader of the Communists in the Reichstag, gave himself up to the police on February 28, while Georgi Dimitroff, Blagoi Popov and Wassil Tanev, three Bulgarian Communists, were arrested. These four men were to become, along with van der Lubbe, the accused at the Reichstag fire trial.

On September 21, after seven months of preparation, the trial opened in the Supreme Court in Leipzig. It lasted until December 23, when all the accused except van der Lubbe, the self-professed incendiary, had to be acquitted, because it was proved beyond all doubt that they could not have been there at the time. Conducted in public, before the eyes of the international press, it was a complete failure from the point of view of the Nazis. In spite of being a foreigner with an incomplete mastery of the German language, Georgi Dimitroff insisted on conducting his own defense; continuously shouting and protesting, he caused such uproar in the court that he frequently had to be excluded by the presiding judge. Goering, who appeared as an important witness for the prosecution on November 4, was driven by Dimitroff to lose his temper in front of a courtroom filled with journalists, ministers and diplomatic representatives.

Goering arrived with a uniformed entourage and himself wore the plain brown uniform adopted by the Nazi leaders now they were in power. He looked, according to Martha Dodd, daughter of Dr. William E. Dodd, the American ambassador, "pompous and yet a little nervous." Speaking in evidence, he gave the history of his preparations for the final destruction of the Communists, and he claimed that the terrorist acts of which the Nazis were accused in the notorious Communist *Brown Book* were acts committed by Communists themselves wearing Nazi uniform. He had been accused of being too prepared to take action after the fire, as if he had known about it in advance. That was not so. The fire, he said, came at an inconvenient time. "I was like a commander in the field who is about to put into operation a considered plan of campaign, and by an impulsive action of the enemy is suddenly forced to change his whole tactics." He then gave his own account of what happened on the night of the fire, adding, "I then took my measures against the Communists . . . I intended to hang van der Lubbe at once, and nobody could have stopped me. I refrained only because I thought, We have one of them, but there must have been many. Perhaps we shall need him as a witness . . . I knew as by intuition that the Communists fired the Reichstag . . . Let the trial end as it will, I will find the guilty and lead them to their punishment."

When Dimitroff rose, anxiously leaning forward to start putting his questions to Goering, the courtroom became completely silent and concentrated. After certain preliminaries about who actually gave the orders for the arrest of the Communists and why Goering had claimed there was a Communist Party membership book in van der Lubbe's pocket when the police had testified there was not, Dimitroff led through to his final courageous attack on Goering:

DIMITROFF: Since you, in your position, have accused the Communist Party of Germany and foreign Communists, has that not directed investigation into certain channels and prevented the search for the real incendiarist?

GOERING: For me this was a political crime and I was convinced that the criminals are to be found in your party. Your party [*shaking his fist at Dimitroff*] is a party of criminals and must be destroyed!

DIMITROFF: Is the Minister aware that this party rules a sixth of the earth, the Soviet Union, with which Germany maintains diplomatic, political and economic relations, from which hundreds of thousands of German workers benefit—

PRESIDING JUDGE: I forbid you to make Communist propaganda here.

DIMITROFF: Herr Goering makes National Socialist propaganda . . . Is it not known that Communism has millions of supporters in Germany . . . ?

GOERING [*shouting*]: It is known that you are behaving insolently, that you have come here to burn the Reichstag . . . In my opinion you are a criminal who should be sent to the gallows!

JUDGE: Dimitroff, I have told you not to make Communist propaganda. You must not be surprised if the witness gets excited.

DIMITROFF [*quietly*]: I am very satisfied with the Minister's reply.

GOERING [*still shouting*]: Out with you, you scoundrel!

JUDGE: Take him away!

DIMITROFF [*as he is being led out by the police*]: Are you afraid of my questions, Herr Ministerpräsident?

Goering was now beside himself with rage. His voice rose to a scream, his face turned deep red and he choked; to one observer he even seemed to show signs of fear as he tried to drown Dimitroff's insolent, impassioned sarcasm. He turned on the Bulgarian as the latter was being dragged from the courtroom and shouted, "You

wait until we get you outside this court, you scoundrel!" Then, overcome, he leaned against the witnesses' table.

Throughout the whole of Goering's appearance in court, Diels
stood near him, listening to every word, watching every movement.
Up to the last few minutes Goering had evidently been aware of
this, for he had made changes in his voice or manner while Diels
circled round him like a stage director. Diels with a certain suggestion of pride had persuaded Martha Dodd, with whom he was
on friendly terms, to come along to watch the trial that day, and she
believed that Goering made an almost disastrous mistake in losing
his temper with Dimitroff; the atmosphere, she says, became "de-
moniac."[13]

Goering felt the need to make a dignified retreat from the courtroom. Before he left he made a statement about the legal inquiry
into the causes of the Reichstag fire which was taking place in
London; at this inquiry, in which Sir Stafford Cripps played a prominent part, circumstantial evidence had been put forward that the
Nazis, not the Communists, had fired the Reichstag.[14] "I would
like to know," said Goering, "what the English, the French or the
Americans would think if they were conducting a political trial and
the Germans interfered in such a manner. And, as England has
been made the home of this inquiry, I would like to suggest to the
English that they study the history of the burning of their own
Parliament a few hundred years ago. There they will see that a trial
like this was not held. Even today the anniversary of this outrage
is celebrated, and a straw effigy hanged to show that the place for
such people is the gallows." But the only man who could be found
to face this fate in Germany after fifty-seven days of public examination of the evidence collected by Goering's men was van der
Lubbe, who through almost every moment of the trial had sat im-
passive, his face vacant. He alone, on January 10, 1934, shambled
in a daze up to the block, where he was dispatched with an ax by
the public executioner; the latter was dressed as tradition demanded
on so formal an occasion, in full evening attire, with white gloves
and a top hat.

Goering, furious at the way he had been treated at the trial, complained bitterly to Hitler that he had felt he was the person being
cross-examined, not the Communists. Hitler replied that little
could be done to change the nature of the courts of law while Hindenburg was still alive.

The election of March 1933 followed hard on the fire. Having set the machinery of his blind justice in motion, Goering, excited and roaring with energy, broadcast to the German people on the night of February 28 and then turned once more to the election campaign.

On March 3, two nights before Germany was once more pushed through the polls, Goering was shouting at Frankfurt am Main: "My measures will not be crippled by any judicial thinking . . . I don't have to worry about justice; my mission is only to destroy and exterminate, nothing more!"[15] March 5 was designated the day of national awakening, and concentrations of marching men filled the streets; their thudding feet were to become the new heartbeat of Germany, while the endless rallies made the night hideous. The radio, with loudspeakers strung up in the streets, thrust the voices of Hitler, Goebbels and Goering into every ear. To vote against such heavy pressure was an act of courage, but on March 5 over twelve million votes were cast against the voices and the violence. But the Nazis and their allies, the Nationalists—led by Papen and Hugenberg—with a total of over twenty million votes cast in their favor, at once proclaimed a great victory, though their 240 seats gave them only a bare majority of sixteen in the Reichstag. As night fell, the bonfires of victory lit up the hills.

It was now, in March 1933, that the concentration camp system was fully established. Goering wished the camps to be thought of as rehabilitation centers for those suffering from varying degrees of political delinquency, but in any case the growing thousands placed under arrest made it impossible for normal imprisonment to be practicable. At Nuremberg, Goering testified that his orders were that "these men should first of all be gathered in camps—one or two camps were proposed at that time—because . . . I could not tell for how long the internment of these people would be necessary, nor how the number would be increased."

The camps authorized by him ("two or three in Prussia") were immediately supplemented by the so-called *Wilde Lager*, unauthorized camps set up by individual Nazis; Goering mentioned at Nuremberg a camp near Stettin set up by Karpfenstein, Gauleiter of Pomerania, another at Breslau established by Heines, and a third near Berlin, of which Karl Ernst ("whom I had always suspected of acts of brutality") was the founder. Goering had these camps closed.

The history of the concentration camps will never be easy to disentangle. Goering claimed that he took the idea initially from the internment centers set up by the British during the Boer War, and in the German encyclopedia the word *Konzentrationslager* was followed immediately by "First used by the British in the South African War." Goering put his own camps under Diels, and at Nuremberg he admitted that brutalities took place, adding, "Of course I gave instructions that such things should not happen. That they did happen and happened everywhere to a smaller or greater extent I have just stated. I always stressed that these things should not happen, because it was important to me to win over some of these people for our side and to re-educate them." He then repeated the well-known story of his friendly treatment of the leader of the Communist Party, Ernst Thaelmann. Thaelmann had been beaten during interrogation, and Goering, hearing of this, had him brought to his office in order to express his regrets. "My dear Thaelmann," he said, "if you had come to power, I would probably not have been beaten, but you would have chopped my head off immediately." He then told Thaelmann he should always feel free to complain of ill treatment should it ever recur, and returned him to his captors. He had done what he felt best for the record of his humanity, but, as he said himself, "Wherever you use a plane, you can't help making splinters."

The early history of the camps is bound up closely with the deep personal rivalries between Goering, Roehm of the S.A., and Heinrich Himmler, head of the S.S. Goering, as we have seen, had control over the police of Prussia, which involved a large part of Germany, at the beginning of February, and had augmented their powers by recruiting a further fifty thousand auxiliaries from the S.A., the S.S., and the Stahlhelm. At the same time he had set up a secret police force, the political police, under Diels. While this was happening Himmler became police chief for Bavaria, which he regarded as a starting point for building up his own secret force, especially when it became evident that Hitler favored the idea of establishing a unified police force independent of the separate state administrations. Reinhard Heydrich, sportsman, S.S. member and dismissed naval officer, joined Himmler to screen the members of the force. To keep the Prussian political police under his own control, Goering removed them on April 26 from under the roof of the Prussian administration to separate headquarters at 8 Prinz Albrechtstrasse, near his own ministry. In doing this, he laid the foundations for the future Gestapo, the Geheime Staatspolizei (Secret State Police), as it became known officially when reconstituted in June 1933. He called himself "Chief of the Political Police and of the Secret Police." Himmler meanwhile gradually took over the police of the rest of the German states and by the following year was able to represent successfully to Hitler that Goering's Gestapo should be added to his own. As Goering put it at Nuremberg, "At that time I did not expressly oppose it. It was not agreeable to me, I wanted to handle my police myself. But when the Führer asked me to do this and said it would be the correct thing and that it was proved necessary that the enemies of the State be fought throughout the Reich in a uniform way, I actually handed the police over to Himmler, who put Heydrich in charge." Himmler in fact took over officially on April 20, 1934.

Roehm, the leader of the S.A. directly responsible to Hitler, was developing ideas concerning the use of the S.A. which were diametrically opposed to those of Hitler and Goering. Roehm wanted the S.A. in effect to displace the Army, with himself as commander in chief; Hitler wanted to keep the Army firmly on his side and to let the undisciplined ranks of the S.A. gradually decline, since the political use of street fighting and rowdyism had become more of an embarrassment than a necessity with the consolidation of power. Goering also wanted ultimately to become Commander in Chief of the Army of the Reich. The S.A., however, had its own private accounts to settle, and with the suspension of civil liberties on February 28 Roehm and his men, as we have seen, began to set up their own concentration camps in more or less secret defiance of Goering's official centers of detention. By the end of 1933 some fifty concentration camps were in existence—a somewhat different figure from Goering's "two or three."

The scandal of the brutality practiced in these camps slowly began to leak out. Beating was followed by blackmail; ransoms were charged to release prisoners from *Schutzhaft*, protective custody. Murder became common, and it was not difficult by 1933 to find many men capable of actively enjoying the exercise of sadism. If, on his own admission, cruelty was practiced in Goering's camps and prisons, this was but the smoke that issued from the fires of pain that were being lit in the secret places controlled by the S.A. and the S.S. Both Hitler and Goering made a show of protest against

these excesses, perhaps as a matter of formality. Dachau was
founded by the S.S. in the spring of 1933, and in April S.S. men
actually fired on Goering's men when the latter attempted to investigate an unauthorized camp discovered near Osnabrück; Hitler
on this occasion forced Himmler to intervene and break up the
camp. Soon, however, Goering's man Diels was to find himself outclassed by such violent Nazis as the Berlin S.A. chief Ernst, and
Goering was to lose his power as the national police controller before the determined self-advancement of Himmler. Heydrich established an office in Berlin in direct defiance of Goering, the S.D.
(Sicherheitsdienst—Security Service), a special secret service formed
from the S.S. Goering by now had an active fear of Roehm, who
had been made a member of Hitler's Cabinet the previous December. He felt the need for alignment with someone who represented
power, and he chose to ally himself with Himmler. By this time,
in any case, Goering's main power interest had turned elsewhere.

The story of Goering's police activities cannot, therefore, be separated from his particular pursuit of power. He acknowledged his
position as second man to Hitler in the new State that was being
created, and his initial strength had been in the establishment of
control through the police.

The new Reichstag was opened on March 21 at Potsdam with
pomp and circumstance, preceded by services in both the Catholic
Pfarrkirche and the Protestant Garnisonskirche. Speeches were
made by the President and the new Chancellor before the altar in
the Garnisonskirche; Goering's own speech was reserved for his
re-election as president of the Reichstag when that body assembled
later in the Kroll Opera House in Berlin; he spoke of the holy fire
of revolution and the need to unify Germany through Hitler.
"Weimar has been overcome," he said. "It is symbolic that the
new Reichstag has found its way back to the town from which
Prussia, and with Prussia Germany, sprang." He reminded them
that March 21 was the anniversary of the day when Bismarck had
faced the first German Reichstag in 1870 and the German family
had been reunited in a German parliament. On the same day decrees were promulgated granting amnesty for criminal acts committed by the Nazis during the period of struggle for power, and
setting up special courts to deal with political offenses against the
new regime. Three days later, on March 24, came the notorious
Enabling Act, giving Hitler dictatorial powers in the State, and

passed by a Reichstag assembly in which many members could not be present because they were under arrest. S.A. and S.S. men stood around, while Goering intimidated those deputies who showed hostility, by shouting, "Quiet! The Chancellor is settling accounts!"

Early in April Goering went on holiday in Italy. There he met Mussolini, who warned him against the Nazi insistence on anti-Semitism; various anti-Jewish decrees were being announced in Germany at this particular time. Italy, according to Mussolini, could not afford to support Hitler on this issue. Goering also met Marshal Balbo, head of the Italian Air Force. On April 10, while he was still in Rome, he received a telegram from Hitler appointing him Premier of Prussia and requesting him to take up his duties on April 20; Hitler thanked him effusively for his services and for "the unique loyalty with which you have bound your faith to mine." According to Goering, this had been prearranged; as he told it later, "I also got Herr von Papen . . . to retire from his post of Commissioner for Prussia in order that the Leader could give the post to me."[16] Goering returned in good time to establish the future Gestapo on April 26.

Goering could now afford to expand his domestic life. He lived in his luxurious flat on the Kaiserdamm, which also served as a personal office; there were a Prussian police officer and an S.S. man on guard, and messengers from the various ministries streamed in and out. A side room off the main hall contained an oil painting of Carin seated on a green slope, surrounded by flowers and backed by snow-capped mountains. The room was decorated in blue-green and gold and richly carpeted. Underneath the portrait was a table with a bowl of flowers and two heavy brass candlesticks. The room was like a shrine.

Carin had now been dead for eighteen months, and Goering had hardened into a single-minded man living the life of a bachelor, with a retinue of official servants and underlings. It was at this time that Robert Kropp, who was to be his personal servant for the next twelve years, saw an advertisement that a valet was required by a gentleman occupying a very important position; the telephone number of an intermediary was given, and an appointment was arranged for Kropp after he had been warned that his potential employer was Hermann Goering. Goering kept him waiting some hours, then saw him and discussed his qualifications, inquiring if he could drive a car and pilot a motorboat. Kropp said he was able to fulfill both these requirements. Goering asked him what wage he wanted; Kropp requested the normal wage for a first-class valet, which was 140 marks a month, with residence. Goering thought for a moment and then offered him only ninety marks, but told him that if he proved good this wage would soon be raised. Goering warned him that the work would be hard and that he would have to be prepared for duty at all hours. Kropp, who was unmarried, agreed to the terms. Three months later his wages were doubled, with the increase backdated to the day he entered Goering's service.[17]

Goering remained unmarried for three and a half years. It was in 1932 that he first met the woman who was to be his second wife; this was the actress Emmy Sonnemann, whom he saw in a play at Weimar and to whom he asked to be presented. At first she refused; she was very vague about politics and was uncertain whether it was Goebbels or Goering who wanted to meet her. She soon met him, however, under more formal circumstances at a reception, and Goering became a close friend, seeking relaxation in her company away from the battleground of the Reichstag and the negotiations that led to Hitler's appointment as Chancellor. When, on August 30, 1932, he was elected president of the Reichstag, the first letter he sent out on the presidential stationery was a note to Emmy Sonnemann at Weimar, which read, "*Ich liebe dich. H.*" He had been a widower for less than a year, and this handsome blond woman in her middle thirties gave him the admiring sympathy of a warm and very feminine nature that his temperament, essentially dependent under the hard crust of masculinity that he displayed to the public, always needed.[18]

Emmy Sonnemann had been married to an actor named Köstlin, but the marriage had ended in divorce. At the time she first met Goering her mother had just died, and the sentimental attachment they felt for each other was nurtured by the losses both of them had endured. Emmy Sonnemann's reputation as an actress was a sound one, though confined for many years to the State theaters of such cities as Hamburg, Vienna and Weimar, the city associated with Goethe and Schiller and her favorite center.

Although there was talk of love between Emmy and Goering as early as August 1932, no formal engagement was to be announced until March 9, 1935. During this period Goering was, of course, deeply involved in his activities of state. But the gap is a long one, and there were rumors of his attachment to other actresses, more especially to the opera singer Margarete von Schirach, sister of the Nazi youth leader Baldur von Schirach, and to Käthe Dorsch.[19] Though Goering loved Emmy, he also wanted to remain faithful to the memory of his first wife. Carin was never to be forgotten, and he always remained in touch with her family. He flew to Rockelstad Castle for the marriage of Carin's niece in June 1933 and at the same time visited his wife's grave in the cemetery at Lövoe.

When Goering became Premier of Prussia in April 1933, he was entitled to another official residence in addition to that of president of the Reichstag. But, like most men tasting the first fruits of power, he was dissatisfied with the stale palaces of a dead regime; he wanted to express himself through something new. While Goebbels, who had been appointed Minister of Propaganda and Public Enlightenment in March 1933, was tearing down the stucco and changing the interior decoration of the Leopoldpalast on the Wilhelmplatz ("I cannot work in the twilight," he said), Goering decided to clear a site on the corner of Prinz Albrechtstrasse and Stresemannstrasse, the name of which he had had changed by the local authority to Hermann Goeringstrasse. Here he built himself a town house at the taxpayers' expense next door to the new headquarters of the Gestapo, for whose activities Diels had commandeered the premises of the Berlin Folklore Museum. The new palace was completed early in 1934.

From this period, Goering's financial status was inextricably entangled with the perquisites and prizes of office. His officially declared salaries were relatively small: president of the Reichstag, 7,200 marks a year; Cabinet minister, 12,000 marks; Air Commissioner, 3,000 marks; president of the Prussian State Council, 12,000 marks. Some of these offices carried expense allowances or exemptions from taxation. Hitler was always prepared to enable Goering to entertain lavishly when it was necessary. In addition, Goering began, by virtue of his powerful positon, to gather substantial business interests in the form of shares, and the influential newspaper, the *Nationalzeitung* of Essen, became his particular mouthpiece.

Thyssen states that many industrialists, including himself, thought that Hitler would re-establish the monarchy. Goering was known to have been the guest of the former Kaiser at his residence in Holland, and, although Goering told Thyssen that the Crown Prince had made deprecating remarks to him about Hitler after a dinner party, the Prince was invited to occupy a prominent box at the first of Goering's Opera Balls. Certain of the industrialists were impressed by this show of favor to the Hohenzollerns.

On February 20, 1933, Goering invited a carefully selected group of industrialists to his Reichstag President's Palace to meet Hitler —among them Schmidt, Krupp von Bohlen, Voegler of United Steel, and Schnitzler and Bosch of I. G. Farben. Goering explained that the purpose of the conference was to create a fund for the March elections. After a speech by Hitler, three million marks was subscribed, and Schacht was invited to administer the fund on behalf of all the right-wing parties. "The elections will certainly be the last for the next ten years," said Goering confidently to his distinguished audience. To the working classes, on the other hand, the Nazis cynically offered socialism in their election speeches. Heiden reports Goering as saying at a mass rally in the Sportpalast in April, after the elections were over, "Not only has German National Socialism been victorious, but German socialism as well."[20]

Thyssen, as one of Hitler's more loyal supporters, was rewarded by Goering with the office of Prussian state councilor for life, and he attended a few meetings—until Goering turned them from debates into cramming sessions "in a course on National Socialism," and even Streicher was invited to lecture! Thyssen had been kept in line during the final days before Hitler became Chancellor by a telephone call from Goering warning him that spies had brought information of an incipient Communist putsch in the Ruhr and that Thyssen headed the list of their proposed hostages. "How could I have doubted his words?" writes the pathetic capitalist, the head of German industry. "I therefore began to collaborate openly with the regime."[21]

Later, when Thyssen had fled from Germany and, among the comforts of Cap-Ferrat, was dictating his diatribes against the Nazis, he cried out, "What a fool I have been . . ." and went on to reveal his knowledge of the graft practiced by certain leaders of the Nazi Party, Goering particularly. Goering's debts were as far as possible left unpaid, Thyssen claims; from poverty he rose suddenly to become one of the richest men in Germany, drawing his revenue alike from private and public resources. As Premier of Prussia he became administrator of all the state domains, and these he distributed to himself and others. To Hindenburg, who made him a general in August 1933,[22] he gave additional lands at Neudeck, known in Germany as "Naboth's vineyard" and later as "the smallest concentration camp," because the President, now eighty-six, spent more and more time there and barely emerged to take part in affairs of state or in social life. For himself Goering took over the vast woodland estate of Schorfheide, where Carinhall was to be built, and staffed it with servants, wardens and gamekeepers who were all supported by the state. Similarly in Berlin his private palace was a state concern. In the Bavarian Alps he was presented by the Premier of Bavaria with a site facing Hitler's own property; here a villa was constructed.

Soon an organized system of sweetening Goering by presents, in particular presents given on his birthday each January, became accepted as part of the Nazi system. Schacht describes the banquet given by Goering to celebrate his birthday in 1934, and the rich publisher who was allowed the seat of honor beside his host; he had given Goering a shooting brake and four horses. Schacht himself presented Goering with "a very fine picture of a bison."

Goering had lived on the fringes of big business and on the door-steps of men of wealth and power since his return to Germany in 1927. He had been brought up in circumstances that led him to believe that the best in life was his due, and that ever since the defeat of Germany in 1918 he had been deprived of this natural birthright. Now the door had swung open and he had stepped immediately into the surroundings of ownership. It was hardly to be expected that he would have developed any refinements of conscience in the roughhouse of German politics during the past five years. Power was for use as well as ornament, and with the new offices and uniforms, the ministries, palaces and servants, came the unmitigated hunger for possessions. Goering, fed from youth on the images of the princes of the past, began to accumulate his horde of booty. He liked now to picture himself as a Renaissance grandee.

By 1933 he had become a very fat man, and his weight, approaching its maximum of 280 pounds, gave him great trouble. His energy made him a voracious eater, but only at times. He was, in fact, a sporadic eater, who tended to absorb big meals only when he was entertaining guests at a favorite restaurant, such as Horcher's. On his own, he would usually take sandwiches and beer, adjusting his eating habits to whatever he was doing, but he frequently roused Kropp in the night and demanded beer and sandwiches, specifying just what cheese or sausage he wanted in them; after this he would go on to his favorite food, which was cake—the sweet, creamy patisserie which, like Hitler, he managed to eat in great quantities. He seldom went to bed before two or three in the morning, and he loved to have films projected privately late at night, another taste he shared with Hitler and also with Goebbels. Kropp, having been kept up to the small hours supplying his master with food, was nevertheless under orders to wake Goering at about six-thirty each morning. He seldom had to rouse him, for Goering suffered from insomnia. He usually found Goering up, shaved and showered; he insisted on shaving himself with an old-fashioned Gillette safety razor, and he always manicured his own hands, taking great care of their appearance. He had a very soft skin and, like most German gentlemen at that time, powdered his face after shaving; this, according to Kropp, was the origin of the rumor that later in his life he used make-up.

In certain matters he was lazy. He disliked having his hair cut, and Kropp always had to bully him into giving time for this to be done by the barber from the Kaiserhof, who was often kept waiting for hours but placated in the end with a generous tip. Above all, Goering was lazy about dressing himself. Although he was cultivating an inordinate taste for dress, he disliked getting into his clothes, and Kropp had actually to dress him. He was fond of wearing specially made coats that reached almost to the ground, making him look not only large but imperious. Tight clothes always troubled him; as often as he could he wore one of the many huge housecoats which he had made specially to avoid constriction round his body.

For sleeping he wore a silk nightgown with puffed sleeves; he disliked pajamas. In the daytime as he became fatter he had to change his clothes more frequently; he sweated to an exceptional degree and went in constant need of clean linen. In vain attempts to control his fat he sometimes went for vigorous walks in the country at weekends.[23]

When he was promoted a general he began to take an increasing interest in the variety of uniforms his various offices required. His uniforms had always been made at Stechbarth's, the fashionable Berlin tailors who specialized in service dress. Cap, their chief cutter, spent many years working for Goering, fitting and refitting his clothes to the changing shape of his body. Cap maintains that rumor greatly exaggerated the actual size of Goering's wardrobe. He had his variety of uniforms (some of which he designed himself), his civilian suits (never more than about twenty of these available at one time to wear), his special garbs (which worried Cap because of their extravagance), and his informal clothes for relaxation. He loved soft leather jackets and fancy waistcoats. Goering often kept Cap waiting for fittings, but then would always be charming and jovial and apologetic. He would even accept advice in good part; once he discarded a heavy fur coat that he had had made, because Cap pointed out with as much tact as possible that the Herr Reichsminister was much too fat for it.

Other responsibilities besides those arising from the creation of a police state were placed on Goering during 1933, and one of the most important of these was the development of Germany as an air power.[24] On May 5, 1933, the office of the Reich Commissioner of Aviation became the Air Ministry, and Goering was appointed Air Traffic Minister, since the pretense was still to be kept up that Germany was not planning the establishment of an air force. The flying clubs and gliding clubs were merged into the German Air Club and the German Air Sport Union under Bruno Loerzer, assisted by Ernst Udet and other famous names in German aviation. Goebbels' press began to take up the theme of flying and the need for an air force, and a great National Flying Day was organized at the Tempelhof Airport on June 15.

In the Pact of Paris made in 1926, Germany had been permitted to establish "air police" units and means of defense in the air. Goering at once took advantage of this and set up the Reichsluftschutzbund, the German Air Defense Union, an organization which gave him control of antiaircraft artillery and civilian air-raid precautions. On April 29 he announced the formation of this German Air Defense Union and issued a manifesto to the German people warning them of the vulnerability of a disarmed Germany to attack from the air; the nations surrounding them, he claimed, had ten thousand war planes which could at an hour's notice fill the skies of Germany. Everyone was urged to join the Union as an air-raid warden and prepare his home for defense against attack; a journal called the Syren was published for the movement and a training scheme set up. A small subscription was charged. In order to provide an appropriate "incident" to use as a lever with the Allied powers, on June 23 all the newspapers published a scare article headed "Red Plague over Berlin: Foreign Planes of an Unknown Type Escaped Unrecognized; Defenseless Germany." Blood-Ryan,

Goering's prewar English biographer, says that he telephoned Goering the same day and asked for his views. Goering replied, "Yesterday's incident shows how defenseless Germany really is. I have not one single plane which I could have sent up in defense and pursuit. I am going to do my utmost to build at least a few police planes to be prepared against any further attacks. These police planes will not become a question of military defense, they are an absolute necessity."

Soon Goering's ministry was in touch with the British embassy in Berlin asking for export permits from the British government so that "police" planes and engines might be bought from British manufacturers. The permits were granted. Hanfstaengl recollects helping to entertain Sir John Siddeley in Berchtesgaden in the late summer of 1933, and how Sir John and Goering "sat out on a balcony with great illustrations and blueprints of British military aircraft it was hoped Germany would buy."[25]

Goering began to gather round him his old associates of the First World War. Colonel Karl Bodenschatz joined him as personal assistant and chief adjutant, and Erhard Milch became State Secretary of his ministry. In the spring of the same year a young Lufthansa trainee-flyer, Adolf Galland, who had already undergone secret instruction which anticipated the needs of a fighter pilot, was summoned to Berlin. He found himself in the presence of Goering, who explained that he and certain other pilots were to be sent to Italy for further secret training in the Italian Air Force; the young man, though impressed by Goering's enthusiasm, was "amazed at his girth and displacement." He returned from Italy "an almost perfectly trained fighter pilot" in the autumn; in February 1934 he passed from civil flying to the "active list" and in October received his commission. He adds, significantly, that Hitler's purge of Roehm and the S.A. in June 1934 "aroused little excitement in the garrison . . . it seemed to be mainly an 'internal party affair.' "[26] Galland was later to become one of Goering's senior officers in the Air Force and one of his sternest critics.

Although the existence of the German Air Force was not formally acknowledged until March 1, 1935, Goering set about building up the air consciousness of Germany in every way he could. Industry was ordered to produce aircraft for civil flying and transport. Under cover of the expansion of civilian air services, pilots and planes were developed side by side.

Once commissioned, Galland found himself (though a civilian in appearance) expected to train other fighter pilots at Schleissheim, which he describes as the first fighter school of the German Luftwaffe. Goering himself came in February 1935 to explain what the Luftwaffe was to be, and the uniform they were soon openly to wear was put on display. In April Galland was attached to the fighter group commanded by Wolfram von Richthofen, near Berlin; he found both airfield and quarters only half finished, but a new Heinkel-51 fighter was safely delivered. He would soon be ready for Spain.

The foundations for all this work were laid during 1933. During weekends Goering liked to break away from his desk and his conferences whenever he could and visit the forests north of Berlin. As if to reward him and make his sport part of his official duties, Hitler permitted him to become Reich Master of the Hunt in May 1933 and also Master of the German Forests, for which a special ministry was established in 1934. As Hitler's Master of the Hunt, Goering designed himself a special uniform including a white silk shirt with his favorite puffed sleeves, over which he wore a sleeveless belted jacket of soft leather.

Goering merged the various powers over forestry and game that were held by the provincial states. Germany's extensive forests are important to her economy, and he began a series of reforms in forestry which were to be of permanent benefit. His love of the countryside was expressed in reafforestation schemes, irrigation and the preservation of areas of natural beauty. He introduced laws to protect wild life and preserve such dying species as the elk, the bison, the wild boar, the wild swan, the falcon and the eagle.

It was now that he became increasingly interested in the Schorfheide, a great tract of forest and moorland infiltrated with lakes that stretched from the north of Berlin away to the Polish border (as it then was) and the Baltic coast; he restocked this area with wild life and decided he would acquire an estate there for himself. He also visited the Rominten Heide, or Heath, on Germany's eastern border. He brought in bison and elk from Sweden, Poland and Canada for experiments which were not always successful, but were intended to revive the breeding of these animals. In July 1934 he tightened the German game laws, forbidding shooting except under a strictly defined quota, and then only by those whose license proved they knew how to handle a gun. All hunters had to be accompanied by a retriever so that wounded animals could be found and killed. Goering passed a law forbidding the vivisection of animals, and he forbade all forms of poaching, hunting on horseback and the use of claw and wire traps, artificial lights or poison against animals. "He who tortures an animal hurts the feelings of the German people," he said.

During 1933 he began to plan his great country house of Carinhall. As the second man to Hitler in Nazi Germany, as Premier of Prussia, as Reich Master of the Hunt and as Master of the German Forests, he felt himself entitled to the finest territory that could be found within reasonable distance from Berlin. He chose an area in the Schorfheide where there was a German imperial hunting lodge built of wood, near a lake called the Wackersee. Here he had a hundred thousand acres set aside as a state park reserved as far as possible for himself, to be the center for the house he planned to build and the game reserve he had decided to establish for his shooting parties.

The Schorfheide was undulating and wooded, its heath and moorland interspersed with pine, oak and beech. The juniper bushes turned the scene a golden brown in autumn, while hawthorn, barberry bushes and broom varied the colors of the landscape, which was broken by marshes with their rushes and sedge and by small lakes edged with pines and firs. Woodpeckers tapped in the trees, and wild swans floated below on the lake water with their cygnets. Goering made the Schorfheide a sanctuary for the deer, the buffalo, the elk and the wild horse and then began to plan the house, which, while it perpetuated the memory of his wife, must bear the stamp of his living personality.

Carinhall was to become unique among the monuments built by princes and millionaires as expressions of their pride. Hitler, Goering and Goebbels were all amateur architects with marked tastes in building, interior decoration and furnishing which their political success let loose in an orgy of construction. But of all the structures set up during the Nazi regime, Carinhall was the most unusual, a cumulative symbol of its builder's dreams, considerably augmented and enriched over the years. Helped by two young architects, Helzelt and Tuch of the Prussian State Department of Architecture, Goering tried to realize his ambitions, his sentiments, his memories and his vanity in stone, timber, metal, plaster and thatch. He designed every detail himself down to the door handles;

he called it his *Waldhof,* and the result was a monumental curiosity, a kind of ancient German baronial hall equipped with every luxury and combining a massive simplicity with showmanship of wealth and power. As Gritzbach put it, "Hermann Goering conceived the ground plan and the structure on lines that expressed his own strong and self-willed personality." Expanding year by year, it gradually developed into a manor house of extraordinary size and appearance.

A great avenue of trees led to the steep-roofed mansion, which was built around three sides of an extensive courtyard containing flower beds, a lily pond and a fountain topped by a statue of a horse with a nude rider. An ambulatory, its roof supported by thick beams and columns of oak, circled the courtyard, while magnificent gates, importations from the south, were set into the heavy wood and stone of the main architecture, for which granite blocks of varied colors were used. The building itself was designed so that every outer window commanded a view of either lake or forest, and, with its thatched mansard roof, pebble-dashed white walls and gray stone borders, it was meant to symbolize the German tradition in architecture. The central façade was in the Gothic style, and when Goering became a Reich Marshal his arms—a mailed fist grasping a bludgeon—were engraved on a pediment over the porch. In addition to the first main courtyard there was a quadrangle divided into a series of lawns with trimmed hedgerows and bronze statues of Apollo, Artemis and Ceres. Another courtyard was enclosed by climbing plants, and a reproduction of the Porcellino of Florence stood half hidden among the rosebushes.

In the central part of the building was the entrance hall, some hundred and fifty feet wide, forming the principal art gallery in which Goering was to take so much delight, the center into which would flow the gifts of works of art and other treasures he was now beginning either to buy or to acquire—pictures by the old Flemish masters and by the German artist Lucas Cranach, whom he admired greatly, and Gobelin tapestries. Twin flights of stairs with gleaming white bannisters led from this entrance hall to the floor above. Other principal rooms included a council chamber in medieval style, center for official work, with its great beams and granite chimneypiece, the main library, the reception rooms for visitors, and the map or card room, where staff conferences were held under the portraits of Frederick the Great and Napoleon. Later there

appeared a vast banquet hall with columns of red Veronese marble.
Here the table was covered with silk, the chairs were white and up-
holstered in leather, the curtains were embroidered with the letter
H in laurel wreaths stitched in gold thread. The walls were covered
by tapestries depicting allegorical figures of Youth, Health and
Joy; from the ceiling hung great crystal chandeliers. The windows
were controlled electrically and would open to display an unim-
peded view of the gardens and the forest. Outside on the paved
terrace guests would be served by footmen in riding boots and green
doublets and breeches, or by girls in buckskin boots and green
jackets and skirts. The main drawing room had two anterooms, the
Gold Room and the Silver Room, in which Goering was to display
the fabulous gifts he received. The staircase to the upper floor was
adorned with the relics and trophies of Goering's hunts. It was in
a large attic here that he installed his model railway, with which
so many distinguished visitors were to be invited to play. The room
was some eighty feet long, and the railway had a length of straight
track running sixty feet. The trains were operated from a control
panel placed beside a large red armchair.

Goering also had a small, secluded workroom with antique Tiro-
lean furniture and with access to a private library where he kept the
books he treasured most, including works on Nordic history, historical and topographical volumes on Germany, studies of military
science and aviation, and books on art, travel and exploration. In
summer he used an entirely private loggia for his work, which enabled him to sit in the open air and look out over the lake.

Carinhall had a basement, in which there was a gymnasium, a
dimly lit swimming pool adorned with sculptures, and a gameroom.
In the gymnasium Goering was able to practice marksmanship by
shooting at moving pictures of animals projected onto the wall;
in the gameroom there was an electrically powered system of model
airliners and railways on a map. At night the gymnasium became a
cinema, where the servants sat. Each had his appointed seat as if
this were the church of some lord of the manor. The guest rooms
for visitors and staff and the servants' quarters were all comfortable
and well appointed; Goering wished to be recognized as a model
employer.

Carinhall as so many visitors have described it was the result of
constant changes and extensions which continued into the early
years of the war. The initial building was much smaller, an elabo-

rate hunting lodge completed by an army of builders within a period of ten months. Opposite to it, by the lakeside, Goering constructed a mausoleum of Brandenburg granite which he intended
should contain the body of his wife, whose grave at Lövoe in
Sweden, had, as he claimed, been desecrated by Swedish anti-
Nazis. (Goering had put a new tombstone emblazoned with the
swastika over Carin's grave, and when visiting Sweden he had
placed a floral swastika on her tomb. This the Swedish anti-Nazis
removed, leaving a note saying that "the German, Goering," had
committed an act of vandalism and should not use his wife's grave
as a means for propaganda.) The new vault was set beneath the
ground with a flight of steps leading down into it. Goering ordered
a vast pewter coffin from the firm of Svensk Tenn, whose luxurious
displays of furnishings and metalwork had attracted him when he
was in Stockholm and could ill afford such decorations. The pewter
coffin was designed on such a scale that it might eventually contain
the body of Goering himself as well as that of Carin. He was as
proud of the vault as he was of Carinhall itself, and in the conducted tours which he never tired of undertaking whenever guests
came to visit Carinhall the vault was normally included.

One of the earliest of the elaborate housewarming parties organized by Goering, on June 10, 1934, was attended by some forty
people, including the British and American ambassadors. Sir Eric
Phipps, the new British ambassador, sent Sir John Simon a long,
ironic description of the whole proceedings.[27] Goering arrived late
at the place in the forest where the guests were assembled; he drove
up in a fast racing car, dressed in "aviator's garments of india-
rubber, with top boots and a large hunting knife stuck in his belt."
First he delivered a lecture on German forestry and fauna, speaking
in a loud voice and using a microphone. He then attempted to
make one of his bull bisons demonstrate mating with some cows,
but this was a failure; the bull "emerged from his box with the
utmost reluctance, and, after eyeing the cows somewhat sadly, tried
to return to it." Goering then disappeared, leaving his guests to
drive in their cars through the woods to Carinhall itself, where he
received them again—dressed now in white tennis shoes, white
drill trousers, white flannel shirt and a green leather jacket, with
the large hunting knife still stuck in his belt—and took them round
the house: all the while he carried a "long, harpoon-like instrument." Emmy Sonnemann was there, and she presided over an

excellent meal; Goering introduced her as his private secretary.

Ambassador Dodd, telling the story in his diary, wrote that Goering—whom he described as "a big, fat, good-humored man who loves display above everything"—showed them about the estate later "and displayed his vanity at every turn, often causing his guests to glance amusedly at each other." Finally they were led to see the vault, "the most elaborate structure of its kind I have ever seen." Goering "boasted of this marvelous tomb of his first wife where he said his remains would one day be laid." Dodd says that he and Phipps grew "weary of the curious display" and hastened back to Berlin.

A few days later, on June 19, Carin's body, transported in its sarcophagus on which the arms of the Goering and Fock families were emblazoned, was interred in the vault with macabre pomp. After a simple service at Lövoe the coffin, covered by a swastika flag, had been placed in a railway car lined with evergreens and filled with flowers. Goering's wreath of white roses bore a card on which he had written, "To my only Carin." Guarded by a corps of Nazis, the coffin went by ferry to Sussnitz and then by rail through the towns of northern Prussia, which were put in a state of mourning while it passed, until it finally reached Eberswalde, where it was placed on a cart and taken by road to Carinhall. Uniformed party men lined the route, and a military band played Siegfried's Funeral March from Götterdämmerung. Hitler was there. But the ceremony so elaborately planned was suddenly interrupted. Himmler arrived late, pale and shaken. He claimed that an attempt had been made on his life and that the windshield of his car had been shattered by a bullet. He was uninjured and had heard no sound of the shot being fired. For a few minutes the interment was delayed while Himmler whispered his story to Goering and Hitler. Then, while hunting horns and trumpets sounded, the sarcophagus was edged down into the vault, where six candles stood burning. After the bearers had filed out, Goering and Hitler went down the steps to pay silent homage.[28]

V

Hitler's Paladin

As GOERING BEGAN to discover the possibilities for wealth and power that his high position in the State could command, his initial interest in the development of police control and its administration waned. He was a man of impulse, of lavish activity so long as his attention was fully absorbed; he disliked painstaking detail or following through the schemes that he originated with such undisciplined energy.

Power brought its own deep satisfaction, but it also brought anxiety. The natural distrust that the Nazi leaders had for one another was immeasurably increased once they had acquired the means to destroy each other. As a result, alliances were formed among the members of the hierarchy surrounding Hitler; each man chose his temporary friends with some misgiving and appointed deputies whose loyalty he hoped he might succeed in holding. Roehm was the man whom Goering most feared; Himmler was the man with whom he made his alliance; Diels was the man he chose for his first deputy.

The organized forces in Germany during the first year of the regime were deeply divided. The Reichswehr, the established German Army, was nominally under the civil authority in the persons of the President and the Minister of Defense; but in fact it had its own high command, and the Minister of Defense was an Army general, Blomberg, the man chosen by Hindenburg. Opposed to the Reichswehr were the private forces of Nazism, the S.A. and the S.S., which in turn were divided against each other. The S.A. at this time numbered perhaps between two and three million men, a vastly greater though far less disciplined force than that of the Reichswehr. Roehm commanded this army of the Brownshirts, whereas the S.S., the black-shirted elite of violence, although nominally still part of the S.A., had been under Himmler's special authority since 1929. Himmler, like Goering, hated Roehm, and it was natural that the two men should ultimately recognize a common interest. Goering's Prussian police and his Gestapo organization were through this alliance united with the police departments of the remaining German states, which Himmler, supported by Goering, so rapidly gathered under his control during the latter months of 1933.

A preliminary trial of strength was won by Roehm when Goering made a bid to display his prestige as Premier of Prussia at the opening of his new State Council on September 15, 1933. Goering's plan for himself included a state drive followed by a review of the S.A. and the S.S. at a special march-past that he suggested they should stage in his honor. But Goering's informants are said to have brought him word that Roehm and Ernst had arranged that if the march-past took place it should be performed so carelessly that the Premier would find himself publicly insulted. In self-defense Goering was forced to retract this act of personal self-glorification and share the honors of the march-past with both Roehm and Himmler. Ambassador Dodd, who was present officially, estimated that a hundred thousand uniformed men lined the streets for the ceremony.

After Goering had delivered a speech in which he referred contemptuously to the parliamentary system which the Third Reich had superseded, the march-past took place, with a special display of the goose step. This empty act of personal aggrandizement by Goering during a ceremony at which Hitler was not present was watched by the diplomatic corps as well as by prominent men from art, industry, politics and the church whom the Premier had invited to become state councilors on the very eve of the period when any form of independent authority exercised by the German states was to be abolished by Hitler.

Roehm was a man of undoubted ability, and Hitler's own attitude to him was complex and ambiguous. Except for his period abroad, he had belonged to the party for longer even than Hitler himself. He was a professional soldier, and in his way he had done almost as much as Goering to ease Hitler into the bargaining position which had won him the chancellorship. He had always seemed on terms of intimacy with the Leader, calling him *du*, a privilege denied to everyone else, including Goering. Hitler's instinctive regard for Roehm, perhaps not untinged with fear of the consequences of upsetting him, permitted a long period of stalemate to develop between them, a situation which became a growing threat to the Führer's activity. Hitler's vision was wider and subtler than Roehm's; Roehm believed in barefaced, not legalized, power. He believed the S.A. should become Germany's revolutionary army, at once absorbing and eliminating the Reichswehr, and that he should be Hitler's Commander in Chief. Hindenburg's influence gradually waned as he withdrew to live in a state of virtual retirement, and the question of who should eventually gain legal command of the Reichswehr correspondingly intensified. Roehm's views were widely known; he made no secret of them in his public speeches. On the other hand, Hitler did everything he could to encourage the confidence of the high command. At the same time he thought it best to make Roehm a member of his Cabinet on December 1, 1933, and permitted the publication the following January of a letter of tribute accompanying the appointment in which the familiar *du* appeared and Roehm was thanked for his "imperishable services." These favors both angered and alarmed Goering.

Roehm was a noted pederast, as were many of his associates, in particular Edmund Heines, head of the S.A. in Silesia, a convicted murderer whom Hitler had dismissed in 1927 for his undisciplined conduct, then reinstated in 1931. Although Hitler did not trouble about the private morals of his followers, he cared a great deal for any weakening of the party's prestige that such notorious behavior might bring about. Even so, he was astonishingly tolerant of practices which had for some time been common knowledge and the constant cause of complaint by parents whose sons had been enticed into the bedrooms of their commanding officers. Meanwhile Goering encouraged the compilation of any evidence that was damaging to Roehm; this included, according to Papen, the discovery that arms for the S.A. were being secretly brought in from Belgium. Goering and Himmler collected assiduously both facts and rumors that blackened the names of the S.A. leaders—their misappropriation of money, their drunken behavior in public places, their anti-Catholic propaganda in the universities, their gross forms of homosexuality. Roehm, now seated at Hitler's council table, unconsciously assisted them by alienating the traditionalists among the Cabinet ministers, as well as the Führer himself, with his persistent demands on behalf of the S.A. In February, the month Roehm presented a memorandum proposing that the S.A. should be combined with the regular Army and the S.S. under a Ministry of Defense of which he clearly desired the control, Hitler assured Anthony Eden, then Lord Privy Seal of Britain, who was in Berlin to discuss the disarmament problem, that he was prepared substantially to reduce the strength of the S.A. Relations between Roehm and the other members of the Cabinet responsible for defense were deteriorating still further when Hitler learned that Hindenburg was not likely to survive longer than a few more weeks. Hitler acted quickly; during April and May he had secret talks with the commanders of the Army and the Navy and in effect promised them the dismemberment of the S.A. if they would support his assumption of the Presidency on the death of Hindenburg.

Meanwhile, Goering was not slow to sense the smell of change. If Chancellor Hitler no longer needed the S.A. rabble and wanted to forget its undignified associations with the street, Premier Goering no longer wanted to be thought a policeman whose men were increasingly associated with excesses he was either unable or unwilling to control. Hitler's genial "paladin," master of two great palaces in Berlin, owner of the splendid Carinhall, the Führer's special ambassador, the official host of diplomatic and foreign representatives, the Reich Master of the Hunt, the lover of art and the administrator of the Prussian state theater, the recognized associate of a well-known actress, could no longer afford to be directly responsible for the other great cause of public scandal and international criticism, the blood of tortured men and women that seeped through the walls behind which the S.S. and the Gestapo conducted their specialized forms of interrogation. Goering made what show he might of his clemency during this first year; for example, in the case of the camps, he was later to point to his having "helped the families of the inmates financially" and ordered at Christmas the release of five thousand prisoners.[1] As we have seen, in 1934, with (as he put it) a gesture of generosity toward his Führer, he offered no opposition to the transfer of the Prussian Ministry of the Interior (with its police, the Gestapo) to the Reich Ministry of the Interior, and on April 1 Himmler took charge of the national police, becoming therefore chief of Goering's "beloved children" as well as of the S.S. On the same day Rudolf Diels was appointed police chief of Cologne and so was removed from his central office; handsome Reinhard Heydrich became Himmler's principal assistant. Goering then began to build another small and private police force, the Landespolizeigruppe, based near Berlin, at Lichterfelde, to give him some personal security in the likely event of trouble.[2]

The field was now almost ready for battle, and the deployment of the forces involved was being gradually clarified. The first phase was the discussions held late in May and early in June; Goering maintained at Nuremberg that he had had Roehm brought to him and had charged him with the rumors then circulating that he was planning a *coup d'état* with his old friend Schleicher and with Gregor Strasser. Even Prince August Wilhelm seemed to be involved. But Gritzbach, the authorized biographer, says that Goering went to Roehm and pleaded with him to remain loyal. However this may be, the principal discussion was one that took place between Hitler and Roehm in which, according to Hitler's account, Roehm promised "to put things right." Hitler then personally announced that the storm troopers as a whole were to go on leave for the month of July. Roehm replied by going on "sick leave" himself with his favorite youths. He retired to Bavaria on June 7, but issued an ominous statement which claimed in effect that the S.A., in spite of what might be done to prevent it, would reassemble in full force after its period of leave and must be regarded as "the destiny of Germany." He then invited Hitler to confer with the leadership of the S.A. in Wiessee, near Munich, on June 30. Hitler accepted. Goebbels himself, playing what may well have amounted to a double game, kept in touch with Roehm, ostensibly on Hitler's behalf. Like Roehm, he was a radical; like Goering, he was beginning to enjoy the fuller fruits of power. But he was as near a friend as Roehm could find among Hitler's immediate circle, and he may well have done some double-thinking about his relationship with Roehm in case there were a putsch that turned out to be successful. Goebbels' prime concern was to keep his position at the top. So he went to Munich to see Roehm at the famous Bratwurstglöckle. Hitler, subject now to mounting pressure from Goering to take action against Roehm, left for Venice, dressed like a depressed commercial traveler, and there met Mussolini, who was resplendently uniformed.

The tension mounted when Papen, inspired by an appeal made to him personally by Hindenburg, delivered a speech at the University of Marburg on June 17, in which he made the last public gesture to come from the ranks of the Cabinet itself of opposition to the imposition of Nazi rule and to the underhand methods that were being used by his colleagues. It was a notable act of courage and of atonement by the man who had done so much to give Hitler the power against which he now felt bound to protest. He spoke as a Catholic and on behalf of Catholics, and he risked his life to do so. The tone of the speech, though its publication was immediately suppressed, soon became widely known and seemed likely to rally public opinion both inside and outside Germany against the Nazi Party. It therefore helped to determine Hitler to take action while there was still time. On the very same day he was himself conferring with Goering and other party leaders at Gera, in Thuringia, and he referred to "the pygmy who imagines he can stop, with a few phrases, the gigantic revival of a people's life." On January 20, speaking at the Prussian State Council, Goering admitted that there was unrest and that "dissatisfaction" had broken out "here and there." Then, referring to talk of a second revolution in Germany, he added, "The first revolution was ordered by the Führer and ended by the Führer. If the Führer wants a second revolution we shall be ready, in the streets, tomorrow. If he does not want it we shall be ready to suppress anybody who tries to rebel against the Führer's will."

The following day, June 21, Hitler went to see Hindenburg at Neudeck, but was told by Blomberg that unless he modified both the policy and the practice of his party, martial law would be proclaimed by the President himself. Distressed and worried by the threat, Hitler retired once more to determine what must now be done; it is evident that he hated the thought of precipitating violence in his own ranks and feared the repercussions of any drastic action during this initial period in the consolidation of his power when so many forces in the State were ready to oppose him. It was many weeks since he had promised the high command that he would suppress the S.A., and it was plain they were impatient to see him do it. For a few more days his nerves demanded distraction from the action he was being pressed to take from every side, by

Roehm's intransigence, by Hindenburg's and the Army's increasing criticism of his leadership, by Goering's insistence that now was the time once more to cleanse the Augean stables.

The distraction he took was to fly to many different places in Germany, like a frightened bird diverting attention from its nest. Between June 21 and June 29 he was in Bavaria inspecting a mountain road, in Essen attending the wedding of Gauleiter Josef Terboven and touring the Krupp plant, and in Westphalia inspecting labor camps. In Berlin the Army was alerted on June 25 and Roehm formally expelled from the German Officers' League on June 28, the same day Goering went with Hitler to visit the Krupp plant and to act as a witness at Terboven's wedding. That evening during the wedding festivities Himmler arrived in Essen from Berlin with further reports of Roehm's alleged designs. Hitler was seen to whisper in Goering's ear, and they withdrew together to a private room in the Kaiserhof, where they talked until midnight. Then, according to Gritzbach, they parted and Goering returned to Berlin. The campaign was being planned. Himmler's S.S. and Goering's police had already been ordered to stand by for action. In Munich Roehm, who had received confirmation that Hitler would attend his S.A. conference on June 30, made arrangements for a banquet at the Vierjahreszeiten Hotel.

On Friday, June 29, Hitler and Goering, again according to Gritzbach, kept in direct touch with each other by means of dispatches sent by air over the three hundred miles that separated them. Even so, Hitler distracted himself with a tour of some local labor camps, returning afterward to his hotel in Godesberg. There he was joined in the evening by Goebbels, who brought the news that Karl Ernst had placed his Berlin S.A. men on the alert, in spite of Hitler's order that they should go on leave on July 1. Hitler had also heard that a specialist had been summoned to attend Hindenburg. The men with Hitler now were, apart from Goebbels, Viktor Lutze, a reliable S.A. leader, and Otto Dietrich. Meanwhile Goering waited in Berlin for the final order from the Führer and took close counsel with Himmler and Blomberg.

Later, Hitler was to claim that he received alarming messages from Goering by telephone announcing that an S.A. putsch was about to take place in both Berlin and Munich. In the small hours he sent a telegram to Roehm to say he was on his way to join him and then hastened into a plane on an airfield near Bonn for the two-hour journey to Munich. When he landed with Goebbels, Lutze and Dietrich at four in the morning, he found that the local S.A. leaders had already been placed under arrest by the Bavarian Minister of the Interior. With the help of Army transport, Sepp Dietrich's S.S. *Leibstandarte* special detachment, some seven hundred strong, had been brought from Berlin to provide the necessary gunmen. Then Hitler and his supporters and a detachment of Sepp Dietrich's men left Munich in a fleet of cars that drove in swift formation down the road to the lakeside forty miles away. There Roehm was sleeping unguarded in the Hanslbauer sanatorium. In the room next to him lay Heines, embracing a boy. Hitler's convoy sped along the autobahn that cut through the shadowy forests in which misty shafts of light from the early morning sun were beginning to slant; then the cars turned south to reach the shores of the Tegernsee.

Hitler's self-control was by now uncertain; he had been virtually without sleep for a considerable time, and the moment was approaching when he had to face Roehm. The cars drew up, and the avengers, led by their Führer, crept silently in. Heines, according to Otto Dietrich, presented "a disgusting scene"; he and the boy with him were taken out, hustled into the back seat of one of the cars, and there shot. Dietrich describes Hitler pacing up and down in front of Roehm with huge strides, "fiery as some higher being, the very personification of justice." Roehm, still dazed with sleep, would not speak. Hitler took his prisoners back to Munich, where they were put into the Stadelheim prison. There they were kept while Hans Frank, the Bavarian Minister of Justice, did what he could through the rest of the day to save their lives. Hitler left them and shut himself away in the Brown House. Eventually Sepp Dietrich's men complained that it would soon be too dark for the firing squads to shoot, and urgent phone calls to Berlin for instructions as to who should be shot among those whose names appeared on the hastily prepared lists led finally to confirmation that nineteen of the two hundred men held should be killed at once. They were hurried out to be shot in the gathering dusk, and others were assassinated the following day. Roehm was not among them; two days later, on July 2, he was invited to commit suicide. When he refused, he was shot down in his cell by two S.A. officers while, stripped to the waist, he stood contemptuously to attention.

There was none of this inefficient, squeamish uncertainty of action about the proceedings in Berlin. There, like the generals in *Julius Caesar*, Himmler and Goering had their death lists ready and in proper order.

> *These many then shall die; their names are prick'd . . .*
> *He shall not live; look, with a spot I damn him.*

Goering was determined on immediate action against the proscribed without any reference to the formalities of justice, which might have caused the same unfortunate delays as were happening in Munich once Hitler's back was turned. The Ministry of the Interior was bypassed. Arrests and examinations began during the night on the direct instructions of Goering, who conducted the purge from his personal residence in the Leipzigerplatz, assisted by Himmler and Heydrich and by his aide Paul Koerner, who belonged to the S.S. Liveried footmen served sandwiches while men taken from their houses or from the streets and dragged to Goering's house under guard stood about in anterooms in a state of apprehension. As the names of the latest arrivals were called, Goering could be heard shouting, "Shoot him! Shoot him!" With their names pricked on Goering's lists, they were hastened away for death at the cadet school of Lichterfelde, where men attached to Goering's Landespolizei stood by to provide the firing squads.

The area round Goering's palace was cordoned off by S.S. guards armed with machine guns. Through this display of armed force, Papen was led by Bodenschatz, who had been sent by Goering to fetch the Vice-Chancellor from his office, to which he had been summoned early in the morning by his anxious staff. Goering told him the situation and bluntly refused to let him take any action or even to inform President von Hindenburg of what was happening. He was, he said, in complete control. Meanwhile Himmler had stolen out of the room to give the signal for a raid on Papen's Vice-Chancellery, where the principal members of his staff were either shot or arrested. Goering, his desk covered by a flood of incoming messages, ordered Papen out; he was placed under house arrest with his telephone cut off. Papen admits that by doing this Goering undoubtedly saved his life, and that both Goebbels and Himmler had wanted to have him assassinated. Goering, sensible of the effect Papen's murder would have had on public opinion, prevented it; Papen was, after all, still Vice-Chancellor and a close friend of the President.[3]

Goering broke away from his bloody assize to conduct a foreign-press conference in the late afternoon at the Chancellery. He spoke briefly and brutally about the purge to an agitated gathering of journalists. When the name of Schleicher was mentioned, Goering smiled. "Yes," he said. "I know you journalists like a headline. Well, here it is. General von Schleicher had plotted against the regime. I ordered his arrest. He was foolish enough to resist. He is dead." With that he left the conference.[4]

The arrests and killings went on throughout the day and the night. Schleicher and his wife had already been shot in their house at Neu Babelsberg; Karl Ernst, who may well have known more than was wanted about the Reichstag fire, was captured on the road to Bremen while traveling with his bride on their honeymoon, taken to Berlin and shot as he cried the words "Heil Hitler!"; Papen's advisers Herbert von Bose and Edgar Jung were shot; Kahr, who had defied Hitler in 1923, was killed now, at the age of seventy-three, and his hacked and mutilated body thrown into a swamp near Dachau; Erich Klausener, the leader of the Catholic Action, was shot; Gehrt, in spite of his former position as Air Force captain in Goering's squadron and holder of the Pour le Mérite, was, according to Heiden, ordered to wear his decorations so that Goering might strip them from his uniform before sending him to the shooting wall. Other victims were General Kurt von Bredow, a friend of Schleicher's, Willi Schmid, a music critic (killed in error for Willi Schmidt, an S.A. leader), and Father Bernhard Stempfle, who was said to know too much about the death of Geli Raubal. Quickly the circle widened and private feuds were being settled in many parts of Germany by men supposed to be carrying out the process of the purge. Gregor Strasser was flung into the Prinz Albrechtstrasse prison, where the bullets fired into him burst an artery and splashed the walls of his cell with blood. The bodies of the men shot were cremated.

During the evening Hitler flew to Berlin from Munich with Dietrich and Goebbels. Gisevius watched the scene at Tempelhof airport, the blood-red sky from which the plane descended, the pale, unshaven face of Hitler, who had not slept for forty hours, the "diabolic" grinning face of Goebbels, the ghostly formalities as Goering, Himmler and Frick stood in line to greet the Führer, the ominous silence broken only by the sound of their clicking heels. Behind them a guard of honor presented arms. Himmler took from

his pocket a long, tattered list of names, and in the angry twilight
Hitler, Goering and Himmler stood on the runway. The Führer
stared at the list with dull eyes and a gray face while the others
whispered at him with insistent gestures. Hitler ran his finger down
the list and then stopped at one name, probably that of Strasser;
then he silenced the whispering of his subordinates with a savage
toss of his head. No more was said, and he went at once to his car.

The shooting and the killing and the suicides, real or induced,
went on through the following day, and Hitler, rested now, gave
a garden party at the Chancellery. The streets of Berlin seemed
quiet when Ambassador Dodd, anxious about the fate of his friend
Papen, drove slowly by his house but could see nothing untoward.
The names of the dead were coming through, but the papers were
filled with the most pedestrian news. Only the foreign journalists
were trying to penetrate the rumors and reach the full story of the
night of the long knives.

Goering ordered all papers and any other evidence connected
with the purge to be destroyed. The German press was silenced by
Goebbels. In the version of what happened presented by Hitler
himself to the Reichstag on July 13, Roehm's name was blackened
and the essential details were veiled. "Everyone must know for all
future time that if he raises his hand against the State, then certain
death is his lot," said Hitler. He, and he alone, had been the supreme justiciar of the German people during this period of national
danger, and that was why trials in the courts of justice had been put
aside. The events in any case were hallowed by the telegrams sent
from Hindenburg to both Hitler and Goering on July 2; that addressed to Goering read: "Accept my approval and gratitude for
your successful action in suppressing the high treason. With kind
regards and greetings. von Hindenburg." Hindenburg was too old
and ill by now to know what he was saying or what was being said
for him. The reward to Himmler was more substantial than kind
thoughts or telegrams: the S.S. was made a force in its own right
independent of the S.A., which was immediately disarmed and
reduced in status to a civilian athletic organization. Papen, released after a few days from his detention, vehemently protested his
innocence and resigned as Vice-Chancellor. At the end of July
Hitler told him he was to become the German minister to Austria,
and he accepted in spite of what had happened.

Goering was well satisfied with his organized liquidation of the men he considered guilty, until, rather late in the weekend, his instinct for moderation began to assert itself and he felt that the massacre had gone far enough. At Nuremberg he claimed that he intervened with Hitler at noon on Sunday and arranged for him to issue an order to stop all further executions. "I was worried that the matter would get out of hand as, in fact, it had already done to some extent . . ." He then claimed that only seventy-two people had been executed, the majority of these in southern Germany. No final figure for the number of murders that took place is ever likely to be known. Hitler's total, as given in the Reichstag, was fifty-eight executed and nineteen killed; Gisevius at Nuremberg made his estimate between one hundred and fifty and two hundred persons and said that, in addition to the official list of numbered names compiled by Goering, Himmler and Heydrich, there were other secret, subsidiary lists of men whom Himmler and Heydrich wanted to have removed under the cover of the purge. In the provinces there were many local assassinations, which one estimate puts at almost a thousand.

In August, when Hindenburg died, Hitler took over the power of the Presidency and so secured control of the Army, every member of which took an oath of allegiance to him. Goering called the officers of the Luftwaffe together in the large hall at the Air Ministry and told them of Hindenburg's death in a subdued voice, speaking like an actor in a tragedy. He added that the powers of the Reich President would devolve on the Reich Chancellor, and he drew his sword and told them all to swear the new oath of allegiance. Milch stepped forward and put his hand on the sword, and while an adjutant read out loud the words of the oath every man present raised his hand and repeated it solemnly. The oath made no mention, as in former times, of the constitution of the nation; the allegiance of all fighting men was to be paid without reserve to the person of Adolf Hitler.[5]

These first years of control were a period during which Goering's character was shaped in its final mold. As he adjusted his bulk to the seat of power, as he took stock of what was good for him, as he changed from the combination of impoverished flat-dweller, petty businessman and political demagogue to a man accustomed to the life of palaces and ministries, as he leaned back on the cushion of servants and secretaries and contemplated the endless perspective of his subordinates, as he experienced the unlimited resources of wealth that came to him without having to be earned, Goering in fact became more vulnerable precisely because he had much more to lose. Power developed his weakness of character rather than his strength. The uncomplicated physical courage of the fighter pilot, the rock climber, or the aerobat was not a moral courage; now that Goering had great possessions he became more than ever subservient to Hitler. Displacement could lead to ruin and the loss of everything he had labored hard to come by. From this time he did everything that Hitler told him, glorying in his subordination and compensating for it by indulging in displays of self-glorification that were to become increasingly childish and by developing an unreliable and exacting nature when dealing with his staff. Expediency, the commonest of motives in the conduct of an authoritarian society, became the key to Goering's character. He was Hitler's principal organization man, his spokesman, his shadow. "If the Führer wants it, two and two make five," he said.

Goering's attitude to the Jews is typical of the man. With Hitler, anti-Semitism was congenital; with Goebbels, it was one of his acquired convictions, a ruthless part of his personal desire for vengeance on the Jewish publishers and theater directors who had refused to respond to his artistic pretensions in his youth. The great Jewish community in Germany, with its prominent intellectuals and artists and with its business houses, both great and small, formed an obvious target for the vengeful greed of these extreme nationalists and their fellow travelers whose real instincts lay in loot or in sadism. But Goering was not anti-Jewish from emotional needs; he became anti-Jewish because the party policy required him to do so. If he liked a man enough he was quite prepared to overlook the Jewish blood in his veins. The case of Erhard Milch, whose father was a Jew, is notorious; in order that Milch should become the State Secretary of Goering's Air Ministry, his mother was required to sign a declaration that she had conceived him with a non-Jewish lover. "It is I," said Goering, "who decides if anyone is a Jew!"[6]

In *Germany Reborn*, Goering's book dictated in a few hours for the benefit of Britain, he claims that it was the Jews who had ruined the economy of Germany and "pitilessly strangled their economically weaker German hosts." He states that they "provided the Marxists and Communists with their leaders," and that the revolt of the German people against them had been an "ordered, bloodless" revolution. In 1934 Neurath reported to Ambassador Dodd that Goering had become "a moderate" on the Jewish problem, and Goering's official biography written by Gritzbach has little in it about his campaign against the Jews. "Goering himself is not anti-Semitic," wrote Thyssen. Yet Goering was in 1935 to become the advocate in the Reichstag of the Nuremberg Racial Laws and later to become an active persecutor of the Jews, more particularly through the economic decrees which he initiated against them.

There is no doubt that Goering wanted to be regarded as a moderate man. He liked comfort, and fanaticism made him feel uncomfortable. He liked to avoid the kind of trouble that could breed more trouble. He thought of himself as a great and imaginative organizer, a man with a genius for making things work, an inspired diplomat whose task was to reconcile Hitler's wishes with what was practicable in the State. He approached the Jewish problem cautiously, therefore, knowing that it could be the cause of great economic upheaval and could not be settled profitably by pogroms and the more savage forms of persecution. He preferred legalized extortion.

Similarly, he was considered "moderate" in his attitude to the churches in Germany. Although, as he himself said at Nuremberg, he was "not what you might call a churchgoer," he liked it to be thought that he supported the principal rites of the church—marriage, christening, burial—and, as second man in the State, he felt he should set what he called "weak-willed persons" an example in this respect. He believed he could be a useful go-between for Hitler in religious matters; after all, as he said, his mother had been a Catholic while he himself was a Protestant, so that he "had a view of both camps." But he was well aware that the churches could be dangerous, and he was determined that the price the priests must pay for the luxury of being left unmolested was silence in political matters. As he said at Nuremberg: "I told Himmler on one occasion that I did not think it was clever to arrest clergymen, and that as long as they talked only in church they should say what they wanted." Himmler disagreed with him, and those priests who were fearless in their denunciation of the regime received the same treatment as laymen in the night and fog of the concentration camps.

To Goering it had seemed at first better to include the churches in his patronage; accordingly, he had appointed prominent Protestant and Catholic clergy to his Prussian State Council. In July

1933, a concordat had been completed with Pope Pius XI through Cardinal Pacelli, his Secretary of State, in which it was agreed that the Nazis should leave intact the principal Catholic religious and social institutions, in return for an undertaking that His Holiness would forbid his priests in Germany to engage in political controversy; at the same time Hitler undertook to see that the Protestant clergy were made subject to a similar prohibition.

Hitler had sought to impose the leadership principle on the Protestant churches through the "German Christian" movement, which was led by a military chaplain called Ludwig Müller; this movement gave unqualified support to the Nazis but represented only a small section of the Protestant community·in Germany. To unify and control the various Protestant sects, Hitler had created a Reich Bishopric for the supervision of all church affairs and the regulation of the clergy, and had made it quite clear that he expected Müller to be formally elected Reich Bishop, as it were by the will of the clerical majority. This plan was, however, momentarily forestalled, for the clergy preferred Pastor Friedrich von Bodelschwingh, an anti-Nazi, who was prepared to resist the demand that no man of Jewish origin could remain a Protestant church member. Goering, as Prussian Premier, ordered the local church organizations that had supported Bodelschwingh to be dissolved. Through the Prussian Minister of Education he immediately imposed civil supervision on the clergy and at the same time assumed control of the church himself. "I learn with great regret," he announced, "of the church dispute that has broken out. Until the revolution of 1918 the King of Prussia was the Summus Episcopus of the Prussian Church. In my opinion, these functions of Summus Episcopus have devolved upon the Prussian Ministry of State, that is upon the Prussian Prime Minister, and therefore upon me. For this reason no alteration in the constitution of the Church is conceivable without my sanction. No intimation has been received by my government from the Church concerning the proposed appointment of a Reich Bishop."

In this way Bodelschwingh was summarily disposed of and Müller was elected the first Reich Bishop to be officially recognized by the State. According to Heiden, however, Hitler, who had been summoned in June to Neudeck to see Hindenburg, was told by the President that Goering's interference with the freedom of the churches was intolerable and that the conduct of church affairs should be placed elsewhere. Hitler, aware of the dangers, handed over the supervision of the churches to Frick's Reich Ministry of the Interior.

Relations between church and State were soon to deteriorate, and the virulent paganism of the Nazi leadership aroused antagonism in Catholic and Protestant alike. Pastor Martin Niemöller, who had originally been sympathetic to Hitler, became leader of the Protestant movement opposed to the Nazis. Ambassador Dodd records the threats of Goering, who, he said, walked uninvited into one of Reich Bishop Müller's conferences with other bishops and church leaders and attacked them, saying that he had a record of their telephone conversations and that they were spreading discord in the State and were "on the borderline of treason." Eighteen months later, in July 1935, the ambassador recalls in his diary the "glaring red ink headlines calling attention to Goering's declaration of war on the Catholics," whose freedom of speech was no longer to be tolerated.

Goering was ready now to change his manner of life. His intimate friendship with the actress Emmy Sonnemann had already lasted for over two years, and their affection for each other was well known. Their engagement was officially announced on March 9, 1935, and they were married on April 10.[7]

Goering's second marriage was the occasion for festivities that were organized on an imperial scale. On April 9, the night before the wedding, a vast reception was held in the great hall of the Opera House, after which Goering and his guests took their places for the gala performance of the second half of *Lohengrin*, which had been delayed for one hour while the reception took place. Outside, the streets had been decorated and a formation of Goering's new fighters had flown over the city roaring their might into the deafened ears of the people.

The ceremonies of marriage took place first at the Town Hall and then at the cathedral. Tickets for the cathedral were sold at twenty marks each. The streets were lined by N.S.D.A.P. guards keeping back the cheering people as Goering, in a new uniform of general of the Air Force, trimmed with white braid, white stripes on his trousers and large white wings on his breast, drove in a car decorated with narcissi and tulips to the Town Hall, where the civil wedding was to take place. Hitler, who was to act as witness, drove from the Chancellery, and Emmy was carried in another car until the line of limousines converged into a procession. The excitement of the crowds heightened, and once more the fighter aircraft cut across the sky. Outside the Town Hall bride and groom were greeted by a fanfare of trumpets.

At the cathedral the civil wedding was blessed by the church. The Nazi Reich Bishop, Ludwig Müller, officiated; the words "Though I speak with the tongues of men and of angels, and have not charity, I am become as sounding brass, or a tinkling cymbal" were the text for his sermon to the great congregation of Nazi leaders and diplomats. Then came another great procession of cars to the wedding feast at the Kaiserhof. After this was over Goering and his wife drove to Carinhall with some of their more intimate friends. There Goering left them all for a while to pray by the coffin of Carin in her mausoleum.

The day after the wedding, Goering invited certain press correspondents to the palace of the Prussian Premier to see the lavish display of wedding presents. Louis Lochner, who was among them, noticed the costly Gobelin tapestries in the large central hall, and a Wurlitzer organ. Behind a Dutch painting was concealed a cinema screen. With an expansive gesture Goering spoke of the love shown him by his people in the form of the presents they had sent him.

Hitler's gift was a portrait of Bismarck by Lenbach. Goering's gift to Emmy was a tiara of amethysts and diamonds. Lochner learned that the gifts had been most carefully selected, and that the more sensible donors, including municipalities, organizations, museums and industries as well as certain wealthy friends, had inquired in advance what Goering would most like to have.

Goering and Emmy spent their honeymoon in Wiesbaden and then traveled down to stay in a villa at Ragusa on the Adriatic. Another era in Goering's life had begun. Emmy, kindly, motherly, uninterested in politics and used only to the public life of the theater, now found herself the first lady of Germany and mistress of Goering's official establishments.

Goering at the time of his second marriage was forty-two; his wife was the same age. The degree of influence she had over him was relatively small. By now he had a firm conception of himself as a shrewd man of affairs, and he enjoyed most of all displaying the geniality for which it pleased him to be famous. Like many men of the world he did not wish to be thought too clever; smartness, shrewdness, sharp-wittedness—all these qualities were good to have, but not mere cleverness, the trained intelligence that could be hired and then dismissed, put back on the shelf where it belonged, like a work of reference. Goering preferred to keep his wits about him while posing for himself and the world as the common man of genius, the self-made man who had come to the top through hard work, great determination and strength of purpose. Such men deserved the love and admiration of women. But Goering did not mix his marriage with his politics except to require his wife to be the charming hostess that she was by nature. She created for him the background of a home life to which he returned whenever he willed. With her he was always happy, and through her his love of the theater and the arts increased and gave him one more face which he might display to the world—that of the art collector. Collecting was soon to become an obsession.

From the social aspect of Goering's nature developed the great balls, receptions, shooting parties and other entertainments that increased with the happiness of marriage and the need of the Nazi leaders to make themselves known, and if possible liked, by the representatives of the world outside Germany. Hitler, remote, introspective, idiosyncratic and subject to the lower depths of mood, untutored too in the manners of society, left such meetings as far as possible to his ministers, and most of all to Goering. Hitler had his own entourage to whom his monologues and his moodiness were no doubt exciting, since they were accepted as part of his particular genius. Goering never belonged to this more intimate circle that sat and listened into the long nights by the fireside. He was not, he could never be, the antisocial recluse that Hitler was inevitably to become. One by one, Hitler placed successive cloaks of public power across the broad shoulders of his "Paladin": the control of the Air Force, the control of the economy, and the representation of his will in the world of diplomacy and industry. This was the life that Goering most enjoyed, moving from one interest to another before matters of detail began to pall, and using his talents as host and sportsman to further the aims of his master.

Nothing excited the jealousy of the other Nazi leaders in public life more than Goering's great entertainments, such as the annual Opera Ball which he organized each January from 1936 on to celebrate his birthday, and which was continued well into the years of war. It was modeled on the magnificent imperial balls of past times, and those members of the royal family and the nobility who favored the Nazis came to add the splendor of their titles to the occasion. Tickets for the balls were expensive, and so were the food and drink. But the society of Berlin poured in to shake hands with the Minister President and his wife, and to dance the night through. The proceeds were intended for the Winter Relief work and the fund for the State theater. Soon the ministers began to vie with each other in the lavishness of their hospitality when state occasions demanded it; even Goebbels, normally critical of such extravagances, organized an all-night reception on the lake island of Wannsee when the Olympic Games were held in Germany in the summer of 1936, and Goering responded with a floodlit garden party held in the grounds of his palace in Berlin; actors and actresses danced in costumes of the eighteenth century, and Udet arranged a display of aerobatics. As the August weather was cold, electric heaters were placed among the hundreds of tables in the gardens.

Hitler had for some while been using Goering as a roving ambassador through whom he could make contact abroad. Hitler disliked leaving the familiar environment of Germany and resented the formalities involved in negotiating with foreigners. He disliked the rules and conventions of professional diplomacy and deeply distrusted the officials of his own Foreign Ministry. Paul Schmidt, who in March 1935 became Hitler's interpreter and was frequently to work for Goering as well, observed the Führer closely on the occasions he acted for him at his meetings with foreign statesmen. When in full control of himself, Hitler was emotional, emphatic, long-winded and obsessed by what he was saying, often seeming quite unaware of the men in his presence. He often spoke for twenty minutes before breaking off to allow Schmidt to interpret. Goering, on the other hand, cultivated a manner of tough good nature that hid what Schmidt soon discovered to be a considerable diplomatic skill and adroitness. Schmidt, it must be remembered, was a man of great experience, an established official on the Foreign Ministry staff, who had acted as interpreter for Brüning and Stresemann. He was not a Nazi, and in spite of his great responsibilities he avoided joining the party until 1943.

"I saw him," wrote Schmidt of Goering, "in very delicate situations, which he handled with a finesse which the German public would not have believed possible in this swashbuckling heavyweight . . . In contrast to Hitler, he was amenable to suggestion and argument."[8] He had long conversations with Schmidt on the many occasions when they traveled together, and he was interested in the accounts Schmidt gave him of his past experiences. But he remained contemptuous of the Foreign Office as a whole. "They spend the morning sharpening pencils and the afternoon at tea parties," was Goering's judgment of the diplomatic corps.

"Foreign policy above all was the Führer's very own realm," said Goering at Nuremberg. Goering himself became closely identified with Hitler's negotiations with the foreign powers. Hitler's ambitions lay in the expansion of Germany by gradually uniting peoples of German blood into a single unified Fatherland, which, having thrown off the humiliations of Versailles, would emerge as the central power of Europe. This he wanted to achieve by the old principle of "legality" without the cost and effort and disruption of war, but he knew that the fear of war latent in the Allies and the surrounding countries was his most powerful weapon in any negotiation that he had to conduct, whether through diplomatic channels, the private conferences of his special representatives or the open forum of his speeches or pronouncements. On three occasions between the spring of 1935 and that of 1938 he took deliberate action which involved the risk of some form of retaliations that might have proved damaging or even fatal to him; strangely enough, all of these deliberate actions took place in March—the public announcements of the existence of the Air Force and of conscription for the Army in 1935, the reoccupation of the Rhineland and the open repudiation of Versailles in 1936, and the occupation of Austria in 1938.

By now Hitler was beginning to take the measure of the national weaknesses and the division of policy between France and Britain. He was learning how to play their statesmen, how to balance an affront to their principles with a placating speech that quieted their fears and led them one stage further by the nose. He was also measuring both the power and the weakness of Mussolini and assessing the preparation needed for the struggle that must ultimately take place with the hidden strength of the Soviet Union. But for the most part he was content to bide his time, indeed to wait upon events, taking advantage of every sign of weakness or diplomatic move that worked in his favor while he continued to build the strength of his own nation. He had the short-term advantage that belongs to all unscrupulous politicians: it was he who could keep the others guessing, he who could choose the time to make the calculated moves, he who could offer spectacular agreements in the name of peace and extinguish the fears he had himself raised in the startled breasts of nervous statesmen only too anxious to keep things quietly as they were. Goering, the hospitable sportsman, the man of such engaging directness of speech and of the helpful word passed on in confidence, became Hitler's principal spokesman in Poland and Italy during this delicate period, the brief breathing space in Europe's power politics.

In 1933, apart from meetings with Mussolini in May and again in November, Goering was preoccupied by affairs at home, but in October 1934 he went to Belgrade to attend the funeral of King Alexander of Yugoslavia, who during his visit to France had been assassinated along with the anti-Nazi French Foreign Minister, Barthou. While he was there, Goering made allegations that the Hungarians had been involved in the assassination, which led the Hungarian government to complain to Neurath. Goering, in fact, had gone to the funeral solely to improve relations between Germany and Yugoslavia at the expense of France.

The years 1934–35 were the test of Hitler's capacity to bring pressure to bear beyond the borders of Germany. Austria was the initial target of his ambition to unite the German-speaking peoples; while moving in the direction of ultimate union with Austria, Hitler had to allow for Mussolini's interest in maintaining her independence, an interest temporarily aroused by the assassination of Chancellor Dollfuss by the Austrian Nazis in July 1934, when Mussolini had rushed in troops to guard the Brenner Pass. Hitler immediately dissociated himself from what had happened, and talked of peace pacts to soothe the rulers of France, Britain, Poland and Italy. The Soviet Union joined the League of Nations in September, and in the national Peace Ballot sponsored in Britain six million people voted for war against an aggressor. In January 1935 the Saar returned to Germany after an overwhelming vote in favor of Hitler, and the public announcement of the existence of Germany's Army and Air Force was followed, after formal protests, by Ribbentrop's singular triumph—the naval pact with Britain signed in June, in which Britain, without consulting either France or Italy, permitted Germany to establish a fleet at a level representing thirty-five per cent of her own. The fall of the year saw Hitler's anti-Jewish laws proclaimed at Nuremberg, the sanctions against Mussolini proposed by Britain at the League following his attack on Abyssinia (sanctions which were ineffective and only served to drive Mussolini into direct alliance with Hitler), the Franco-Soviet pact (which gave Hitler his moral right to repudiate Locarno and the courage to risk reoccupation of the Rhineland in 1936), and finally the cynical Hoare-Laval plan of December, which aimed to impose sacrifices on the Emperor of Abyssinia through the League, an immoral demonstration of how to stop fascist aggression by partitioning other people's lands. The plan was exposed in the press and was repudiated by Prime Minister Baldwin, and the matter was left in abeyance until, by May 1936, Mussolini had conquered what he wanted and driven Emperor Haile Selassie into exile—to the shame and ultimate destruction of the League. It was, as A. J. P. Taylor has pointed out in his *Origins of the Second World War*, a rehearsal for Munich.

The moral of these events in 1935–36 was not lost upon Hitler, who during this period had employed Goering principally in Poland and the Balkans. In January 1935 Goering had made the first of many visits to Poland, whose Premier, Pilsudski, had no illusions about Hitler in spite of the nonaggression pact he had signed with Germany in January 1934. Relations between Germany and Poland were of necessity strained by history; their territory had been traditionally a no man's land for war and for occupation by the peoples of Germany and Russia. Hitler at this period was anxious to maintain Polish opposition to the idea of an Eastern security pact involving France, the U.S.S.R. and Poland. Goering, who had been invited to a hunting party in the Polish forest of Bialowieza, spoke of "the strength and dynamic power of Poland" and laughed off any idea of some future bartering of Polish territory between Nazi Germany and Bolshevist Russia. "A common German-Russian frontier," said Goering, "would be highly dangerous to Germany." He even hinted at "an anti-Russian alliance and a joint attack on Russia" and was puzzled when the professional diplomats warned him to go easy on such suggestions with Pilsudski.[9]

In April Józef Lipski, the Polish ambassador in Berlin, who was friendly toward Hitler, visited Goering on one of those diplomatic shoots which delighted the Master of the Hunt, since on these occasions he could combine the pleasures of the chase in both fields at once. Hitler, he told Lipski, had asked him to specialize in developing Polish-German relations "independently of official channels," and had spoken once more against the Russians, whether their regime were Soviet or anything else; Goering also complained of the hostility of Mussolini. In May, when Marshal Pilsudski died, Goering represented Hitler at the state funeral, which was also attended by the French Foreign Minister, Pierre Laval, fresh from signing his alliance with the Soviet Union. Goering, intent on the chance of talking to Laval, took Schmidt with him, traveling in a special coach attached to the normal train. Schmidt found himself accommodated in the kitchen compartment and Goering apologized to him for this with a laugh. In Warsaw the weather was very hot, and Goering, wearing the uniform of an Air Force general, marched beside Schmidt in the long procession that took four hours to pass through the streets of Warsaw behind the gun carriage bearing Pilsudski's body. Panting and covered with sweat, Goering tramped along with the rest, and he marched again the following day in the second procession at Cracow, where the Premier, national hero of Poland, was finally buried. During the period for refreshments offered to the foreign representatives, Goering met both Marshal Pétain and Laval; a formal meeting with the French Foreign Minister was arranged for the afternoon.

Schmidt was now able to watch Goering in action and to note the way in which he repeated Hitler's arguments, even using exactly the same phrases. Goering lost no time in attacking the recent agreement. "I trust you got on well at Moscow with the Bolshevists, Monsieur Laval," he said. "We know the Bolshevists better in Germany than you do in France . . . You will see what difficulties your Paris Communists will cause you." Then he crowded the conversation with statements and proposals—statements about German rearmament and the League, proposals, vague and generalized, for an air pact and for an improvement in Franco-German relations. Such generalizations, expressed in "the language of the man in the street," observed Schmidt, were Goering's technique in diplomacy. He gave the impression of great sincerity whether he was belaboring the Russians or earnestly assuring Laval that there was now absolutely no reason at all why Germany and France should not become good neighbors. Germany, he said, had nothing but admiration for France, and the old causes of dispute, such as Alsace-Lorraine, no longer existed. Laval cunningly represented the Franco-Soviet alliance as a diplomatic gesture of security for the French people which would in fact make establishing friendly relations with Germany more easy. On the way back to Berlin, Goering talked at length to Schmidt and agreed with him that the conference with Laval had shown France quite genuinely wanted an understanding. Later, in September, Goering invited Polish representatives to shoot in Germany, and he was in turn the guest of the Polish General Staff at Bialowieza in February 1936.

During an extension of his honeymoon in May 1935, Goering and his wife visited Budapest. The visit was brief, and they then went on to Sofia, Dubrovnik and Belgrade. The tour lasted until June 8. In each of the capital cities, Goering was received by the head of state and he saw the principal ministers, and his visit, though described as a honeymoon, was evidently a political one inspired by the need to counter the effects of the Franco-Russian and Czechoslovak-Russian pacts.

On March 7, 1936, Hitler took his first grave risk and occupied the Rhineland, and Goering was later to admit to Sir Ivone Kirkpatrick, first secretary at the British embassy in Berlin, that this was a period of intense anxiety. Hitler himself spoke in the Reichstag at noon, announcing the end of the Locarno Pact (invalidated by the Franco-Soviet alliance), offering new proposals for peace—including nonagression pacts both with France and Belgium and with her eastern neighbors, an air pact with Britain and a demilitarized zone along the Franco-German frontier—and expressing his desire to start negotiations for the re-entry of Germany into the League of Nations. The Reichstag was then dissolved by Goering. During the following week, once it was clear that France and Britain would have to accept the reoccupation as a *fait accompli*, Goering and other Nazi leaders stumped the country emphasizing on platform and radio the generosity and farsightedness of Hitler's foreign policy. On March 29 another so-called plebiscite gave cover for an official announcement that 48.8 per cent of the adults qualified to vote in Germany had said '*Ja*' to Hitler's policy.

Goering then returned to Berlin to fulfill a new destiny in Germany, that of becoming master of the German economy. But before he could give his full attention to this new and exciting work, he had one other matter to deal with abroad, the intervention of the Luftwaffe in the Spanish Civil War.

The Civil War broke out on July 17, 1936, and Hitler, who was attending the Bayreuth Festival, received a letter from rebel General Franco asking for help. After consultations with Goering and Blomberg, he decided that he would support Franco with men, arms and aircraft. The matter was secret and no speeches could be made, but following a conference on July 26, over which Milch presided, a small group of airmen set out in plain clothes for Africa, where their aircraft had been flown out for them. This was the first stage in the formation of the Condor Legion. During the whole period of the Civil War Luftwaffe pilots fought in Spain, serving comparatively short terms of duty so that the maximum number of men could gain experience in a hot war. For Goering the Spanish Civil War came as a blessing; it gave his men active service in hostilities that did not affect Germany. Guernica was a most convenient rehearsal for Warsaw, Belgrade and London. But Goering did not involve himself greatly in this small but important undertaking. The German economy was his new obsession.

Goering's interest in taking part in the economic life of Germany had begun during 1935, when, after consultation with Dr. Schacht, Hitler's Minister of Economics and (after May 1935) Plenipotentiary-General for War Economy, he had made a speech in Hamburg on the German rearmament program in which he boasted of the need to sacrifice butter for guns. "What does butter do but make us fat?" he cried, and the crowd under the floodlights roared in response to Hermann's wit. Hitler's open proclamation, in March, of conscription to bring the Army up to thirty-six divisions, and then again, on April 1, of the official existence of Goering's Luftwaffe, dropped the transparent veil of secrecy surrounding German rearmament. Schacht, ever since his national appointment as Minister of Economics in September 1934, had acted in Hitler's interest with speed and skill, printing special paper money which did not even have to be accounted for in the published statements of the banks in order to pay the armaments manufacturers. He built up foreign credit like magic on the basis of barter, so that raw materials for the war industries might be imported. Such actions appealed to Goering, and he longed to play his part in them. As far as any knowledge of economics was concerned, he knew he was entirely ignorant, but he trusted his flair in this wide-open field just as he did in the field of diplomacy, and he shared Hitler's dislike of the professionals with their long-winded reasons why what was wanted could not be done. Schacht, in a matter of months, had maneuvered the German economy onto a war basis, organized the manufacture of tanks, aircraft and guns, and, by encouraging government expenditure, continued the spectacular conquest of unemployment, which had already been more than halved by December 1934.

Goering's first official step toward economic control of Germany came when Schacht asked Hitler for help from someone of high authority in the party to deal with currency abuses abroad which were being practiced by party officials at a time when Germany's resources in other countries were strained. Schacht suggested Goering, and on April 27, 1936, Hitler announced that the Minister President would in future take charge of foreign-exchange control and the import of raw materials. Goering accepted this new charge with alacrity, if only for the purpose of using it as a means toward extending his range of power; his nephew, Herbert Goering, was an official in the Reichsbank and anything Goering did not understand he could quite easily resolve within the family. Two weeks after his appointment he convened the first of a series of meetings at which Schacht was present; at these conferences he emphasized the necessity to develop synthetic raw-material substitutes and answered objections to the prohibitive costs involved by saying, "If we have war tomorrow we must help ourselves by substitutes. Then money will not play any part at all."

Hitler found economic planning both troublesome and uninteresting except insofar as he could understand the subject in terms of political expediency. He regarded the plebiscite of March 27 as an overwhelming reassurance from the German people that his policy was approved by all. This convinced him that the German nation was ready to pay the price of rearmament, and that the most popular man among his leaders was necessary to rally the people and symbolize the cause.

During the summer Hitler drew up the model for a Four-Year Plan for the German economy; according to Gritzbach, Goering was summoned to Berchtesgaden to hear it and returned dazed with admiration. "Never have I been so impressed by the strength of the Führer, by his logic, and by the boldness of his ideas . . . There will be consternation abroad!" At a meeting of ministers at which he presided on September 4, Goering's new interest was already much in evidence, though his appointment had not been announced. He lectured his colleagues on the need to make German industry self-sufficient as if the nation were already at war. Germany must do what Russia had done; after all, he said, it was inevitable that one day Germany and Russia would be at war.[10]

The first announcement of the plan and of the appointment of Goering as its Commissioner was made at the annual party rally at Nuremberg in September. This rally was the most spectacular yet staged and matched in splendor, pageantry and the magnificent organization of its processions and its patterns of massed humanity the grandeur that had been Germany. The formal proclamation giving Goering his new powers followed on October 18; he was authorized "to issue decrees and general administrative directions" and given the right to "question and issue directives to all, including the highest Reich authorities." The plan was due to come into operation by February 1937, and Goering stated that his job was "to put the whole economy on a war footing within four years."[11]

It is characteristic of Hitler that he gave this far-reaching authority to Goering without first consulting Schacht, who was merely informed a few days in advance that a new economic program was to be announced. He was expected to run his ministry alongside Goering's new department, which at once began to accumulate a large staff of officials and to increase the administrative complications involved in a controlled economy. It was inevitable that Schacht and Goering, who had formerly been on terms of friendship, should soon begin to differ. To Schacht the Four-Year Plan seemed little but a crude and unprofessional hastening of the measures he had himself taken. In his later writings he mentions as instances the extraction of benzine from coal and the extension of mining operations and of the whaling fleet; Goering simply took over Schacht's plans and inflated them. At the same time he mounted the platform and turned the rough lessons he had learned about economics into popular speech, hammering the message home with the blows of patriotism. "Never again must a foreign hand grip us by the throat . . . Our plan *must* succeed—say that over and over to yourselves as you get up in the morning . . . I shall suppress all parasites . . . hoarders will be treated as swindlers . . . A great age demands a great nation." The audience filling the Deutschlandhalle on October 28 listened to the familiar voice vibrating through the loudspeakers, and the microphone on the platform carried the words throughout the land in a broadcast to the German people. Much was made in the press of the public response to this mighty harangue, and the sentimental stories grew of the party man who collected 637 wedding rings from the fingers of his comrades to help the nation and of the little girl who sent her golden bracelet as a gift to Goering. Later he himself stood in the streets of Berlin laughing and shaking a collection box while people pressed around him to push foreign coins into the slot.

Goering had already announced his first labor decree on October 24, ordering additional labor for harvesting vegetable crops. On November 9 further decrees were issued to recruit labor for the rearmament program. As economic dictator of Germany, Goering gloried in his amateur status. "I do not acknowledge the sanctity of any economic law," he said. "Economy must always be the servant of the nation . . . I have never been a director or on a board of directors and never shall be. Neither am I an agriculturist. Except for a few flower pots on the balcony I have never cultivated anything. But I am ready with all my heart and soul, and with firm belief in the greatness of the German nation, to devote all my energies to this mighty task."

In December Goering held a conference of industrialists, and Schacht was shocked to hear him invite his audience to bring foreign bills of exchange into the country by any method, legal or illegal, and urge industry to produce whether it made a profit or a loss. Schacht claims that he responded by telling a similar audience a few weeks later that evasions of the laws of exchange were still punishable as far as he was concerned, and that to produce at a loss would be to "consume the very life substance of the German people." When Goering complained of this, Schacht refused to change his attitude, so Goering took over the responsibility for placing all orders for armaments from Schacht's ministry.[12] Having established his department, he placed his old friend Pilli Koerner in charge of it with the rank of Secretary of State. This was to prove a grave error; Koerner was quite incompetent to deal with the intricate problems of industry, of which he had no understanding whatsoever.

In foreign affairs, the second six months of 1936 saw the gradual closing of the gap between Germany and Italy. Mussolini had approved the "gentleman's agreement" negotiated by Papen with Dr. Kurt von Schuschnigg, successor to Dollfuss as Federal Chancellor of Austria, and signed in July; in this Hitler had recognized the sovereignty of Austria in exchange for the right of the Austrian Nazis to share political responsibility in the State—an important step toward the future *Anschluss*. Mussolini's open intervention in

Spain hardened Britain against Italy, while British sponsorship of sanctions in the League Assembly hardened Mussolini against Britain. By November the Duce was using the term "axis" in reference to Italy's relations with Germany and was losing interest in giving active support to the independence of Austria, where Papen was slowly but successfully preparing the way for the *Anschluss*. Ribbentrop was appointed ambassador to Britain to keep relations with Britain as favorable as could be, and in May 1937 Neville Chamberlain became British Prime Minister, with Lord Halifax as his Foreign Secretary.

In January 1937 Goering went to Italy to exercise what influence he could on Mussolini, who had just signed what Papen would have called a "gentleman's agreement" with Britain, in which both countries guaranteed to maintain the freedom of the Mediterranean. On the other hand, Mussolini was equally aware of Ribbentrop's attempts to win support in Britain for Germany's territorial ambitions. At the beginning of 1937 Hitler's attitude to Austria still remained the most serious stumbling block in the path of friendship between the two dictators.

Goering traveled by train from Berlin to Rome with Count Massimo Magistrati, a senior official on the staff of the Italian embassy and the brother-in-law of Count Galeazzo Ciano, the Italian Foreign Minister. Goering was in the habit of talking against Britain to Magistrati, and, like Hitler, he was annoyed about the naval agreement. On the train he said that Italy and Germany must prepare for the final clash with Britain; militarily speaking, Germany would be ready for this in three years; he explained that discussion of the Austrian problem was the principal reason for his journey, and that Italy need never fear to have a common frontier with Germany. "In any case," Goering added as the train neared Rome, "Germany will indulge in no surprises, and whatever decision she makes on questions so vital to her as those of Austria, Danzig or Memel will be preceded by understandings with Italy." When Mussolini received the report of this conversation, he expressed anger that Goering should think he feared having the Germans at the Brenner.[13]

Goering took Schmidt with him to Italy to interpret, and, after some discussions with Count Ciano on mutual aid to Franco, they went in the afternoon of January 15 to the Palazzo Venezia to meet Mussolini. Goering and the *chef de protocol*, standing stomach to

stomach, filled the only lift available, and Schmidt had to run up
the stairs and round the rising carriage to be ready to meet his chief
at the upper door. They passed along passages hung with armor,
through the Hall of the Fascist High Council with its furnishings
covered in dark-blue velvet, into an anteroom where Ciano was
waiting for them, ready to take them to Mussolini's large but
sparsely furnished study, with its marble floor and large globe of the
world. Mussolini rose in the distance and walked the full length of
the room to greet them. He gave Goering the Fascist salute, and
they sat down.

They spoke of Spain, the bravery of the Spaniards and their poor
tactics, and the unofficial, "voluntary" help Italy and Germany
were giving to Franco. Mussolini was very guarded in what he said.
Goering, less guarded, boasted enthusiastically of the German
transport planes that were carrying Franco's Moroccan troops into
Spain. "Franco has much to thank us for," he added. "I hope he'll
remember it later."

When they turned to the discussion of Europe, the conversation
went less well. Mussolini showed his anger about sanctions; Goering
was blunt about the coming of the *Anschluss* in Austria. Mussolini,
who understood and spoke some German, watched Goering closely
while he talked, but he asked Schmidt to translate what Goering
said into French and then shook his head vigorously, though he said
nothing. He sat upright, short and squat, his brown eyes fixed on
Goering; in most matters except Austria he expressed agreement in
short, concise sentences with Hitler's view of Europe as Goering explained it.

Yet it was to gain ground on the Austrian question that was the
principal reason for Goering's visit. Ulrich von Hassell, the German
ambassador in Rome, was particularly anxious that he should be
reticent. When Goering had told him, "Italy should keep her hands
off Austria and recognize her as a German sphere of interest so that
even an *Anschluss* could be carried out if we so desired," Hassell had
replied that the Duce did indeed now recognize that a union of
some sort was inevitable, but feared that Hitler's ambitions would
tempt him to expand further south than the Brenner frontier; he
urged Goering to make the whole matter seem as long-term as possible and to assure Mussolini that he would be consulted before any
action was taken. Goering was to see Mussolini again on January 23

after a brief trip to Capri; meanwhile in Rome he made no secret in various conversations he had that the Nazis were being persecuted in Austria.

At the second of his talks with the Duce, on January 23, Goering urged Mussolini to use his influence with Schuschnigg to keep the Austrians "loyal" to the July agreement; he claimed that sinister international forces were using Austria to keep Italy and Germany apart. But there would be no surprise in the relationship between Germany and Austria, he added, remembering Hassell's warning— unless, of course, there were any attempt to restore the Hapsburgs. Mussolini let this go, but warned Goering that his influence in Austria was confined to reassuring her of his respect for her independence. The Italians regarded the meeting as an unhappy one, and Goering had found in the visitors' book in his hotel at Capri a scribbled note: "*Non svastica in Mediterraneo!*" Mussolini thought Goering "flashy and pretentious."[14]

On April 20 Goering, who was reported to be ill and on his way to southern Italy for a rest cure, once more left Berlin. He visited both Ciano and Mussolini in Rome on April 26 with the intention of discovering what had taken place between the Duce and Schuschnigg, who had met on April 22 in Venice. Mussolini had tried to explain to the Austrian Chancellor Italy's need for understanding with Germany in spite of differences of outlook on many matters, including that of the independence of Austria, which could now, he said, be best maintained by friendship with Germany; the war in Spain and a possible visit of Mussolini were also reported to have been discussed. Goering paid a third visit to Italy, this time to Venice only, in May, when he also visited Bled, Yugoslavia, in an effort to improve Germany's relations with that country and encourage an increase of trade between the two.[15]

The coronation of King George VI in London on May 12 led to an embarrassing situation for Goering. When the Labor member of Parliament Ellen Wilkinson learned that Goering intended to represent Germany at the coronation, a ceremony of the kind in which he most enjoyed taking part, she made a savage attack on him and his "blood-stained boots" and demanded in the House of Commons assurances from the Foreign Office that he would never be allowed to insult the country with his presence.[16] Ribbentrop sent a copy of the speech to Hitler with the recommendation that damage to German-British relations might result from Goering's visit, and Hitler appointed General von Blomberg in his place. Goering was furious. He decided to make a private visit to London and arrived in a Junkers 52 at Croydon Airport; Ribbentrop met him there and drove him to the embassy, where the matter was explained to him bluntly and he was dissuaded from showing himself. Ribbentrop had managed to keep the visit secret from the press, and the following morning Goering, deeply humiliated, was driven to the airport and flown back to Germany. Only the British Foreign Office and the police knew of his visit.

Goering's informal contacts with the British were happier than this. The late Marquess of Londonderry, a former Air Secretary, was a frequent guest for shooting in the Schorfheide. Paul Schmidt often acted as their interpreter; he first went to Carinhall for this purpose in February 1936. Goering boasted then about the growing power of the German Air Force and was very open in discussing technical details. "If Germany and England stand together," he would say, "there is no combination of powers in the whole world that can oppose us." Sometimes Lord Londonderry would bring his wife and daughter, traveling in his private plane to Berlin. Schmidt noticed their friendly amusement when Goering put on his hunting clothes and strode along wielding his spear and blowing his horn to attract the bison. Hitler was in favor of these meetings, because they might lead to a better understanding with Britain. In the autumn of 1937, Londonderry attended the German Army maneuvers in Mecklenburg which Mussolini witnessed; afterward Papen was invited by Goering to join Londonderry and himself in a stag-and-bison shoot, and in the conversations round the fire at night Papen said the British should negotiate directly with Hitler and repudiate the last shackles of Versailles—advice that Chamberlain was to take. In October, Goering, wearing uniform and decorations, entertained the Duke and Duchess of Windsor at Carinhall; though formally dressed, he managed to demonstrate the massage apparatus he had recently installed in the basement gymnasium. In the attic he showed off his vast model railway, over which a toy airplane flew dropping little wooden bombs.[17]

The ambassadors and senior members of the diplomatic corps in Berlin differed considerably in their attitude toward the Nazis. Their work was complicated by the rivalries among the Nazi leaders, for though Goering, Neurath (Hitler's Foreign Minister until February 1938), and Ribbentrop (Neurath's successor) all received their instructions from Hitler, their interests, emphases and mutual distaste for each other led to many differences in their statements of policy, and these in turn were subject to Hitler's own sudden changes of front. Ambassador Dodd, who was in Berlin from 1933 to the end of 1937, was a democrat who hated the Nazis, but he was both inexperienced as a diplomat and out of touch with the Nazi leadership; he was a sick man, and unpopular with Sumner Welles, the powerful American Under-Secretary of State from 1937, but he had the ear of President Roosevelt. To him Goering was a man un- fit to rule, and after 1935 he had no social relationship with him whatsoever. His high-spirited daughter Martha, however, enjoyed considerably the social life in Berlin and has written vivid and gossipy accounts of Goering. She admired Emmy, but criticized her husband for his morbid worship of Carin's memory, and she found him boorish and unpleasant in company.

During this period André François-Poncet was the French ambas- sador in Berlin. He was right-wing in politics, accepted the revival of German nationalism and made it his aim to establish friendship between France and Germany. He regarded Goering as the most approachable of the Nazis leadership, even though "he concealed badly enough that he had a special distaste for France." Goering afforded him ironic amusement, especially on one occasion when he claimed, the ambassador wrote later, that if Hitler "disappeared . . . Goering would be his successor." He noted that Goering periodically purged off his weight and then put it on again, and he knew that he still underwent periodic cures for his tendency to morphine. But François-Poncet also recognized Goering's quick and supple intelligence. He was less amused when Goering in his presence demonstrated his model railway to a group of guests by showing a bombing attack on the replica of a French train. The ambassador referred to *"ses yeux clairs, froids, dont l'expression est dure et inquiétante"*; his successor, Robert Coulondre, who became ambassador in November 1938, thought Goering's eyes *"obliques."*[18]

The rumors about Goering's drug addiction were still current in Berlin, but he was naïve enough, according at least to Diels, to be- lieve that once the documentary evidence of his case in Sweden had been procured by his agents and safely put in his hands, he had up- rooted and destroyed all memory and record of these past troubles. The cure in Sweden, however, had not proved permanent, and every year he underwent, in the strictest isolation, an intensified treatment administered by Professor Hubert Kahle, who had devised a special method for the abrupt withdrawal of narcotics which had had a very high percentage of success since he began it in 1921. Many of the patients at his sanatorium near Cologne were airmen who for one reason or another had become addicts.

The drug addict's disposition was described by Professor Kahle as a condition in which the nervous system becomes greatly excited and there are variations in pulse and breathing, an excessive activity of certain glands and an outpouring of vital energy. The use of drugs removes these symptoms and brings the addict a temporary state of calm, which is really an artificial form of subjection of his nervous and glandular troubles. If a man addicted to drugs is deprived of them, he suffers the most acute withdrawal reactions, such as nausea, vomiting, diarrhea, acceleration of pulse and breathing, salivation, and pains in his limbs. It is difficult for him to sleep without soporifics. The basis of Kahle's cure was to remove the dangers and the pains of this condition of excitement, calming the nervous system by a form of treatment that introduced a state of balance within it. To achieve this state of calm the patient was given a complex dosage of secret prescriptions which put him into a twilight sleep. During this time the toxic effects of the original drug were removed from his system and he should wake feeling free from any desire for his previous addiction.

This was the treatment Goering underwent, but he was unfortunate in that the cure for him did not remain permanent. Every so often, about once a year, he would either attend the professor's clinic or Kahle would himself come to Carinhall, where Goering would shut himself away for treatment in one of the chalets on the estate. This intensified treatment began with drinking a brandy glass of the preparation brought by Kahle, which sent Goering into a deep sleep lasting some twenty-four hours, during which he sweated continuously. When at length he woke, he had to repeat the dose, sleeping and sweating virtually without nourishment while Kropp attended him and wiped the sweat from his body during the period needed for the cure. In order to control the revival of the rumors about his addiction, Goering actually attended the performance of an opera immediately after one of these drastic treatments because he had heard there was gossip that he was at the professor's sanatorium. Kropp, who went with him to the theater, had to hold him up from behind when he rose to acknowledge the cheers of the audience.

The glandular disorder which led to his excessive weight also subjected him to constant sweating. He took what exercise he could in the country, and after discovering that there was a sauna establishment in the Leipzigstrasse he frequently went there with Kropp after hours until he was able to install a sauna room in the basement at Carinhall. It was at this establishment in Berlin that he discovered his other manservant, Müller, who was a masseur there; Müller was later engaged as Kropp's assistant in the personal service of the Reich Minister. As a further attempt at exercise, Goering would occasionally indulge himself in a form of tennis; he would play with anyone who was prepared to observe his personal rules for the game, which were that the ball should always be directed by his opponent to a spot near to where he was standing so that he need not run after it. "Can't you see where I'm standing?" he would shout if the ball fell out of reach.

In February 1937 Goering went to Poland as the guest of its President, Ignacy Mościcki, to shoot lynxes and to reassure him of Germany's peaceful intentions. He met Marshal Śmigly-Rydz in Warsaw on February 10 and told him Germany was completely satisfied with her present frontiers with Poland and had no intention of seizing the Polish Corridor. "We don't want the Corridor," he is reported to have said. "I say that sincerely and categorically. We don't need the Corridor." They could take his word for it. Germany wanted a strong Poland because if she were weak this would only encourge an attack by the Soviet Union, and the one thing Germany did not want was an extension of Russian power, whether Communist or monarchist. It would pay Poland, he said, to "deal with a friendly-disposed Reich," and he repeated again and again how he hoped the friendly and peaceful intentions of Hitler toward Poland would be reflected in a better understanding between the Polish and German peoples as a whole. Then he slipped in a reference to Danzig and "the advent of the Hitler regime in the Free City," and the facilitating of German entry to East Prussia through Poland. In Berlin on November 4 in a conversation with Count Szembek, the Polish Under-Secretary for Foreign Affairs, he returned to the same subject—that, as the Count reported it, "the Third Reich was not nursing the least idea of aggressive intentions

against Poland and regarded her territorial integrity as inviolable."
(This was the day before Hitler's notorious meeting with his ministers and military chiefs at which the future expansion of Germany
at the expense of her neighbors would be plainly stated in a speech
lasting four and a half hours.) Incidents in Danzig, said Goering,
were unimportant; "nothing could happen in Danzig against
Poland."[19]

The British ambassadors during the Nazi regime were Sir Horace
Rumbold, who left Berlin in May 1933, Sir Eric Phipps (May 1933
to May 1937) and Sir Nevile Henderson (May 1937 to September
1939). Before he left for Germany, Henderson was instructed by
both Baldwin, the retiring Prime Minister, and Chamberlain, who
was to follow him, to do his "utmost to work with Hitler and the
Nazi Party as the existing government in Germany." In Henderson
Goering was to find at first a friend, for the new British ambassador
—"the man with the flower," as Hitler called him—enjoyed both
good sport and good society. Henderson wrote:

Of all the big Nazi leaders, Hermann Goering was for me by far the
most sympathetic . . . In any crisis, as in war, he would be quite ruthless. He once said to me that the British whom he really admired were
those whom he described as the pirates, such as Francis Drake, and he
reproached us for having become too "debrutalized." He was, in fact,
himself a typical and brutal buccaneer, but he had certain attractive
qualities, and I must frankly say that I had a real personal liking for him
. . . I liked Frau Goering as much as her husband, and possibly for
better moral reasons.[20]

Henderson first met Emmy Goering at an embassy lunch he gave
for the Prime Minister of Canada in June 1937. He found her
simple, natural and easy to like. The brief conversation he had with
her turned on a remark on vanity in men and women. "I approve of
vanity in men," said Emmy.

Henderson's reaction to Goering was one of the most favorable
to come from a professional observer of men who was not himself a
Nazi, though it should be pointed out that Goering was to make a
similar impression on the Swedish businessman and would-be
peacemaker Birger Dahlerus during their series of meetings in 1939,
and on Sumner Welles when he visited Carinhall in 1940. Henderson's picture of Goering presents him fully established as the sec-

ond man in Germany ("he had always given me to understand he was Hitler's natural successor as Führer," wrote Henderson, echoing what Goering had said to François-Poncet), a man of great possessions, happily married and soon to be a father, his range of responsibilities delegated to subordinates while he was free to conduct any negotiation along lines determined for him by Hitler. Henderson was impressed by his utter self-effacement before the Führer: "Everything had been done by Hitler, all the credit was Hitler's, every decision was Hitler's, and he himself was nothing . . . However vain he may have been in small ways . . . he was quite without braggadocio over the big things which he had accomplished." Henderson liked his Falstaffian sense of humor, his love for children and animals ("however little compassion he may have had, like so many Germans, for his fellow men"), his fondness for playing with trains and airplanes that dropped bombs (it was not, he said to Henderson, part of the Nazi conception of life to be excessively civilized or to teach squeamishness to the young). Apart from Hitler, he was the only one of the Nazi leaders for whom the German people had any genuine regard.

As a negotiator, Henderson found him readily accessible, quick to take a point, "a man to whom one could speak absolutely frankly. He neither easily took nor lightly gave offence . . . he was invariably ready to listen and eager to learn." Henderson concludes:

My own recollections of Goering will be of the man who intervened decisively in favour of peace in 1938, and would have done so again in 1939 if he had been as brave morally as he was physically; of the hospitable host and sportsman; and of a man with whom I spent many hours in friendly and honourable dispute and argument.

It was with high hopes, therefore, that Henderson looked forward to the November visit of Lord Halifax to Goering's international hunting exhibition in Berlin, for which Henderson had successfully managed at the last minute to secure a small grant from the British Treasury so that Britain might be represented among the other nations exhibiting. Halifax was then Lord President of the Council, but he was soon, in February 1938, to succeed Anthony Eden as Foreign Secretary and so form the combination with Chamberlain that brought appeasement to a fine art and wrecked all chance of peace. Halifax, like Henderson, was a sportsman; the Berliners

called him "Lord Halalifax" (*halali* means "tallyho"), because he
was a master of foxhounds and this was given out as his qualifica-
tion for the visit; but it was Chamberlain's purpose that he should
meet the Nazi leaders and work for that diplomatic ideal known as
"a better understanding." After visiting the exhibition, Halifax
went on November 18 with Neurath and Paul Schmidt to see
Hitler at Berchtesgaden, and provoked him at once by opening the
discussion with the remark, "I have brought no new proposals
from London." The conversation went badly, Hitler complaining
of the British press and lecturing Halifax about the German demands. Halifax's response was that Britain would be prepared to
discuss any solution to these problems that did not involve the use
of force.

(In July, soon after his arrival in Berlin, Henderson had asked
Goering to send him a memorandum on Germany's specific griev-
ances against Great Britain "in the matter of our alleged attempt to
hem her in," and also to state what were her ultimate aims in Europe. Goering never sent the memorandum, and when some weeks
later Henderson reminded him, he said he would talk to Hitler
again and perhaps supply the answers if Henderson would come for
a shoot and stay with him at Rominten at the beginning of October. There Goering was friendly but blunt; it might be necessary, he
said, to revise the Anglo-German naval agreement if Britain persisted in her refusal to collaborate with Germany. Henderson replied that this kind of action would only end in war. Goering "re-
gretfully admitted that this might be so." On another occasion during this period Goering asked Henderson which nation he thought
had gained most in the end from the World War. When Henderson gave Italy and the Slav states as his choice, Goering's reply was
a strange one. "No," he said, "Germany. Without such a war and
such a defeat, German unity would have been impossible.")

Halifax was due to lunch at Carinhall after his return from
Berchtesgaden; meanwhile Schmidt, his work at Berchtesgaden
done, hurried to Carinhall ahead of him to tell Goering the meeting with Hitler had not gone well. During Halifax's visit Goering,
who had received very precise instructions from Hitler, went over
the Führer's arguments again for his benefit, but expressed them
more tactfully and pleasantly. Everything, even including the pressing matter of Austria, could be settled by negotiation, said Goering,
though he stressed that any German government would in the end

regard it as essential that Austria, the Sudetenland and Danzig should return to the Reich. Peace, went on Goering, with a nice touch of flattery, depended less on Germany than on England, because England would be able to contribute so much to the peaceful solution of these questions. "Germany," he added, "does not want to go to war over these issues. Under no circumstances shall we use force. This would be completely unnecessary."

Halifax thought Goering immensely entertaining, and considered he looked like Robin Hood—"a composit impression of film-star, gangster, great landowner . . . Like a great schoolboy, full of life and pride in all he was doing. He was dressed in brown breeches and boots, green leather jerkin and he had round his waist a green belt with a dagger enclosed in a red leather sheath." He took Halifax for the inevitable drive round the estate, and then they had luncheon, waited on by maids in peasant costume and footmen in eighteenth-century livery—"green and white plush breeches, gaiter-spats, reversed cuffs and caught-up tails of the coats."

After Halifax had gone, Goering said to Henderson, "Does the Prime Minister really mean business?" Halifax on his return to England reported to Chamberlain, "Both Hitler and Goering said separately, and emphatically, that they had no desire or intention of making war, and I think we may take this as correct, at any rate for the present." Only a short while before Halifax's visit, Goering had been assuring Count Szembek in Berlin that he considered Polish territory to be inviolable. He repeated the same assurances to the Hungarian ministers when they visited Berlin that same month, November. Was he merely fulfilling Hitler's instructions, or was he sincerely trying to bring about a peaceful solution to the problems Germany was pressing upon Europe, because he himself dreaded the thought of war? It may be significant that in November he became finally certain that Emmy was pregnant, and life took on a new meaning for him; he wanted to be free to enjoy it.

Yet at the now famous meeting on November 5, attended by Goering and the others most immediately concerned with forwarding Germany's aggressive power—Blomberg (now Minister of War and Commander in Chief of the newly renamed Wehrmacht, the armed forces), Foreign Minister von Neurath and the Commanders in Chief of the Army and the Navy, General von Fritsch and Admiral Raeder—Hitler had talked for over four hours on the future of Germany and Europe: of her need to reach the peak of her striking power by 1943 and of her need to expand her territories in the face of the opposition of Britain, France, Russia and the countries immediately surrounding her. He had spoken of the possible need to overrun Austria and Czechoslovakia, of the need to keep the Spanish Civil War active, of the need to sustain the neutrality of Italy, Poland and Russia until Germany's strength was expanded and consolidated. This meeting may have been the result of a mood of elation, for Italy was about to sign Hitler's Anti-Comintern Pact, which had already been signed by Japan the previous year.

During the early months of 1937 Goering was, as we have just seen, preoccupied with international affairs. On June 21, however, he made a speech to the delegates of the International Chamber of Commerce, who were meeting in Berlin. He tried to prove that the attempt by Germany to make her economy as self-sufficient as possible would do no harm to world economy, since world economy was itself dependent on the sound national economies of individual nations. Germany's researches and inventions, he claimed, would be of benefit to everyone; in fact, she was now setting an example to others. But she would not permit other nations to dictate what she might export and what import! Germany, said Goering, was determined to maintain equality of rights in the world economy. His speech was received somewhat ironically by the professional economists.

In July Schacht was once more taken completely by surprise when Goering commandeered the iron and steel industry. Germany was dangerously impoverished in her iron and steel resources. He founded the Hermann Goering Works at Salzgitter, and this concern was given the right to acquire compulsorily (in exchange for shares in the new combine) the mining rights of other firms, more especially those whose iron-ore resources were, in his opinion, underdeveloped. Germany was rich only in low-grade ore, and the deposits at Salzgitter were thought to be the most suitable for smelting. Goering protected his combine from the huge losses in which it was soon involved by compelling other steel works to acquire shares which they were later forced to sell at a loss. In this way he hoped within four years to increase Germany's home-produced iron ore from twelve and a half to fifty per cent of her needs.

By now the German economy was hidebound by decree. Prices were pegged, dividends and wages controlled; credit was unlimited for State-approved developments, projects for the ersatz, the synthetic, were lavishly endowed, imports drastically reduced. Small businesses were dissolved and the larger firms encouraged, while the network of State-controlled chambers of commerce ensured the complete subjection of the employer to the economic decrees which never ceased to flow from government to industry. The workers were similarly tied; the unions had been abolished and replaced by the State-controlled Labor Front, and the Charter of Labor of 1934 ensured that workers stayed where they were needed, worked the hours they were required to work, received the wages it was decreed they should receive, paid the taxes and compulsory contributions required by decree, and enjoyed the leisure activities, sports and holidays organized for them through the movement known as Strength through Joy.

Schacht, the initial architect of this economy, found quite intolerable the ruthless pace set by Goering to accelerate rearmament, as well as the methods he introduced to achieve this. Time and again Goering failed to consult him over matters that lay within the province of his ministry. In August 1937 Schacht wrote Goering a long letter in which he criticized his policy in some detail, especially the drastic reduction of German credit abroad, the provision of credit without cover for his iron-ore projects, and the reckless allocation of labor and raw materials to new undertakings, which meant serious reductions in the production of goods needed for both export and home consumption. He refused any longer to be party to Goering's activities or to appear to share with him this uneven responsibility for Germany's economic future. "You will remember," he wrote, "that I declared to you months ago that uniformity is indispensable to economic policy, and that I urged you to arrange matters in such a way as to enable you to take over the Ministry of Economics yourself." He sent a copy of the letter to Hitler, who summoned him at once to a conference on the sun-drenched terraces of Berchtesgaden, flattered him and then urged him to come to some understanding with Goering. Schacht claims that, unknown to him at the time, Hitler had already committed Goering to the policy he was adopting to develop rearmament at all costs, and was utterly opposed to Schacht's efforts at moderation. It is characteristic of Hitler that he avoided any unpleasantness with Schacht, whose outstanding talents he felt were still necessary to him. All the Minister was able to extract from the Führer was a promise to consent to his resignation if, after two months, he had come to no form of working agreement with Goering. Then Hitler saw him to his car and talked about the weather, not showing his resentment until after Schacht had gone.

No working agreement was reached. An exchange of letters with Goering led nowhere, and Schacht went on leave in September. In October he repeated his view that the position of Minister was intolerable and that his ministry and Goering's department could not effectively function side by side. On November 1 he met Goering again at Hitler's request. When Goering ended by saying, "But surely I must be able to give you instructions," Schacht left him with the words, "Not to me—to my successor!" Hitler reluctantly gave way at the end of the month and accepted Schacht's resignation, though the latter remained a Minister without Portfolio and president of the Reichsbank in order that the dissension should not be made too public. Goering, entering Schacht's room in the Economics Ministry, exclaimed, "How can one indulge in great thoughts in so small a room?" Then he telephoned the former Minister at the Reichsbank and shouted, "Herr Schacht, I am now sitting in your chair!" They were not to meet again until eight years later when they were taken under guard to a washroom and squatted side by side in the prison baths at Nuremberg.

VI

Peace or War

Early in 1938 there occurred the notorious cases against Blomberg and Fritsch, both representatives of the German military caste, in which lay the remaining roots of opposition to Hitler. Blomberg, now a field marshal, was both Minister of War and Commander in Chief of all the armed forces; General von Fritsch was Commander in Chief of the Army alone. Both were in varying degree regarded by Hitler as reactionaries; they had opposed the risks he ran in reoccupying the Rhineland, and they did not approve of the speed with which he sought to build up armaments and the manpower to use them. Fritsch had openly expressed his disagreement at the notorious session on November 5 the previous year.

Goering and Himmler had their own additional reasons for wanting to remove the two military chiefs. Goering wanted Blomberg's command for himself; Himmler wanted to bring the influence of the S.S. to bear on the Army, whose Commander in Chief was deeply opposed to Himmler's extraneous form of armed power.

It was a woman who came to their aid. Blomberg, a widower of sixty, wanted to marry a young girl called Erna Grühn with whom he was infatuated. She was not the kind of woman a member of the officer caste would normally marry, and this worried the Field Marshal sufficiently for him to consult Goering in private as to the suitability of the marriage. There was also another man in love with her. Goering reassured Blomberg, undertook to send the unwanted rival abroad and mentioned the matter to Hitler, who raised no objection. Goering even consented to act as a witness at the marriage along with Hitler himself, and the ceremony finally took place on January 12. The honeymoon was spent, very properly, in Capri.

Within a matter of days it became known that the Field Marshal's wife had a police record for prostitution and had even at one time posed for indecent photographs. Goering was hastily consulted by Keitel, to whom the evidence had been given by Count von Helldorf, police chief in Berlin. Goering himself saw that the matter was placed before Hitler, who agreed to dismiss Blomberg from his ministry and his command. Goering broke the news to the Field Marshal the same day. Blomberg offered to divorce his bride, but Goering turned the offer aside and left him to go back to his honeymoon, after he had had a final interview with Hitler the following day. The Blombergs stayed in exile for a year and then returned to Germany and lived in retirement.

In order to forestall any suggestion that Fritsch should succeed Blomberg, another dossier was produced by Himmler and the Gestapo which alleged that the General was guilty of homosexuality, and on January 26 Hitler confronted him with this evidence in the presence of Goering. Fritsch, disgusted and angry, denied the charge, but refused to defend himself; he had known something of what was to happen, since he had been warned in advance by Colonel Hossbach, Hitler's aide, who was furious at this second attack on the honor of the officer caste. In support of the charge, Himmler had a man called Hans Schmidt, an inveterate blackmailer who specialized in victimizing homosexuals, brought into Hitler's presence; Schmidt swore that he knew the General and had been levying blackmail on him for several years. Goering, according to Hossbach, became suddenly excited and rushed from the room shouting, "It was he, it was he!" Hitler suspended Fritsch and put him on indefinite leave. The General Staff, in spite of Fritsch's obstinate contempt and refusal to fight the charge, were determined to investigate the case against him, and on January 31 they forced Hitler to agree to an inquiry.

Goering now held himself in readiness to receive his reward from Hitler—the command of Germany's armed forces. On February 4, however, Hitler summoned his Cabinet for the last time and announced that he himself would become Commander in Chief in addition to being Supreme Commander, the position he already held as head of state. At the same time he abolished the Ministry of War and replaced it with the O.K.W., the High Command of the Wehrmacht, which would be responsible directly to him as Supreme Commander; as its chief of staff he appointed General Wilhelm Keitel. In Fritsch's place as Commander in Chief of the Army he appointed General Walther von Brauchitsch, who was, curiously enough, about to be involved in a divorce action. Hitler also dismissed sixteen of his generals, and he took the opportunity to dismiss Neurath from the Foreign Ministry and replace him by Ribbentrop. Goering was merely promoted to field marshal. According to the affidavit he swore at Nuremberg in 1945, Blomberg suggested to Hitler that Goering should succeed him, but the Führer turned the proposal down at once with the remark that Goering was neither patient enough nor diligent enough for the job.

The preliminary investigations into the case against Fritsch were conducted by the Army during February and revealed an active conspiracy against him developed principally by Himmler and Heydrich. The Army was secretly elated and awaited the outcome of the court of honor which Hitler agreed should take place on March 10 with Goering as president, supported by Brauchitsch and Raeder as commanders in chief respectively of the Army and the Navy. But the date was a fatal one. The Austrian crisis suddenly came to a head; the president and the commanders were needed elsewhere, and the court was postponed. When it was eventually reconvened on March 17, the *Anschluss* was over and Hitler's credit was once more at its height. Goering, who always realized the tactical advantages of generosity, himself intervened to help clear Fritsch of the accusation against him by forcing the prosecution's chief witness, the blackmailer Hans Schmidt, to confess that the Gestapo had threatened to murder him unless he consented to testify against Fritsch. Apparently the plot had originated when someone had discovered that Schmidt had once blackmailed a Rittmeister von Frisch after spying on his homosexual practices. Having gone as far as this, Goering, satisfied that Fritsch could be declared innocent, neglected to press any further with the charges against the Gestapo, his beloved children, or by now perhaps rather less dear stepchildren. Himmler waited anxiously for the outcome. According to Walter Schellenberg, a member of his staff, he revealed his superstitious nature by assembling twelve S.S. officers in a room near the place where the trial was being held and making them sit in a circle and concentrate their minds in order to exert a telepathic control over the proceedings.

The trial concluded the following day and Fritsch was acquitted. No mention of the inquiry or the verdict appeared in the press. Fritsch remained deposed; he decided to challenge Himmler to a duel, but the message, sent through General Gerd von Rundstedt, was apparently never delivered. A Polish machine-gunner dispatched him the following year while he was serving with his regiment outside Warsaw. As for Goering, Fritsch could only express his gratitude after the inquiry; he said to Rundstedt that Goering had "behaved very decently." Raeder declared at the Nuremberg trial that "it was entirely due to Goering's intervention that he [Fritsch] was cleared without friction." Goering, however, talking to Henderson a month or so after the Fritsch verdict, openly justified Hitler's dismissal of Fritsch, on the grounds that he disapproved of the Führer's foreign policy. Fritsch too must have modified his opinion of Goering early in December. Hassell records in his diary that Fritsch called Goering "a particularly bad specimen, always engaged in double-dealing," and considered he had begun to conspire against him after the Roehm purge in 1934.[1]

It is impossible now to determine the exact degree to which Goering was directly involved in planning the downfall of Blomberg and Fritsch. That he was ready to take advantage of any circumstances that might arise to remove them seems to be certain. His chief accuser remains Gisevius, who claimed at the Nuremberg trial that it was Goering who, in order to make Blomberg's position untenable, encouraged the Field Marshal's marriage to a woman he, Goering, already knew to be disreputable, and that in the case of Fritsch it was Goering himself who threatened Schmidt with death at a meeting in Carinhall if he refused to testify before Hitler about the blackmail he was supposed to have levied. Gisevius alleged that the case, with its mistaken identity, had been on the Gestapo files since 1935, but that Goering raised the matter only when Hitler mentioned the possibility that Fritsch might be suitable to take over Blomberg's position. Goering was sufficiently uneasy at Nuremberg to send Gisevius threatening messages in an attempt to stop him from saying too much about the Blomberg case. On the other hand, Meisinger, the man responsible for preparing the case against Fritsch, is said to have admitted he also faked evidence against Erna Grühn, using her mother's dossier to do so, and that until after Blomberg's wedding neither Hitler nor Goering knew of the matter in this form, prepared for Heydrich.

It was during 1938 that Goering dissolved the Prussian administrative courts (*Verwaltungsgerichte*), which protected the individual in matters where the civil courts did not offer protection. No
citizen could challenge a police decree or protect himself against
the new and fundamentally illegal decrees that poured out from the
Nazi administration.

Between the dates set for the court of honor, March 10 and
March 17, Goering had been involved in one of the triumphs of his
diplomatic career, the conquest by telephone in the Austrian
Anschluss.

The situation in Austria had come to the point where, with a
sudden exertion of pressure, the Nazis were able to disintegrate the
fragments of opposition left in their path. Papen, whom Hitler had
removed from the office of minister to Austria in the previous
month, had served him well in Vienna. As we have seen, he negotiated the "gentleman's agreement" of July 1936 which had given
the Austrian Nazis the right to share political responsibility in return for Hitler's empty recognition of Austrian sovereignty. Chancellor von Schuschnigg resisted the slow penetration of Germany
into Austrian affairs which it was Papen's principal duty to bring
about, and he leaned as long as it was possible to do so on the broad
shoulders of Mussolini. Mussolini's support for an independent
Austria weakened when the Rome-Berlin Axis was created in 1937,
and the Nazi underground, impatient at delay, was planning a
putsch. Throughout 1937 Goering had been in correspondence with
Guido Schmidt, the Austrian Under-Secretary for Foreign Affairs,
after Schmidt had noticed at Goering's hunting exhibition a map
of Europe on which no frontier was marked between Germany and
Austria. "Good huntsmen know no frontiers," Goering had remarked with a grin. Later he had invited Schmidt to Carinhall in
an attempt to maintain friendly relations, but in a letter written on
November 11 he had stated categorically that Austria and Germany
should adopt a common policy integrating their economy and their
military forces. It was a clear enough indication of the way things
were going.

Schuschnigg's position grew gradually intolerable; when Papen
was recalled to Germany in February, he brought a message to Hitler from the Chancellor asking for conversations. Hitler immediately extended the period of Papen's duty as minister in order that
he might take charge of the arrangements for the meeting. Accord-

ingly Schuschnigg traveled overnight to Salzburg on February 11 and drove with Papen and Guido Schmidt up the mountain roads to the Berghof. There Hitler abused and threatened him for two hours, then gave him lunch and flung him into the ready hands of Ribbentrop and Papen. They presented him the text of an ultimatum which amounted to the amalgamation of the two countries; it included an amnesty for imprisoned Nazis and the appointment of the Nazi Seyss-Inquart as Minister of the Interior with full control of the police. Otherwise, force. Schuschnigg could do nothing; Hitler saw him again and demanded his signature on behalf of the Austrian government. When Schuschnigg raised the point that such far-reaching terms would have to be discussed and ratified, Hitler shouted for Keitel and turned him out of the room. Later, with a show of magnanimity, he allowed him seven instead of four days to get the agreement ratified. But the presence of Keitel and other generals in the Berghof was not lost on the Austrian Chancellor, who returned to Vienna by the night train after Papen had reminded him suavely, "You know, the Führer can be absolutely charming!"

Seyss-Inquart was duly appointed Interior Minister on February 16 and the amnesty for the Nazis was proclaimed. On February 20 Hitler made his long-awaited speech in the Reichstag, praising Schuschnigg but ending with an ominous warning that ten million Germans lived outside the Reich in Austria and Czechoslovakia and that their position as oppressed minorities was "intolerable." This was a threat to Prague as well as Vienna. Schuschnigg himself spoke on February 24; although carefully avoiding any affront to Hitler, he stood firmly by Austrian independence. Meanwhile the Austrian Nazis redoubled their violent demonstrations, and in the town square of Graz they tore down the Austrian flag during the broadcast of Schuschnigg's speech and put up the swastika in its place. In a desperate attempt to rally an opposition to the Nazis, Schuschnigg (whose government was still a one-party dictatorship) agreed to recognize the Social Democrats, whose party he had originally suppressed along with the Nazis. Having done this, he bravely determined to hold a national plebiscite on Sunday, March 13, in which the Austrian people as a whole could declare whether they were for independence or for absorption into Germany. Hitler did not hear of this until March 9.

This was the last thing he wanted. He immediately assembled his

ministers and generals in Berlin, and on March 10 orders were given
for the Army to be prepared to invade Austria two days later. Nervous of Mussolini's reaction to this, Hitler sent him a private letter
by Prince Philipp von Hessen, who immediately flew to Rome.

We have seen that the principal part so far played by Goering
in the *Anschluss* had been the preparation of Mussolini to receive
just such a letter in this form from Hitler, in which he all but
pleaded with the Duce to recognize the desperate position he was
in, with Austria (as he asserted) conspiring with the Czechs to restore the Hapsburgs and with Schuschnigg breaking his promises
that he would stop the cruel oppression of the Austrian Nazis. He
gave Mussolini the most solemn assurances that he regarded the
Brenner as the ultimate boundary between Germany and Italy.
Meanwhile, German Army formations were moving toward the
Austro-Bavarian frontier, and Goering's bombers were flying in to
line the airfields.

Seyss-Inquart had now replaced Papen as the seemingly respect-
able instrument of Hitler's will in Austria. He was a young lawyer,
a Catholic and a churchgoer, and Schuschnigg still felt he might
negotiate with him. There was always hope when dealing with a
Christian and a gentleman, who would know how to compromise
and make special agreements. Without instructions from Hitler,
Seyss-Inquart even agreed to the plebiscite.

It was at dawn on March 11 that Schuschnigg was wakened with
the news that German forces were massing along the Bavarian
frontier, which had been sealed. Soon after six the Chancellor was
kneeling at Mass in St. Stephen's Cathedral; he then went straight
to his office. It was not until ten o'clock that Seyss-Inquart and
Glaise-Horstenau, another Nazi minister in Schuschnigg's Cabinet,
who had just brought Hitler's instructions by air from Berlin, told
him bluntly from Hitler that the plebiscite must be called off. After
consulting President Wilhelm Miklas, Schuschnigg finally agreed
to this early in the afternoon.

It was at this point that Goering took control of the negotiations,
working entirely by telephone from Berlin. By his own order a
transcription was kept of twenty-seven separate interchanges between his office and Vienna during the afternoon and evening of
March 11. By the time Goering and his agents had finished, Austria
belonged to Germany.[2]

These abrupt, excited and confused conversations, in which Goering imposed his will at long distance on the men who were struggling to carry out his orders and bury the obstinate corpse of an independent Austria, are deeply characteristic of him. He leaped from one point of instruction to another as it occurred to him, which resulted in a muddled and disorderly expression of what he wanted them to do. There was no self-discipline, no compunction in him, only a highly charged, temperamental thrust. It was the final travesty of legal form when force is beating at the door.

Hitler through Goering demanded the resignation of Schuschnigg as Chancellor, the appointment of Seyss-Inquart in his place by President Miklas and the immediate formation of a National Socialist Cabinet. Wilhelm Keppler arrived from Berlin in the afternoon to replace Papen, bringing with him the wording for a telegram which Hitler instructed Seyss-Inquart to send back to Berlin as soon as he was legally the Chancellor. The telegram requested the help of German forces to put down disorders in Austria. Keppler, Seyss-Inquart and Glaise-Horstenau formed a cabal in the Austrian Chancellery while Schuschnigg stood helplessly by. It was President Miklas himself who proved the final obstacle while Goering roared at now one person, now another, in the German embassy, getting confused and contradictory information from anxious but ill-informed officials.

At 5 p.m.:

DOMBROWSKI [*at the German embassy*]: Seyss-Inquart has talked to the Austrian Chancellor until two-thirty, but he is not in a position to dissolve the Cabinet by five-thirty because it is technically impossible.

GOERING: By seven-thirty the Cabinet must be formed and several measures must have been taken . . . I want to know what is going on. Did he tell you he is now the Chancellor?

DOMBROWSKI: Yes.

GOERING: As just transmitted to you?

DOMBROWSKI: Yes.

GOERING: Good, go on. What time can he form the Cabinet?

DOMBROWSKI: Possibly by nine-eighteen.

GOERING: The Cabinet must be formed by seven-thirty.

DOMBROWSKI: By seven-thirty.

GOERING: For that purpose Keppler is about to arrive . . . The demand to legalize the party must also be made.

DOMBROWSKI: All right.

GOERING: All right, with all its formations, S.A., S.S. . . . The Cabinet must be entirely National Socialist.

DOMBROWSKI: Good, that also has been settled, by seven-thirty that must be—

GOERING [*interrupting*]: That must be reported by seven-thirty, and Keppler will bring you several names to be incorporated . . . The party has definitely been legalized?

DOMBROWSKI: But that is—it isn't even necessary to discuss that.

GOERING: With all of its organizations?

DOMBROWSKI: With all of its organizations within the country.

GOERING: In uniform?

DOMBROWSKI: In uniform.

GOERING: Good . . . Be careful, the daily press must leave immediately, and our people.

DOMBROWSKI: Well, as to the man whom you mentioned with regard to the Security Department—

GOERING: Kaltenbrunner. Yes, he is to get the Security Department, and then, mark this, immediately the press representatives . . . (overtalking, with Dombrowski saying "Yes" several times).

At 5:20 P.M.:

GOERING [*to Franz Ullrich Hueber, his brother-in-law*]: Look, Franz, you take over the Ministry of Justice, and, corresponding to the wish of the Führer, you also take over for the time being the Ministry for Foreign Affairs. Later on someone else will replace you in this . . . The Cabinet has to be formed by seven-thirty, otherwise it's all for nothing; otherwise, things will take their own course, and very different decisions will be made . . . And then another important factor which I forgot to mention before: The Reds, who were given arms yesterday, have to be disarmed in the quickest way, and just as well in a ruthless manner; that is rather a matter of course.

At 5:26 P.M.:

SEYSS-INQUART: The Federal President has accepted the resignation [of Schuschnigg], but his point of view is that no one but the Chancellor is to be blamed for Berchtesgaden and its consequences, and therefore he'd like to entrust a man like Ender with the chancellorship.

GOERING: Yes—now, look here. This will change the whole situation. The Federal President or someone else has got to be informed this is entirely different from what we were told. Dombrowski said at your request that you had been given the chancellorship . . . that the party had been restored, the S.A. and S.S. had already taken over police duties, and so on.

SEYSS-INQUART: No, that is not so. I suggested to the Federal President that he entrust the chancellorship to me; it takes usually three to four hours . . .

GOERING: Well, that won't do! Under no circumstances! The matter is in progress now; therefore, please, the Federal President must be informed immediately that he has to turn the powers of the Federal Chancellor over to you and to accept the Cabinet as it was arranged.

The conversation was then interrupted by the arrival of a fresh message that the Federal President would respond only to diplomatic action from the Reich and had refused to see the three National Socialists charged with pressing acceptance of Goering's requirements on him.

GOERING: Give me Seyss. [To Seyss-Inquart] Now, remember the following. You go immediately together with General Muff and tell the Federal President that if the conditions which are known to you are not accepted immediately, the troops that are already stationed at or advancing to the frontier will march in tonight along the whole line, and Austria will cease to exist . . . Please inform us immediately about Miklas' position. Tell him there is no time now for any joke; just that, as a result of the false report we received before, action was delayed, but now the situation is that tonight the invasion will begin from all the corners of Austria. The invasion will be stopped and the troops will be held at the border only if we are informed by seven-thirty that Miklas has entrusted you with the Federal chancellorship . . . Then call out all the National Socialists all over the country. They should now be in the streets. So remember, a report must be given by seven-thirty. . . . If Miklas could not understand it in four hours, we shall make him understand it now in four minutes.

SEYSS-INQUART: All right.

At 6:34 P.M.:

GOERING: What does he have to say?

KEPPLER: Well, he would not agree to it.

GOERING: Well, then, Seyss-Inquart has to dismiss him. Just go upstairs again and tell him plainly that Seyss will call on the National Socialist guards, and in five minutes the troops will march in by my order.

The telephone connection broke down; during the interval Keppler went to see the President again. When the line was restored, Seyss-Inquart spoke to Goering to report on the position.

GOERING: Well, how do we stand?

SEYSS-INQUART: Please, Field Marshal, yes.

GOERING: Well, what is going on?

SEYSS-INQUART: Yes, ah, the Federal President won't budge from his original position . . .

GOERING: But do you think it possible that we shall come to a decision in the next few minutes?

SEYSS-INQUART: Well, the conversation can't take longer than five to ten minutes. I reckon it can't take longer.

GOERING: Listen. So I shall wait a few more minutes . . . Then you inform me by priority call in the Reich Chancellery, as usual. But it's got to be done fast . . . If it can't be done, then you will have to take over the power all right.

SEYSS-INQUART: But if he threatens?

GOERING: Yes.

SEYSS-INQUART: Well, I see, then we shall be ready.

GOERING: Call me on priority.

At 8:03 P.M.:

SEYSS-INQUART: Dr. Schuschnigg will give the news over the radio that the Reich government has presented an ultimatum.

GOERING: I heard about it.

SEYSS-INQUART: And the government itself has abdicated . . . They are waiting for the troops to march in.

GOERING: Well, they were appointed by you?

SEYSS-INQUART: No.

GOERING: Did you dismiss them from their office?

SEYSS-INQUART: No. No one was dismissed from his office, but the government has itself pulled out and let matters take their course.

GOERING: And you were not commissioned? It was refused?

SEYSS-INQUART: It was refused now, as before. They are taking a chance with the invasion and expect that, if it actually takes place, executive power will be transferred to other people.

GOERING: Right. I shall give the order to march in, and then you make sure that you get the power. Notify the leading people . . . that everyone who offers resistance or organizes resistance will immediately be subject to our court-martial, the court-martial of our invading troops. Is that clear?

SEYSS-INQUART: Yes.

GOERING: Including leading personalities. It doesn't make any difference.

SEYSS-INQUART: Yes, they have given the order not to offer any resistance.

GOERING: Yes, that doesn't matter. The Federal President did not authorize you, and that also can be considered as resistance.

SEYSS-INQUART: Yes.

GOERING: Well, now you *are* officially authorized.

SEYSS-INQUART: Yes.

GOERING: Well, good luck. Heil Hitler.

The obstinate courage of President Miklas, who resolutely refused to yield to any outside pressure concerning whom he should appoint as Chancellor, spoiled the legal game that Goering was trying to play. The streets were filled with Nazi demonstrators yelling for the blood of Schuschnigg, who, realizing that there was nothing more that he could do, broadcast a brief farewell to the Austrian people. "We have yielded to force," he said, "since we are not prepared even in this terrible hour to shed blood. . . . God protect Austria!" Deserted now by everyone, President Miklas continued his stubborn resistance in the face of Seyss-Inquart's direct challenge to his authority. He did not finally give in until midnight; then and then only did he yield to the appointment of Seyss-Inquart as Chancellor.

After Schuschnigg's broadcast Goering returned to the telephone.

GOERING [*to General Muff, military attaché at the embassy*]: Tell Seyss-Inquart the following. As we understand it, the government has abdicated, but he himself remains, so he should continue to stay in office and carry out necessary measures in the name of the government. The invasion is going to happen now, and we shall state that everyone who puts up any resistance will have to face the consequences . . . I should try to avoid chaos.

MUFF: Seyss will do so. He is already making a speech.

GOERING: . . . Best if Miklas resigns.

MUFF: Yes, but he won't. It was very dramatic. I spoke to him almost fifteen minutes. He declared that he will in no circumstances yield to force.

GOERING: So. He will not give in to force. . . . What does this mean? He just wants to be kicked out?

MUFF: Yes. He doesn't want to move.

GOERING: Well, with fourteen children you can't move as you like! Well, just tell Seyss to take over.

Urged on by Goering, Seyss-Inquart himself broadcast at 8 P.M., demanding that the people should keep calm and offer no resistance to the German troops.

At 8:48 the telephone was busy again.

KEPPLER: The government has ordered the Army not to put up any resistance.

GOERING: I don't give a damn.

KEPPLER: Might I ask you if a prominent personality in Berlin wants to add a few words for the Austrian people?

GOERING: Well, I don't know yet. Listen, the main thing is that Seyss takes over all powers of the government, that he keeps the radio stations occupied—

KEPPLER: Well, we represent the government now.

GOERING: Yes, that's it, you are the government. Listen carefully. The following telegram should be sent here by Seyss-Inquart. Write it down: "The provisional Austrian government, which after the dismissal of the Schuschnigg government considers it its task to establish peace and order in Austria, sends to the German government the urgent request to support it in its task and to help it prevent bloodshed. For this reason it asks the German government to send German troops as soon as possible."

KEPPLER: Well, the S.A. and the S.S. are marching through the streets, but everything is quiet.

GOERING: . . . Seyss-Inquart has to take over . . . and appoint a few people—the people we recommend to him. He should now form a provisional government. It is absolutely unimportant what the Federal President may have to say . . . Then our troops will cross the border today.

KEPPLER: Yes.

GOERING: Look, and he should send the telegram as soon as possible. . . . Well, he does not even have to send the telegram—all he needs to do is to say, "Agreed!"

KEPPLER: Yes.

GOERING: Call me either at the Führer's or at my place. Well, good luck. Heil Hitler!

Goering leaned back. The matter was in effect settled. He cared nothing about the misgivings of his agents in Vienna. After Miklas had resigned at midnight, Seyss-Inquart, Keppler and Muff all tried to prevent the march into Austria ordered for daybreak, but they telephoned Berlin in vain. Hitler was determined on direct action in the face of the President's opposition, and he was further relieved and encouraged when, at 10:30 that night, Prince Philipp, his agent in Rome, telephoned at last with a message from Mussolini: "He sends you his regards. . . . Austria would be immaterial to him." Hitler's relief sprang hysterically to his lips: "Please tell Mussolini I will never forget him for this. . . . Never, never, never, no matter what happens! . . . As soon as the Austrian affair is settled I shall be ready to go with him through thick and thin—through anything! . . . I thank him from the bottom of my heart. Never, never shall I forget it. . . ." He could not stop repeating gratitude upon gratitude. As for France and Britain, Hitler guessed they would do nothing, and he was right. His Majesty's Government had declined to offer any advice to Schuschnigg when he appealed to them by telegram on March 11; he was merely informed that Britain was "unable to guarantee protection." Ribbentrop was back in London paying farewell visits before leaving his embassy to take up his duties as Hitler's Foreign Minister; he was in fact lunching at Downing Street with Chamberlain and Halifax when official news arrived reporting the German ultimatum to Austria. Winston Churchill, who was present at this lunch, describes Chamberlain's embarrassment at receiving the news and his endeavors to get rid of Ribbentrop and his wife, who lingered on in order, no doubt, to prevent Chamberlain from hastening into action.

Within the hour of closing his campaign by telephone, Goering was playing another part administering sedatives to the anxious neighbors of Germany. He went straight from a consultation with Hitler to a grand ball in the Haus der Flieger at which he was the host. Henderson was there with over a thousand other guests, including many of the diplomatic corps, all of whom were as anxious as the Germans themselves to know what was happening in Austria; all they knew was what they had read into the broadcasts of Schuschnigg and Seyss-Inquart. The curiosity of the whole assembly was raised when Ivone Kirkpatrick suddenly arrived and demanded an urgent consultation with his ambassador; all he had brought with him was the draft of the formal note of protest which the British government instructed the ambassador to send to the German Foreign Minister. Henderson approved the draft, and Kirkpatrick, feeling, as he put it, like Cinderella at Goering's Ball, slipped away to transmit the message, while a thousand pairs of eyes followed him out, trying to gather from his expression what form of intervention Britain might be considering.

Goering arrived late from his meeting with Hitler, but before joining his guests he talked in private with Dr. Vojtech Mastny, the Czechoslovak minister in Berlin, who was at the ball and was desperate to receive some form of reassurance. Goering had responded warmly at the sight of him and said how glad he was to find him there, "for he wanted to declare to me on his word of honor that there was not the least reason for Czechoslovakia to feel any anxiety. . . Germany had no hostile intentions of any kind toward her, but, on the contrary, wished to continue advancing toward a *rapprochement*." The entry of Reich troops into Austria was only, he said, "a family affair." However, Goering added that he had heard rumors of Czech mobilization. Mastny hastened off to his legation to check this.

Goering then joined the assembly, shaking hands with a few of the principal guests, including Henderson, who tried to make his handshake seem specially cold. Goering appeared very nervous and taken aback by this form of greeting from his British friend. Soon everyone was invited to sit down to watch the performance of a ballet by the State Opera; the circumstances could not have been less appropriate for music and dancing. Goering anxiously scribbled Henderson a note: "Immediately the music is over I should like to talk to you, and *will explain everything to you.*" The last words were underlined five times. The moment the ballet finished, Goering withdrew with Henderson to a private room. Henderson claims that he argued resolutely on behalf of Schuschnigg and the anti-Nazis in Austria, urging moderation in their treatment. Privately, however, Henderson believed that Schuschnigg had behaved foolishly, and that it had been inevitable that Austria and Germany should eventually unite. When he returned to the embassy in the middle of the night to report his conversation with Goering, he included a sentence stating that he had "reluctantly" admitted "that Dr. Schuschnigg had acted with precipitate folly." Halifax reprimanded him for making any such remark to Goering, and the following month he was warned again to be careful what he said in private and unofficially about the next point of action on Hitler's agenda, the Sudeten question.

Meanwhile, Mastny had returned to the Haus der Flieger to tell Goering no mobilization had been ordered. Goering then repeated his reassurances to Mastny in the name of Hitler, and he took the trouble to telephone him again the following midday to remind him of what he had said and extract once more from Mastny official confirmation that the Czechs were not mobilizing. The next day, March 13, Henderson obtained Goering's permission for Chamberlain to refer in the House of Commons to the reassurances he had made to Mastny; the same day Henderson confirmed in writing that he had reported to the British government Goering's assurances on the night of March 11 that German troops would be withdrawn from Austria as soon as the situation was stable and that free elections would take place "without any intimidation whatever." However, in a note to the German minister in Hungary written on March 21, Ribbentrop was more careful and specified that Goering's assurances referred exclusively to "*ad hoc* measures connected with carrying out action in Austria."[3]

Nazi celebrations in Austria followed hard upon the tanks that crossed her borders at daybreak on March 12. Neurath, still Acting Foreign Minister in Berlin while Ribbentrop was preparing to leave London, sent a curt reply to the British note of protest; this was a wholly German affair, he stated, and the German forces were entering Austria in response to an urgent telegram from the new Aus-

trian government. In the afternoon Hitler followed his troops into
Austria and made a triumphal entry into Linz, where he had been at
school; he was received by Himmler and Seyss-Inquart. Hitler, over-
whelmed by the tumult of the crowds, demanded that a law be
drafted immediately making the *Anschluss* a total one; Austria was
to become a province of the Reich with the Führer as its President.
This law was promulgated on Sunday, March 13, by the new Austrian government under the signature of Seyss-Inquart; Goering was
to be among the signatories for Germany. There was to be "a free
and secret plebiscite" on April 10 on the reunion with Germany,
held under Hitler's and not Schuschnigg's auspices.

That evening from Carinhall Goering made another of his exult-
ant telephone calls, this time to Ribbentrop in London.[4] The almost one-way conversation was to last forty minutes.

GOERING: There is overwhelming joy in Austria. That you can
hear over the radio.
RIBBENTROP: Yes. It's fantastic, isn't it?
GOERING: Yes, the last march into the Rhineland is completely
overshadowed. The Führer was deeply moved when he talked to me
last night. . . . Well, this story that we had given an ultimatum is
just foolish gossip. From the very beginning the National Socialist
Ministers and the representatives of the people presented the ultimatum. . . . The Ministers asked us to back them up, so they
would not be completely beaten up again and subjected to terror
and civil war. . . . Then you have to remember that Schuschnigg
made his speeches, telling them the Fatherland Front would fight
to its last man. One could not know they would capitulate like that,
and therefore Seyss-Inquart, who had already taken over the government, asked us to march in immediately. . . . These are the
actual facts which can be proved by documents. . . . The following is interesting, the absolutely complete enthusiasm for National
Socialism, which is surprising even to us. . . .
RIBBENTROP: So it seems that all Austria is on our side.
GOERING: Well, let me tell you, if there were an election tomorrow . . . I have already told Seyss-Inquart he should invite representatives of the democratic powers; they could convince themselves that this was really an election carried out on a democratic
basis—and we should have ninety per cent votes in our favor. Absolutely! . . . Responsible people from England and France should

be asked to come over here and to watch what is actually going on. The biggest trick ever played was done here.

RIBBENTROP: I believe that this conviction will grow here.

GOERING: One thing I want to say: If it is claimed that we overpowered the Austrian people and took away their independence, then one should admit at least that just one little part of it was put under pressure—not by us—and that was the government which existed on such a small basis. The Austrian people have only been freed. . . . I also want to point out that yesterday . . . they were saying the most serious things, war, and so on; it made me laugh, because where would one find such an unscrupulous statesman who would send again millions of people to death only because two German brother nations—

RIBBENTROP: Yes, this is absolutely ridiculous; they realize that over here. I think they know pretty well over here what is going on.

GOERING: Ribbentrop, I would call attention to one fact particularly. What state in the whole world will get hurt by our union? Do we take away anything from any other state? . . . They could only have one interest, to create hostile feelings against Germany . . . Besides, I do want to point out that the Czechoslovakian minister came to see me yesterday and he explained that the rumor Czechoslovakia had mobilized was taken out of thin air and they would be satisfied with one word from me that I would not undertake the slightest thing against Czechoslovakia. . . . It was then that I said: The German troops are supposed to stay fifteen to twenty kilometers away from the border on their march through Austria; and north of the Danube in the whole sector only one partial battalion was to march, merely so that these villages can share in the joy and pleasure. . . . Tell the following to Halifax and Chamberlain: It is not correct that Germany has given any ultimatum. This is a lie by Schuschnigg. . . . I want to state that Seyss-Inquart asked us expressly by phone and by telegram to send troops. . . .

RIBBENTROP: Goering, tell me, how is the situation in Vienna? Is everything settled yet?

GOERING: Yes. Yesterday I landed hundreds of airplanes with some companies, in order to secure the airfields, and they were received with joy. The Austrian troops did not withdraw but . . . fraternized immediately with the German troops, wherever they were stationed.

RIBBENTROP: That had to be expected.

GOERING: . . . The whole affair is turning out as it was supposed to. . . . In no way are we threatening the Czechoslovakian Republic, but it has now the opportunity of coming to a friendly and reasonable agreement with us . . . on condition that France remains sensible. . . . Naturally, if France now organizes a big mobilization close to the border, then it won't be funny.

RIBBENTROP: I believe that they'll behave all right.

GOERING: We have a clear conscience, and that is a decisive factor. Before history we have a clear conscience. . . .

RIBBENTROP: I had a long, intensive conversation with Halifax, and I told him our basic conception, also about the German-English understanding—

GOERING: That was what I wanted to say. You know yourself, Ribbentrop, that I always was in favor of a German-English understanding. Anyone would be if he also recognized that we too are a proud and free nation. After all, we also represent two brother nations.

RIBBENTROP: I can tell you one thing, Goering. The other day I spoke to Chamberlain . . . and I got a very good impression of him. . . . I do not want to speak about it over the phone, but I have the impression that Chamberlain also is very serious about an understanding. . . . I also said to Halifax . . . that we honestly do want to come to an understanding, and he replied that his only worry was the Czechoslovakian Republic.

GOERING: No, no, that is out of the question.

RIBBENTROP: I told him then that we were not interested and we did not intend to do anything there. . . . I got the best impression of Halifax as well as of Chamberlain. He thought it would be a little difficult with public opinion, because here it looks like force. I have the feeling that the normal Englishman, the man in the street, will say, "Why should England bother with Austria?" . . .

GOERING: I must say Mussolini behaved wonderfully.

RIBBENTROP: Yes, I already heard about it.

GOERING: Wonderful.

RIBBENTROP: Very good indeed. We always thought so!

GOERING: Marvelous!

There followed a gossipy interchange in which Goering described how Schuschnigg used to rig the votes, counting all torn voting papers as affirmative votes; Goering then impersonated a Herr Meier who went from booth to booth voting yes in each. They then went on to discuss the election that was to come in Austria, and how Germany intended to alleviate the economic situation there.

GOERING: Let me tell you the following, confidentially. The Führer, who is usually well controlled, has his heart too much involved in all this, since it concerns his homeland. I believe if he receives any threat in the Austrian question he will never give in, and, I have to make it clear, neither will the two nations. It would be a matter of fanaticism, in Germany as well as in Austria.

RIBBENTROP: That's clear.

GOERING: There is no doubt. Whoever threatens us now will strike at both peoples, and both will put up a fanatical resistance. . . . The weather is wonderful here. Blue sky. I am sitting here on my balcony all covered in blankets, in the fresh air, drinking coffee. Later on I have to drive in, I have to make a speech, and the birds are twittering, and over the radio I can hear the enthusiasm, which must be wonderful there.

Goering ended by praising an article written by Ward Price from Linz, in which he quoted Hitler as challenging him to say if this welcome he had received looked like the result of force!

Goering now had new territory to bring into his economic plan for Germany. Toward the end of March he too went to Linz as part of a triumphal visit modeled on that of Hitler. There he spoke of the "great plans" he had for Austria. "There will be power stations, a new autobahn, armament works, new industries, harbors, social measures. Unemployment will be banned completely. . . . Now you must work hard!" Speaking on March 26 in Vienna, he said, "The city of Vienna can no longer rightfully be called a German city. . . . Where there are three hundred thousand Jews, you cannot speak of a German city. Vienna must once more become a German city, because it must perform important tasks for Germany in Germany's Ostmark . . ." He then directed that Jewish commerce must be made Aryan, "systematically and carefully, . . . legally but inexorably."

During his tour of Austria, Goering did not fail to stop at Mauterndorf and stage a triumphal entry into the village where he had been so often as a boy at the home of his guardian Epenstein, and where Marianne, his former fiancée, still lived. Like Hitler at Linz and Goebbels at Rheydt, Goering enjoyed receiving admiration and applause in the places where he had once been undistinguished, and to make sure that the village was crowded and gave him a fine welcome he brought with him a large number of soldiers.

By now the reign of terror had begun behind the walls of cheering people. Himmler's security arrangements for Hitler's entry into Vienna (which had been delayed until Monday, March 14, because of the numerous breakdowns that the Nazi tanks and motorized units had suffered on the road) led to the first wave of arrests, which in Vienna alone were soon to amount to 76,000. There were many suicides, and a great exodus of Jews began. Goering is reported to have said in a broadcast, "I can't help it if the Jews do away with themselves. I cannot put a policeman behind every Jew to prevent suicide!" Henderson claims that Goering did his best to encourage moderation in Austria and indeed ordered the release of some thousands of persons, but that the Austrian Nazis and Himmler were entirely unaffected by any scruples of this kind and rearrested those whom Goering had freed.

On April 26 Henderson met with Goering at Carinhall in an effort to obtain the release of Schuschnigg and certain other Austrian leaders held by the Nazis. Goering spoke with great bitterness and said the British drove him "mad with rage"; they always seemed to try to stand in Germany's path. Henderson replied that public opinion was roused about Austria. Goering said he hated the thought of the two great Germanic peoples fighting each other; Germany in any case would be fully satisfied with the settlement of the Sudeten question. Then he talked "wildly," as Henderson put it in his report to Halifax, about dividing the "appendix" of Czechoslovakia among Poland, Hungary and Germany. In May Goering was reported as forecasting that the Czech affair would be liquidated in the summer, and on June 22 Henderson and Goering met again at Carinhall. Henderson found him obsessed by the problem of Czechoslovakia and the need for an understanding with Britain; the ambassador felt he was "genuinely anxious" for this. They agreed about the Czech problem while driving round the woods inspecting elk. "For once," wrote Henderson, "the Field Marshal refrained from bluster of any kind. He seemed, in fact, more depressed and anxious and less confident than I have ever known him."[5]

During the final eighteen months before the invasion of Poland

and the outbreak of war, Goering was ceaselessly involved in forwarding Hitler's foreign policy. But in the middle of the year he paused for a moment to exult over another form of success—the birth of his daughter, Edda, on June 2. Goering's uxorious nature was filled with joy over fathering a child. He had hoped for a son for dynastic reasons, but he was from the first devoted to his baby daughter. When Emmy had recovered, he took her away with the baby for a holiday by the sea on the island of Sylt. During the summer he was ill with a glandular trouble and high blood pressure, which were to recur in February the following year.

Goering's relationship with Hitler was complicated by the arrival of Ribbentrop in Berlin. Vain, ambitious, cunning rather than intelligent, the new Foreign Minister decided that he should become Hitler's brightest star. His successes in Britain and Rome had brought him the favor of the Führer, and he was determined to be master in his own field of foreign relations, subject only to Hitler himself. Neither he nor Goering had forgotten the affair of the latter's unfortunate visit to London. Goering, who of course regarded himself as second only to Hitler, was intent on keeping the position he had won as Hitler's roving ambassador. The position was anomalous, like much else in the administration of Nazi Germany. Hitler liked a situation where two men were competing to serve him, and it disturbed him little that a bitter rivalry developed between Goering and Ribbentrop, and that they put very different slants upon Nazi foreign policy in their diplomatic discussions.

Goering's movements in 1938 show that his principal activities were in foreign affairs, though this does not mean he neglected to apply some of his driving energy to his deputies and officials concerned with the Air Ministry and with the economic organization of Germany. There are records, for instance, of an address he gave on July 8 to a number of leading aircraft manufacturers whom he invited to Carinhall for a conference. Here he confided that war with Czechoslovakia was imminent, that the German Air Force was superior to the British and that a victorious Germany would be rich, with markets that dominated the world. "For this goal," he said, "risks must be taken." Rearmament on a huge scale was the subject of a similar conference held in Berlin on October 14, shortly after the Munich agreement had been reached. The concentration, he urged, must be upon offensive weapons. Everything thought of beforehand, he said, was now "insignificant." Exports must be increased, the Air Force must be multiplied fivefold, the Navy must be armed, and tanks and heavy artillery must be supplied in "large amount." Brutal methods were necessary; if private enterprise was no good, he would make "barbaric use of his plenipotentiary power given to him by the Führer" and go over to a State economy. Hours of work must be increased, women drafted into industry, mutinous workers sent to the forced-labor camps. At a session of the Reich Defense Council on November 18, he spoke for three hours to an assembly that included the Reich ministers and the commanders of the armed forces with their chiefs of staff; although the economy was already strained, said Goering, the production of armaments must be increased threefold. In the same month he was even pressing the Foreign Ministry to renew negotiations for trade with Russia, whence the raw materials so badly needed by Germany might be obtained; but these negotiations were to break down the following year because Germany was unable to supply Russia with anything in exchange.[6]

Goering's principal speech of the year was delivered to the Labor Front at the Nuremberg party congress, where he defended his use of compulsory labor and contrasted its success with the conditions of unemployment and the strikes that disfigured the democracies. He spoke of the need to secure Germany's food supplies; the Austrians, he said, should have white bread and the Bavarians more beer! Then once more he challenged the Czechs, and he sneered at the trouble the British were having in Palestine. "It is the states which stand for order, Germany and Italy, which have brought back peace to the world . . . but if hatred wins the day we are utterly and courageously determined to obey our Führer's call in whatever direction he may lead us."[7]

It was in the sphere of economics that Goering felt best able to give his full official support to the persecution of the Jews. His aim, as he was to admit at Nuremberg, was to drive the Jews out of German finance and business, as they had already been driven out of German political and cultural life through the racial apartheid of the Nuremberg Laws, which, as president of the Reichstag, he had announced in 1935. The matter came to a head after the pogrom which Goebbels instigated on the night of November 10 following the murder in Paris on November 7 of a German embassy official by a Jewish youth of seventeen. Goering was angry at the pogrom not because of the suffering caused to the Jews but because of the serious loss of property that it entailed. All Jewish-owned property had been required to be registered earlier in the year, following a decree issued by Goering in April as part of his Four-Year Plan. Now, in a single wave of lawless violence, some of that property had been either stolen or destroyed. Goering was traveling from Munich to Berlin on the night of the pogrom, and when he learned what had happened he complained at once to both Goebbels and Hitler. The outcome was a now-famous meeting at the Air Ministry on November 12, over which he presided; among those present were Goebbels, Funk, Schacht's successor as Minister of Economics, Heydrich and Schwerin von Krosigk, the Minister of Finance.[8]

Goering opened with a lengthy speech. The meeting, he said, had been convened by Hitler's orders to solve the Jewish question one way or another. The problem was mainly an economic one, and these uncoordinated demonstrations, as he termed the pogroms, only in the end harmed him and not the Jews! "Because it's insane to clean out and burn a Jewish warehouse and then have a German insurance company make good the loss! The goods that I need desperately, whole bales of clothing and what not, are being burned; and I miss them everywhere." What was necessary was to eliminate the Jews from the German economy and have their property transferred to the State. The Jews would be compensated in the form of interest on the value of what was confiscated from them as determined by a State trustee. "Naturally this amount is to be set as low as possible," he added. This process of confiscation he called "Aryanizing." On the other hand, he would not tolerate unqualified people seizing Jewish property on the grounds that they were party members; only qualified people should be allowed to take over. He then went into certain details about the method of confiscation to be adopted, adding for good measure that German Jews who had acquired citizenship elsewhere would be entitled to no compensation at all. "We shall try to induce them first through slight and then through stronger pressure and clever maneuvering to let themselves be pushed out voluntarily."

The debate then ranged freely over the methods for segregating the Jews. Heydrich reported 101 synagogues destroyed by fire, 76 demolished and 7,500 stores ruined. Goebbels, by far the most vindictive member of the group, wanted the Jews to be subject to *apartheid* as far as German social life was concerned; Goering just joked about it. When Goebbels seriously put forward the idea of segregation in trains, Goering replied, "I'd give the Jews one coach or compartment. And should . . . the train be overcrowded, believe me, we won't need a law. We'll kick the Jew out and he'll have to sit all alone in the toilet!" Give them their own beaches for bathing, parks for sitting in! Goebbels was not to be fobbed off by Goering's jokes. He felt this was a serious matter requiring legal sanction.

An insurance consultant called Hilgard was then brought into the meeting by Goering. When the windows of stores were broken, said Hilgard, glass had to be imported from abroad and paid for in foreign currency—three million marks' worth. "One could go crazy!" cried Goering. Many broken windows turned out to belong to property rented by Jews and owned by Aryans, who therefore held the insurance policies. Then there was the case of the Markgraf jewelry store, which had been stripped; the insurance claim amounted to 1,700,000 marks. Goering was outraged. "Daluegue and Heydrich," he shouted, "you'll have to get me this jewelry through raids staged on a tremendous scale!" Considerable looting, said Hilgard, was still going on.

There followed a debate on how best to save face and money at the same time.

HILGARD: . . . If we now refuse to honor clear-cut obligations, imposed on us through lawful contract, it would be a black spot on the shield of honor of German insurance.

GOERING: It wouldn't the minute I issue a decree, a law sanctioned by the State.

HILGARD: I was leading up to that.

HEYDRICH: The insurance may be granted, but as soon as it is to be paid it will be confiscated. That way we'll have saved face.

HILGARD: I am inclined to agree with what General Heydrich has just said. First of all use the mechanism of the insurance company to check on the damage, to regulate it and even pay—

GOERING: One moment! You'll have to pay in any case, because it is the Germans who suffered the damage. But there'll be a lawful order forbidding you to make any direct payment to the Jews . . . but to the Minister of Finance.

HILGARD: Aha!

GOERING: What he does with the money is his business. . . .

HEYDRICH: Seven thousand five hundred stores in the Reich . . .

GOERING: I wish you had killed two hundred Jews, and not destroyed so much property.

Among other business discussed was the closing of Jewish businesses in Austria. Goering learned that the plan there was to close some fourteen thousand of the seventeen thousand Jewish-owned stores by the end of the year, and that the rest would be "Aryanized."

GOERING: I must say that this proposal is grand. This way, the whole affair would be wound up in Vienna, one of the Jewish capitals, so to speak, by Christmas or by the end of the year.

FUNK: We can do the same thing here. I have prepared a law elaborating that, as of January 1, 1939, Jews shall be prohibited from operating retail stores and wholesale establishments . . .

GOERING: I believe that we can agree with this law.

The meeting, which was to last nearly four hours, continued with discussion of the problems of expropriating shares and bonds held by Jews and the profits made from such properties as apartment houses and from moneylending. Then the ministers and their colleagues moved on to the expulsion of the Jews from German and Austrian territory; Heydrich gave the figures that so far fifty thousand had left Austria, but only nineteen thousand had left Germany. But prior to expulsion there must be segregation.

GOERING: But, my dear Heydrich, you won't be able to avoid the creation of ghettos on a very large scale, in all the cities. They will have to be created.

Ghettos and complete segregation, thought Heydrich, might lead to slow starvation, disease and crime; how to organize a community within a community where the minority can conduct no business of their own and the majority is unwilling to have any dealings with them? The ministers became more and more entangled in their various ideas for regulations. They decided it could not be achieved in stages. Then Goering had the brilliant idea of fining the Jews a billion marks as a punishment for the murder they had committed in Paris.

GOERING: I shall close the wording this way: German Jewry shall as a punishment for their abominable crimes, et cetera, et cetera, have to pay a fine of one billion. That will work! The swine won't commit another murder. . . . I would not like to be a Jew in Germany!

Had he known the nature of Goering's attitude at this meeting, Hassell would scarcely have recorded in his diary the following month that, after condemning the pogrom openly, Goering had said more privately that this was the last filthy business to which he would lend his name. Hassell regrets Goering did not take the opportunity to join General von Brauchitsch and overthrow Hitler; he is just another appeaser, like France and Britain! He believed that Goering was deeply afraid not only of Hitler, but also of Himmler and Heydrich, although he had told them after the pogrom that he would burn his honorary S.S. uniform. Emmy too had been openly critical. Johannes Popitz, the Prussian Minister of Finance, told Hassell that when he had said to Goering that those responsible should be punished, Goering had replied, "My dear Popitz, do you wish to punish the Führer?" Nevertheless, Popitz said Goering was deeply troubled by the pogrom. On January 24, 1939, Goering signed a letter to Frick as Minister of the Interior informing him that a Central Emigration Office for Jews was to be established in his ministry with Heydrich in control, adding that Heydrich was empowered "to solve the Jewish question by emigration and evacuation in the way that is most favorable under the conditions prevailing at present." When he signed that, Goering introduced Heydrich to the problem of ridding Europe of the Jews, a matter which was soon to be resolved by the "final solution" of genocide.[9]

Goering's methods of work as Plenipotentiary for the Four-Year Plan reveal his nature. He had an excellent memory and was very quick to grasp the essentials of any situation presented to him by his assistants and experts. His interest lay always in policy and seldom in technical details; as Kesselring put it, "Goering . . . could be made to work, and when he felt the need for it he worked with remarkable concentration and perseverance." He enjoyed tossing out ideas that set everyone running. A few hasty words would lead to days of work for his staff. He scribbled his notes in a large diary, writing with an oversize pencil which, according to Diels, "he

held like a dagger." As points arose in conference, he would interrupt the discussion to send telegrams up and down the country;
these telegrams were often unintelligible until checked back with
his office. When Diels complained to him in 1938 about the arbitrary methods that existed in the call-up of women for work in the
munitions factories, Goering broke off and sent a telegram to the
Minister of Labor: "No differences of rank in the women call-up."
He never drafted his decrees; these were left to the experts in his
various departments. Diels, like others, complained bitterly of the
incompetence of Koerner, whom Goering had put in charge of the
Four-Year Plan. He claims that he told Goering in 1939 that Koerner would lose Germany the war, and that the industrialists refused
to consult him because he was unable to understand what they were
saying; to this Goering replied, "He is my friend and I will not
allow anyone to speak badly of him." It was one of Goering's greatest weaknesses as an administrator that he sometimes gave responsible posts to old friends rather than to men qualified for the work.

One of the most acute observers among the Nazi leadership was
Albert Speer, a brilliant young architect whom Hitler suddenly
created Minister of Armament and War Production in 1942. When
he was interrogated about Goering after the war, Speer said, "He is
intelligent, has a flood of desultory ideas and considerable perception, but he lacks the toughness with which to put them into effect.
Some of his ideas are so bad that they outweigh his intelligence. He
undertakes too much. His ideas were at the same time his danger,
because he was not enough of a realist. . . . Until 1939 he was in
good mental shape and carried out the great work of the Four-Year
Plan against the wishes of industry. Until then he showed a great
deal of energy with good and bad qualities. After 1939 his energies
slumped, and only the bad qualities remained." According to Speer,
the Four-Year Plan was Goering's only worth-while effort before
the war; Koerner, in Speer's opinion, as in the opinion of so many
others, was totally incapable of undertaking his great responsibilities.[10]

In July 1938, Goering, unknown to Ribbentrop in Berlin, had
made some confidential inquiries in Britain to discuss whether an
official visit by him would be encouraged by the government.
Chamberlain welcomed the idea, provided "the atmosphere should
be as favourable as possible," particularly in connection with
Czechoslovakia, and Dirksen, the German ambassador in London,

reported in August that it was known Lord Halifax was very enthusiastic about Goering's proposed visit. In addition, certain informal conversations took place with the knowledge of the ambassador between Sir Horace Wilson and Wohltat, an official acting
on behalf of Goering, in which Wilson suggested that Britain
would be willing to sign a nonaggression pact with Germany as a
result of which she might become free to shelve her obligation to
Poland. When the discussions came to the knowledge of Ribbentrop, he bitterly resented these attempts by Goering to interfere
with foreign affairs.

Nevertheless, during the nine months prior to the Munich settlement Goering was constantly conferring with the representatives of
foreign countries. In February he went to Warsaw to continue with
his efforts to keep Poland reassured at the time when the crisis in
Germany's relations with Czechoslovakia was mounting. Pointing
to a picture of the Polish King John Sobieski coming to the relief
of Vienna in 1683, Beck, who was Goering's host, had laughed and
said, "That will not recur." During one of Goering's discussions
with Ambassador Lipski, his aide Bernd von Brauchitsch heard him
reveal what seemed to be secret information about the Luftwaffe.
Afterward, when they were alone, Brauchitsch asked why he had
given away this information. Goering merely laughed and said the
facts he had revealed were ascertainable with a little research by
Lipski; having found them to be true, Lipski would be all the more
ready to believe anything else Goering cared to tell him at the subsequent meeting, whether it were true or false. "That's politics,"
said Goering.[11]

He was now, however, gradually to increase the harshness of his
references to Czechoslovakia. The assurances given to Mastny the
previous November were conveniently forgotten. In April he spoke
of Czechoslovakia as "the appendix" when talking to Henderson,
who noted that this was now Goering's favorite term. The appendix, he said, should be cut up and divided among Poland, Hungary
and Germany. On another occasion he declared that "the incorporation of the Sudetens into the Reich" would be "sooner or later
inevitable." One night, after dining at the French embassy, Goering asked François-Poncet quite openly what France would do if
Germany were to remove the appendix of Europe. The ambassador
replied formally that France would respect her obligations and give
assistance to the Czechs. At this Goering looked savage and

growled, "Well, so much the worse." To the King of Sweden he talked of pushing the Czechs back to Russia, "where they belong," and the British ambassador in Prague recorded in May that "Goering has lately been making no secret of his intention to liquidate Czechoslovakia this summer."

On the night of May 21, while Henderson was dining with friends in Berlin, some demolition work nearby sounded for the moment like bombing, and he tactlessly remarked that the war seemed to have begun. Goering heard of this later and told him that he too had been startled by the noise, but that his reaction had been, "Those cursed Czechs have begun it!" This story is not so trivial as it sounds, for on the preceding day the Czech government had manned the frontier posts and called up the reservists because, it was declared, Hitler was about to invade. No one knows what lay behind this sudden demonstration. In fact no German troops had been moved, so Hitler was free to make what political use he could of the heightened tension caused by the action of the Czechs.

On May 28 Goering, along with Keitel, Brauchitsch, Raeder, Ribbentrop and others, attended a conference convened by Hitler, at which the Führer gave full expression to his anger with Czechoslovakia and with the sympathy its plight was causing, more particularly in France. While informing the Czechs that he had no aggressive intentions against them, he said to his subordinate leaders and chiefs of staff, "It is my unshakable will that Czechoslovakia shall be wiped off the map." He ordered preparations to be made for military action on October 1.

During the summer, in both June and July, Goering had conversations with Sztójy, the Hungarian minister in Berlin, concerning Hungary's part in the attack on Czechoslovakia, which should, he suggested, follow a day or two after any German invasion, the aim being to forestall the Poles (who also had minority claims to make). For, said Goering, "she ought not to rely on Germany's pulling the chestnuts out of the fire all alone." The Hungarian minister replied proudly that Hungary did not wish "to receive anything as a gift." It was obvious, added Goering, that any invasion by Hungary must be preceded by the necessary provocation. On August 11, Lipski reported that during an informal conversation the previous day Goering had told him that Czechoslovakia would soon cease to exist, and that "he realized the necessity for a common Polish-Hungarian frontier." He added, according to Lip-

ski, that if there were a war over the Sudeten question, the Italians
would be most unlikely to let France attack Germany.[12]

During the uneasy summer of 1938, Hitler mastered his generals,
in spite of a movement led by General Ludwig Beck, Chief of the
Army General Staff, to oppose his plans to wage a war for which his
armies had neither the necessary strength nor readiness. Beck resigned and became involved in one of the first major conspiracies
designed to remove Hitler from power. The question in everyone's
mind, and not least in Hitler's as he spent the summer fulminating
in Berchtesgaden, was the action that might be taken by France
and Britain if and when Germany used open force against Czechoslovakia. Both Marshal Balbo, the Italian Air Minister, and later,
General Vuillemin, head of the French Air Force, visited Germany
and were Goering's guests at Carinhall. When Goering asked Vuillemin what France would do should war break out between Germany and Czechoslovakia, the General could say nothing except
that France would keep her word. But privately he expressed his
view to the French ambassador that the French Air Force would
not last a fortnight against what he had seen in Germany. The following November Wolfram von Richthofen was to recommend
that the Condor Legion in Spain be trebled to ensure a victory for
Franco, a demand he would justify on the grounds that this would
be good for German rearmament.[13]

There were many indications that Chamberlain wanted the matter settled at the expense of the Czechs; there were even signs that
Britain was becoming angry with Czechoslovakia. "The moment
has come for Prague to get a real twist of the screw," wrote Henderson to Halifax in July. Chamberlain felt that Britain should mediate and get the matter settled once and for all by diplomatic means.
Meanwhile, the anti-Hitler movement in Germany was trying
through its spokesmen in London to persuade the British to stand
up to Hitler, and had even given Halifax knowledge of Hitler's
plans and the existence of the generals' plot in Germany to overthrow him should he order an attack on Czechoslovakia. But the
British had by now decided to put pressure on Czechoslovakia's
President, Eduard Beneš, rather than on Hitler, and Chamberlain
instructed Henderson to let Hitler know that he was ready to visit
Germany and act between him and Beneš.

The war tension in Europe grew. Everyone waited for the sullen
man from Berchtesgaden to speak his mind at Nuremberg, where

the party was due to assemble for its annual week of speeches and celebrations on September 6. The words so much feared were first uttered by Goering on September 10 when he spoke of the Czechs as "this miserable, pygmy race" and their country as "a petty segment of Europe." They were, he shouted, "oppressing a cultured people," and behind them lay "Moscow and the eternal mask of the Jew devil." In Czechoslovakia gas masks were distributed, and the Jews began hastily to leave the country. On September 12 Hitler roared his hatred of his neighbor, but issued no ultimatum. A revolt in the Sudeten area had to be suppressed by force; the French, fearful of having to fulfill their obligations to help the Czechs, now begged Chamberlain to intervene, and to Hitler's astonishment he was informed on September 13 that the British Prime Minister would fly (for the first time in his life) to Germany in order to examine with Hitler "far-reaching German proposals . . . take part in carrying them out, and . . . advocate them in public."

This was the Führer's chance. Everyone in Germany except Hitler himself was dubious of the success war might bring to Germany; even Goering, according to a dispatch from the British embassy dated September 11, did not "regard Germany's prospects in a general war too optimistically." Chamberlain's gesture to Hitler at the same time revealed Britain's hidden hand. The relief was intense everywhere, except in Prague, and not least at Berchtesgaden itself. Hitler smiled.

Goering was at Berchtesgaden when Hitler received Chamberlain on September 15, and he did not mind at all when Chamberlain's desire to speak to Hitler alone, except for the interpreter Schmidt, led to the exclusion of Ribbentrop along with himself from the first conference. Ribbentrop's revenge was to refuse to let Chamberlain have a copy of Schmidt's notes on the three-hour conversation. Chamberlain won nothing from Hitler but a brief period of waiting while he returned to London to consult his colleagues about the proposed secession of the Sudeten region from Czechoslovakia on the basis of the right of self-determination. "I got the impression that here was a man who could be relied upon when he had given his word," said Chamberlain.

On September 17 Henderson went to Carinhall and found Goering "still unwell." Henderson begged Goering to intervene with Hitler and keep him from the precipitate action that Ribbentrop would no doubt encourage. Goering talked loosely about the bad effects of any "catastrophic" action in Czechoslovakia; otherwise he was sure Hitler would now behave with restraint, though he agreed about Ribbentrop. Goering remained "deliberate and restrained in his language" and later spoke in a "very admiring and respectful manner" of Chamberlain.

Meanwhile Hitler continued with preparations for war within three weeks and brusquely urged both the Poles and the Hungarians to lay parallel claims in the name of their minorities to assure the total dismemberment of Czechoslovakia. They did so on September 21 and 22. In the files of the German Foreign Ministry there is a memorandum on a conversation that had taken place between Goering and Hungarian Minister Sztójy at Carinhall on September 16. Goering had urged that Hungary was not "doing enough in the present crisis"; the Hungarian minority in Czechoslovakia was far too silent, and the government was not demanding, as it should have been, the restoration of the Czech areas to Hungary. He also assured the minister that Yugoslavia would take no action if Hungary joined in any conflict with Czechoslovakia on the third or fourth day after any action initiated by Germany.[14] On September 19 Lord Runciman presented to Beneš the British and French proposals that the Sudetenland be handed over to Germany without even holding a plebiscite, in return for which Britain and France would guarantee the new Czech frontiers against unprovoked aggression; an answer to the proposals was required by September 22, when Chamberlain was due to see Hitler for the second time. Beneš refused. Extreme pressure was brought to bear once more; Britain and France, their governments declared, would withdraw all help if Beneš did not accept these terms. On September 21 Beneš capitulated; he had, he said, been "basely betrayed."

Chamberlain returned to Germany and met Hitler at Godesberg on September 22, in the hotel from which Hitler had planned the final stages of his campaign against Roehm. The Prime Minister was appalled to find that Hitler was now no longer satisfied with the Czech capitulation; he demanded immediate military occupation of the Sudetenland by his forces. Hitler did not want capitulation, he wanted the destruction of Czechoslovakia. A military occupation of the Sudetenland would humiliate Beneš and demonstrate his own strength in Europe. Chamberlain, angry, worried and grieved, but still ready to act as mediator, retired to his hotel on the opposite bank of the Rhine. Notes were exchanged across the river between the two hotels, while the world's press grew hungry for hard news. Finally Chamberlain and Hitler met with their advisers in the middle of the night, over the memorandum which Hitler had produced in response to Chamberlain's request, and which the latter felt was an ultimatum to Czechoslovakia. No, said Hitler, not an ultimatum, a memorandum, and, as a simulated concession to Chamberlain, he altered the date of the occupation from September 26 to October 1, the date he had always had in mind. Ribbentrop, but not Goering, was present at this meeting. While Chamberlain flew back to London, Henderson in deep depression knelt in the vast emptiness of Cologne Cathedral and prayed for peace.

In the matter of Czechoslovakia, Goering, along with the generals whom Hitler despised, was on the side of moderation. In taking this position he sacrificed to some extent the warmth of his relationship with the Führer to his rival Ribbentrop, who, new to the experience of power, took every cue from Hitler in order to retain his master's favor. In the current situation, it was a matter of who dared to bluff longest, and Hitler had most to gain by bluffing and the right temperament to play the game. When he learned that the Godesberg ultimatum was rejected not only by Prague but also by the cabinets of France and Britain, he delivered a wild, violent, uncontrolled speech against Beneš at the Sportpalast on September 26, claiming he would have the Sudetenland at any cost by October 1. He went to the limit in challenging the timidity of Britain and France, but, in doing so, brought protests on his head from other quarters, including the remote and isolated United States. Prague now claimed to have a million men under arms, and France was mobilizing. The German public were utterly unresponsive to the idea of a noble war. Hitler, according to Schmidt, who translated his urgent letter to Chamberlain on the night of September 27, seemed to be shrinking from the "extreme step," but Goering had told Henderson during the day that if the Czech government did not accept the terms of the Godesberg memorandum by two o'clock the following day, mobilization and action would follow. He was "neither nervous nor excited, but absolutely confident," wrote Henderson to Halifax. On September 28 Hitler kept in touch with Goering, the generals and Ribbentrop. Goering, according to Jodl, was saying, "A great war can hardly be avoided any longer. It may last seven years, and we will win it." Even the British fleet was mobilized. During the morning the British, French and Italian ambassadors all intervened under instruction; François-Poncet had to seek Henderson's help to secure an interview with Hitler. Henderson telephoned Goering and told him that it was a matter of fresh proposals, and that peace or war would result. Goering did not wait to hear what the proposals were. "You need not say a word more," he said to Henderson. "I am going immediately to see the Führer."

Goering saw Hitler and again urged a peaceful solution by negotiation. He was supported by Schwerin von Krosigk and Neurath. According to Henderson, who regarded Goering at this supreme moment in the light of a friend and an ally for the British and French ambassadors, he most vehemently accused Ribbentrop of inciting war. It was even said that he "shouted that he knew what war was, and he did not want to go through it again," though of course, if the Führer ordered it, "he would go himself in the first and leading plane," and that "Ribbentrop should be in the seat next to him." How much of this Goering roared in the presence of Hitler and how much to the men congregated in the anterooms of the Chancellery cannot now be determined, but Henderson maintained that Goering called Ribbentrop a "criminal fool" in front of Hitler. How far Goering was influential in diverting Hitler from war also cannot be known, for it was at this juncture that Mussolini himself intervened with a plea for the postponement of hostilities and an offer to join personally in mediation with the Czechs. Arrangements were made for Mussolini, Chamberlain, French Premier Daladier and Hitler to meet in Munich the following day. When Chamberlain announced this in the House of Commons the hysterical outburst of relief created a wild and disturbing scene. Jan Masaryk, the Czech ambassador to Britain, was there and looked on appalled by this shameful display. No representative of Czechoslovakia had been invited to Munich. Simultaneously, the German generals canceled their plot to remove Hitler from power, and forever after they used Chamberlain's and Daladier's assent to Munich as their excuse for inaction.

Goering used the intervention of Mussolini to edge Ribbentrop out of being a principal in formulating the Munich agreement. At Nuremberg he described how Attolico, the Italian ambassador to Germany, telephoned him at the orders of Mussolini before seven in the morning and insisted on seeing him personally and not Ribbentrop. Goering claimed that, accompanied by Attolico and Neurath (who was still influential with Hitler and held the artificial title of chairman of the Secret Cabinet Council, a body that did not exist), he went to see Hitler and persuaded him to accept Mussolini's offer. When in the afternoon Goering learned from François-Poncet that Daladier would join the conference, he cried, "*Gott sei Dank! Bravo!*" Goering, Neurath and Baron von Weizsaecker, State Secretary of the Foreign Ministry, who was deeply distressed at what he regarded as Ribbentrop's irresponsibility, together drafted a written proposal which should be presented the following day as Mussolini's personal solution to the problem. When Hitler had approved also, Schmidt translated it into French at their request, and the translation was given to the Italian ambassador for presentation by Mussolini the following day, when it reappeared at the Munich conference in Italian and was duly retranslated into German by Schmidt. The proposals contained in this much translated document were designed to circumvent further trouble, and Mussolini's authority was needed to forestall a plan that Ribbentrop was anxious to put forward himself. It was, in Henderson's words, "a combination of Hitler's and the Anglo-French proposals," and Mussolini accepted the subterfuge in order to smooth the path to peace and avoid what everyone present, except perhaps Hitler himself and his shadow Ribbentrop, regarded as "a futile and senseless war." Before Goering had left for Munich he had told Bodenschatz that he would do everything he could to avert hostilities.

Hitler was in a bad mood throughout the negotiations. When the protocol was at last ready for signature at two in the morning both Goering and Mussolini were "jubilant" and the atmosphere grew relaxed, though Hitler was nervous and moody; he sat glaring, crossing and uncrossing his legs. When the time for signature came, the inkstand was found to contain no ink.

When all was done, Goering emerged from the conference room and exclaimed to everyone, "This is peace." On October 1 German troops crossed the frontier into the Sudeten territory. The same day Goering summoned Mastny to his office and told him Hitler would no longer tolerate Beneš as the Czech head of state. Unless he resigned, Germany would be completely ruthless. Beneš resigned on October 5, left Prague the following day and stayed on his estate in southern Bohemia until, on October 22, he finally left his country and went into exile in England. He was succeeded as President by Dr. Emil Hácha, an elderly and frail judge.

For a few more months Czechoslovakia was kept in being, though both Poland and Hungary seized, on threat of force, a further 8,150 square miles of territory in which there were Polish and Hungarian minorities. The country was ruined, both militarily and economically.

Czechoslovakia's loss was Germany's gain; for example, Germany acquired the Skoda works. Within a matter of days Hitler was planning the "liquidation" of the remainder of the country and looking ahead to the occupation of Memel. At a staff conference Goering had held on October 14, he was blunt about the future exploitation of the Sudetenland and added that "Czechia and Slovakia would become German domains," and that "everything possible must be taken out." On October 17 Ferdinand Durcansky, the Slovak leader, and Franz Karmasin, a leader of the German minority in Slovakia, met Goering in Berlin to discuss the establishment of complete independence for Slovakia, following the autonomy she had secured after Munich. They wanted, they said, "very close political, economic and military ties with Germany." Goering noted afterward, "A Czech State minus Slovakia is even more completely at our mercy. Air base in Slovakia for operation against the East is very important." When he met Durcansky again on November 11, he said that he himself favored the creation of an independent Slovakian State and "an autonomous Ukraine oriented toward this independent Slovakia."[15]

During October, Hitler endeavored to create a diplomatic split between France and Britain. He took François-Poncet up to the high mountain retreat known as Eagle's Nest and there tempted him by expressing his love for France and his hatred for Britain, in spite of the little certificate of peace he had signed at Chamberlain's request to sweeten the Prime Minister's return to Britain. Goering was quoted in the press as saying, "With a man like Monsieur Daladier it is possible to make politics." A Franco-German agreement was proposed.

The notes made by Goering after a conversation he had with Lipski on October 21 survive. "Maintain contact; avoid misunderstandings," he scribbled, and then he noted the principal worry expressed by Lipski, which was over Carpatho-Ukraine, a territory of Slovakia where Poland was afraid there might be a Communist uprising. Lipski wanted this particular area to be ceded to Hungary, but not the whole of Slovakia, which lay along her southern frontier. Poland by now, in fact, was beginning to play the part of a European power, and it pleased Germany for a while to flatter her; nevertheless, Ribbentrop now began to bargain for Danzig, using Carpatho-Ukraine as a lever. That these were not the first conversations on such matters with Poland is suggested by a report to Halifax by the British ambassador in Warsaw dated October 25 saying Goering had been bargaining along these lines with Lipski before that date.

On November 2 Ciano met Goering in Vienna. He was, Ciano noted, wearing a flashy gray suit, an old-fashioned tie passed through a ruby ring, with more rubies in the rings on his fingers, and he had a large Nazi eagle set with diamonds in his buttonhole. Ciano thought he looked like Al Capone. Goering tried in vain to interest Ciano in his denunciations of the Hungarians, who, he claimed, were in league with the democracies. Then he attacked King Boris of Bulgaria for planning a union with Yugoslavia. Ciano remained bored and Goering returned to Berlin, where the November pogrom was about to take place, and gave his attention to the economic problems presented by the Jews.

Robert Coulondre, the new French ambassador to Berlin, first met Goering toward the end of November and was most surprised when Goering deliberately suggested that he should circumvent any difficulties he might experience in dealing with Ribbentrop by coming directly to him. Goering took the ambassador aside and warned him of the gravity of the general strike which was due to take place in France the following day—the work, he warned, of the Communists.

During January and February 1939, Goering's health began to trouble him increasingly and interfered with his work. Ever since his attitude prior to the Munich Conference he had been out of favor with Hitler, and the range of the duties he had undertaken began to weigh down on him. He spent more time at Rominten and Carinhall, and the field of foreign affairs was left open to Ribbentrop. On February 18 Henderson reported to Halifax that Goering, whom he had seen that morning, had told him he was extremely tired; he "had taken off forty pounds in weight and wanted to remove sixty." So he was going away soon for a holiday. "People can make what mistakes they like," he said to Henderson. "I shall not care." Goering went on to say how much he feared British rearmament if her comparatively unstable government fell and was replaced by one with Churchill as Prime Minister. Henderson tried to allay his fears and said that the threat lay rather in unremitting German rearmament, "just as if Munich had never been." Goering then claimed that Germany was unable to afford her rearmament; both he and Hitler would far rather be spending the money on beautiful buildings and the improvement of social conditions. Henderson came away convinced of Goering's sincerity. "I believe, in fact, that he would now like in his heart to return to the fold of comparative respectability," wrote Henderson. "As the Field Marshal said to me this morning, tyrants who go against the will of their people always come to a bad end."

Goering was in need of a holiday. He was suffering from an inflammation of the jaw which resulted in an abscess that had to be treated for three weeks by one of his doctors, Professor von Eiken. Goering had been invited by Balbo in 1938 to visit Tripoli, and at the end of February, when he was convalescent, he decided to accept the invitation and combine it with a holiday in San Remo. He and Emmy went to Tripoli from Naples on the German ship *Monserate*. On the way back Goering wanted to put into Spain to meet Franco, but when the ship was in sight of Valencia the visit was suddenly cancelled, much to Goering's annoyance, and the party landed at Genoa and then traveled by land to San Remo. Ribbentrop had heard of the projected visit and effected its cancellation. On March 12, when they were in San Remo, Hitler suddenly ordered Goering to return at once to Berlin.

Throughout the winter the Czechs had been subjected to merciless bullying by Hitler and Ribbentrop which reduced their government to a state of vassalage, and the promised guarantee to their frontiers was not ratified by either France or Britain. Only once did the Czech government rebel against this endless provocation. This was early in March, when Hácha dissolved the troublesome autonomous governments of Slovakia and Ruthenia, arrested their leaders and, on March 10, proclaimed martial law. It was a fatal decision; it gave Hitler the excuse he wanted to use force and at the same time Chamberlain and Daladier an opportunity to turn their faces away from the dismembered country whose frontiers they were supposed to protect. On March 13 he forced the Slovak leaders to declare their independence, and on the same night the pathetic scene took place in Berlin when Hácha, old and abject, his face flushed with agitation, pleaded for what was left of his country before the contemptuous eyes of Hitler and Ribbentrop.

Hitler realized instinctively the values of melodrama and the effectiveness of conducting one-sided negotiations in the small hours of the night, when the world outside is dark and empty and both courage and the capability to resist are at their lowest. The lights were shaded in Hitler's study. Hácha was alone at the Chancellery except for his Foreign Minister, Chvalkovsky, and they had been kept waiting in an anteroom until after one o'clock. Hitler listened to the President's broken voice and then coldly informed him invasion would begin at six o'clock. It rested with him, said Hitler, whether the German entry would be accepted peaceably by the Czechs or made the occasion for armed resistance and immediate bloody defeat.

Hácha had sat motionless while Hitler talked; only his eyes, said Schmidt afterward, showed he was alive. He suffered from a weakened heart. Helplessly he asked Hitler what he could possibly do in the time left to him. Hitler told him to telephone Prague at once and make the best arrangements he could; then he was dismissed and conducted from Hitler's presence by Goering and Ribbentrop, who began at once to urge him to make an immediate decision. Schmidt, meanwhile, was attempting to reach Prague by telephone, only to find that the line was out of order. While Ribbentrop raged at the telephone exchange, Goering bullied Hácha. At Nuremberg he admitted threatening to bomb Prague in order, as he put it, "to accelerate the whole matter."[16] The line to Prague was cleared, but when Hácha began to speak it failed once more. Ribbentrop was beside himself with anger, but all he could do was threaten the dismissal of the telephone supervisor and the operating staff. Suddenly Goering's voice could be heard shouting for Dr. Morell, Hitler's physician, who was in attendance, it seemed by some thoughtful prearrangement. "Hácha has fainted!" cried Goering, in great agitation. "I hope nothing happens to him. It has been a very strenuous day for such an old man." The one thing no one wanted was for Hácha to die in Hitler's Chancellery. Using a hypodermic needle provided by Goering,[17] Morell revived the President by administering injections, and he recovered sufficiently to speak to Prague when a line was hastily improvised. By four o'clock in the morning of March 15 Czechoslovakia's independence was signed away, and by evening Hitler stood triumphant in Prague. He had at last overcome the frustrations of Munich, but in doing so he had finally destroyed the mood of appeasement in both Britain and France.

On March 16, while Hitler was still away, Lipski, the Polish ambassador, called on Goering and complained bitterly that for five days he had been trying vainly to see either Ribbentrop or Weizsaecker. He protested that such treatment was intolerable when Germany was taking an action in Slovakia that vitally affected Poland. Goering passed the matter off as innocently as he could, saying he had only just come back from his holiday in Italy. Poland was in fact alarmed at this sudden extension of her frontiers with Germany, and she was even more discomfited when, less than a week later, on March 22, Lithuania ceded Memel to Germany. It provided only too likely a precedent for Danzig, over which there was a growing dispute between Ribbentrop and Józef Beck. By the end of the month the rift between Poland and Germany over Danzig and the Corridor was public knowledge, and on March 30 Chamberlain so abandoned his policy of appeasement as to give Beck assurances of British and French support in the event of any threat to Polish independence. On March 31 Chamberlain repeated these assurances in the House of Commons. On April 3 Hitler, after fulminating in public over Britain and Poland, issued his top-secret orders (the famous Operation White) requiring the German forces to be ready by September 1, 1939, to make a surprise attack on Poland. On April 6 Britain signed a pact of mutual assistance with Poland, in spite of the latter's obsolete Army and Air Force and the foolhardiness of her militaristic leaders. Meanwhile, a visit by the president of the British Board of Trade to Germany was canceled, and Goering expressed, according to Henderson, "the utmost indignation that it should be cancelled for such a trifle!"

Goering revealed at Nuremberg that the "whole matter" of the occupation of Czechoslovakia "had been carried out for the most part over my head." He never visited Prague, then or on any subsequent date. Hitler, he said, had rejected the advice he had sent him in a letter from San Remo to take a moderate line with Czechoslovakia and achieve his aims through economic penetration and not by force of arms. Economic penetration no doubt represented the thinking behind a memorandum Goering had written on February 18 to the German Foreign Ministry, in which he urged the acquisition by the Reichsbank of a large section of the gold reserve of the Czechoslovak National Bank, since this reserve was "urgently re-

quired for the execution of important orders given by the Führer."
When Goering, in response to Hitler's summons, had arrived in
Berlin on the morning of March 14, the Führer had claimed to
have evidence that Russian aviation commissions were present at
certain Czech airdromes in flagrant violation of the Munich agreement. When Hitler went to Prague to survey his conquest it was
Ribbentrop, not Goering, who went with him.

It was Ribbentrop's turn to be mortified, however, when Goering
visited Rome the following month. Mussolini had on April 7 sent
his army across the water to seize Albania, which gave the Axis a
valuable foothold in the territory bordering Greece and Yugoslavia.
On April 13 France and Britain offered guarantees to both Greece
and Rumania. The following day Ciano was welcoming Goering in
Rome, later noting in his diary how harshly Goering spoke of Poland. On April 15 Goering met Mussolini; they agreed, among
other matters, that economic settlements with Russia were important for both Germany and Italy, and that both countries must
concentrate on rearmament. Goering believed war to be inevitable,
but hoped they would manage to postpone it until 1942 at the
earliest; by then their combined forces would be so strong they
would be invincible. Nevertheless, he added, Italy and Germany
should remain in a steady state of mobilization even though this
should not be apparent to the world outside. He returned to Berlin
by train on April 17.

Goering was bitterly affronted that Ribbentrop and not he was
presented by the King of Italy with the coveted decoration of the
Collar of the Annunziata when the military alliance between Germany and Italy known as the Pact of Steel was signed in Berlin on
May 22. Dino Alfieri, who was later to become ambassador in
Berlin, was present at the banquet inaugurating the Pact of Steel
and saw Goering in a quiet moment slip into the dining room and
reverse the cards on the dinner table that had placed him on
Ciano's left and Ribbentrop on the right. When, however, he
returned to the reception and saw Ribbentrop receiving the Collar,
the result was what Alfieri could only describe as "a tragedy in
miniature," and it was with great difficulty that Goering was restrained from leaving the embassy immediately.[18] Goering felt,
indeed he knew, that it was he who had laid the foundation of the
German-Italian alliance, and Ciano, his sharp eyes always alert for
signs of human weakness, noted in his diary the tears of envy that

stood in Goering's eyes as he looked at the Collar of the Annunziata hanging from Ribbentrop's neck. The German ambassador
reported to Ciano that Goering had "made a scene," and Ciano
promised he would try to get another Collar for Goering. It was to
prove a most difficult business that dragged on until May of the
following year. Goering blamed Ciano for mishandling the matter,
and every effort was made through diplomatic channels to prise
another Collar out of the King. The tragicomedy of Goering and
the Collar became a refrain underlying the relations between the
two countries. Eventually Ciano interceded with Mussolini, and
Mussolini with the little King, to whom, as Ciano put it, "the
pitiful situation of the tender Hermann" was described. The King
proved both difficult and obstinate, postponing his consent for as
long as possible, until Mussolini had to intervene once more, saying
it was "a lemon" His Majesty must swallow for the good relations
between the two countries. The King finally consented in May
1940, but raised difficulties over sending the usual telegram of con-
gratulation. Goering, however, insisted on having a telegram with
the Collar, and the King could only complain angrily how distaste-
ful the whole thing had become to him. Goering finally received
both his Collar and his telegram from Alfieri, the newly appointed
Italian ambassador.

During May 1937, the German ambassador in Spain complained
of both Goering's and Goebbels' attempts at wholly independent
action in Spain. Goering wanted to be invited to represent Germany in a victory parade, and at the same time to hold discussions
with Franco, but he had instructed Bernhardt, his Four-Year-Plan
representative in Spain, to negotiate this visit. He told Bernhardt
that the ambassador should be prevented from knowing anything
about the matter; he knew that Ribbentrop would scarcely approve.
The ambassador finally heard what was going on and insisted on
taking the arrangements out of the hands of Goering's agents; the
visit, however, was finally abandoned. Ribbentrop himself drafted
a letter of rebuke to Goering about the way in which the whole
matter had been handled, but although the draft of the letter was
filed, it was apparently never sent.

It was at this period that reports of Goering's ill-health recurred;
he had returned to San Remo.[19] Bodenschatz told the Polish military attaché, who passed the news on to the British embassy, that
"there was no hope of restoring . . . Goering's health, and his

political eclipse at the hands of . . . Ribbentrop was now complete." By the middle of May, Henderson gathered that these rumors were exaggerated, and that Goering had "a form of diabetes," but was improving under a doctor's care in San Remo. "There is, on the other hand," added Henderson, "no doubt that he is out of favor with Hitler at the moment."

On May 23, the day after the signing of the Pact of Steel (in which the signatories openly stated that they were "united by the inner affinity of their ideologies" and were "resolved to act side by side and with united forces to secure their living space"), Hitler summoned Goering and thirteen other senior officers for the purpose of briefing them on the war to come. Poland, once she had been isolated, was to be attacked at the first suitable opportunity; Germany was to expand her living space east into the granaries of the Ukraine; the people of the subject territories would provide Germany with forced labor. If Britain and France declared war, then they must be vanquished in a campaign striking through Holland and Belgium. Hitler seemed in a mood to take on everyone simultaneously. In the minutes of this meeting there is no record of either questions or dispute; these were the Führer's orders.

On May 28, Henderson reported a conversation he had had the previous day at Carinhall, in which Goering had complained bitterly of British hostility to Germany. Henderson described to him the shock that the German action on March 15 had been to the British people and to himself; it had undone all the work he had tried to do in establishing friendly relations between Germany and Britain during the past two years. It was the work, he said, of the "wild men" of the party; at this, according to Henderson, Goering became "a little confused" and explained that, after all, he had been away at San Remo. Then he blamed the obstinacy of the Czechs and tried to persuade Henderson that if Britain went to war over Poland she would stand to lose more than Germany by such an action; the Polish-British alliance, in fact, was only encouraging Poland to adopt a foolishly intransigent attitude to Germany's fair demands. Henderson pointed out that there was always a limit to Polish compromise, and that the wild men must not push the Polish issue or the issue of Danzig too far. After this exchange of diplomatic threats, Goering showed the ambassador the extensions to Carinhall and the colored sketches of certain "naked ladies" representing the Virtues in some sixteenth-century Flemish tapestries which he intended to buy for the decoration of his dining hall. "I got the impression that Goering was pleased to see me," added Henderson in a supplementary report. "Goering is not much better than the others really, but at heart I feel sure he does not want war, and hates Ribbentrop."[20]

A month later the Army's plans for the conquest of Poland were placed on Hitler's desk, and a special meeting of the Reich Defense Council was convened on June 23. Goering, who presided over this meeting of civil and military chiefs, made it clear the war was very close upon them and that the total mobilization of the country to meet it was the purpose of the conference. Seven million men were to be called up, and the deficiency of labor in the war plants and on the farms must be made good by men brought in forcibly from Czechoslovakia and drafted from the concentration camps.[21]

Later, in July, further meetings of the Council were called to plan improvements in the fortification of the West Wall in order to deter French and British intervention when Poland was attacked. Detailed surveys were discussed of the labor force available in Germany and the use of labor drawn from the occupied territories and the concentration camps. On August 24 the British ambassador in Warsaw reported that the Polish ambassador in Berlin had talked to Goering that afternoon. Goering had apparently admitted that "his policy of maintaining friendly relations with Poland . . . had come to nought," and that his influence was now small. He had then added significantly that the chief obstacle to removing tension was not Danzig but Poland's alliance with Britain. Nor would Goering be sidetracked by what seemed to him to be irrelevant issues. During August Albert Voegler, an industrialist in steel who was also a Nazi deputy in the Reichstag, presented Goering with a report that his company had received from America which pointed out that if Britain went to war the United States would eventually follow, and that her war industry could easily outclass that of Germany. Goering merely scoffed at the report; he considered America far too remote to be taken seriously in European politics.[22]

There is no question, therefore, that Goering did not know exactly what Hitler had in mind—a major war of conquest timed to suit Germany's rearmament (of which Goering himself was in general charge) and seizure of those territories Hitler wanted when they were no longer available through diplomatic blackmail.

The moment of ignition might well be September 1, or later; this depended on the reactions of Poland, Britain and France. And, not least, on the reactions of Russia, with which Hitler now saw the advantages of some sort of pact, however temporary. The coldness of Britain and France toward the Soviet Union had not passed unnoticed at the Chancellery. If they were prepared to reject an alliance so patently to their advantage, he was not. The scathing references to Bolshevism usual in Nazi speeches and propaganda slackened noticeably. Early in May, Goering sent Bodenschatz to the British and French embassies to hint that Germany and Russia might soon be reaching an agreement, in the hope that this would modify the attitude of their governments.[23]

Every month that passed without war was to Germany's advantage; this was Goering's view as well as that of all the responsible senior officers. The arbitrary dates decreed in secret by the Führer were always too soon for them. Hitler, isolated for the most part in his mountains, grew more and more egocentric, more and more intolerable to serve. Goering, moreover, was still a sick man. The responsibility of war was the last thing he wanted. "A war is always a risky and unsure business," he said to Bodenschatz. He was forty-six years of age, happily married, with a wife and a baby daughter, both of whom he adored. And he liked to be regarded as the richest man in Europe.[24]

Goering in fact was rich solely because he had to pay for so little; he was rich in perquisites and possessions. Carinhall, Rominten and his house in Berlin on the Leipzigerplatz were maintained by what his accountant, Herr Gerch, called "representation funds." Goering's private life was so involved in official entertainment that he and his wife seldom ate alone, and the expenses that would normally be regarded as private—such as those connected with his daughter—were either absorbed into the general house accountancy or were so negligible as to be easily offset by Goering's official salaries, which totaled some fifty-four thousand marks a year. Gerch, a senior administrative official in Goering's household, estimates that Goering need only have used some fifteen thousand marks a year on such purely personal expenditure.

Goering's comparatively small official income was substantially increased by the earnings from the books published by him or about him; he claimed a substantial part of the royalties earned through the authorized biography which Gritzbach had written for him and on which he also worked himself. Gerch's estimate of these accrued royalties from his biography and other publications is some 840,000 marks. Gerch also confirmed that from industrialists who wanted his favor Goering received substantial sums of money which went into his private account, as well as valuable gifts which went into his art collection. His personal art possessions were kept strictly separate from those acquired for the nation and paid for from Hitler's special *Bilderfond* on Goering's authority. Gerch maintains, against the evidence of other witnesses from his household staff, that Goering never directly asked for presents. It seems, however, that he was frequently consulted as to what he would like to receive from official bodies. He was also by now beginning to deal in art, buying and selling works, which brought him further personal profit.[25] Goering's bank accounts, held by the Thyssen Bank and the Deutsche Bank, were divided into "private" (for his official salaries), "special" (for capital sums and gifts) and "military" (for funds provided by the State).

Early in 1939, Goering acquired further property. Epenstein's widow, Frau Lilli von Epenstein, who had maintained contact with Goering after the Nazis had come to power and who had been a frequent guest at Carinhall, died suddenly and left all the Epenstein property, including the castles of Mauterndorf and Veldenstein, to the Goering family. She specified that Mauterndorf should go to Edda, but Goering did not take the trouble to establish his daughter's legal right to the property, and both castles became nominally his.

Goering thus had everything to lose if Germany went to war unprepared and failed to succeed in the fabulous encounter of which Hitler dreamed. He therefore talked both war and peace, according to the occasion and the men he was with. As his wealth increased, so his spirit for adventure declined, and he no longer stood side by side with the Führer as his friend and comrade. Like the other senior officers, he began to fear Hitler and was soon to dread the fearful summons to the Chancellery or to Berchtesgaden. He retired as much as he decently could to the luxury of Carinhall.

Once again the long days of summer were drawn out like a nerve stretched in tension. Hitler had always gained by waiting for the move his opponents would make under the stress of his threats. He followed this principle with Poland, as he had done so successfully with Czechoslovakia. The tentative approaches to the Soviet

Union by Britain and France on the one hand and by Germany on the other dragged on; for Chamberlain it was sufficient that negotiations for an unwanted mutual-assistance pact were kept as desultory as possible; for Ribbentrop the matter assumed urgency only when he thought the Allies might succeed in bringing Russia into line against German action in Poland. When on August 5 the Anglo-French military mission set sail on a slow boat to Leningrad, Hitler and Ribbentrop decided to step up the pace of their negotiations. Ribbentrop offered to visit Stalin. If a nonaggression pact could be signed, then the ground would be snatched from under the feet of the Allies, and those feet would in consequence be subject to cold.

Meanwhile a strange, unexpected intervention occurred in German-British relations. An idealistic Swedish businessman, Birger Dahlerus, felt inspired to bring Britain and Germany together and stop the drift toward an inevitable war. He sensed that some block existed in the official communications between the leaders of the two countries which a wholly independent mediator might well be able to remove. He was acquainted with Goering, whom he had approached in 1934 when difficulties had been placed in the way of his marriage to a German widow; Goering had stepped in then and solved the matter for him. Subsequently he had been able to help Goering by procuring a business training for his stepson Thomas von Kantzow, who was living in Stockholm, and this led to regular meetings between them in Germany.

Dahlerus had a great love for Britain, where he had lived and worked for ten years and where he still had influential contacts among the industrialists. His visit to Germany convinced him that the Nazis were both ignorant and suspicious of British intentions. He knew the hard core which lay concealed under the seemingly soft surface of the lazy national temperament of the British people, and he felt that this was tempting Hitler to misjudge their real strength. He believed progress might result if a representative of the Nazi leadership were to meet, for informal discussion, some prominent Englishmen outside the diplomatic circle. On the German side he considered that Goering was the right man to approach because he already knew him and because he realized that Goering "did not like the idea of war." Certain friends of Dahlerus in Britain responded seriously to this idea, and on Wednesday, July 5, he obtained an interview with Goering at Carinhall.

He was amazed at the extent of the enlargements to Goering's "sumptuous castle" since he had first seen it, in 1935; even at this time of economic stringency in Germany, he noticed that hundreds of workmen were engaged on these further extensions. A garden party was about to begin, but Goering, in spite of constant summonses to meet his guests, insisted on staying for over an hour to talk to Dahlerus about German-British relations. Goering said that he considered Britain was bluffing and was determined to hamper Germany's proper development. However, he favored the idea of the meeting and agreed to talk to Hitler while Dahlerus consulted his British friends. It was finally agreed that a secret meeting should take place at a house belonging to Dahlerus' wife, a mansion called Sönke Nissen Koog, situated in Schleswig-Holstein, close to the Danish frontier.

Halifax, with whom Dahlerus next discussed the matter, considered the meeting might prove useful, but retained his doubts of Germany's intentions. Hitler permitted Goering to undertake the mission because he saw in it a further way of eliminating British intervention, in which by now, under the influence of Ribbentrop, he no longer seriously believed. As for Ribbentrop, he knew nothing whatsoever about the conference at this stage; later, when he learned about it, he resented these secret meetings with Dahlerus, which were to continue until September 4, four days after the invasion of Poland. Goering regarded the whole affair, therefore, as a most unexpected and welcome opportunity to spike Ribbentrop's guns.

Seven British businessmen attended the conference at Sönke Nissen Koog on August 7.[26] They had stayed there overnight and waited in some state of excitement for the arrival of Goering, who traveled from Berlin by special train accompanied by Bodenschatz and Koerner. Dahlerus, who was so tense with expectation that he had been quite unable to sleep the previous night, opened the conference, and Goering at once adopted his usual frank and friendly manner in answering the questions the Englishmen put to him. He explained at length why the Nazis felt that England was cold and hostile and lacked any understanding of the change that had taken place in Europe as a result of the rebirth of Germany. The English then criticized Hitler's aggressive and "offhand" methods of dealing with the German minority questions. Goering chose this moment to give his audience his "sacred assurance as a statesman and an officer" that Germany did not intend to encircle Poland, and that the settlement of the problems of Danzig and the Corridor would not be followed by demands for territories elsewhere. At lunch Goering proposed a toast to peace, and the outcome of the discussion, which finally ended at six-thirty in the evening with further friendly toasts, was an agreement to recommend that a delegate conference authorized by the British and German governments should meet on Swedish soil to resolve the deadlock over Poland.

Dahlerus has been called an interloper, and there is no doubt, to judge from the tone of his book *The Last Attempt*, that he obtained an intense personal gratification from his self-appointed mission. There is, indeed, an odd air of comedy about the whole affair, as if some intrusive character in a complicated play had grown so insistent on joining in the plot that all the weary protagonists accepted his presence and then made use of him to serve their particular ends. Dahlerus' intervention, therefore, inevitably confused events before the war, and for Goering he became a means of keeping himself at center stage at a time when both Hitler and Ribbentrop were confining him to the wings as a misguided appeaser of Britain.

As the days passed, Goering's motives in his relations with Dahlerus became more and more mixed. Hitler's only interest in Goering as a diplomat was to use him to sever Britain and France from Poland; Goering, aware of this, exploited the situation as much as he could to sever Hitler from Ribbentrop and so regain his influence as the advocate of negotiation. So long as he could keep Dahlerus in active contact with Britain, his own initiative with Hitler could be maintained, if only on the telephone. On the British side, the weakness and desperation of the government are revealed by the degree to which they confided in Dahlerus and made full use of him, though he only met Halifax for the first time on July 19, Chamberlain on August 27, and Henderson on August 29. The final disillusionment of this amateur diplomat was not to be expressed until he was cross-examined at Nuremberg in 1946; yet, at the time, his desire to help seemed to shine like a "good deed in a naughty world." But the professional diplomats soon defeated his honesty and wrapped his goodness in their winding

sheet. In the end he became a ghostly counselor unable to penetrate the gathering mists in spite of a courageous persistence that
lasted even after war had been declared.

Like so many others, he failed to understand sufficiently the
complex character of Goering and to see through the combination
of mainly selfish motives that divided him at this time, though he
certainly saw Goering's lack of moral courage in his relations with
Hitler. What he failed to realize was Goering's inability to resolve
the dilemma created by his circumstances and his character, his
innate desire to be prominent in either of the divergent paths of
peace or war. Goering had to maintain his difficult position beside
a master whose authority he accepted as absolute, while in his heart
he dreaded the trouble, the labors and the losses that total war
would bring to the luxurious existence he had come to regard as
essential to him.

Dahlerus was to meet Goering eighteen times between July 5
and September 4, and to have many other meetings with ministers
and diplomats in London and Berlin. In addition he undertook
innumerable difficult telephone conversations with Goering and
with various British representatives. In the same period he was to
travel between England and Germany and back again twelve times;
four of these journeys were undertaken during the critical three
days of August 25–27. No one could have been more patient or
more desperately hopeful.

The day after the conference at Sönke Nissen Koog, Goering
invited Dahlerus to the island of Sylt, where he was having a brief
holiday, for a further conversation; Bodenschatz had flown to
Berchtesgaden to give Hitler an account of the discussion. Meanwhile Goering said that in his opinion the proposed conference
(now increased by mutual consent to a four-power level to include
Britain, Germany, France and Italy) would be acceptable, provided it was prepared for in advance and its terms of reference were
strictly defined. This was confirmed a few days later and telephoned
by Dahlerus to London. Then followed a long, exasperating silence; most of the British negotiators, it was explained to him, were
away on their annual holiday. He was not to know that the silence
was due to the rival negotiations which were then proceeding in
Moscow and which resulted in the pact between Germany and
Russia and the abandonment of the Russians' halfhearted talks
with the British delegation. The pact provided in public for mutual

nonaggression and in private for the mutual disposal of the territory of Poland and the Baltic States. The announcement of the pact came as a severe shock to Dahlerus.

Meanwhile Goering had been wearing his other guise of the resolute war leader. It was in August that he repeated his famous boast about the Luftwaffe which made headlines in the press: "Germany will not be subjected to a single bomb. If an enemy bomber reaches German soil, my name is not Hermann Goering; you can call me Meier!"[27]

On August 14 he attended with the other commanders in chief a war conference called by Hitler at Berchtesgaden, where the Führer claimed that Britain's leaders were not of the caliber that wages war, that Poland must be defeated within a week and that Russia (he dropped a hint here only of the negotiations that were afoot) was interested in the "delimitation of spheres of interest." There is no sign in the record of the meeting that Hitler had learned anything from the conference organized by Dahlerus, or that Goering spoke up against the preparations which he must have realized were far more likely than not to lead to war with Britain. On August 22, the day after the conclusion of the pact with Russia, Hitler called a further staff conference, at which he expressed his triumph by declaiming his genius, surveying the situation at inordinate length, and harping continually on Britain and her ineffectual position, and on the significance of Russia's alignment with Germany. According to one report, Goering leaped on a table and offered Hitler "bloodthirsty thanks and bloody promises." He hotly denied this story at Nuremberg, pointing out that he did not have the habit of jumping on tables in private houses; to have done so would have shown "an attitude completely inconsistent with that of a German officer." But he agreed that he had led the applause for the speech. After lunch Hitler told them all to close their hearts to pity and "act brutally."

Bloodthirsty thanks or not, Goering was still trying to make contact with Britain. On August 21, writes Lord Halifax in his memoirs, "a cryptic message" was received from Germany that Goering wanted to visit England and see the Prime Minister.[28] Arrangements were made for him to fly in secretly on Wednesday, August 23, and be taken by car to Chequers, the official country seat of Britain's Prime Ministers. He never came, and it appeared subsequently that Hitler had canceled the visit as unlikely to be useful.

So Goering, unable to succeed on his own, decided once more to resort to Dahlerus, from whom he had heard nothing since the conversation at Sylt on August 8. On the morning of August 23, the day after the conference at Berchtesgaden, Goering telephoned Dahlerus, told him the situation had worsened and asked him to come to Berlin. After hasty consultations with the Swedish Prime Minister (who was also on holiday and pooh-poohed the idea that the situation was grave), Dahlerus, acting strictly as a private citizen of Europe, went to Berlin, where he was told by a Swedish friend, a banker, that Goering's influence was less than it had been, because of his "definite repugnance to a war." The friend added that Dahlerus might well be arrested if he discussed peace plans with Goering against Hitler's will. Nevertheless he went, on Goering's invitation, to see him at Carinhall. Goering told him of Germany's strengthened position as a result of the agreement with Russia and "with great eagerness" urged him to fly to London and impress on the Foreign Office that "forthcoming developments would be wholly dependent on British attitude and initiative." He made it plain that Ribbentrop, now on his way back from Moscow, would do nothing to ease the situation. Goering then drove Dahlerus back to Berlin in a sports car; the people in Berlin recognized Goering at the traffic lights and, to his delight, cheered him on his way.

Goering had told Dahlerus he was about to see Lipski and then Hitler. In the conversation with Lipski which followed he said how sorry he was that his policy of maintaining friendly relations with Poland had "come to naught," but he no longer had the influence to do any more.[29] What mattered was not so much the future of Danzig, Goering said, as Poland's alliance with Britain.

That night, speaking on the telephone, Goering renewed Dahlerus' hopes that he might still be useful if he went immediately back to London. He flew there by passenger plane the following morning, Friday, August 25, and gathered, after conversations with Halifax, that the governments were in active touch once more; Henderson was seeing Hitler. That night, with official help, Dahlerus managed to speak by telephone to Goering, who left a conference with Hitler to take the call. Goering sounded nervous and uneasy; he said war might break out at any minute. The situation had worsened, he added, because of the pact England had signed that afternoon with Poland. On Saturday morning, August 28,

Dahlerus saw Halifax once more, told him what Goering had said and added that "Goering was the only man in Germany who might be able to prevent a war." The Prime Minister then approved Dahlerus' suggestion that Halifax should send Goering a personal letter confirming Britain's desire to reach a peaceful settlement.

Dahlerus returned to Berlin immediately by special plane and was taken that evening by car to Goering's personal train, which he found halted at a wayside station not far from Carinhall. Goering was "very grave," repeated some standard complaints about the ill-treatment of German minorities in Poland and for a while would scarcely let Dahlerus speak. For a whole hour they talked while Dahlerus purposely withheld the letter, delivering it finally as a climax to his assertions that Britain was eager for peace. Goering fell on the letter, opening it quickly and nervously; he became impatient with his uncertain English and asked Dahlerus to translate it with care in order to bring out every shade of meaning. He listened tensely and seriously, and then they left the train and drove immediately to the Chancellery in Berlin.

It was midnight. The place was in darkness and Hitler had gone to bed. Goering sent Dahlerus back to his hotel to wait while he stayed on in the hope that the Führer could be roused to study the letter. Dahlerus did not know that August 26 had been the day scheduled by Hitler for the invasion of Poland, and that on the previous day, when the Anglo-Polish pact was announced and Mussolini had admitted by letter he could not offer Germany military assistance, Hitler had telephoned Goering canceling the operation.[30] Goering had asked if this was temporary or for good, and Hitler's reply had been, "No, I will have to see whether we can eliminate British intervention."

No wonder, therefore, that Goering thought Hitler would not mind being disturbed. No sooner had Dahlerus reached his hotel than he was chased back to the Chancellery, where he was amazed to find the place transformed from darkness to light, like a stage where the curtain has suddenly risen on a scene filled with activity. There followed one of those fantastic interviews with Hitler that revealed the disturbance of his mind. Dahlerus was led over the exquisite carpets of the famous long gallery in the new wing of the Chancellery, past walls on which hung masterpieces of art, and between masses of orchids that lined the path to the Führer. Hitler stared at him with a fixed gaze, then welcomed him and proceeded to give him the customary lecture on German history and policy, during which he became more and more excited. Dahlerus managed after some considerable time to break in and say that he had lived in Britain as a workingman, and this so captivated Hitler's curiosity that he broke off to question him at length about this unique and unexpected experience. Then, "his face stiff" and his movements "peculiar," Hitler returned to the set groove of his own arrogant ambition, the greatness of his Army and his unconquerable Air Force. Goering, who had been silent as a schoolboy in the headmaster's study, "giggled contentedly" as Hitler praised the Luftwaffe. When Dahlerus, speaking very quietly because he realized that Hitler's "mental equilibrium was patently unstable," pointed out the strength of Britain and France and their ability to blockade Germany, Hitler's behavior became suddenly abnormal. His voice blurred, and he started to jerk out words and phrases as he stood in the center of the room, his eyes staring: "If there's war, then I'll build U-boats, build U-boats, U-boats, U-boats, U-boats . . ." He choked. When he had gained some self-control, he shrieked out violently, "I'll build aircraft, aircraft, aircraft, and destroy my enemies!" Dahlerus was horrified and looked toward Goering, but Goering "did not turn a hair."

Hitler continued, his eyes glazed and his voice unnatural, revealing a fanatical belief that Germany's strength could overcome any form of opposition. The discussion culminated in a proposal from Hitler that Dahlerus should return to London and explain the German case. Drawing on his experience as a businessman, Dahlerus said he would do so if the exact nature of Germany's demands on Poland could be explained to him, for example about the Corridor to Danzig. Hitler gave the solitary smile his visitor saw that night, and Goering at once tore a map of Poland from an atlas and marked off with quick, rough strokes the territory Germany wanted. Then this strange conference in the small hours of the night turned into an attempt to fix in Dahlerus' mind—he was allowed to write down nothing, for security reasons—the terms of a pact offered by Hitler to Britain if she in her turn would help Germany obtain Danzig and the Corridor, and, for good measure, the former German colonies in Africa. Hitler became excited and difficult to pin down to essentials; Goering was self-satisfied and silent most of the time. His "strictly formal and obsequious behavior toward his chief" came as a deep shock to Dahlerus, who "resented" Hitler's manner to Goering, while the latter's fawning humility seemed to him utterly repellent.[31]

The interview ended about four o'clock in the morning; it was now Sunday, August 27, and some twelve hours later Dahlerus was in Downing Street with Chamberlain, Halifax and Sir Alexander Cadogan of the Foreign Office, trying as clearly as he could to elucidate the points in the German offer in an atmosphere of calm skepticism. It was finally decided to use Dahlerus as a secret messenger to test Hitler's advance reactions to England's response to the German proposals. Goering was telephoned; he consulted Hitler, who agreed to receive Dahlerus a second time in the capacity of unofficial diplomat. Once more the Swedish messenger settled down to learn by heart what might not be put on paper.

While the doors opened and closed on these secret conferences, the public atmosphere in both Germany and Britain was very tense. Dahlerus' business friends had clustered anxiously round him, acting as a screen against curiosity, when his special German plane landed at Croydon. Air communications between the two countries had been severed. In Britain there was partial mobilization; families were parting; trains were running hours late. In Germany rationing of food, soap, coal and clothing was being announced, while troop movements were only too obvious.

By a quarter past eleven that night Dahlerus was back in Berlin with Goering. The British reaction did not please Goering, and he rubbed his big nose. Dahlerus, who fully realized the solemnity of the moment and was determined to make the Germans understand the British position, was careful to make every detail clear. Goering said in the end, according to Dahlerus, that "he, personally, quite appreciated what Britain felt, but that he doubted if Hitler would do the same." He saw Hitler and obtained an unexpectedly reasonable response from him; Goering telephoned that the Führer was ready to receive a British note along the lines explained by Dahlerus, who surprised the British embassy by telephoning them shortly before two in the morning requesting an immediate meeting. The coded telegram explaining the nature of his mission did not arrive until an hour later!

After leaving the embassy, Dahlerus, who had not been to bed for two successive nights, bathed and then went straight by car to Goering's special train. Goering received him in a green dressing gown fastened at the waist with a jeweled buckle; he was in a

cheerful mood and showed off the skill of the German Intelligence
Service by giving his guest an exact account of his telephone call
to the embassy and the surprise that it had caused. There was no secrecy about the matter as far as Goering was concerned. Dahlerus
met many senior members of Goering's staff—Koerner, Milch,
Udet and Bodenschatz. No secret was made about the preparations
for war; they all had lunch in the open air under the shade of the
surrounding beech trees, and Goering showed Dahlerus where the
attacks would be made if war broke out. He also described his
Luftwaffe headquarters at Oranienburg, which had been blasted
out of a cliff near the railway. Goering confided in him that his
relations with Ribbentrop were bad, and Dahlerus "received the
definite impression that there was a battle of wills going on between Goering . . . and other members of the government."

All seemed set for negotiations to start. Dahlerus, in spite of his
excitement, was at last able to get some sleep. The following day,
August 29, he went to Goering's office, where "Goering dashed up
to me, pressed my hand, and said excitedly: 'We'll have peace.
Peace has been assured.' "

Dahlerus went straight to the British embassy; there he met
Henderson for the first time and found him deeply skeptical, even
about Goering, who, he said, was slightly different from the other
Nazi leaders but was frequently guilty of lying when it suited him
to do so. Nevertheless, they agreed that Goering was a far easier
man to deal with than the rest. Henderson, who looked tired, said
how much he dreaded meeting Hitler that evening to receive the
German reply to Britain's formal communication.

That night Dahlerus learned how badly the meeting had gone.
Hitler had inserted a new demand as the next stage in his plan to
make any negotiations with Poland abortive, while at the same time
putting Britain as far as possible in a position where she would be
unwilling to use force. Evidently the influence of Ribbentrop was
again replacing that of Goering. The demand was for Britain to see
that a Polish representative would be in Berlin the following day,
August 30, to negotiate on behalf of his government. Henderson
had protested violently at this ultimatum, as he called it.

While Forbes of the British embassy was telling Dahlerus this
disastrous piece of news, Goering himself telephoned, "exceedingly
nervous and upset," and asked Dahlerus to visit him at once.
Dahlerus found him not only nervous but angry. Goering put the

blame squarely on Henderson and fiercely underlined with his red pencil the points in the German note that he considered specially significant. He talked now like Hitler, against Britain, against Poland, near whose borders the German Army was massing. "Sixty German divisions—about one million men—are there waiting, but we all hope nothing will happen. The Poles are mad . . ." Only the hope of an agreement with Britain was preventing Hitler from marching in to stop the atrocities the Poles were at that moment practicing against the German minorities. Hitler was working on a plan to present to the Poles. Again Goering tore a page from an atlas and marked off the territories it would suit Germany to acquire. He begged Dahlerus to return to London in a special German plane; he then thanked him for what he had done, in case they never met again, hinting that there were certain people who were determined to prevent Dahlerus from "getting out of this alive." By "certain people" he meant Ribbentrop. At five o'clock on the morning of Wednesday, August 30, the indefatigable Swede left by air for London, where elaborate precautions were taken to shield him from publicity.

In Downing Street the atmosphere still remained one of skepticism of Hitler's and Goering's intentions. Britain would not encourage Poland to send any representative to Berlin; negotiations should take place on neutral territory. Dahlerus telephoned Goering with this suggestion, but Goering turned it down flat. "Nonsense," he said. "The negotiations must take place in Berlin, where Hitler has his headquarters." Dahlerus flew back to Berlin with further assurances from Britain that they still wanted Hitler to negotiate. Still sleepless, he left Berlin shortly after midnight on the morning of Thursday, August 31, to meet Goering on his train —just, in fact, as Henderson was leaving a stormy interview with Ribbentrop following the British answer to Hitler's "ultimatum." Ribbentrop had in the most insolent manner read Henderson the text of Hitler's terms to Poland in such a way that he could not grasp them, and had then refused to give him a copy for study, declaring that it was too late in any case, since it was past midnight and the Poles had failed to send their representative within the time limit that had been set by Hitler. When Goering boasted to Dahlerus about the generosity of Hitler's terms, a copy of which he had with him, Dahlerus asked permission to telephone the embassy. When he found out what had happened, he begged Goering to intervene and see at least that the ambassador received a copy of the terms. Goering paced about nervously, then said suddenly, "I'll do it. I'll take the responsibility! You can telephone him." While Dahlerus dictated the terms to Forbes at the embassy, Goering kept hurrying him, anxious for the call to be over, because, it seemed, of his fear of Ribbentrop. Goering then persuaded his visitor to spend the rest of the night on the train.

On August 31, Weizsaecker, Ribbentrop's deputy and the moderate man on the Foreign Ministry staff, felt the situation to be so dangerous that he begged Hassell to intercede and warn Goering about Ribbentrop's intolerable attitude in recklessly encouraging Hitler to make war. "Carinhall will go up in flames," was in his view the best way to put it to Goering. Hassell was able to speak to Goering on the telephone through the help of the latter's sister, Olga Rigele, who was a friend; Goering maintained that the Poles must send a negotiator at once and told him to impress on Henderson the absolute necessity for this. Hassell was left with the impression that Goering genuinely wanted peace, and Olga Rigele told him with tears in her eyes how Goering had embraced her and said, "Now, you see, everybody is for war. Only I, the soldier and field marshal, am not." But Goering had kept himself apart, at his "battle station" at Oranienburg, though he returned to Berlin later that day.[32]

By ten o'clock on the morning of August 31, Dahlerus was back in the British embassy, and Forbes took him to meet Polish Ambassador Lipski, with whom Henderson had been in constant touch since the small hours of the night. They found Lipski too distraught even to study Hitler's proposals, so Dahlerus dictated them to a secretary and left. Meanwhile Lipski had told Forbes that if there were war between Germany and Poland the Germans would rise against Hitler and the Polish Army would march into Berlin. Shortly after midday Hitler issued the final order to his commanders in chief for the invasion of Poland to start at dawn on September 1. The directive included the words, "It is important that the responsibility for the opening of hostilities should rest squarely on England and France."

At one o'clock Dahlerus was back with Goering, whom he found instructing his secretary about the disposal of the art treasures in his Berlin palace in the event of war. An adjutant brought in a copy of an intercepted communication between Warsaw and Lipski, at

the Polish embassy, which made Goering bound out of his chair
and pace about in fury. It proved, he shouted, that the Poles had
no intention of negotiating. He made a copy of this message in
his own handwriting and gave it to Dahlerus for Henderson.[33] After
further raving, he proposed they should lunch together, and ended
by inviting himself and his adjutant to eat at Dahlerus' hotel in the
public restaurant, which led to the maximum publicity. Dahlerus
decided to give his self-invited guest the finest possible meal, which
ended with a cognac that so appealed to Goering's palate that he
immediately ordered two bottles of it to be sent out to his car.
Dahlerus, satisfied that Goering was mellow with food and drink,
appealed to him to take over the negotiation with Henderson himself. Goering went off to get Hitler's permission to discuss the
matter with the ambassador. Hitler consented, provided a neutral
person were present, and the result was a strange tea party at Goering's residence, to which Henderson, Forbes and Dahlerus were
invited. After rather elaborate civilities, the discussion began in
vague terms, and it was agreed that Goering's proposal for Anglo-
German negotiations, with Britain representing Poland, should be
investigated. At the same time Goering showed Henderson the
intercepted message from Warsaw. He spoke of the horror of war;
he would hate, he said, to bomb England. When Henderson replied that he might die as a result, Goering promised to fly over
England himself and drop a wreath on his grave as a final act of
friendship.[34]

Henderson came away from this lengthy conversation convinced
that Goering was prepared to give him so much time only because
preparations for war were complete and there was nothing left for
him to do but make a "forlorn effort" finally "to detach Britain
from the Poles." He was equally convinced that Goering did not
want war, but Henderson remembered only too well what Goering
had once said about Hitler: "When a decision has to be taken,
none of us count more than the stones on which we are standing.
It is the Führer alone who decides." He also hinted that a military
pact was being negotiated with Russia.

After a depressing evening and a little sleep, Dahlerus joined
Goering on his train at eight o'clock on the morning of Friday,
September 1. Goering seemed very depressed, and eventually he
admitted that the German Army had crossed into Poland and that
his Air Force was now destroying that of the Poles. Goering then

abused both the Poles and the British, who had forced him to take this unnecessary action. Having said what Hitler wanted him to say, he agreed with Dahlerus that the war might be limited in its effect if Hitler were to permit him to meet the British representatives. He then left for the Kroll Opera House, where the Reichstag was assembled to hear the Führer give his own explanation of the failure of the negotiations on which he had pretended to place so much hope, after which Hitler proclaimed himself "the first soldier of the German Reich." He also legitimized Goering as his rightful successor and so made legal and public the claim that Goering had been making for so many years in private.

Goering arranged a final meeting between Dahlerus and Hitler, at which the Führer performed lunatic gesticulations in order to emphasize his ability to fight Britain. Even Goering turned his back on the spectacle, though as they went in he had spoken with pride of his new right of succession. When they returned together to Goering's palace, Dahlerus noted that the works of art were still being packed off for safety. They met again that afternoon to discuss the same vain topic. By now Britain had delivered her conditions for not going to war with Germany. Goering was plainly caught up in the war fever, as if for him the die was finally cast. He presented Koerner and Gritzbach with swords of honor in Dahlerus' presence and ordered them to fight with glory. That night Berlin was blacked out for the first time.

Dahlerus, still persistent in hope, visited Goering on his train early on Saturday, September 2, and learned that Mussolini had offered to mediate. He carried the news at once to the British embassy and with the speed of Mercury dashed back and forth between the British and German centers, until he finally ended up by spending the whole afternoon lunching at the Esplanade with Goering, who had returned to Berlin and seemed, in spite of waging a war in the air against Poland, to have considerable time at his disposal. The British were demanding the withdrawal of German troops from Poland as the prerequisite for any further talk of negotiation, whether inspired by Mussolini or anyone else; this was followed by the firm ultimatum handed to Ribbentrop the following morning, Sunday, September 3. Dahlerus was told of the ultimatum by the embassy an hour before Ribbentrop, and he tore through the streets of Berlin in a German staff car to Goering's train, which was stationed near Potsdam, to give him this final news. The drive out of Berlin took forty minutes.

Goering seemed to know little of what was going on, to be "at sea," as Dahlerus put it. He was utterly surprised by the British ultimatum, which expired at eleven o'clock, and as he talked he seemed to be able only to lay the blame for the war and its extension on Britain. He telephoned Ribbentrop while Dahlerus was out of the room, and when they met again it was plain to Dahlerus that Ribbentrop had won the struggle for influence over Hitler. At this moment of supreme decision, Hitler made no approach himself to Goering, whom only a brief while before he had proclaimed the second man of Germany. Dahlerus, speaking from a telephone in a vestibule situated between the dining car and the kitchen, pushed his way through the blocked telephone system to the Foreign Office in London to implore the British government not to ask too much of Germany—a standstill, possibly, as distinct from a withdrawal. He then begged Goering to offer to fly to London and conduct negotiations himself on Hitler's behalf, leaving before eleven o'clock although it was now already past ten. Goering rang Hitler.

Again Hitler gave his consent. While Bodenschatz hastened off to make arrangements for a plane, Dahlerus wormed his way once more through telephone connections to the Foreign Office in London, only to be told that Goering's visit could be considered only after Hitler had replied to Chamberlain's ultimatum. By now only twenty-five minutes was left, and Goering was angry at this further example of what was, in his opinion, British intransigence. He asked Dahlerus to leave him and spoke again to Hitler. Then he came out, said nothing of how Hitler had responded, and sat in a chair under the beech trees. He looked hopeless and disappointed. The idea of a momentous visit to Britain had appealed to his imagination. Now, like the rest of the Germans, he had to sit and wait for the Second World War to begin. About half an hour later Koerner brought him the news that Britain had declared war. It was then, and only then, that he was summoned to the Chancellery.

Dahlerus saw him once more, on the following day. Goering promised to conduct the war as humanely as possible and said Germany would initiate no hostilities against France and Britain. Meanwhile, war in Poland would take only a month, and her territories would then be divided between Germany and Russia. He only hoped the rapid defeat of Poland would compel Britain and France to have second thoughts about extending the war. Goering talked on and on, until Dahlerus grew fearful of missing his train. He was tired and all he wanted now was to return to Sweden.

At the Chancellery the previous day Goering had turned to Schmidt, who had brought the British ultimatum to Hitler, and said, "If we lose the war, then God have mercy on us."

VII

Blitzkrieg

THE GERMAN INVASION of Poland was completed in three weeks. The Polish Air Force resisted bravely, but many of their machines were destroyed on the ground during the first two days of the war. By September 17, when the Russians moved in to occupy their share of Polish territory, the struggle was all but over. On October 5 Hitler rode in triumph in the streets of Warsaw.

The strategy that had conquered Poland was new in warfare and was used with devastating suddenness and savagery—the combined operation of Brauchitsch's fast-moving mechanized ground forces, commanded by Guderian, and Goering's air arm, commanded by Richthofen.[1] The Luftwaffe struck first, using the blitzkrieg method to destroy the Polish Air Force and annihilate the Army; when the Poles attempted to make a final resistance in Warsaw, the city was bombed by men who had been well rehearsed at Guernica. When the German blitz was over, movie cameras in aircraft flying low over the endless streets of roofless, gutted houses pried on the bones of Warsaw for *The Baptism of Fire*, Goering's film of praise for the might of the Luftwaffe. Once more the Stukas dropped screaming from the sky to hurl their bombs into the smoking streets, and the handsome blond airmen grinned in the summer sun.

The immediate success of this blitzkrieg confirmed both Hitler and Goering in their long-standing prejudice in favor of the bomber, a prejudice which was in the end to cost them the defeat of the Luftwaffe. The theory was that wars could be won cheaply and quickly from the air; the enemy's defense could be broken or immobilized, and the fast-moving panzer divisions could move in and occupy relatively undefended territories in a matter of days. The quick and bloodless occupations of Austria and Czechoslovakia could be followed now by the equally swift, if bloody, conquest of large territories in Europe. "Leave it to my Luftwaffe," became Goering's favorite boast, and in a broadcast from a munitions factory on September 9 he threatened fearful retaliation if British or French planes attempted to bomb Germany. This might, he said, be a long war.

The Luftwaffe was designed for short-range operations; the production of heavy, long-range bombers had been suspended as early as 1937. The emphasis from then onward was on the production of medium bombers, dive bombers (such as the Junkers 87) and fighters (such as the Messerschmitt 109); Germany did not develop a heavy bomber of the kind that was used later by the Allies and that she needed desperately when the range of the war front extended. Telford Taylor claims that the Luftwaffe "was shaped by aviators who were amateur soldiers, and soldiers who were amateur aviators."[2] The old high-spirited aces, such as Udet and Robert Ritter von Greim, found themselves serving alongside soldiers such as Generals Albert Kesselring and Hans Jeschonnek. In any case, the Luftwaffe was to be controlled as much by Goering's personal vanity as it was by Germany's war needs, and most of those to whom he gave authority came into conflict with him when the Luftwaffe began to face defeat. Nevertheless, the German Air Force was never designed to have the strategic independence from the Army that both the British and the Americans gave to their air forces. In addition to the friction that developed at Goering's headquarters, there was friction also between Goering and the high commands of the other services, more especially at first between Goering and Raeder, Hitler's energetic and far-seeing naval Commander-in-Chief.

Goering's Luftwaffe intelligence misinformed him about the capacity of the Royal Air Force. The experiment of using the Graf Zeppelin during May and August 1939 to test Britain's radar defenses failed to give him the information he needed, and Major Schmid, his chief of intelligence, responded to his vanity by underestimating the strength of the R.A.F.'s fighters in the same year.

The notorious period of stalemate followed the fall of Poland. The pact with the Soviet Union gave Hitler the breathing space he needed to develop the war in the west. The German generals still felt themselves ill-equipped to face the combined armies of France and Britain, which were as unprepared as the Germans themselves to start hostilities in the west on September 3. There was once again talk about peace, and this was sufficient to bring Dahlerus hurrying back to Berlin on September 26. He met Goering and Hitler, and discussion turned on the best way to enable the British to conclude peace terms without loss of face; Goering thought representatives of the two countries might meet secretly in Holland and prepare the ground for later talks which would take place at the invitation of Queen Wilhelmina. After visiting Chamberlain in London, Dahlerus returned with uncompromising terms: the British government would negotiate only with a new German government, not that of Hitler. Dahlerus bore these terms back to Germany with a heavy heart, and on October 1 he met Goering at Carinhall. They talked there in the garden, and Dahlerus asked Goering directly whether he served Germany or Hitler. Goering asked him to return the following day and meanwhile arranged that he should meet Admiral Canaris, head of the German Intelligence Service and a man known to a few to be critical of Hitler. Nothing came of this meeting, except the possible indication that Goering was not unaware of the existence of an underground movement planning the overthrow of Hitler.

On October 6 Hitler made his lengthy speech in the Reichstag offering to conclude a peace which should be followed by conferences to determine the outstanding problems of Europe as he saw them. Meanwhile, however, he set his military chiefs to prepare for war in the west, which excited them to produce a catalogue of reasons why this was impossible without months of delay. Only Raeder seemed anxious to strike; he had commenced his operations by sinking the British liner *Athenia* on the very day war had been declared. Hitler proceeded to browbeat the generals and forced upon them dates for attack that gave them barely a month in which to prepare. Brauchitsch, a weak man, took the full brunt of Hitler's anger when he pleaded for more time.

The secret plans to overthrow Hitler, which had always in the past failed to reach the point of action, now stirred uneasily once more. Warnings of incipient invasion were sent out through underground channels to both Belgium and France. Independently of this, an almost certainly bogus attempt on the lives of Hitler and the principal Nazi leaders was staged in Munich on November 8 at the annual reunion to celebrate the 1922 putsch. Goering alone was absent through illness, and the bomb that had been "planted" to kill the whole of the Nazi leadership exploded only after Hitler, who spoke for eight minutes instead of his customary two hours, had left. Whether this attempt was bogus or not, Goering told Bodenschatz that had Hitler been killed, he as successor to the Führer would have stopped the war by withdrawing German troops from all non-German territory.[3]

There seems to have been no doubt that certain of the recalcitrant generals considered that Goering might be the man to head the government after the removal of Hitler by a military *coup d'état*. There is evidence of this, for instance, in the diaries of Hassell. "It is significant that in desperation everyone looks to Goering as the only hope," he wrote on October 19, "significant because it makes clear how little hope there really is, for basically Goering is not a man in whom one can have confidence. He lacks both character and real determination to see things through." The following month Hassell received hints that Goering was on bad terms with Hitler and even considered he was mentally ill, but he also noted Goering's "paralyzing fear of the Gestapo" and the fact that he "will not listen to unpleasant things if he can help it."

Goering, as far as we can tell, gave no direct encouragement to these moves. His part in the campaign against Poland had been a resounding success and had done much to reinstate him in Hitler's eyes. During October he was involved in the spoliation of that part of Poland which on October 8 was incorporated into the Reich by an order of which he and Hitler were signatories.[4] In directives dated October 19 and October 30 and signed by Goering as Plenipotentiary of the Four-Year Plan, instructions were issued on the economic organization of Germany's new eastern territories. The directive of October 19 included the "complete incorporation" of industry "into the Greater German economic system at the earliest possible time" and the removal of all raw materials and machinery needed for the German war economy; to this Goering added the statement, "Enterprises which are not absolutely necessary for the meager maintenance of the bare existence of the population must be transferred to Germany." The expropriation of the Jews was naturally involved. Goering also signed a secret decree on October 7 which gave Himmler power to "Germanize" Poland. Nor were his staff concerned alone with raw materials, machinery and produce; they were interested in the confiscation of human labor. Goering needed a million men and women to work in agriculture and industry in the Reich, and he sent this request to Hans Frank, the Governor General of Poland; arrangements were made for their forcible transfer in 1940. Goering's signature underwrote document after document that initiated the terrorization and the expropriation of millions of men and women whose lives and labor lay at the mercy of the agents of Nazism.[5]

The attack on the West which Hitler demanded of his generals was postponed no fewer than fourteen times between November 1939 and the spring of 1940. The bad weather was frequently blamed for these delays. Goering wanted to bomb Britain, but Hitler insisted that such attacks should only accompany a land offensive. But when Raeder asked for air support to help his inadequate Navy attack British merchant shipping, Goering was uninterested. Meanwhile Goering concentrated on the production of planes, more especially the short-range bombers.[6] At a reception held at the Soviet embassy in Berlin on November 7, the day the Queen of the Netherlands and the King of the Belgians offered to mediate for peace, Goering boasted to a group of American journalists (including both Shirer and Lochner) about the fine planes that were being produced in Germany, and how they would be more than a match for the Allied air forces even though they were now able to buy planes from America, where the Neutrality Act had recently been repealed. Asked why he was merely bombing enemy ships and not their ports, he said, "We're humane. You shouldn't laugh—I'm serious. I *am* humane!"

On November 12 the German people received a severe shock at the stringency of the clothing allowance when their ration cards were issued; they realized what Hitler had meant when, in a broadcast on November 8, he had told them that it would be a long struggle and that he had ordered Goering to prepare for a five-year conflict on the day Britain and France had entered the war. Later in the month Goering lectured an assembly of high-ranking officers on the poor morale in the Army as compared with the Navy and the Air Force.

It was at this time that the rifts began to show between Germany and Russia, on the one hand, and Italy on the other. Germany and Russia were driving the hardest possible bargain with each other on the exchange of commodities, such as grain and oil from Russia for war material from Germany. On November 1 Goering protested about the loss this entailed to the German armed forces, even though in a speech on September 6 at an armament works he had emphasized the importance of the economic agreement with Russia to German victory.[7] But to Hitler the trading of German armaments to Russia was the high price that had to be paid to keep the Russians out of the conflict that lay ahead in the west. On the other hand, Stalin in person complained at the charges that were being made for German aircraft! Meanwhile, Mussolini's alarm was growing at this expansion of German-Soviet co-operation and the sudden spread of Russian power into Poland and the Baltic. The Russians started their war against Finland on November 30.

At the beginning of the war in Poland, Goering had told Magistrati at the Italian embassy in Berlin that Italian neutrality suited Germany; he had even hinted that Russia was going to intervene in Poland and absorb a part of Polish territory. But during the autumn Germany's awareness that Hitler had been let down by Mussolini in August, and that as a result Britain and France had been encouraged to support Poland, began to intensify. On November 12 a further conversation took place between Magistrati and Goering, in which Goering confirmed his opinion that the majority of the Germans were satisfied the Duce and the Führer had agreed amicably on Italy's remaining neutral; this in fact was far from the truth about German opinion, but Goering still wanted his Annunziata order. However, when Mussolini sent Hitler his letter of January 4 in which he strongly criticized the pact with Russia, Hitler summoned both Ribbentrop and Goering, and the three of them discussed the letter angrily for several hours. Only six weeks later, on February 20, Ciano was writing in his diary that Goering had shown his anger to the Italian military attaché in Berlin over "the Italian position"; and he added of Goering, "He is the most human of the German chiefs, but he is emotional and violent and might become dangerous."[8] The Duce agreed to send Germany 3,500 tons of copper the following day, which emphasized the shortage of raw materials that led Goering to decree on March 14 that German citizens must give up to him any articles they had which were made of copper, bronze, zinc, brass, tin, lead or nickel.[9] On April 2 Ciano noted that Goering was once more applying pressure on Italy to hasten her preparations for war, and that Mussolini replied at once that he was doing so. At the end of the month Goering assured the Duce he would be given at least a fortnight's notice before any German offensive was launched in the west.

On January 3 an official announcement had reaffirmed that Goering was absolute dictator of Germany's economy, and this enabled him on January 10 to put further pressure on the industrialists of the Rhineland, whom he gathered together for a conference at the Chancellery. On January 30 he received General Georg Thomas, chief of the Economic and Armament Department of O.K.W., the Armed Forces High Command, and told him Hitler expected soon to be master of France, Belgium and Holland, and that "the decision follows to exploit everything of ours to the utmost in 1940, and to exploit the raw-material reserves at their expense in later years."[10] It was part of the Army's duty to appoint economic liaison officers to reconnoiter captured territories and prepare for the shipment to the Reich of all valuable raw materials, "trainload upon trainload." After the fall of France, so great was the pressure of German big business to get its hands on the wealth of the occupied countries that Goering had to step in and call a halt to this rapacity with a decree on June 19 that stated, "The endeavor of German industry to take over enterprises in the occupied territory must be rejected in the sharpest manner." But in August he was once more advising economic penetration in Norway, Holland and Belgium. In a memorandum dated August 2, Goering impressed on the Reich commissars in these countries the absolute necessity for economic penetration through share purchases by German enterprise and take-over bids for firms made by German capital, and also by preventing firms in these territories from transferring their titles of ownership to interests in such neutral countries as the United States or Switzerland.

The year 1940 began with an event that further delayed Hitler's plans for attack on the West. Major Helmut Reinberger, a staff officer in the Luftwaffe, lost his way while flying to a conference and made a forced landing in Belgium; he was carrying the complete plan of attack in the west, together with maps. He twice attempted to destroy the documents, and indeed managed to send a report that they were sufficiently burned to make them unintelligible. There was consternation in Berlin, however, and Hitler, Goering and Keitel held a conference on January 13, trying to determine how much might now be known. According to General Kurt Student, while Goering raged at this accident, Hitler kept calm.[11] For a week the matter was anxiously debated, and then the German ambassador in Brussels was summoned by the Belgian Foreign Minister and told flatly that the plans for an invasion were known. On January 20 Hitler gave a stern warning on military security to his commanders, including Goering, who had dismissed General Felmy, the able commander of the air fleet to which Reinberger had been attached; Felmy's place was taken by Kesselring.[12]

The attack was now set back until the spring. Because of the need to protect the all-important flow of Swedish iron ore, which during the winter had to be shipped through Narvik, it was planned to begin with an invasion north into Denmark and Norway, where Major Vidkun Quisling was only too anxious to encourage a German occupation. There was also some fear that Britain might occupy Norway to blockade Germany and bring assistance to Finland. Hitler signed the directive for this operation on March 1, having ten days previously, quite independent of his military chiefs, appointed General Nikolaus von Falkenhorst commander for the invasion of the Norwegian ports. When the directive arrived on Goering's desk on March 1, he was furious that he had not been consulted.

On March 5 Hitler called an urgent conference to stop the dispute that had broken out among his commanders. General Alfred Jodl, operations chief of O.K.W., records in his diary how Goering "vents his spleen because he was not consulted beforehand" and "dominates the discussion and tries to prove that all previous preparations are good for nothing." Hitler made concessions to Goering, but insisted that the plan in general should proceed, though with heavier commitments by the Army and Navy.[13]

During the period of this dispute, Sumner Welles, the American Under-Secretary of State, arrived in Germany on what was intended to be yet another well-meant mission to restore peace, inspired this time by President Roosevelt. The visit was also a tour of investigation by a man who opposed America's isolationism. He talked at length to Mussolini, Ciano, Hitler, Ribbentrop and Goering, and he included Paris and London in his tour. Hitler issued special directives to anyone who should have conversations with this visitor to let him do most of the talking, to put full blame for the war on

Britain and France, and to stress that Germany was prepared to fight on.

Sumner Welles has given his own account of his mission to Europe in his book A Time for Decision; the German account of these talks has survived through the elaborate notes kept by Paul Schmidt, supplemented by the description of the meetings in his book published after the war. The Germans found Sumner Welles reserved, cold and intelligent. He spent only three days in Berlin and saw Goering at Carinhall during the afternoon of March 3. In Schmidt's view, Goering's handling of Sumner Welles was most skillful, though for some reason he did not offer him the usual lavish meal, sending him back to Berlin after several hours of conference in a state of starvation.

Welles found Carinhall in its normal state of extensive reconstruction and thought it would end up by being about the size of the National Gallery in Washington when the work of building was finished. A trained observer, he noticed Goering's high color and thought at first that his face was heavily rouged, but as the unnatural flush faded during the course of their meeting, he put the effect down to some form of "physical maladjustment." "His hands were shaped," he wrote, "like the digging paws of a badger." On his right hand Goering wore a great ring set with six large diamonds; on his left hand he had his favorite emerald ring, the stone of which appeared to be about an inch square.

Goering was very unaffected and friendly in his manner, and he gave his own account of Germany's case in European politics, claiming that he personally had done everything he could to maintain peace in the face of the provocative attitude of the British and the French; the war was solely the result of their persistence. As for the war itself, Germany had "all the trumps in her hand"; the German Air Force was supreme and would remain so. Whether the war was short or long was quite immaterial; Germany had more than sufficient raw materials, and was even producing butter and other fats from coal!

While they sat and talked in easy chairs by the fire with the snow falling in swirling gusts outside, Welles, like others before him, found he was more impressed by Goering than he had been by the other Nazi leaders. He found him just as ruthless and untouched by human feelings as they were, but he felt that Goering was capable of taking a wider view of Germany's relations to other European countries and to the United States. But when Welles pointed out that the American poeple could hardly remain un-affected by a war that devastated Europe, Goering replied naïvely that he could not see how a war in Europe touched "the vital inter-ests" of the United States. Welles countered this by reminding Goering that the American people, though equally determined to keep out of the First World War, had been quick to enter it once they came to accept that their national interests were indeed threatened, and that even now they were "profoundly moved" by German cruelty to the Jews. Goering tried to answer this by claim-ing that the Americans supported in their own attitude to the colored races the very policy they condemned in Germany's atti-tude to the Jews. When Welles pointed out the difference between an active government policy of discrimination and repression and the practice of these things by misguided groups against the gen-eral feeling of both the nation and its rulers, Goering said no more on this issue, but returned to the safer ground of abuse of Britain's determination to develop the war against Germany instead of fol-lowing the policy of peace that had been offered her so repeatedly by Hitler.

Goering then insisted on taking the hungry Under-Secretary on a tour of his galleries, where, he explained, he had himself arranged every object and work of art. He showed him his gifts from foreign governments, including recent acquisitions from Japan; he showed him his Cranachs and other pictures in his growing collection of Old Masters. The reception room and the halls were hung with "hundreds of paintings," but Welles felt that "it would be difficult to find an uglier building or one more intrinsically vulgar in its ostentatious display." He drove away through the gathering twi-light, passing through electronically operated gates at successive points along the drive leading to the main entrance and the road back to Berlin. As he drove he thought how the only deterrent to the armed might of Germany would be to form once more a united front of the Western European democracies and the United States, and how impossible it would be to achieve this with the American electorate in its present mood of isolation. The people in the streets of Berlin, he thought, looked glum and unsmiling.

Goering's evasive answer to the charge of German cruelty to the Jews was typical of his ambivalent attitude to unpleasantness and

cruelty. He was not unaware of the massacres, tortures and evic-
tions which were being carried out by the S.S. in Poland under
Frank, Himmler and Heydrich. The deportation of Jews from
Germany to Poland had already begun, and stories of death from
ill-treatment and exposure were being reported by American observers and relief workers, who were still present in Poland. The
foreign press published stories of appalling cruelty to men, women
and children who had been forcibly taken from their homes. Goering, as president of the Reich Defense Council, was ultimately
responsible for the deportation orders, and at a meeting held on
February 12 at Carinhall he advised Himmler that the movements
should cease for the time being on account of these reports, although Himmler suggested to him that thirty thousand racial Germans in Lublin should be moved out to allow for the expansion of
the ghetto. At the same meeting Goering said that "the strengthening of the war potential of the Reich must be the chief aim of all
measures to be taken in the east." But partly through personal rivalries among the Nazi bosses, partly through sheer mismanagement
in the handling and canceling of orders, the sad migrations of frost-
bitten victims went on. Later, on March 23, when the report of
deaths during further movements of the Jews came in, Goering
ruled once more that they should be suspended, though he was
challenged by Greiser, governor of the Warthegau, who said that
he had been promised the evacuation of two hundred thousand
Jews from Lódz and that Goering's suspension did not come into
operation until May. Meanwhile Himmler was bringing in vast
numbers of racial Germans from those eastern territories which
were in the Russian-occupied area or the Russian sphere of influence.

Hitler was impatient to get his war in the west begun and finished. He was happy for Mussolini to take on a supporting role,
his entry into the war to be timed only after the Germans had
delivered the initial, fatal blow. On April 2, Hitler summoned
Goering, Raeder and Falkenhorst to a conference, the result of
which was that the invasion of Denmark and Norway was ordered
to begin at one hour before dawn on April 9. The German Navy
began to sail for Norwegian waters on April 3. On April 9 the governments of Denmark and Norway were informed they were to be
placed under the protection of the Reich in order to forestall Anglo-
French occupation. Denmark submitted in the unequal struggle

with scarcely a shot fired. The Luftwaffe made a token flight over Copenhagen so that the roar of its engines might express the will of Germany. In Norway the resistance proved greater, but the Luftwaffe took possession of Sola airfield. By noon the principal ports were in German hands, but not Oslo. The King and his government fled to the mountains. When they refused to capitulate or accept Quisling as Prime Minister, the Luftwaffe was sent to destroy the village where they were thought to be. With British and French aid, the initial Norwegian resistance lasted for the rest of the month against the blitzkrieg of the Luftwaffe. The German Navy suffered heavily, losing ten destroyers and three cruisers, and sustaining heavy damage to the *Scharnhorst*, the *Gneisenau* and the pocket battleship *Lützow*. This was to help deter Hitler from launching his invasion of Britain later in the year.

What was of equal importance was the nervous reaction of Hitler to the initial reverses in Norway, and Goering remained on edge during this period for fear that his authority or the prestige of the Luftwaffe might be overshadowed.[14] It is significant that in the diary of General Franz Halder,[15] Chief of the Army General Staff, there is no mention of either Goering or the Luftwaffe throughout the whole Danish-Norwegian campaign. In Jodl's diary, however, he is mentioned on April 19; he "criticizes that the behavior against the civilian population is not energetic enough," adding that "the Air Force cannot do everything." On April 22, Jodl notes that the Field Marshal is "somewhat quieter today, in view of the good weather forecasts," and he is mentioned as present at Hitler's daily discussions on April 24, May 2 and May 3, when he was angry again because Milch's name did not receive equal weight with that of others of the high command, and then made an "onslaught" aimed at getting the naval air units under his control.

The Luftwaffe's part in the campaign had, in fact, been an essential one. A large fleet of transport aircraft carried German infantry to Norway, and some four hundred bombers were in action against the centers of resistance. Few fighters took part in the operation, since opposition in the air was negligible.

After considerable vacillation, Hitler finally decided that Operation Yellow, the code name for the invasion of the West through Holland and Belgium, should begin on May 10. In less than six weeks the Germans, to their own surprise, became the masters of Holland, Belgium and France.

By the time this devastating campaign was launched, the Luftwaffe had become the world's largest air force. Goering had some
3,500 operational aircraft for the invasion, organized in two air
fleets commanded by Kesselring and Sperrle. Kesselring's command
included naval air operations and mine laying, and the all-important paratroop division commanded by General Student. This
division and the dive bombers were prominent in the strategy, as
they had been in Scandinavia; it was the main landing of Goering's airborne troops that took the Dutch by surprise. The invasion involved the merciless bombing of Rotterdam by Stukas
in which over eight hundred persons were killed and many thousands injured at the very time the surrender of the city was being
negotiated.

The ruthless bombing of Rotterdam was a further sign of Hitler's
aggressive cruelty. Though it was a defended city and its capitulation had not taken place at the time of the attack, both Goering
and Kesselring should have been aware that the negotiations for
surrender were in progress; Student, who had initially asked for
the attack, had sent a radio message at noon to that effect and saying that the proposed raid should be postponed. It has been
assumed that Goering and Kesselring deliberately launched the attack to hasten the negotiations, and that there was confusion over
the flares put up to cancel it. Kesselring refers to "hours of heated
conversation with Goering" about the raid and whether it should
take place at all. The effects of the raid were seriously aggravated
by the fire department's being put out of action, and by flaming oil
from a margarine factory. But whether Goering was deliberately
careless of the lives of the Dutch or not, ruthlessness is revealed
by his public announcement on May 28 that all captured French
airmen would be put in chains because the French were reported
to be ill-treating German airmen whom they had taken prisoner;
he declared that he would shoot five French prisoners for every
German airman shot, and that he would increase this to fifty if a
German flyer were shot while parachuting to earth.

It was at this time that the King of Italy consented at last to
award Goering his Collar of the Annunziata. Ambassador Alfieri
hurried at Ciano's orders to the battlefront and there met Goering
in his armored train, which was covered with camouflage netting,
surrounded by antiaircraft guns and stationed near a tunnel in case
of emergency. Goering's voice quivered with emotion as he thanked

the ambassador for the decoration he had coveted so long; after the little ceremony of presentation, he told him about the successes of the Luftwaffe and the invincible strategy of the blitzkrieg. The war, he claimed, would soon be over. Then he squeezed himself sideways through the door to the dining saloon, and returned almost immediately wearing his Collar. He called for the photographers and carefully posed for them displaying his new order. It had taken far longer for him to overcome the resistance of the King of Italy than to conquer the armies of the West.

The attack on Belgium proceeded at such a dramatic pace that Hitler had a nervous crisis. He was "frightened by his own success," as Halder noted at the time. He halted the advance of his armored divisions twice at the very time they most needed to press on. The second of these halts was on May 24 twenty miles outside Dunkirk, where he appeared to have the northern Allied armies completely cut off and at his mercy. On May 28 the King of the Belgians capitulated without consulting his allies.

The reason for Hitler's decision to halt has been debated ever since it happened. The evidence collated by Shirer, and based to a considerable extent on a letter from Halder, makes Goering ultimately responsible. The German armored columns were halted by Hitler and General von Rundstedt, who were in conference at the latter's Army Group A headquarters at Charleville. Halder noted bitterly in his diary, "Finishing off the encircled enemy army is to be left to the Air Force!" Goering had intervened and offered to bomb the enemy into submission; he was overheard saying to Hitler, "My Luftwaffe will complete the encirclement and will close the pocket at the coast from the air." Halder wrote later to Shirer:

During the following days it became known that Hitler's decision was mainly influenced by Goering. To the dictator the rapid movement of the Army . . . became almost sinister. He was constantly oppressed by a feeling of anxiety that a reversal loomed . . .

Goering, who knew his Führer well, took advantage of this anxiety. He offered to fight the rest of the great battle of encirclement alone with his Luftwaffe, thus eliminating the risk of having to use the valuable panzer formations. He made this proposal . . . for a reason which was characteristic of the unscrupulously ambitious Goering. He wanted to secure for *his* Air Force, after the surprisingly smooth operations of the

Army up to then, the decisive final act in the great battle and thus gain the glory of success before the whole world.[16]

Guderian, the panzer leader, also said, "I believe it was Goering's vanity that caused Hitler to make his momentous decision." The only Army intervention Goering wanted was a simple mopping-up operation which should follow the major action that he would initiate. Meanwhile the paralyzed panzers would stand by at a safe distance to keep the human target hemmed in.

The order to halt was withdrawn two days later, on May 26, but by that time the British evacuation plan was under way and the German tanks found themselves faced by three British divisions supported by heavy artillery. The Luftwaffe failed to vindicate Goering's boasts, for two reasons. The first was that bad weather frequently grounded the planes (which in any case did not at this stage fly at night, when the evacuation was continued), and the second was that the Luftwaffe met its first strong opposition by an air force that was to prove its match. The Messerschmitts met the Spitfires, which, although outnumbered, outclassed the German fighters in performance.

The Luftwaffe bombed Dunkirk harbor on May 27, but did not completely destroy it; it was still usable on May 28, when the bad weather combined with smoke from the stores and fuel that had been set alight to obscure the action below. By May 29 the Germans realized the extent of the evacuation that was going on, and the Luftwaffe began to attack the boats. The R.A.F. retaliated, often above the clouds, which led to the unfortunate belief among the beleaguered soldiers that they had been deserted by their Air Force. On May 30 the Luftwaffe was grounded by the weather, but it renewed its attacks on the ships on May 31. "We are now paying for our failure to cut off the West, due to interference from above," wrote Halder in his diary. On June 1 came the greatest battle in the air, and each side lost some thirty planes. After this the evacuation continued only at night until the weather once more turned in its favor and the Luftwaffe was again grounded. The evacuation ended only on June 4, when the German ground forces, not the Luftwaffe, overcame the Allied resistance (Raeder, his Navy either sunk or confined to Norway, could do little to oppose the British at sea); but by that time 338,000 Allied troops, including some 60,000 French, had been rescued. Goering turned this failure into the semblance of a triumph by going with his staff into Dunkirk and gloating over the vast piles of undestroyed booty left by the retreating enemy.

On June 5, the day after Dunkirk had fallen, Milch joined Goering in his train, which was drawn up in a tunnel near the Channel coast, and proposed that a carefully co-ordinated series of mass parachute landings should be made on the R.A.F. fighter stations in England. Goering agreed to put this to Hitler.[17] Further meetings to discuss it were held on June 18 and 27, by which time France had capitulated.

Hitler, however, still hoped for peace, and he gave another, and this time a political, reason, which Halder duly noted, why he did not want the decisive battle against the Allies to take place on Flemish soil; he regarded the Flemish as cousins to the Germans, and he wanted to keep their land intact. Also he was beginning to think he could persuade the British to accept peace now that Germany was dominant in Western Europe. He seems to have accepted Goering's failure in good part, perhaps for this reason. He invited Mussolini to join in the final defeat of France once the French Air Force had been liquidated. Mussolini entered the war on June 10, but his forces made no headway in the south, while the French high command refrained from any offensive action against Italy. The victory was Hitler's, and the armistice terms that he dictated to France were entirely of his making. On June 18 Hitler said to Goering, "The war is finished. I'll come to an understanding with England." Goering, greatly moved, beamed and said, "Now at last there will be peace."

The old railway coach in which the 1918 armistice was signed was torn from its museum and set up in a sunlit clearing in the forest of Compiègne, a forlorn relic isolated beneath the trees. There Hitler, accompanied among others by Goering, Ribbentrop, Keitel and Hess, arrived in a car at three-fifteen on the afternoon of June 21. Goering carried his field marshal's baton. Together they looked at the granite block on which were inscribed the words, "Here on the eleventh of November, 1918, succumbed the criminal pride of the German Empire—vanquished by the free peoples which it tried to enslave." The film cameras recorded every moment of the scene as Hitler's face took on its pathological expression in which contempt and triumph were horribly matched. Then they entered the coach and there received the group of Frenchmen sent to negotiate the terms of armistice. Hitler left Keitel in charge of the discussions, which continued for two days. The railway coach at Compiègne was then taken to Berlin, and the granite plaque that had offended Hitler and Goering in the moment of their glory was blown to pieces. Hitler went for a sight-seeing tour of Paris, while Goering took advantage of the moment to make the first of his many visits to the city which was to become one of the principal centers where he could forget war and indulge his pursuit of works of art for the great collection he was now assembling.[18] Halder noted in his diary on July 4 that Goering was demanding that an economic commission should be set up parallel to the armistice commission to settle all aspects of French economic life, including confiscation of raw materials for Germany.

On July 19 in the Kroll Opera House Hitler proclaimed the victories of his genius to an assembly of the Reichstag; then he offered Britain peace. After this, he made the principal agents of his power into field marshals and generals. Goering was proclaimed the "Reichsmarschall des Grossdeutschen Reiches." Shirer, who was present at the ceremony, describes Goering sitting on his president's dais scribbling out his own speech while Hitler spoke, chewing his pencil and frowning "like a schoolboy over a composition," clapping his hands "with Gargantuan gestures" and waving his arms "like a boxer in the ring" when Hitler announced that Milch, Kesselring and Sperrle were to become field marshals, and even "sneaking a glance under the cover of the lid" when Hitler handed him the box containing his special baton.[19]

In July Goering entrusted Walther Funk, Reich Minister of Economics, with the task of forming the plan for the German New Order in Europe. This New Order was created gradually by a succession of statements and decrees and never existed in the form of a charter or published plan. The integration of industry throughout the whole territory under German control formed a major part of the scheme, with specialization of production in different countries, and with an increase of agriculture (a less profitable occupation than industry) in the countries outside the Reich. The whole idea was based on the Golden Age—but golden for Germany, not her tributaries.

When Churchill rejected Hitler's propagandist peace offer, the problem was thrown back to Hitler and his commanders whether

or not to proceed with the invasion of Britain. Both Kesselring and
Student, like Milch, were said to have been in favor of invasion
after Dunkirk, but Goering rejected this immediately. If Britain
was to be beaten, bombing must come first. So Air Fleets 2 and 3
were concentrated along the newly captured Channel coast during
June and July, when Hitler was turning over in his mind the various
ways in which Britain could be brought to the point of negotiation
or capitulation.

Hitler hated the sea. As Halder noted, he thought crossing the
Channel would be very hazardous, and the German high command
had had no experience in naval operations, except for the none-too-
encouraging action in Norway which had seriously depleted Germany's small Navy. All the preliminary, theoretical planning in
1939 for Operation Sea Lion, the projected invasion of Britain, had
led to doubts from one source or another, and now when the time
had come to take advantage of Britain's weakness (in July Britain
could have armed only some six divisions on her own soil, whereas
arms were available for twenty by September), controversy and in-
decision dominated Hitler's headquarters. Goering had a habit of
trying to curry favor with Hitler by showing up the deficiencies of
the other commanders. The feud between Raeder and Goering,
which had started over the Scandinavian invasion, intensified.[20]
Goering had sent Raeder a grossly insulting telegram telling him to
mind his own business, in reply to the Admiral's request that a
strong air force be kept to protect the German naval base at Trond-
heim. Because of the uselessness of the Navy during the western
campaign, Raeder came to Hitler's headquarters bursting with
plans for transporting German troops to the shores of England.
Rundstedt's counterproposals were unacceptable to the Navy.
Milch mulled over the idea of dropping paratroopers on the English airfields, and Kesselring, convinced that landings would be possible on the beaches he could see with the naked eye from Cap
Gris-Nez, chafed at the inaction forced upon him. With Hitler's
and Goering's approval, "deception drops" of fake paratroop materiel, maps and instructions were made by the Luftwaffe to un-
nerve the British and give them rumors to publish in the press.
When, in late June, the R.A.F. sporadically bombed Germany,
Goering wanted to strike back, but Hitler still restrained him,
though very minor operations over England were outlined in a directive issued by Goering on June 30. By mid-July, Hitler had ap-

proved the final invasion plan, and at a conference convened by
Goering on July 21 he told his staff that they now had a new task
ahead of them: inflicting damage on the British Navy in the
United Kingdom. By the end of July Hitler was persuaded by Raeder to consider giving up the idea of invasion during 1940, but
meanwhile to unleash the Luftwaffe against Britain. The order was
issued on August 1. Sea Lion, over which the Army and the Navy
continued to wrangle, would depend on the results.

Meanwhile, on July 24, Goering had cordially entertained
another peacemaker at Carinhall—Dr. Albert Plesman, head of the
Dutch K.L.M. airline, in which Goering's nephew, Peter Goering,
had served as a pilot. Plesman wanted to do precisely what Dahlerus had done, fly between Germany and England as an informal
negotiator between the governments. He had his own plan for
peace, with neatly defined spheres of influence extending to Africa.
Goering smiled and promised to talk to Hitler when the Führer
returned from Berchtesgaden. The plan reached Lord Halifax by
late August and was rejected; by September Goering was at pains
to dissociate himself from it when Dr. Plesman ran him to earth in
The Hague and tried to stop him from making London the target
for mass raids.

Goering, as always, was optimistic about the destruction the
Luftwaffe would inflict on Britain. In an order dated July 11, he
directed that when the time came both the British air armament
industry and the Royal Air Force must be destroyed "at the earliest
possible moment by the first blows of the attack." The defenses of
southern England, he estimated, would last only four days and the
R.A.F. four weeks; Goering felt the Luftwaffe could underwrite the
invasion for Hitler within a month, and on July 21 he sent a message to Hitler in Berchtesgaden that he would like "to be given
freedom to launch attacks against Britain's fighter pilots, Air Force,
aircraft industry, ports, industries, oil centers, and the Channel
area." Goering even thought his success might make invasion unnecessary, and by September he was reported as saying that he did
not believe Operation Sea Lion would ever take place. Nevertheless, plans for paratroop landings were prepared during August, and
raids on the ports were carried out along with the other targets. On
August 2, following Hitler's directive, Goering issued his orders for
the destruction of the R.A.F. Nothing had happened by August 10,
however, because by the time the Luftwaffe was ready to undertake

its first major raid the fine weather had passed. Raeder could not let this chance go; the Naval War Staff put on record that, for reasons not known to them, the Luftwaffe had "missed opportunities afforded by the recent favorable weather." Meanwhile, Goering at his headquarters near Paris raged at the weather reports that were spoiling his major operation. The heavy raids on the ports began eventually on August 11, and the attacks on airfields on August 13 and 14. On the fifteenth, 801 bomber and 1,149 fighter sorties were flown. The Battle of Britain had begun, but in such difficult weather conditions that Goering was driven to despair.

Goering was based on his famous wartime railway cavalcade, the mobile headquarters which were called by the code name Asia. His personal train was preceded by a pilot train of normal coaches together with cars for the transport of automobiles; this was followed by Goering's own train, which had open cars at either end on which antiaircraft gun crews were stationed. The coach in which Goering traveled had two bedrooms, a small study and luxurious toilet arrangements and was joined immediately to a second coach, designed as a sitting room, with film projection facilities. A third coach held Goering's command post and operations room, and a fourth was his dining saloon. Other coaches were attached for the comfort of guests and senior staff. The trains were normally stationed where they could easily be shunted into a tunnel in the event of air raids. Goering took with him Kropp, a staff doctor and his devoted nurse, Christa Gormanns, who had charge of his medicines; Hitler was constantly on the telephone, demanding progress reports, and Goering was often driven to a state of nervous exhaustion.

The story of the blitzkrieg on Britain has been told from every point of view, describing the experiences, excitements and sufferings of men and women in the air and on the ground. It lasted in its full extent from mid-August 1940 to mid-May 1941, with a brief period of relief in the height of winter, from January 18 to March 8, when only a few comparatively light raids took place. The raids began on the ports, the airfields, the radar stations and the aircraft plants; experiments in night bombing, although they affected the civilian population, missed for the most part the targets for which they were intended. German superiority in numbers kept the British fighter pilots working round the clock at an appalling strain; on average, Goering sent about a thousand aircraft a day over Britain, six hundred or more of them fighters which were intended to keep the R.A.F. at bay.[21]

Goering was deeply dissatisfied with the progress made; there was no question by now that the Spitfires were more than a match for the Stukas as well as the twin-engine and even the single-engine Messerschmitts, and that the bomber losses were becoming serious. The R.A.F. could not be tempted to commit the majority of its planes to the air at one time, a move which could have led easily to its disintegration, nor could it be destroyed on the ground. The Royal Air Force remained intact in spite of the efforts of the Luftwaffe to destroy it. On August 18 Goering summoned his leaders and told them with heavy sarcasm to attack the aircraft industries and "not the lightship off Dover," and then sent them back to their bases. He summoned Galland to Carinhall. Galland flew to Berlin and noted with some disgust how little the pleasure-loving capital seemed to care about the struggle on the coast in which so many young men were losing their lives. Then he was driven to the luxurious Carinhall, was decorated by Goering with the Gold Pilot Medal with jewels and was told that younger blood was needed in the command to improve the fighter service. He was promoted a group commodore. Later, when Goering was at the front grumbling at his men, Galland told him that what was needed to carry out his wishes was "an outfit of Spitfires."[22]

It was out of revenge for a small raid on Berlin that Hitler agreed to launch the blitz on London, and this operation, so costly to the Luftwaffe, began on September 7.

Goering, who preferred to direct all his operations from his headquarters in Paris, went in person to the coast for the first time on September 7 to direct the flow of aircraft to London. He stood on the hillside near Cap Blanc-Nez, which was an air command post for Air Fleet 2, and broadcast to the nation about the destruction of London and the flight of the Luftwaffe to strike "right into the enemy's heart." Over six hundred bombers and six hundred fighters flew to London within twenty-four hours. He was prodigal with his aircraft, and he paid for it proportionately.

Goering took his nurse, Christa Gormanns, to the front with him, and on occasion she took messages and telephoned orders on his behalf. He began to vacillate in his attempts to avert the increasing losses inflicted on the Luftwaffe, mixing his changes of tactics with wishful thinking, such as his remarks on September 16:

"Stick by the enemy; then, in four or five days, his fighters will be out! Then aircraft-producing centers must be eliminated. . . . Sea Lion must not disturb or burden the Luftwaffe operations." Meanwhile, the R.A.F. was itself bombing the vessels and equipment assembled along the coast in preparation for Sea Lion. Hitler, blowing now hot, now cold, was beginning to think of Russia and the possibility of winning golden victories in the east while leaving England pinned down like a broken butterfly by the Luftwaffe.

On September 17 Hitler decided "to postpone Sea Lion indefinitely." This was a bitter blow to Goering, who realized that this was Hitler's formal acknowledgment of his failure. His staff, according to General Karl Koller, noticed the change in him. He ordered his train to be made ready to leave and told his commanders to bomb Britain mercilessly—but by night, when her fighters were immobilized.[23]

Galland had a private conversation with Hitler on September 24 when he came to Berlin to receive the oak leaves to the Knight's Cross, the highest award that could be given apart from the Grand Cross, which was reserved for Goering alone. He expressed his admiration for the R.A.F.; Hitler agreed with him and said it was tragic that the Germans and the British should be at war; the destruction of Britain would leave "a vacuum . . . which it would be impossible to fill." Galland then went to Rominten to shoot with Goering, who met his young air commodore in his favorite leather jacket, silk blouse, and belt with the hunting knife. They stayed in Rominten with the stags for three days, during which time the Luftwaffe sustained one of its worst series of losses. At this time Goering permitted a release to the foreign press that he had himself recently flown over London, but this was withheld from the German papers. There was, in any case, no truth in the report.

Russia, meanwhile, had not been idle while Hitler was preoccupied. In June she had, after a semblance of negotiation, occupied the Baltic States and taken over Bessarabia and northern Bucovina from Rumania by threat of force. In late August, Hitler, anxious about the Rumanian oil fields, had countered by forcing Axis arbitration onto Hungary and Rumania. King Carol had fled the country, and Hitler's friend Antonescu had become dictator. Neither Russia nor Germany had consulted each other about these actions. By August, when Hitler's interest in the invasion of Britain had first begun to recede, the plan to attack Russia in the spring of 1941 became the principal occupation of the high command. On July 31 Halder summarized Hitler's remarks at a staff conference held in the mountain seclusion of the Berghof: "Something strange has happened in Britain! The British were already completely down. Now they are back on their feet. . . . Russia needs only to hint to England that she does not wish to see Germany too strong and the English, like a drowning man, will regain hope. . . . But if Russia is smashed, Britain's last hope will be shattered. . . . Russia must be liquidated. Spring 1941." Goering on August 14 dropped a hint that the normal deliveries of products to Russia were to be maintained "only till the spring of 1941" so that the supply of raw materials from the Soviets would continue till the last possible moment.[24] The General Staff was kept busy with the details of this secret plan during the next few months, while in September the Tripartite Pact between Japan, Italy and Germany was signed, ostensibly against America, but actually against Russia.

It was a difficult winter; Franco could not be edged into the war or persuaded to block British entry to the Mediterranean; Mussolini, in foolish wrath against Hitler's move in the Balkans, attacked Greece through Albania in November and thus threatened German strategy in this troublesome area, which had become the primary open cause of strife between Germany and Russia. Raeder had always pressed for war in the Mediterranean and now he had got it against Hitler's will; the Führer decided Germany must go to Italy's aid not only in Greece but in North Africa, where Wavell had routed Graziani.

Meanwhile Goering had continued the campaign from the air against Britain. The docks and the East End of London suffered during the first phase of the bombing of London in September. During this period the Luftwaffe learned that it paid to bomb by night rather than by day, and the dreaded periods during the autumn became the nights when "the bomber's moon" was shining. On October 18 Goering decided to praise his young men: "Your indefatigable, courageous attacks on the head of the British Empire, the city of London . . . have reduced the British plutocracy to fear and terror." The night raids continued on both London and the provincial centers until January 19; the heavy raid on Coventry took place on November 14. There was a lull until March 8, when the bombing of London and the provinces was resumed on a large scale and lasted until May. Neither the antiaircraft barrage nor the night fighters were at this stage very successful; on the other hand the bombing itself was frequently inaccurate, and the Luftwaffe sustained heavy losses through flying in bad weather. The Luftwaffe fighter pilots were angry when a third of their Messerschmitts were converted into fighter-bombers; Goering retorted by saying this had to be done because of their failure to protect the bombers from the R.A.F. The result was that the fighter pilots dropped the bombs anywhere merely in order to be rid of them; they did not regard themselves as cargo carriers. With an eye on morale and personal popularity, Goering gave all the pilots in the Channel area a free skiing holiday in the new year, withdrawing the units one by one for rest and refitment during the period of January and February when the ground was unsuitable for take-off. The British were able to recover some of their lost sleep.

When spring arrived the night fighters became increasingly successful, but Hitler was determined to keep the raids heavy for as long as possible before the Russian campaign began, if only as a reprisal for the growing number of raids the R.A.F. was now mounting against Germany. By the end of May 1941 the period of the great raids on Britain was over, and Kesselring was ordered to move Air Fleet 2 to Poznań in readiness for the assault on Russia on June 22.

Goering claimed at Nuremberg that he was deeply troubled about the war with Russia and that he was told nothing about it until the late autumn of 1940 in Berchtesgaden. Although this is hardly compatible with his orders on August 14 concerning the stoppage of deliveries of goods to Russia in the spring of 1941, there is little doubt that he sought to dissuade Hitler, as any sane person in a position to give advice would have, against allowing his forces to be spread out in simultaneous actions east, west and south. He preferred to concentrate on removing Britain from the war, and the only extension of activity he favored was in the Mediterranean.[25] For once he agreed with Raeder, who strongly supported this policy. Goering wanted to take Gibraltar by the old strategy of bombing followed by dropping paratroops on the Rock. Then, the western entrance to the Mediterranean having been closed to the British, an army group under Rundstedt would invade Morocco and Tunis, while a second group under Field Marshal Fedor von Bock descended via Italy and crossed to Tripolitania. A third army, com-

manded by Field Marshal Sigmund List, was to take Greece, the
Balkans, the Dardanelles and Ankara, then cross to close the Suez
Canal to the British. After this, Goering thought, the British would
be at the mercy of Germany, and it would be easy to come to an
arrangement to join forces to oppose Russia. On November 14
Halder noted that Goering was unwilling to consider a mission by
the Luftwaffe against the Cape Verde Islands, the Azores and the
Canaries, but that on the other hand he wanted complete freedom
of action in Spain. At the end of January, Goering and Student
were summoned by Hitler to the Obersalzberg to discuss the future
use of the paratroopers on the various campaigns that were being
considered. Student came with several proposals for the invasion of
England which were discussed at length, including the idea of occupying the Devon-Cornwall peninsula and Northern Ireland. Student then retired and left Goering and Hitler together. On the way
back to Berlin Goering said, "Don't bother yourself needlessly
about Ulster. The Führer doesn't want to invade Britain. From
now on Gibraltar will be the main task for you."

Hitler, however, was not to be deterred from his grand strategy—
Operation Barbarossa against Russia. "When Barbarossa starts," he
said, "the world will hold its breath and make no comment." Goering, therefore, fell into line, planning the operation, as he said at
Nuremberg, with the familiar strategy: "The decisive thing at the
time of the first attacks was, as before, to smash the enemy air arm
with full force as the main objective." When Milch himself first
heard of the campaign, he claims he told Goering that he must at
all costs stop Hitler, saying, "It's your responsibility to do this to
save the Fatherland." Goering merely replied that it was hopeless
to try to change the Führer's mind at this stage, and threatened to
have Milch court-martialed if he tried to intervene himself. "I will
not tolerate having a leading Luftwaffe man branded a defeatist,"
he said angrily.[26]

Before the great Russian venture, Hitler had to settle matters in
the Balkans. During February an army of two thirds of a million
men entered Rumania and Bulgaria, which were now Germany's
tributaries, but a popular uprising in Yugoslavia precluded Germany's gaining the easy access she wanted to yet a third Balkan territory. Hitler fell into an hysterical rage; postponing the invasion of
Russia for a month, he ordered Goering to flatten Belgrade from
the air and his armies to crush the Yugoslavs. The Luftwaffe visited

the air massacres of Warsaw and Rotterdam on the heads of the civilians of Belgrade. Yugoslavia capitulated on April 17 after eleven days of resistance, and the panzers pushed through her into Greece. By the end of April the Germans were in Athens, and the British division that had been sent from Libya to help the Greeks had to evacuate the mainland as best they could. Student wanted his paratroopers to capture Crete, and without difficulty he excited Goering with the idea. Goering sent him to Hitler, who consented to the campaign. The parachute division succeeded in taking Crete from the British, but only with heavy losses. "No island is now safe," boasted Goering significantly. Halder's note for May 8 on the conquest of Crete is interesting: "Operational control for Crete. [Reich Marshal] will have over-all responsibility. Ground forces will operate under him to the complete exclusion of O.K.H. [Oberkommando des Heeres—Army High Command]. Dangerous business!" Only a month previously, on April 7 during the Balkan campaign, Halder had remarked bitterly on Goering's interference in Army affairs and had added: "This damned back-biting is starting again"; now he is complaining that Goering seems to want to make Crete "an exclusive Luftwaffe domain."

Every British soldier available was needed now in Africa to face the grim struggle with General Erwin Rommel, who had arrived in Tripolitania with an armored division and some units of the Luftwaffe in February and had driven the British back to the borders of Egypt. It was fortunate for Britain in this melancholy spring that Hitler once more rejected Raeder's and Goering's advice to conquer Suez and seal the Mediterranean. The campaign against Russia, now delayed to a serious degree, had to come first, and the armies reassembled for the struggle which Hitler told his commanders must be "conducted with unprecedented, unmerciful and unrelenting harshness." On May 13 he directed Himmler "under his own responsibility" to undertake "special tasks" in the political administration of Russia and ordered Goering to organize "the exploitation of the country and the securing of its economic assets for use by German industry."

But Hitler was to suffer a severe personal shock while his departments were planning the conquest of Russia. On May 10 Hess, the third in the line of succession to the Nazi empire, his mind deranged by astrology, took off in a plane from Augsburg and flew to Scotland. Hitler was in the Berghof, and according to

Schmidt it was as if a bomb had struck him when he received Hess's letter explaining what he was about to do. He telephoned Goering, who was in Veldenstein, and demanded he come at once. After a three-hour drive Goering arrived, and Hitler wanted to know if Hess could possibly reach Britain. Goering said that he could, and then immediately telephoned Galland, ordering him and his group into the air in a vain attempt to stop Hess in his Messerschmitt. Galland, believing everyone mad, ordered some token flights to be made and then telephoned Goering to report the failure of his mission.

During the spring Goering continued to work on the plans for the invasion and economic exploitation of Russia, though he had also to act as host to the Axis representatives who came to Germany. The Japanese Foreign Minister, Yosuke Matsuoka, had visited Berlin at the end of March at the very time Hitler was enraged by Yugoslavia's opposition to his plans. Both Ribbentrop and Hitler hinted to Matsuoka that a conflict with the Soviet Union lay ahead; they spoke about the need to keep America out of the war, and about their hope that Japan might attack Britain through Singapore. This was repeated by Goering when the Minister visited him at Carinhall, where the war effort had not hindered still further enlargements, which the builders had just completed. During the reception Matsuoka leaned across to Schmidt, who was acting as interpreter, and murmured that there were people abroad who said that Goering was mad and that he had once actually been confined in a mental institution. Afterward Goering took him on a tour of the house and demonstrated his model railway, which Matsuoka specially admired.

Hitler's official directive of May 13 had formally confirmed Goering in the job of planning the economic exploitation of Soviet Russia; this was in effect an extension of his power as Plenipotentiary for the Four-Year Plan. In April, with his usual capacity to create administrative overlaps, Hitler had appointed Alfred Rosenberg, the inept philosopher of the Nazi movement, as Commissioner for the East European Region. Friction was inevitable; both Rosenberg and Goering were angry at the very thought of this overlapping of authority.

During May, June and July Goering authorized directives for his Economic Staff East which were so ruthless in their exploitation that they became some of the principal documents quoted by the

prosecution in the Nuremberg trial. He gave detailed instructions
for plundering Russia in the spirit of a memorandum issued on
May 2, which opened: "The war can be continued only if all the
armed forces are fed by Russia in the third year of the war. There
is no doubt that as a result many millions of people will be starved
to death if we take out of the country the things we need."[27] These
directives came to be known as the Green File or Portfolio.

A top-secret report for the staff on May 23 contained this statement:

The German Administration in these territories may well attempt to
mitigate the consequences of the famine which undoubtedly will take
place and accelerate the return to primitive conditions . . . However,
these measures will not avert famine. Many tens of millions of people
in this area will become [redundant] and will either die or have to emigrate to Siberia. Any attempts to save the population there from death
by starvation by importing surpluses from the black-soil zone would be
at the expense of supplies to Europe. It would reduce Germany's staying
power in the war, and would undermine Germany's and Europe's power
to resist the blockade. This must be clearly and absolutely understood.[28]

Industry in the Moscow and Leningrad areas was to be closed down
and the population starved or dispersed; there must be "the most
ruthless cutting down of Russian domestic consumption." The staff
must face "an extinction of industry as well as of a large part of the
people in what so far have been the food-deficit areas."

The assault on Russia began in the small hours of Sunday morning, June 22; it was the very day that Napoleon had chosen for his
invasion of the country. Goering remained at Carinhall. For reasons still to be explained the attack took Russia by surprise, and the
old tactic of destroying enemy aircraft on the ground succeeded
once again.

It is also true that the Germans were as surprised as the Russians.
Only the key men in the invading forces were told the truth, and the
propaganda put out was that all the preparations being made were
for an attack on Britain. In May at the Luftwaffe's Paris headquarters Goering briefed all the commanders of the units stationed in
France, speaking only in terms of the invasion of Britain. But after-
wards he took Galland and Werner Mölders, another senior officer,
aside, chuckled and said, "There's not a grain of truth in it." He

then told them that the invasion of Russia was imminent. It was a
paralyzing shock, says Galland; he believed the basis of Hitler's
strategy was to avoid at all costs waging war on the two opposite
fronts. Goering, however, seemed not the least perturbed; he decried
the capacity of the Red Air Force and said that this was a chance for
the Luftwaffe to shine again and shoot down the enemy like clay
pigeons. As for England, that could be dealt with in a few months'
time when Russia was defeated. Goering posted Mölders to the eastern front and told Galland he would be sent to relieve him six weeks
after the campaign had started. "You will do the rest, Galland," said
Goering in his most fatherly manner. Meanwhile, of course, secrecy must be observed.

The Luftwaffe was now spread wide over the airfields of Europe.
It had a headquarters in Rome, an operational command in Sicily,
whose duty was to neutralize Malta (which was mercilessly
bombed in 1941–42) and to deny the Mediterranean to the British,
and there were bases in North Africa to support Rommel. In 1941
it was, in effect, master of this area, but with the opening of the
Russian campaign the hastily deployed groups who had blazed
through the Balkan skies to capture Yugoslavia, Greece and Crete
were rushed north to support the eastern armies, while two relatively small groups, amounting only to some two hundred operational aircraft each, were left to control Malta and the Mediterranean and to support Rommel. Goering's resources of men and
aircraft were by now showing signs of strain and were successful
only because so little at this stage of the war could be put up in the
skies against them. While the British were building up a strength
which was to begin to show itself during the winter of 1941–42, the
Germans squandered their great period of supremacy by diluting
their strength over an area that soon proved to be far too great.
They failed utterly in the small Iraq campaign; the attacks in the
Mediterranean area lessened in the summer, and the British began
to move over to the offensive on German shipping in the Mediterranean. Though the Luftwaffe had the support of the Italian Air
Force, this was relatively ineffective, and by the autumn of 1941
something like parity was reached in the air between the Axis and
the British. This situation was not to change until January 1942,
when Goering took the risk of withdrawing planes from the Russian front and doubling the Luftwaffe strength in Italy and Sicily
under Kesselring. Then Malta was to suffer again.

The speedy successes of the Russian campaign only increased Hitler's delusions. It took three weeks for the armies to reach Smolensk, two hundred miles from Moscow, and to press north toward Leningrad and south toward Kiev, the capital of the Ukraine, where the food supplies coveted by Germany lay waiting. So successful was the invasion that Hitler was planning in July to disband forty divisions of his armies so that the manpower they represented could be returned to the armament industry. In spite of these successes, Halder on July 1 notes how the Luftwaffe's plans for the massing of the air strength were "again an absolute muddle" due to confusion in the discussions between Goering and Hitler. The Luftwaffe had in any case "greatly underrated the numerical strength of the enemy." A week later, on July 8, Halder recorded Hitler's decision to use the Luftwaffe to bomb both Moscow and Leningrad, "so as to relieve us of the necessity of having to feed the population through the winter."

Goering was among those present on July 16 at a conference held at Hitler's headquarters on the exploitation of Germany's captured territories, which were far better than colonies, as the Führer pointed out. While Rosenberg was weak enough to express some concern for the treatment of the Ukrainians, Goering said all that mattered now was to exploit the granary of the Ukraine. He also asked Hitler to add the Bialystok forests in the Baltic to East Prussia, because they were good for shooting. Hitler, however, said he was determined to take all the Baltic States into Reich territory and raze Leningrad to the ground. Reich territory must also include the Crimea, the Volga region, Baku and eastern Karelia. They discussed staff matters, Goering insisting, against Rosenberg's futile suggestions, that efficiency was what mattered in the organization of agricultural production and transport. He intended putting Luftwaffe training units into Russia, because their lessons in bombing would help discipline the people if there was trouble. After coffee, Hitler said that Europe was now merely a geographical concept; soon the Reich would stretch to Asia.[29]

On September 16, Goering presided over a meeting of German military officials to re-examine the exploitation of the food supplies now available in Russia. He emphasized again what had already been said in the Green File. "In the occupied territories, on principle, only those people who work for us are to be supplied with an adequate amount of food. Even if one wanted to feed all the other inhabitants, one could not do it in the newly occupied eastern areas. It is, therefore, wrong to syphon off food supplies for this purpose, if it is done at the expense of the Army and necessitates increased supplies from home." On November 7 he gave further orders at a conference on the use of Russian workers for heavy labor in the Reich.[30]

Goering was also implicated in the directions for the treatment of the Jews in wartime. On July 31, Heydrich received his commission from Goering in which he was instructed to extend the "final solution of the Jewish problem" to the total area controlled by the Reich in Europe. In this Heydrich was given his formal orders in the correct official jargon:

Supplementing the task that was assigned to you on January 24, 1939, to solve the Jewish problem by means of emigration and evacuation in the best possible way according to present conditions, I herewith instruct you to make all necessary preparations as regards organizational, financial and material matters for a total solution [*Gesamtlösung*] of the Jewish question within the area of German influence in Europe. . . . I instruct you further to submit to me as soon as possible a general plan showing the measures for organization and for action necessary to carry out the desired final solution [*Endlösung*] of the Jewish question.[31]

The exact nature of this "final" as distinct from "total" solution, Hitler's State Secretary Hans Lammers said at Nuremberg, took the form of an order from Hitler which was passed through Goering to Heydrich and was most probably given orally and never written. But by the time this letter was sent to Heydrich, the extermination groups were already at work in Russia.

Six months later, on January 20, 1942, at a conference held at Wannsee to discuss the removal of the Jews of Europe, Heydrich was to find representatives of Goering's Economic Staff East demanding exemption for the Jewish armament workers. In fact, Goering, through his initial intervention in the autumn of 1941, managed to keep the Jewish armament workers and their families free from deportation for about a year. But, as the world now knows, the "final solution" had already become the fearful summons to the mass extermination camps. In spite of his protests at Nuremberg about the comparative innocence of the terms used in his directive to Heydrich, there can be no doubt that Goering knew

in principle that genocide was now the official practice of his colleagues. If any doubt remains, then his ears must have been shut
when, at the meeting over which he presided on August 6, 1942,
Lohse, one of the "Reich commissioners" for the occupied territories, commenting on a report concerning the massacre of 55,000
Jews in White Russia, said, "There are only a few Jews alive. Tens
of thousands have been disposed of."

At a conference on November 7 Goering issued directives
which demanded the ruthless exploitation of Russian civilians and
prisoners of war as laborers. Germany by now held some five million prisoners of war, of whom two million were employed in the
war industries. Goering was quite prepared to order free men to be
seized and employed as prisoners if they would not consent to
work in and for Germany under normal contract.[32]

At the end of August when Germany was beginning to experience the teeth of Russian resistance in front of Moscow, Mussolini
visited Hitler's headquarters on the eastern front, which were in
the forest near Rastenburg in East Prussia, not far from Goering's
shooting estate of Rominten; the headquarters, which were known
as the Wolf's Lair, looked like an Alpine village composed of chalets. There Hitler lectured his lesser warlords on the Russian campaign and admitted that he had underestimated the degree of
resistance his armies were now experiencing. According to Hassell,
Goering was host to both Hitler and Mussolini at a small dinner
party; Mussolini apparently behaved very coldly toward him, although Goering gave the Duce an album of photographs of Bruno
Mussolini's visit to the Luftwaffe's Atlantic bases.

Compared with what was happening in Russia, the air war between Britain and Germany in the summer of 1941 was a comparatively chivalrous affair. The airmen respected each other, and
Goering readily allowed the R.A.F. to parachute a pair of artificial
legs to Wing Commander Douglas Bader, who had been shot
down after a duel in the air. In the autumn Galland, who had been
singled out by Goering as a future member of his senior staff and
was in consequence a frequent guest at his shooting parties, was
summoned to Veldenstein to confer about the increasing weight of
the R.A.F. raids on Germany. To Goering the matter appeared of
only temporary significance; soon all the planes would be back
from the east. The job of the Luftwaffe, repeated Goering end-

lessly, was to attack, not defend. But Galland remained anxious; the fighters had been withdrawn in large numbers to the east, and many were converted to fighter bombers, while in the factories the production of bombers was still given priority. Meanwhile, the R.A.F. was taking advantage of this period of comparative invulnerability to increase the range and scale of its raids. Goering, however, preferred to leave defense to the antiaircraft gunners. In the east the Luftwaffe found it impossible to give the effective support to the Army that it should have done. Its strength was dispersed over a front that had suddenly extended a thousand miles within a couple of months, and it became a secondary force in the German strategy so vigorously opposed by the Russians. The glorious days of the Luftwaffe as a strategic force in its own right were gone, and perceptibly Goering's interest in it slackened.

In November came the suicide of General Udet following a violent scene with Goering, who had placed far too considerable a weight of responsibility on this easygoing, gallant, lighthearted pilot of the First World War. Though popular with the young airmen, Udet had been quite unequal to the task of organizing the development of the Luftwaffe's aircraft research and production.[33] Goering insisted that the suicide remain secret, though the rumors spread around, and Udet's death was officially attributed on November 18 to an accident while testing a new weapon. A state funeral was ordered for November 21, and Werner Mölders, who had recently been appointed general of the Luftwaffe's fighter arm, crashed and died on his way to take part in it. Goering walked behind Udet's coffin in the funeral procession to the Invalidenfriedhof in the north of Berlin, where he delivered an oration, weeping publicly under the floodlights. When he retired to stand beside the Führer, the funeral march from *Götterdämmerung* rose in grand crescendo.

During the period November 24 to 27 Ciano was in Berlin, ostensibly to help celebrate the Anti-Comintern Pact. He met Goering several times, and the Reich Marshal put on a grand formal reception at his Berlin residence. In private conversation Ciano recounted later that "Goering gave the conversation a really friendly character such as I had not encountered in him for a long time." He praised the Italian forces in Libya "with all the marks of his impetuous and enthusiastic temperament." He said he was worried about the food situation in Greece and was considering an appeal to Roosevelt for help; if Roosevelt refused aid, then the blame for Greek starvation would be his!

He added, said Ciano:

On the other hand, we cannot worry unduly about the hunger of the Greeks. It is a misfortune which will strike many other people besides them. In the camps for Russian prisoners of war, after having eaten everything possible, including the soles of their boots, they have begun to eat each other, and what is more serious, have also eaten a German sentry. This year between twenty and thirty million persons will die in Russia of hunger. Perhaps it is well that it should be so, for certain nations must be decimated. But even if it were not, nothing can be done about it. It is obvious that if humanity is condemned to die of hunger, the last to die will be our two peoples.[34]

In Berlin itself, Ciano thought, although the morale seemed high there was no enthusiasm whatsoever for the war.

At Mölders' funeral, which followed that of Udet at the end of the month, Goering called Galland away from the guard of honor by beckoning to him with his baton and told him that he was now general of the fighter arm in Mölders' place. Goering characteristically undertook to pass on Galland's farewell to his command in France, as he was going to visit the grave of his nephew Peter Goering, who had died in battle as a fighter pilot, and then enjoy a period of relaxation in Paris. On December 1 he had a conference with Marshal Pétain; he traveled by special train and was accompanied by Galland, to whom he said on the way, "In twenty minutes I shall have finished with the old gentleman." Goering emerged from the conference after three hours looking angry; according to Schmidt, who interpreted, there seemed no reason why the meeting had taken place at all. It had ended in deadlock—Goering demanding that the French be more energetic in defending their colonies against the British, Pétain replying that he needed larger forces and more war materiel. As Goering was taking his leave, Pétain, aged and cross, forgot his dignity and thrust firmly into the Reich Marshal's pocket a memorandum which Goering had refused to accept.

While Goering talked, shopped and cast an appraising eye over the art treasures gathered for his inspection in Paris, the German armies were experiencing the savage Russian winter for which Hitler had never equipped them. The roads disintegrated, the snow fell and the temperatures were catastrophic. The quick victory declined into deadlock, while the British and the Russians used the valuable months of winter to strengthen themselves for a spring offensive. Galland stationed himself at the Luftwaffe's East Prussian headquarters at Goldap, conveniently near Goering's staff headquarters at Rominten and the Führer's headquarters at Rastenburg. He soon learned how strained were the manpower resources of the Luftwaffe when it came to building up the Fighter Arm for the spring. Milch, as the new head of aircraft production, was increasing the output of fighters; the policy was to dip deeply into the reserves of men in training in order to give them intensive instruction for a second quick, devastating offensive against Russia. Galland agreed with Jeschonnek, the Chief of Staff, who had to interpret this order at great cost to the long-term efficiency of the Luftwaffe.

When Hitler gave Galland a further decoration, the diamonds to the Knight's Cross, Goering looked at it quizzically and demanded to see it more closely. Galland had followed the usual unofficial practice of fastening the ribbon holding the cross with a woman's garter hidden under his collar; when the laughter over this had died down, Goering took the stones, examined them and claimed they were not diamonds at all. He said that the Führer, who knew nothing of such matters, had been duped. Later at Carinhall he gave Galland his decoration back, set by his own court jeweler. "Now," said Goering, "these are the Führer's diamonds and these the Reich Marshal's. Which of us knows something about diamonds?"

The year 1942 was the first in which Germany received the full force of armed retaliation against her. Hitler, working in an ever-increasing mental isolation, blamed the reverses on his generals and withdrew from the counsel of everyone, including Goering, whose failure in the air became openly apparent when the great raids from Britain began in the spring. Germany, feeding on the resources and the forced labor of the conquered territories, used her formidable strength in vain in a war that extended from North Africa through Russia to the Baltic and from Norway through Britain to France and Germany herself. To this on December 11 in the Reichstag he almost casually added the declaration of war on

America, four days after the Japanese had made their surprise attack on Pearl Harbor.

Goering went to Rome in January in an attempt to draw Mussolini closer to the great struggle to come, and to ask for an increase
in military aid. He had celebrated his birthday with a lavish reception on January 12 and had been referred to afterward in the press
by his old and favorite title of paladin of the Führer. Nevertheless, when he arrived in Rome on January 28 he said on getting off
the train, "We are having hard times." In conversation with Mussolini he blamed the Russian stalemate on the generals as if it were
Hitler who was talking; he was skeptical about France making a
useful contribution to the Axis, but he was convinced, he said, that
Russia would yield during 1942 and Britain in 1943. Meanwhile,
he wanted to renew the attack on Malta. "Nothing more can be
done this winter," he added to Mussolini, who stared at him
thoughtfully. Ciano, who still had no love for Goering, describes
him as "bloated and overbearing" and says that he "strutted bliss-
fully" in front of the servile Italian commanders who were his
hosts. On February 4 he had dinner with Ciano and boasted about
the jewels he owned, and indeed displayed on his fingers.

I am told that he plays with his gems like a little boy with his marbles
[writes Ciano with his usual malicious delight]. During the journey he
was nervous, so his aides brought him a small vase filled with diamonds.
He placed them on the table and counted them, lined them up, mixing
them together, and calmed down completely. One of his high officers
said last evening, "He has two loves—beautiful objects and making war."
Both are expensive hobbies. At the station he wore a great sable coat,
something between what motorists wore in 1906 and what a high-grade
prostitute wears to the opera. . . . He is not only accepted in Germany
but perhaps even loved for it. That is because he has a dash of humanity."

In February Goering presided over the court-martial of General
Count von Sponeck and, according to Hassell, made it clear, when
the General was condemned to death for ordering a tactical retreat
in the Crimea, that Hitler expected nothing but obedience from
his commanders. Hitler was now openly insulting his senior officers
at the conferences he called, while he interfered increasingly with

the details of their commands. Constant staff changes were the sign of his impatience and megalomania, and he had finally appointed himself Commander in Chief of the Army in December. Concentrating like a hypnotist in his forest fortress, he willed his generals to hold out in the cruel conditions of the Russian winter, with armies that were inadequately clothed and with frozen weapons the troops could not operate in the icy mud and deep drifts of snow. A third of his Army was either killed, wounded or missing by February 1942.

Goering, no longer able to achieve prominence through the sporadic activities of the Luftwaffe, was still able to give his power some expression through the economy of Germany. The office of the Four-Year Plan issued a decree on January 29 addressed to both the civilian and the military authorities in the occupied territories, stating that "any and all methods must be adopted" to force workers to go to Germany. On March 21 Fritz Sauckel was appointed Plenipotentiary General for Manpower, responsible directly to Goering, and on March 27 Goering issued his enabling decree giving Sauckel the terrible powers that finally brought him to the dock in Nuremberg: "My manpower sections are hereby abolished. Their duties, recruitment and allocation of manpower, regulation for labor conditions, are taken over by the Plenipotentiary General for Manpower, who is directly under me. . . . In the case of ordinances and instructions of fundamental importance, report is to be submitted to me, in advance."[35]

In April 1942, on the suggestion of Speer, the new Minister of Armament and War Production, Goering established the Central Planning Board to allocate and distribute various materials among the three branches of the armed forces. Speer drafted the decree that Goering issued on April 25, and he was in effect Goering's subordinate; Todt, his predecessor, had been on bad terms with Goering precisely because he had not been directly under him. Once more Hitler created administrative networks that tied themselves into knots and hindered his war effort. Speer, however, was to prove remarkably efficient, though he was later to become a convinced anti-Nazi and plan an attempt on Hitler's life. Speer also managed to avoid having Goering present at the meetings of the board, of which he took charge, because, as he put it at Nuremberg, "We would not have had any use for him, for after all we had to carry out practical work." In spite of Allied bombing, he brought German armament production to its peak during the latter part of 1944.

On August 6, 1942, Goering presided at the Air Ministry over a conference of the commissioners for the occupied territories at which he stressed the increased range of his powers as Plenipotentiary. He told the commissioners, "God knows you were not sent to work for the welfare of the populations, but to squeeze the utmost out of them so that the German people may live. . . . It makes no difference to me if you say that your people are starving." Territory by territory he went over the quota of food to be supplied. Even a little blunt humor seemed called for: "It seemed to me to be a relatively simple matter in former days. It used to be called plundering. It was up to the party in question to carry off what had been conquered. But today things have become more genteel. In spite of that, I intend to plunder and to do it thoroughly. . . . Whenever you may come across anything that may be needed by the German people, you must be after it like a bloodhound. It must be taken out of store and brought to Germany." He ended by threatening them: "Gentlemen, I have a very great deal to do and a very great deal of responsibility. I have no time to read letters and memoranda informing me that you cannot supply my requirements. I have only time to ascertain . . . whether the commitments are being fulfilled. . . . I will get what I demand from you, and if you cannot manage I will set up agencies that will get it out of you whether you like it or not." Only for Sauckel does he seem to have had some praise: "What he has done in this brief time in order to collect workers from all over Europe and to bring them to our factories with such rapidity is a unique feat. I must say to all: If everybody in his own area would apply a tenth of the energy which Gauleiter Sauckel has applied, then indeed the tasks which have been assigned to you would easily be fulfilled."[36]

This bluff, aggressive manner was, of course, as normal to Goering in dealing with his agents and subordinates as it is with certain schoolmasters addressing unwilling pupils. But his hectoring manner at this important conference undoubtedly concealed his own uneasiness in authority. Like Hitler, he was hiding from the truth that the war to which he was now fully committed was no longer going well. When Walter Schellenberg, head of Himmler's foreign-intelligence service, presented him with a special report on American war production early in 1942, all Goering would say was, "Everything you have written is utter nonsense. You should have a psychiatrist examine your mental condition." The report gave evidence about the development of the United States Air Force and claimed that the annual steel production in the States was eighty-five to ninety million tons. By March 1942, according to Schellenberg, Goering was no longer important, his prestige had suffered severely through the failure of the air offensive against Britain, and he "seemed to have lost nearly all interest in the great military events." Schellenberg refers to "his increasing dependence on morphia" and says many people attributed his loss of influence to this and to his "increasing morbid indulgence in a life of luxury." Himmler sent Schellenberg in March to see Goering at Carinhall in order to suggest that a special large-scale organization for telephone tapping in Germany and the occupied territories, known as the Goering Research Bureau, should be taken over by Himmler. Goering kept Schellenberg waiting in the entrance hall and then suddenly emerged clad in a toga and sandals and carrying his marshal's baton. While he listened to Schellenberg, he sat at a table on which stood a cut-glass bowl filled with pearls and antique jewelry, and these he fingered with such concentration that he appeared to be in a trance.[37]

Himmler called Goering "the king of the black markets." Nevertheless, in March Goering signed a law against profiteering and illicit dealing, though Goebbels claims its terms were milder than they should have been; in any case, he added, "the behavior of people prominent in political life should be made to accord with them"—which was without a doubt a jibe at Goering himself, whose openly luxurious way of life had always offended the harsh and narrow-minded Minister of Propaganda. However, Goebbels decided in March that it was time he had a discussion with Goering, and he seemed surprised to find him in "exceptionally good condition physically." In his secret diary, Goebbels pays a rather unexpected tribute to Goering's hard work, "enormous successes" and sound common sense. They discussed many matters, including the reprimand Goering had recently sent to two Catholic bishops who had been outspoken against the regime; he had reminded them of their oath, pledged to him personally, of fidelity to the State. On the other hand, he agreed with Goebbels that it was unwise for the party to have insisted on the removal of crucifixes from schools and hospitals. The Christian denominations, they agreed, could wait until after the war for their Nazification. About the war itself, Goering expressed doubts whether the spring and summer offensive would succeed against the Russians. The two ministers gossiped about the shortcomings of the field marshals and generals, and of their colleagues Frick and Rosenberg, and they daydreamed of removing the dividing line between Europe and Asia and forming a vast Eurasian hegemony. Goering, however, was "cautious" in his prognosis. When they parted, they found they had so enjoyed their talk that they decided there and then to meet more frequently.

The following month, Goebbels remarked on the dignified language of the tribute to the Führer which Goering published on Hitler's birthday, but was much less impressed when he made a public appearance on April 26 and introduced Hitler at a session of the Reichstag; he spoke, says Goebbels, "indistinctly and haltingly," and his lack of assurance and apparent carelessness of manner caused considerable criticism.[38] Hitler boldly proclaimed the campaign he was about to wage in Russia, but no doubt the moment was unpropitious for Goering to appear in public, for neither the Luftwaffe nor the antiaircraft defenses had been able to lessen the large-scale raids on Rostock during recent nights.

May was an unfortunate month for Goering. First, he was greatly upset to find that a member of the Luftwaffe staff in the telephone-tapping "Research" Bureau, Lieutenant Harold Schulze-Boysen, the eccentric grandson of Admiral von Tirpitz, was head of an extensive spy ring known as the Rote Kapelle that was working for the Russians and had its agents placed in several of the ministries. The discovery led to over fifty hangings. At the end of the month the State Secretary forwarded to Goering in the strictest confidence the documents of a case against an embezzler called Pieper, in which Goering's name and that of his cousin Herbert Goering frequently occurred. Part of Pieper's defense was that he had been a channel through whom prominent industrialists had given presents to Goering in order to gain his goodwill, and it was suggested by Pieper's lawyer that "publicly to go into this sort of thing in open court undoubtedly would seem to be contrary to the interests of the State." Peter Menthe, one of Goering's adjutants, had made statements that he had given Pieper letters expressing the Minister President's gratitude for the presents received. The documents of the case, which were sent to Goering on May 8, were put under lock and key for a year, after which the State Secretary, Dr. Schle-gelberger, promised Goering he could destroy all but the papers that ought to be kept.[39] In August, Goering thought it wise to confer a flyer's wings on Himmler, who was investigating the affairs of the ministry and possibly his own as well.

No doubt this case did not give Goering much worry; such mat-ters as this could easily be suppressed. But the first thousand-bomber raid, on the night of May 30–31, was a different matter. Cologne was severely damaged. Goering was at Veldenstein; Jes-chonnek and Bodenschatz, who were with Hitler at Rastenburg, had to take the brunt of the Führer's anger. There were conflicting reports as to the scale of the raid: the Luftwaffe report said that two hundred planes had come; the Gauleiter of Cologne reported there had been a thousand or more. Goering was summoned and Hitler in his anger treated him with contempt.

In the Mediterranean the second period of the Malta blitz was less successful than had been expected. Malta had been reinforced by the R.A.F., and the island was most skillfully defended. Goering met Galland in Naples and blamed the lack of success on the fighter pilots. To blame was easy, and Galland resented the criti-cism and the implication of the defeatist spirit behind it. Galland toured Africa and found that the task assigned to the Luftwaffe was beyond the available strength; the report he sent to Goering only led to further charges of defeatism. In October Montgomery opened his counteroffensive at El Alamein; in November the American forces landed in North Africa and the Battle of Stalin-grad began in Russia. Hitler's major successes of the year (apart from his toll on Allied shipping), Rommel's drive toward Egypt and the penetration of the Caucasus, were either countered or reversed. Goering drafted a decree for the call-up of fifteen-year-old schoolboys; the draft was sent by accident to Schacht, who was still a Minister without Portfolio.[40] When the Sixth Army was sur-rounded at Stalingrad, Goering made a desperate bid for reinstate-ment in Hitler's favor by promising to supply General Paulus' forces by air—a matter of attempting the impossible task of trans-porting 750 tons daily through the wintry Russian skies. The Luft-waffe failed, and so did attempts to relieve the Sixth Army by land. Hitler forbade surrender, but Paulus finally capitulated on Febru-ary 2, 1943.

Goering's situation during the winter of 1942–43 lay in the

shadows. He made one of his last public speeches at a harvest festival in the Sportpalast on October 4. Hassell reports it to have been successful, far more successful than Hitler's own speech made a few days previously. Goering tried to hearten the German people. "It is my desire," he said, "that the population of the territories which have been conquered by us and taken under our protection shall not suffer from hunger. If, however, through enemy measures difficulties of food supply should arise, then everyone should know that, if there is to be hunger anywhere, it shall never be in Germany." He also referred as scathingly as he could to the Americans. "Some astronomical figures are expected from the American war industry. Now, I am the last to underrate this industry. Obviously the Americans do very well in some technical fields. We know they produce a colossal number of fast cars. And the development of radio is one of their special achievements, and so is razor blades. . . . But you must not forget there is one word in their language that is written with a capital B, and this word is Bluff."

Late in November Rommel, who was making a fighting retreat with his famous Afrika Korps, flew to Rastenburg to report to Hitler; when he put the point soberly that North Africa should be abandoned, the Führer shouted at his favorite general that Tripoli must be held at any cost in lives. At a second meeting, Goering was called in and ordered to see that Rommel had everything he wanted. Goering responded with alacrity. "You can pile everything on my shoulders," he said. "I shall attend to it all myself." Hitler gave him extraordinary powers to rearm Rommel's men, whose armor and supplies had been devastated by British bombing.

Rommel traveled to Rome with Goering in his special train, and Frau Rommel was invited to accompany her husband. Rommel's account of this journey is one of unmitigated frustration at what he called Goering's "antics," his vanity, his response to flattery from his staff and his endless conversation about jewelry and pictures. According to Rommel, who was deeply depressed, he showed no interest in Africa except insofar as there might be a chance to win laurels for himself through some action by the Luftwaffe or by his so-called praetorian guard, the Hermann Goering Panzer Division, which was then on its way to Tunis. Rommel's bitterness against Goering, who accused him of needless pessimism, broke out. "During the whole of this period, my bitterest enemy was Goering," he wrote. At a staff conference held two months before, in September, Goering had minimized the difficulties in Africa and radiated false optimism. As for the Americans, he had scoffed once more that they only knew how to make razor blades. Rommel was to find Mussolini far more sympathetic and knowledgeable about the difficult situation of the Afrika Korps.

Frau Rommel was also horrified at Goering's appearance and behavior. She had never met him before, and he seemed to her to be a megalomaniac. Later she remarked on his tie secured with an emerald clip, his watch case studded with emeralds, the enormous diamond ring which he displayed to her with the remark, "You will be interested in this—it is one of the most valuable stones in the world." In Rome, Goering stayed with General and Frau Rommel at the Excelsior Hotel. Frau Rommel, who was worried because of her husband's depression over the fate of his army in Africa, shared his despair at Goering's ceaseless talk about pictures and sculpture. Goering avoided all reference to Africa in their private conversations. "They call me the Maecenas of the Third Reich," he boasted, and he spent all the time he could away from staff conferences searching for pictures and sculpture.[41]

Goering stayed some days in Italy and promised Mussolini that three armored divisions would be sent to Africa, the Adolf Hitler, the Hermann Goering and the Deutschland—"three names that mean much to German honor," he added. Goering's aides tried to spread confidence among the Italians they met. Ciano, however, believed that Goering's aim was to "create confusion" and blame bad Italian organization for the failures in North Africa; Goering, according to some German experts at the embassy, merely talked nonsense. After a meeting with Kesselring and Rommel, the Reich Marshal went to Naples to appoint a superintendent of transport. "Can it be that Goering is really thinking of appointing himself Reich Protector of Italy?" wrote Ciano. Having settled his affairs in Naples, Goering returned to Rome to lecture Mussolini on the need to redouble his efforts in Africa.[42] It was pleasant for him to be treated with respect and even servility by the high command of Italy. According to Schmidt, he "ranted and threatened," alienating the Italians and showing "very little psychological insight."

In Berlin in December Goering met the French General Juin, who offered help in North Africa, but not if it involved direct contact with the Germans. "As long as there are still French prisoners of war in Germany, I cannot ask my officers to fight with the

German Army," he said. Goering was also present at a conference at Hitler's headquarters in Rastenburg, where the Führer criticized the fighting quality of the Italians on the eastern front and the shortcomings of the French. At an inspection of newly appointed officers held in the Sportpalast, Goering deputized for Hitler and repeated to these young officers the Führer's reproaches at the ability of his generals—they, not Hitler, he said, were responsible for the position at Stalingrad. Goebbels heard that "the delivery was poor, and some of his remarks about death on the field of battle were in rather poor taste." In addition to the Luftwaffe, Goering still had his own private army amounting to twenty-two infantry divisions formed during this period from the supplementary ground staffs of the bomber force and the parachute divisions, which were to remain under his command till the end of the war. Goering's aim was to keep the maximum number of men under his control in spite of the pressure that was being brought to bear on him to release men for the Russian front; as he put it to Hitler, why should he send his "National Socialist boys," as he called them, where "some general or other would probably get the idea of sending them to church"?[43] General von Thoma, who, with Guderian, was the most famous of Germany's pioneer leaders of the panzer armored-tank divisions, complained bitterly after the war about Goering's obstructionism during the Russian campaign; the division of authority between the ground forces and the air forces (including Goering's paratroopers) led to disagreement in strategy which only a unified command on the spot would have obviated. According to Thoma, "Guderian worked well with Student, who trained the parachute forces, but Goering blocked proposals for combined action with the panzer forces. He always wanted to keep up the strength of the Luftwaffe and was therefore niggardly with such air transport as he had to provide for the parachute forces." In the end the paratroopers, whom Hitler tended to keep in reserve for special projects that seldom matured, disintegrated and formed supplementary ground forces after Goering had lost his initial enthusiasm for the Luftwaffe. Goering had for too long formed the habit of promising what he was in no position to provide. Hitler finally developed into a man deploying false statistics rather than actual forces in the field, and Goering slipped easily into the same unreal strategy; when the Russians began to force the German armies back, he promised Hitler ten divisions of ground troops recruited from the Luftwaffe at short notice, without bearing in mind that the men he was committing to the fearful conditions of the eastern front were trained only for air operations and knew nothing of action on the battlefield. According to General Warlimont, "Goering stirred the fire, interfering with everything without scruple or responsibility. The misshapen Luftwaffe field divisions originated at that time [late in 1942] because Goering could not expect his Air Force men to change their blue-gray uniform for the field gray of the Army."[44]

Goering's illusions of grandeur demanded still further extensions to Carinhall. However serious the war situation, his passion for building never ceased, and he made an official request to the Minister of Finance, Count Schwerin von Krosigk, for a grant of two million marks for extension and redecoration at Carinhall. Schwerin von Krosigk warned him of the damage this work would do to his reputation at a time when the Russian campaign was draining Germany's manpower and resources. Goering promised to think the matter over, but later renewed his demand.[45] Nor did the situation in Stalingrad stop him from organizing the most splendid reception he had ever held to celebrate his fiftieth birthday, on January 12, 1943, while the usual valuable presents and works of art poured in from all quarters. On January 30 while Goering was deputizing for Hitler at the annual party celebration of the ascent to power in 1933, his speech was interrupted by an air-raid warning, and he had to break off and take refuge in a bunker.

Goering, in fact, was trying to live two lives at once—the life he lived at Carinhall, Rominten and Veldenstein, and the life of a man still exerting power and influence in the conduct of Germany's war policy and economy. When the new Swedish minister, Thomsen, arrived to take up his duties in Berlin, he was invited to Carinhall, where he spent the day being driven around the forest and entertained by Goering in his shooting costume. According to the account given by Hassell and recorded at the time in his diary, Goering "changed his costume after the day and appeared at the dinner table in a blue or violet kimono with fur-trimmed bedroom slippers. Even in the morning he wore at his side a golden dagger, which was also changed frequently. In his tiepin he wore a variety of precious stones, and around his fat body a wide girdle set with many stones—not to mention the splendor and number of his rings."

In January 1943 the first daylight raids by the U.S. Army Air Force over Germany began to supplement the night raids by the R.A.F., which had been growing in strength throughout 1942, ever since the massive thousand- or near-thousand-bomber raids had taken place on Cologne and Essen in May and on Essen and Bremen in June. The R.A.F. also carried out special missions by day. One by one the great centers of armament production and of communications were subject to these annihilating attacks. Goering's name was Meier, and the effect of the raids on German morale was naturally very great. But the Germans, like the British, learned how to survive. The Luftwaffe night fighters took a heavy toll of the great bombers; by March 1943 Galland claims that two thousand had been shot down. Galland, as general of fighters, did his best, but he was not in command: "All my attempts to explain to the High Command the seriousness of our position miscarried. . . . They embarked on a path of criminal carelessness. They did not see the danger because they would have had to admit their many omissions. Unpleasant reminders were regarded as a great nuisance." Goering made his public act of self-immolation at what he called the shame of the Luftwaffe by announcing he would forgo wearing his decorations. The Luftwaffe in fact, in spite of its high losses in the Mediterranean and elsewhere, was fighting, supporting and supplying as hard as its inadequate numbers allowed. What was needed was a gigantic program of air armament production and a vast new training scheme for air crews.

By the middle of 1943, Germany, though still powerful, was in retreat in both Russia and the Mediterranean. Goering was in conflict with his own officers. Galland demanded a four-to-one ratio of fighters to bombers; Goering refused to accept the argument that a totally new policy of air defense on a massive scale was all that could save Germany from an increasing weight of Allied air attack. Both Hitler and Goering still favored the production of bombers, but Milch managed to deliver about a thousand fighters a month during the first half of 1943. Hitler's determination to fight over every foot of ground in Russia and the south, where by July the Allies had landed in Sicily and by September had reached the mainland, led to the dispersion and loss of a high proportion of the fighter planes and crews that should have remained in Germany to supply what Roosevelt called the roof over the German fortress, the roof that Hitler and Goering forgot.

The position of Goering himself grew more difficult. Rudolf Semmler, Goebbels' aide who was among those observers of the Nazi leaders who kept a useful diary, returned from a year's service on the Russian front to find that Goering's drug addiction was common gossip among the Nazi leaders, and that Morell, Hitler's quack physician, had told Frau Goebbels that "Goering was becoming more and more a slave to the habit, and that even his doctors were powerless to stop him."[46]

Rommel claims that he was successful in avoiding Goering's interference at his conference with Hitler at the Führer's headquarters behind the Russian front on March 10. He flatly puts the blame for the collapse of North Africa on Goering's "baleful influence" at headquarters and his ambition to supersede the Army. On the other hand, Goering himself admitted at Nuremberg that by this time he had lost the confidence of Hitler:

> The chief influence on the Führer, at least up to the end of 1941 or the beginning of 1942, if one can speak of influence at all, was exerted by me. From then until 1943 my influence gradually decreased, after which it rapidly dwindled. All in all, I do not believe anyone had anything like the influence on the Führer that I had. Next to me, or apart from me, if one can speak of influence at all, Goebbels, with whom the Führer was together quite a good deal . . . This influence wavered for a time . . . and then increased greatly in the last year of the war.[47]

Toward the end the influence on Hitler was exerted "first and foremost," as Goering put it, by Martin Bormann, the Führer's private secretary. Bodenschatz confirms the decline in Goering's position: "According to my personal opinion and conviction, Hermann Goering began to lose influence with Hitler in the spring of 1943."

Nevertheless, the retired and saddened figure of the Reich Marshal was involved briefly in the calculations of Goebbels, whose star was now once more in the ascendant. Goebbels was making his supreme bid for influence over Hitler; he had become convinced that Germany must face facts and bring the whole population into the conflict, and he saw himself as the one man in Germany capable of taking a place alongside the Führer as the plenipotentiary for total war. Although there was much that he despised in Goering— what he regarded as his softness, his lack of moral stamina and, above all, his lapse into luxury—he felt the need to revive Goering's

prestige and form a triumvirate with him and Speer, whose administrative qualities and driving energy in furthering war production
he very much admired. With Goering as a popular figurehead
round whom he believed he could weave a network of revivalist
propaganda, Goebbels hoped to break the inner circle round Hitler
represented by Bormann, Lammers and Keitel. He even hoped to
bring the isolated and secret figure of Himmler into some form of
assocation with him. It was to be an attempt by the remaining
members of the Nazi foundation to oust the newcomers. As Goebbels put it, "As was always the case during the crises of the party,
it is the duty of the Führer's closest friends in time of need to
gather about him and form a solid phalanx around his person."

At the end of February Speer had talks with Goering, who was
down on the Obersalzburg. He found him in a "resigned mood"
and distrustful, but Speer managed to persuade him to see Goebbels and talk over his new policy for the war. On March 1 Goebbels
drove up the mountain road to the wintry quiet of Goering's chalet
high above Berchtesgaden. The Reich Marshal received Goebbels
in a manner the Propaganda Minister described in his private diary
as charming and openhearted, though his dress was "baroque" and
"almost laughable." They reviewed the war situation rather de-
spondently and seemed "somewhat helpless" in the face of the
seemingly endless supply of Soviet armament. But Goebbels, who
thought his host "tired and apathetic," set to work to impress on
him the need to rally Germany for a total war effort. Together they
criticized Rosenberg, Ribbentrop (whom Goering still blamed for
the war with Britain), Lammers, Bormann, Rommel, Keitel and
the other generals at Hitler's headquarters, and they discussed the
unhealthy life that Hitler lived, worrying and brooding in his
bunker. Goebbels then urged on Goering consideration of his main
plan—to rally a group of loyal leaders in order to concentrate on
winning the war and oust the inefficient and undesirable men who
were hampering and misleading the Führer. Goering roused himself and agreed; he seemed heartened that Goebbels had come to
see him. Strangely, he said that he would like to win Himmler over
to the idea. Dictating his diary the following day, Goebbels remarked for the record, "Goering has been standing aside too long
from the political factors which supply the real driving force.
. . . He is no longer closely connected with our political leaders. . . . Goering is fully conscious of his rather weak position

today. He knows that it is decidedly to his advantage for strong men to come to his side." Goebbels says that he spent four hours with Goering; like all the Nazi leaders with a lust for self-expression, Goebbels loved to record how long his endless interviews and speeches lasted.

But when the first approaches were made to Hitler, the mention of Goering's name raised a storm. Hitler said he was thoroughly dissatisfied with Goering's war measures. Speer, who was the first man to suggest Goering's reinstatement, found the Führer "unapproachable at the moment as regards Goering." Goebbels, though he realized Goering was still "somewhat inactive and resigned," was loath to give up his plan to make use of his name. "Goering after all has strong political and military authority which was gained in the course of years and certainly cannot be made to vanish overnight." Goebbels visited Hitler, who criticized Goering "with extraordinary sharpness," considering him the victim of "wishful thinking" and misled by his Luftwaffe generals, just as Goering considered Hitler misled by the generals of the Army. The Luftwaffe generals, said Hitler, merely withdrew to castles and lived the lives of sybarites. Goebbels, thinking the matter over in the course of dictating his diary, felt forced to agree that "Goering likes to hear things that are pleasant." No one, therefore, told him the truth, and the air-raid damage achieved by Allied planes was always minimized in the reports. Goebbels tactfully gave up mentioning the idea of Goering's reinstatement to the Führer, and Speer agreed with him.

Goering, meanwhile, had gone to Italy with Bodenschatz to inspect the supply lines. Bodenschatz returned in time to face the anger of Hitler when Nuremberg was raided on the night of March 8. "Goering now knows it is the eleventh hour for him," remarked Goebbels, who was with Hitler and had heard the Führer's cutting remarks to Bodenschatz because Goering was in Rome at such a time as this. Hitler worked himself into a rage, having ordered Bodenschatz to leave his bed and come to headquarters so that he might be used as an object for the expression of the Führer's hatred of the Luftwaffe. Goebbels magnanimously stepped in to protect Goering in his absence and rescue Bodenschatz. Goering might still be necessary as an ally, and Goebbels was testing his own renewed influence with the Führer. Four days later Hitler ordered Goering to return from Rome so that he could reprove him personally for his inactivity in the face of the increasing strength of the raids on Germany. The following day, March 12, according to Goebbels, "the Führer told Goering what he thought, without mincing words."

On March 17 Goebbels' cabal, which included Funk and Robert Ley, head of the Labor Front, as well as Speer, met Goering, who informed them, no doubt as a result of his experiences a few days earlier, that it was all-important to handle Hitler in the right way at the right time. Goebbels now decided to make use of Goering, who was to accompany Hitler to a meeting with Mussolini on the Obersalzberg; Goering was to recommend to the Führer that "German domestic leadership be made more definite" (that is, placed under Goebbels), and that the defunct Reich Defense Council be revived with Goebbels as deputy chairman, in order to direct the policy of total war. This was all part of the conspiracy to edge Bormann, Lammers and Keitel out of the inflated positions of power they had managed to create for themselves because, as Goebbels said, Goering had failed to summon the Council and use it as it should have been used to keep the power in the right hands. He found Goering ignorant of the extent of damage and loss of life in Berlin, but much more alert and positive than before. "Obviously," wrote Goebbels, "the fact that I told him to wake up had made a deep impression on him." Goebbels was beginning to enjoy bullying the stricken Reich Marshal.

The following month, while traveling with Goebbels to Essen, Milch dared to criticize Goering for having gone to sleep on the laurels of the Luftwaffe's victories of 1939 and 1940. He claimed that Udet had also failed, and that the Air Force would not be in a position to retaliate fully against England for another year owing to the backwardness in the development of new aircraft. Milch told Goebbels about Hitler's "most furious and unrestrained language" before the generals of the Luftwaffe, and how he had not failed to include Goering among the guilty men. Nevertheless, Hitler told Goebbels later that month that although he was "not too well satisfied with Goering," his authority was "indispensable to the supreme leadership of the Reich," and that he was glad Goebbels was establishing a more intimate relationship with him. "When his authority and mine are combined," writes Goebbels, "something useful for the administration of the Reich is bound to result." On Hitler's birthday Goering issued a proclamation to the press, which at least showed he was sufficiently alert to pay his respects at the appropriate moment.

But Goebbels' patience with Goering, like that of Hitler, soon waned. On May 7 he is blamed for not having "succeeded in taking the initiative"; he is, in fact, "rather ill" and needs a holiday. Two days later there even appears in the diary a word of praise for Bormann, and the remark that at least he keeps his promise, which is more than Goering ever does. "One can no longer really depend on Goering," wrote Goebbels. "He is tired and washed out." The kind of statement he was now making in public was "unfortunate" and damaging both to himself and to the regime in its foolish optimism. Since Hitler had issued an order in May that required all broadcast speeches to be shown to him in advance, Goering had declined for a while to speak and had left the field open to his critics. "There are even mumblings of a crisis developing about Goering," wrote Goebbels on May 22. "He has withdrawn to his lonely abode and says nothing . . . lethargically letting things drift. He does nothing to offset the way in which his prestige is falling."

Goebbels, impatient for power, realized that he would have to work for it independently. He left Goering to his decline. There were better ways of dealing with Hitler.

VIII

Maecenas of the Third Reich

W<small>HEN DURING</small> the First World War Goering had been awarded his Pour le Mérite, he had sent his batman to Munich to fetch the diamond ring that his father had bequeathed him. With the ornamental cross of the award suspended from his neck and the diamond flashing on his finger, he felt that he had earned great personal distinction. After the humiliating dependence of his youth spent in a house that could be called home only by virtue of his mother's relationship to his godfather, he began to feel the satisfaction of a certain rank and position which he had acquired for himself.

But the surroundings of his youth had remained firmly fixed in Goering's imagination, and he always referred proudly to "our castles."[1] When Epenstein died at the age of eighty-three in the summer of 1934, Carinhall was scarcely the showplace that Goering would so dearly have liked to display to the old man who, though he had dishonored his mother, had also shown him a way of life that he wanted to regain and then surpass. After Epenstein's death, his handsome widow was invited to Carinhall; she was addressed as "Baronin Lilli" (a form of address to which she was not strictly entitled), and when Goering welcomed her he said, with an expansive gesture to indicate the furnishings and decorations of his new domain, "What a pity the old man could not have lived to see all this. How I would have loved to show him Carinhall."[2] Epenstein would have had to live to the age of ninety to see Carinhall in its wartime glory, the center for what was to become one of the finest private art collections in Europe and itself one of the architectural wonders, or rather perhaps curiosities, of Germany. Epenstein's wealth and possessions would seem very poor in comparison.

After Frau von Epenstein's death, Goering, as we have seen, came into possession of both Veldenstein and Mauterndorf, the castles that had first inspired in him the pride of personal ownership. It is difficult to tell in his case to what extent he was by nature a connoisseur of art, furniture and decoration and how far these possessions were merely an extension of his need to display himself as a man of unique position and power. His abnormal energy and enthusiasm and his unusual memory equipped him to learn many things rapidly, and Hitler himself provided Goering with an example to emulate in his obsession for building (a psychological need in most dictators) and for the acquisition of famous and priceless works of art. Goering spent many years both before and during the war as a student, connoisseur and, indeed, dealer in art, and he had men of considerable knowledge on his staff to act as his advisers. At Nuremberg he referred to his "collector's passion," and his collection amounted in the end to some 1,500 works, including among them many masterpieces. Their total value was estimated after the war at some two hundred million dollars.

Though Goering's need for the experience of art and beauty was a part of his vanity, it was by no means superficial. His love of jewels did not stop at using them for display. He needed to finger them to calm himself in moments of anxiety or nervous strain. As the stresses of his drug addiction built up in him, he turned with relief to the comforts of silken clothes, soft leather, the luxuries of extravagant dress and the physical beauty represented by his *objets d'art*, his antique furniture, his porcelain and the treasures of fine craftsmanship that stood in their cases around him. Their indestructible grace and dignity eased the increasing tension that the war and its failures forced upon him. His mastery over these works of art represented for Goering the final confirmation of prestige. What did the Luftwaffe matter in the face of such permanent beauty as the Hermann Goering national art collection revealed? This would be his monument when all else failed. He was, as he reminded Frau Rommel when her husband was facing defeat in North Africa, the Maecenas of the Third Reich.

When he acquired Veldenstein and Mauterndorf, Goering's passion for building and redecoration, unhindered by national shortages, as we have seen, was extended to his new properties. He improved and modernized them; at Veldenstein he slept in the master's suite that Epenstein himself had used during Goering's youth, and his growing collection of pictures, sculpture, furniture, tapestries, china and objects of silver and gold overflowed from Carinhall to the south.

Goering had appointed a Berlin art dealer called Walter Andreas Hofer to act as his agent and adviser in all matters of art. Hofer became the principal organizer of Goering's collection, planning and tracing acquisitions for the Reich Marshal, selecting the birthday presents from industrialists, State institutions and local authorities, and organizing the Reich Marshal's deals and purchases. Hofer, shrewd, calculating, knowledgeable and loquacious, claimed to have guided not only the nature of the collection but Goering's personal taste in art. As his art manager he became inevitably his principal art tutor, and although he found in Goering a taste to some extent already formed, he was able to develop and extend it as the masterpieces he discussed with his employer increased in range and number. Goering's taste in any event was a traditional one, and he read as widely as time permitted about the work of the masters he most admired, such as Rubens and the Dutch painters of the seventeenth century. Goering specialized in acquiring the works of Lucas Cranach, the sixteenth-century painter and etcher, friend of Martin Luther and portrayer of female nudes. Goering shared with Hitler a detestation of the forms of modern painting such as those exhibited in the notorious Nazi exhibition of "degenerate" art organized by Goebbels in Munich in 1937, which contained works by such artists as Renoir, Gauguin, van Gogh and Picasso. Goebbels planned to destroy these once the exhibition was over, but Goering realized as an economist if not as a connoisseur that such works had value abroad if they had none in Germany, and he acquired many of them to use as barter with dealers and art galleries outside Germany.

Goering claimed at Nuremberg that it was his plan to establish a national collection of masterpieces in his name, and house them in a great gallery which was to be built on his estate near Carinhall after the war. He planned this to coincide with his sixtieth birthday. There is no doubt that this was true; a portfolio of architect's drawings for the gallery dated January 1945 was discovered by the

Americans among his possessions.[3] His collection would rival that of Hitler, whose own great store of paintings remained mostly in crates waiting for the day when a gallery could be built in Linz. In his greedy acquisition of paintings Goering was to become Hitler's principal rival, as he readily admitted at the trial in Nuremberg.

While the foundations of Goering's collection were already established before the war,[4] the opportunities for acquisition, nominally by the state, increased immeasurably once the Nazis began to overrun Europe. Poland became the first center for the wholesale confiscation of works of art by Germany. In October 1939 Goering ordered Dr. Kajetan Mühlmann, an authority on art appointed for the purpose, to "safeguard" Polish art treasures, which soon came to mean their confiscation and removal to Germany. Mühlmann later stated under oath that this was so and claimed that he personally gave Goering thirty-one sketches by Albrecht Dürer taken from Lemberg, and that Goering handed them over to Hitler. Mühlmann was to remain in charge of art confiscation in Poland until 1943.

It was with the formation of a special task force, Einsatzstab Rosenberg, under the leadership of the Nazis' notorious cultural guide and philosopher, Alfred Rosenberg, that the organized looting of masterpieces, principally from the privately owned Jewish collections, began on a large scale with Goering's enthusiastic support. The task force was formed by a special order issued from Hitler's headquarters to the Commander in Chief of the Army on September 17, 1940. Rosenberg was authorized to seize any valuable historical material found in libraries and elsewhere, and this authority was almost immediately extended to include works of art. The order had been anticipated as early as January 29, 1940, when Hitler had made Rosenberg responsible for preparations to set up a center for National Socialist culture after the war. It was to further this scheme that the order made in September was extended to include the confiscation of all Jewish-owned works of art. A further order signed by Goering and dated November 5, 1940, gave instructions on how these treasures were to be handled. They were to be divided into four main groups:

1. Those about which the Führer has reserved for himself the decision as to their use.

2. Those which serve to complete the Reich Marshal's collection.
3. Those works of art and books the use of which seems suitable to the establishment of higher institutes of learning.
4. Those works of art that are suited for German museums.[5]

After the fall of France, the Rosenberg Task Force set up its headquarters in Paris, in the Salle du Jeu de Paume in the corner of the Tuileries Gardens near the Place de la Concorde. Goering in particular was prepared to give Rosenberg every help possible in the huge task of confiscation that lay ahead of him and his staff. It was revealed after the war that in Paris alone some 38,000 homes owned by Jews were sealed and their contents confiscated, stored and catalogued. In all, up to July 15, 1944, over 21,000 works of art were taken and inventoried, including 5,000 paintings, over 2,400 articles of antique furniture and over 500 textiles (including the Gobelin tapestries that Goering so dearly loved). Some of them were photographed so that the problem of assessing their value and ultimate destination would be made easier for the cultural masters of Germany.[6]

Goering tried to give Rosenberg every help that he could, and he soon became a constant visitor to the Musée. Transport was one of Rosenberg's greatest difficulties, though he employed removal contractors on an extensive scale and, according to the reports quoted at Nuremberg, managed to send some 26,000 railroad cars full of looted works and furniture from France to Germany. No wonder that Goering praised him; he wrote:

I was very grateful that a place was at last selected for the collection, although I want to point out that other departments are also claiming the authority of the Führer. First of these was the Reich Minister of Foreign Affairs. . . . In order to avoid misconceptions regarding these articles, some of which I wish to claim for myself, some of which I have purchased, and some of which I want to acquire, I should inform you . . . I have now obtained by means of purchase, presents, bequests and barter perhaps the greatest private collection in Germany at least, if not in Europe.[7]

He went on to list the works he particularly wanted, which included a large and highly valued collection of Dutch masterpieces of the seventeenth century, certain works by eighteenth-century French artists, and a collection of Italian masters.

Goering frequently visited this fascinating collecting center where so many famous paintings were at any moment likely to arrive in the collecting vans to the surprise and delight of the officials responsible for their theft. He would stay for hours, forgetting the affairs of the Luftwaffe as his collector's instinct asserted itself. He came for his first visit on November 3, 1940, and returned again two days later. He often wore civilian clothes for these expeditions, with a long double-breasted overcoat and a felt hat cocked at a rakish angle, and he carried a walking stick shaped not unlike the once famous Richthofen trophy. The following February he was back again, selecting works to be transported home on his special train. He took on this occasion some furniture and fifty-three canvases, mostly acquired from the Rothschild and Seligmann collections—among them Teniers' *Adam and Eve in Paradise*, Rubens' *Atalanta and Meleager* and a Venus by Boucher. He also bought some pictures from the Wildenstein Art Gallery, including a Venus by Cranach for which he was ready to pay only the purely nominal sum of five thousand marks. He returned in May, again in mid-August, and finally in December. As his own representative to work alongside the Rosenberg Task Force he appointed Dr. Bruno Lohse, a young art historian who remained permanently stationed in Paris, holding only the rank of a lance corporal in the Luftwaffe but officially detailed for special service for Goering. Dr. Lohse is among those who vouch for Goering's considerable knowledge of art in those branches of it that he most admired. On one occasion, he says, Goering had the grace to apologize to him, in spite of Lohse's youth, following an argument with him as to the authenticity of a work said to be by Cranach. According to Lohse, Goering gave a certain measure of concealed protection to Jews who had given him valuable service in his art deals.[8]

From time to time Goering was able to protect the Rosenberg Task Force from the criticism that its operations raised in the German Army. A letter survives addressed by General von Stülpnagel, the German commander in occupied France, to Field Marshal von Brauchitsch, dated January 31, 1941, in which he complains ironically of Rosenberg's activities, saying that if Jews and Freemasons had no right to their own property as the chosen opponents of the

Nazi Party, then what of Frenchmen as a whole? Stülpnagel was to be one of the generals involved in the plot of July 1944 and was to pay with his life for this opposition to Hitler. More typical, however, is a note of February 9 written by a senior officer of the military administration in France, which reads:

On February 5 Reich Marshal Goering gave instructions for some works of art which the Führer wants to acquire, and for some other works which are to be the property of the Herr Reich Marshal, to be transferred to Germany at once on the special train of the Herr Reich Marshal. Payment for these works is to be made according to the estimates of a French expert.[9]

A footnote adds that for Jewish property no payment is to be made, since that is considered to be *herrenlos*—that is, "no one's property."

Another "highly confidential" document, a letter that is undated but that probably originated also in February, was written by Dr. Bunjes, an art historian acting as a German liaison officer; he reports that, in spite of protests by the French government, works of art taken from Jews in France are to be transported to Germany and that a selection of them is to be held for disposal either by Hitler or by Goering.

The following year, 1942, Goering had to defend Rosenberg's unit from charges of irregular art dealing. He wrote Rosenberg a personal letter of appreciation on May 30.

MY DEAR PARTY COMRADE ROSENBERG:

Your unit for the acquisition of cultural treasures in Paris has, I believe, been quite wrongly suspected recently of indulging in art dealing, and to some extent this misunderstanding may be due to me. I personally both know and appreciate the work of the unit very well, and I want to state that there is hardly any other unit that deserves so much praise for continuous good work, and that applies to all the members of the unit.

As for this recent suspicion that the unit has been conducting art deals on its own account, I think that I have inadvertently given cause to that rumor's getting about, the reason being that I have repeatedly asked officers of the unit to remember me and my interests whenever, either in Paris or elsewhere in France, they happen to hear about certain art treasures which may be of interest for my own collection that they may find in the hands of dealers or private persons. Since this has happened quite frequently, I have once again asked those officers to do me the favor of acquiring these items, and I have always kept a certain account available for them to draw on for this purpose. So when these officers were particularly keen on making contacts with art dealers, they did it solely as a personal favor to me in helping me to build up my collection. . . .

On the other hand, of course, I personally support the work of your unit quite considerably and wherever I find an opportunity to do so; undoubtedly many of the cultural treasures collected by your unit are due to the fact that I personally and my own various units have done their best to help yours.

On June 18 Rosenberg wrote a reply that had evidently been carefully thought out.

It was very kind of you, Herr Reich Marshal, to express your appreciation of the work done by my unit in France, and it goes without saying that all my colleagues remain at your disposal always and will serve you to the best of their ability. . . .

With a view to the historical importance of the unit's work, and in order to clear the officers concerned, I have ordered a thorough investigation into whatever has been done so far in securing art treasures. This check is now being made, and it seems all the more necessary since in certain circles, as you kindly informed me, my unit has been suspected of indulging in art dealing. . . . Since you have made special accounts available for the art treasures already acquired by you, I should like to be told how you want to dispose of these funds. . . . I do hope you will not resent or misinterpret this question, but I hope you will agree with me that the work of my unit would be impossible but for the successful struggle of our party. Moreover, the Party Treasurer has provided generous funds for carrying out those tasks. I hope you will agree with me that art treasures confiscated from former Jewish property should be considered secured in favor of the party. It would seem to be only fair that great art treasures secured from such sources should one day become the property of the party. Needless to say, the final decision on this must rest with the Führer, but since it was the party that financed the twenty years' struggle against Jewry, it certainly *would* seem that this is a fair decision.[10]

As we have seen, Goering had many private and State accounts from which he could pay for works of art that did not come to him through gift or confiscation. He was in the habit of acquiring what he needed in the occupied territories by means of loans against his various State accounts, as this note of December 6, 1940, an internal memorandum within Goering's household office, clearly reveals:

Lieutenant Colonel Veltjens of the Staff of the Army Commander in the Netherlands, General Christiansen, called at this office today with regard to the reimbursement to the Army Commander in the Netherlands of one million guilders (M.1,333,000) advanced to the Herr Reich Marshal for private purchases. By agreement with Herr Lieutenant General Bodenschatz, I have instructed the Prussian State Bank to remit M.530,000 from the Sonderkonto to the credit of General Christiansen in Amsterdam. Because of this payment, the Sonderkonto, which was recently brought up to M.3,100,000, is exhausted, and fresh funds will be required so as to remit the balance of the amount due to General Christiansen.[11]

The Sonderkonto was a special account which had to be replenished from time to time from State funds. Goering's deals were often on a very large scale, as the case of the Goudsticker property reveals. Jacques Goudsticker was one of the most important of the Dutch art dealers and Goering acquired the whole of his art properties, which were valued at some five million dollars, for a sum considerably less than this; the contract was dated July 13, 1940, and the purchase price two million guilders. The owner was said to be away ill. The pictures Goering wanted from this collection went by train to Carinhall; the rest were left on sale to provide money for other works.[12]

Goering spent many millions of public money in acquiring the masterpieces that covered the walls of Carinhall, Mauterndorf, Veldenstein and his residences in Berlin. He regarded himself as the privileged trustee of the German nation, a trustee who was able to enjoy in private the beauty of those works which would eventually be displayed to the nation at the Hermann Goering Museum. Although he was the kind of man who loved to bargain and had an intense dislike of being duped by astute dealers, he was well aware, as he said later at Nuremberg, that prices tended to rise the moment he or his agents were seen approaching. But money became less real to him as his craving for the possession of art grew greater, and the large sums he authorized, borrowed or acquired were in the end only so many entries on paper to be recorded by his staff. The pictures, the statues, the tapestries and the plate were real.

The Dutch art dealer de Boer has described how Goering and his agents would conduct their deals.[13] Goering, dressed in civilian clothes, visited de Boer's gallery twice with his aides. On the first occasion he merely took a fleeting glance at the pictures and said he would come back soon to make some purchases. Before he returned, de Boer put away some of his more valuable works, but Goering (whose considerable knowledge of Dutch art could not be denied) remembered exactly what he had seen on the previous visit and inquired where the missing pictures were. He bought some twenty or so works, none of them particularly valuable. Then he saw a painting by Jan Steen that he seemed to like particularly. It was quite expensive—somewhere around 80,000 or 100,000 guilders, de Boer remembers; Goering said it was too expensive, more than he wanted to spend, much as he liked the picture. Then he turned to Hofer, who was with him, mentioned one of his own Jan Steen paintings and suggested an exchange. Hofer insisted that the Herr Reich Marshal's piece was more valuable. But Goering replied that he liked the painting here and that he would gladly exchange his own for it. De Boer was still unhappy at making this deal, but Hofer came back alone and made veiled threats that if the Reich Marshal was annoyed it might become unpleasant for certain Jewish relations of Madame de Boer. Goering is described by de Boer as remarkably interested in pictures; the way he became absorbed in them, the dealer has said, one might have thought he had nothing else to think about.

Goering was among those who bought one of the celebrated forgeries painted by van Meegeren.[14] Since these forgeries for a period had deceived the most expert eyes, Goering can hardly be blamed for buying what seemed to be a picture by the hand of Vermeer. The genuine purchase of art treasures, the acquisition of them through looting and confiscation, and the preservation of them from the Allied air raids and other hazards of war all led to the continual flow of works from the occupied countries to Germany, many in crates marked "A.H." for Hitler or "H.G." for Goering. So great was the desire to sell to Goering that even his servants received presents from dealers anxious to establish goodwill in the right place. Robert Kropp recalls how a dealer in Amsterdam gave him a small but valuable picture merely because he had admired it. Kropp was astonished, but took the picture and later asked Goering whether he had been right to accept it. Goering laughed. "Of course you must keep it," he said, but when he saw it he wanted it for himself. He gave Kropp a larger but quite valueless view of Carinhall in exchange and did not hide his pleasure at acquiring another small treasure in this way.

Some of the sales to Goering may well have been conducted under pressure. This was said to be the case by M. Renders, whose valuable collection of some thirty paintings of the fifteenth-century Flemish school was bought by Goering and then reclaimed by their owner after the war. Shortly after the occupation of southern Germany by the American forces, Major Anderson, American Military Government officer with the 101st Airborne Division, traced these pictures to the castle of Zell am See, in Austria, where Emmy Goering remained for a while after her husband's capture. She wept when the paintings were taken from her. Edda's nurse herself gave the Americans a canvas wrapped in a package which Goering had left with her, telling her to look after it carefully, as it was of very great value. It turned out to be van Meegeren's "Vermeer."

Apart from the ruthless confiscation of works of art from helpless Jewish owners, Goering was normally careful to study appearances when acquiring famous works from abroad. He experienced most trouble in his relations with Italy. In surviving confidential documents of considerable length,[15] Hans Georg von Mackensen, the German ambassador in Rome, complains bitterly (if diplomatically) about the trouble and humiliation he was caused due to the acquisition of art treasures for Goering's collection. He had, he writes, unpleasant interviews with the Italian Minister of Education, and even with Mussolini and Ciano. Eventually, in May 1942, he was forced to make public denial of the rumors that important Italian works of art had been sent to Germany, and he announced that in any case the export of masterpieces from Italy would be stopped by law. Nevertheless, Goering continued to buy or acquire Italian pictures; they were stored in crates and kept in an annex to the German embassy in Rome while waiting transport to Germany. He acquired Memling's *Portrait of a Man* from the

Corsini family for 6,900,000 lire, and he paid over ten million for the *Spiridon Leda*, a picture attributed to Leonardo—though this painting he had to relinquish to Hitler. He bought furniture and tapestries from Bellini, an art dealer in Florence, and in June 1941 Hofer paid Count Contini in Florence six million lire for a valuable collection of Renaissance paintings.[16]

The incident that embarrassed Goering most in his uneasy relations with the Italians was the precious birthday present sent him by the Hermann Goering Division after it had taken possession of Monte Cassino. The monastery had been used by the Italian government in 1943 as a repository for art treasures that came principally from the Museum of Naples and included pictures by Titian, Vandyke and Raphael and antique bronzes from Pompeii and Herculaneum. Nearly two hundred cases of paintings and other works of art were deposited there, and arrangements were made to send them to the Vatican for safekeeping—less some fifteen cases which members of the Hermann Goering Division stole and sent to Goering for his birthday in January 1944. Goering was horrified and issued a reprimand. But the paintings did not go straight back to Italy; they were sent to the caverns of the Alt Aussee for safekeeping while they waited for official transport back to Italy.[17]

In all these varied ways the great art collection with its center at Carinhall was gradually massed together ready for permanent exhibition after the war in the Hermann Goering Museum. It remained to the end in the charge of Andreas Hofer, and Gisela Limberger acted as librarian and confidential secretary responsible for the endless correspondence involved in Goering's deals and acquisitions.[18] The photographic record they compiled of the collection filled 217 large albums which came into the possession of the American authorities after the war.[19] Eventually the Carinhall portion of Goering's art collection (he had seven art-filled residences in all) had to be packed and sent south for safekeeping. The Americans confiscated the final load, which included twenty-seven cases of books, four cases of glassware, seven of porcelain, eight of gold and silver plate, and six of rugs. This was, of course, only a fraction of the truckloads and trainloads of precious things that had been sent from the north during the weeks preceding the final evacuation of Carinhall in April 1945.

Goering collected everything of interest and value, including Oriental weapons, alabaster vases and Renaissance sundials. He had

a writing desk which had once been the property of Cardinal Maza-
rin. He had fine examples of eighteenth-century Beauvais tapestries
and some Gothic tapestries which had been carefully chosen as
companion pieces to certain Tournai hunting scenes he had bought
for the bargain price of twenty million francs at a forced sale of the
Sèze collection in France. He owned several altarpieces, such as a
French Passion and Crucifixion of the fifteenth century; the latter
had been confiscated from the art dealer Seligmann in Paris. The
most important of his altarpieces, by the Master of the Holy Kin-
ship, an artist of the Cologne school of the fifteenth century, he
acquired on the basis of an exchange with the Louvre. Also from the
Louvre he acquired the life-size statue of the Magdalene known as
La Belle Allemande, carved in wood, the work of the sixteenth-
century Swabian sculptor Gregor Erhardt. The statue was thought
by the Americans to bear some resemblance to Goering's wife.
Among the pictures he took a special pride in owning were five
portraits by Rembrandt, including the *Bearded Man,* the *Man with
Turban,* and portraits of his wife, her sister and her son, a Veláz-
quez Infanta, Rubens' *Resurrection of Lazarus,* Chardin's *Joueuse
de Volant,* Fragonard's *Young Girl with Chinese Figure,* David's
Mystic Marriage of Saint Catherine, paintings by Frans Hals, Vandyke, van Eyck, Boucher and Goya, and his special collection of
work by the two Lucas Cranachs, the elder and the younger.

The final destination for the last great consignment of Goering's
collection was Berchtesgaden. When it was located by the American experts sent to survey art looting, this consignment was discovered packed in the Luftwaffe's rest house at Unterstein, three
kilometers south of Berchtesgaden. The paintings filled forty
rooms, the sculptures were jammed into four rooms and a corridor,
and another room was piled high with tapestries. Two rooms were
filled with rugs and another two rooms with hundreds of empty
picture frames. Further rooms were piled with boxes and trunks
and barrels full of porcelain. A chapel attached to the rest house
was stacked with fine furniture of the Italian Renaissance. All this
represented one single trainload, which Goering had ordered his
men to store in a large bunker near his property in Berchtesgaden.
But the Allied armies had reached the district before this could
be done, and American soldiers had found most of the collection
still stacked in the nine coaches of Goering's train; Goering's men
had apparently been more interested in emptying two compart-

ments filled with bottles of champagne and whiskey that Goering could not bear to leave behind for the Russians who overran Carinhall.[20] The American soldiers in the end stacked the collection in the rest house. This train represented Goering's final stripping of the contents of Carinhall. The process of removal to the south had been continuous during the weeks preceding, and various consignments had been dispersed in different places. His valuable collection of weapons, for example, was found in the possession of Fritz Görnnert, a member of Goering's staff.

Goering was to the end the most assiduous collector of art among the Nazi leaders. Hitler, obsessed with war, left his great possessions in store unseen. Gradually the treasures looted by Rosenberg found their way into various centers, such as the cool tunnels of the salt mines of the Alt Aussee, where the Americans found six thousand paintings and vast collections of sculpture, furniture and tapestries, as well as valuable books and manuscripts. The whole area of Berchtesgaden was found to be full of art treasures, more or less hidden from the Allies. The chaos represented by the mixture of private looting and genuine removal of valuable objects to places of safety to avoid destruction by bombing was to mean months of checking by the investigating units set up to trace and catalogue the tens of thousands of missing works which their owners wanted returned to them after the war. Many works were irretrievably lost, many were damaged, and some no doubt are still to be found in the places where they have remained hidden. This was another martyrdom that Nazi Germany inflicted: the stealing and displacing of thousands of the masterpieces of European art until they finally came to rest in mine shafts, railway sidings, bunkers and storerooms, or were snatched from the nervous hands of petty agents still trying to steal the precious remnants of their masters' plunder.

IX

Eclipse

THE TWELVE MONTHS preceding the Allied landings in Normandy on D Day, June 6, 1944, saw Germany's empire contract on every front. Mussolini, who had been urging Hitler in vain to make peace with Russia, fell from power in July 1943; by September the Allies were in southern Italy, an Italian armistice had been signed with the Allies, and Hitler had stolen the captive Mussolini from Badoglio—an operation carried out from the air by Himmler's and not Goering's men. In Russia the German forces, after an unsuccessful July offensive, were in retreat during the remainder of the summer, while in Germany itself the great Anglo-American air offensive from Britain grew to devastating proportions, depressing deeply though it did not break the morale of the German people. The network of conspiracy within Germany against Hitler failed time and again to achieve effective action, culminating in the brave but unsuccessful attempt on the Führer's life made by the hostile generals on July 20, 1944. Meanwhile the Allied foothold in Normandy had become an established invasion, and the great Russian offensive had pushed the eastern front back into Poland.

The failure of the Luftwaffe, in spite of great individual courage, was a failure of dilution beyond its strength—a failure in the supply of machines and equipment, of fully trained men, of opportunity to oppose the overwhelming increase in the air offensive of the Allies. In the Mediterranean the Anglo-American air forces were four or five times as strong as those of the Luftwaffe; in fighting power and in reconnaissance preceding the Allied landings in Italy, the Germans markedly failed despite Goering's foolish and misleading optimism in the face of Rommel's warnings. Only the shock of Mussolini's fall from power revived the Luftwaffe briefly in the area of the Ionian Sea and the Adriatic. On the Russian front the situation was the same—neither planes nor air crews were sufficient in numbers or quality. By 1944 the Soviet Air Force could oppose between ten and fifteen thousand modern planes to the declining force of some twenty-five hundred German aircraft, many of which were obsolete. Their duties became entirely defensive. In the west the Luftwaffe's strength, while it waited for the inevitable D Day, barely exceeded that on the eastern front, and most of these planes were occupied opposing as best they could the bomber incursions into Germany. The Allied air force by D Day amounted to some eleven thousand aircraft. Even the Luftwaffe's attempts at reconnaissance before D Day were wholly inadequate. The long-range bomber force ready to oppose the landings barely amounted to 350 planes manned by relatively inexperienced crews. Goering put up every man and every aircraft he could to help protect Rommel's ground forces, but they melted to nothing before the sheer weight of the recurrent waves of Allied bombers and fighter-bombers, while the Luftwaffe's ground organization was smashed and disorganized.

Under Milch and finally under Speer, German aircraft production was greatly expanded. Production plants and repair depots were spread over the whole of German-occupied Europe, and the range of types of aircraft was reduced to facilitate mass production of such machines as the Junkers-88 bombers, the Messerschmitt-109 and Focke-Wulf-190 single engine fighters, and the Messerschmitt-110 and -410 and Junkers-88 twin engine fighters. During 1943–44 an output of some two thousand aircraft a month was achieved, one thousand less than Goering and Milch had planned in 1942. It was only Speer's brilliant organization that brought production to a level of some three thousand aircraft a month by the spring of 1944.

Hitler's determination not to mince words with Goering, and to make him push the Luftwaffe into attempts at retaliation against the British people for what the Allies were now able to make the German civilians suffer, did not encourage the Reich Marshal to attend Hitler's war conferences. But Hitler still had a certain affection for Goering. On July 25 he said to his generals during a staff conference, "The Reich Marshal has been through many crises with me. He is ice-cold in time of crisis. At such a time one can't have a better adviser . . . brutal and ice-cold." After his habit he rambled on, repeating the phrases he liked. "You can't have a better one; a better one can't be found. He has been through all crises with me, through the worst crises. That's when he's ice-cold. Every time it got really bad he became ice-cold."[1] When Goebbels, feeling that the Reich Marshal was no longer capable of directing the Luftwaffe, had suggested a few days before that Goering be replaced, Hitler emphatically refused and told Goebbels he resented such comments and would not tolerate "this kind of conspiracy." Galland, called to Hitler's headquarters, told him that what was needed to drive back the Allied bombers was three or four times as many fighters as the enemy had bombers. But both Hitler and Goering were unshakable in their dream of bombers; fighters that could not bomb the enemy into submission were for them a symbol of defeat. At the same time the twin-engine de Havilland Mosquito, with a speed performance which outstripped the best German fighters of 1943, so irritated Goering that he set up special fighter groups over Galland's head to deal with them, but they too failed. Goering harried and bullied his staff, exasperating them by ineffectual interference until Jeschonnek appealed to Hitler to take over command of the Luftwaffe himself. Goering, hearing of this, told his Chief of Staff he could indict him for insubordination—but hinted he might prefer suicide. Jeschonnek killed himself.[2]

As Schellenberg put it, "By the end of 1943, Goering had lost every vestige of authority or respect."[3] In his diary entry for August 10, Semmler, Goebbels' highly observant aide, records: "Politically, Goering might as well be dead. Rumors have already made him out to be dead. Hitler, with whom Goering surprisingly enough still stands high, has therefore advised that the Reich Marshal should be seen again among his people, to win back his popularity." Goebbels commented contemptuously that Goering, with a staff of be-medaled officers, had visited the Berlin markets and mingled with the people. According to Semmler, voices had shouted out, "Herr Meier!" and men had whistled at the sight of him.[4] Goebbels told Semmler that Goering had been ill-advised to keep for so long out of the public eye, for nothing leads to rumors so readily as this, and he instituted a special press campaign on behalf of Goering. At the

annual Nazi rally in Munich, Hitler made fun in public of the rumors that he had "deposed" his "friend Goering," and even in
September the following year he reaffirmed a certain continuing
faith in him when he renewed his position at the head of the Four-
Year Plan.

After the heavy raids on Hamburg in the summer, the Luftwaffe's commanders, assembled in full conference, convinced Goering finally that the Luftwaffe must be fully equipped for defense.
The conference had taken place at the Führer's headquarters in
Rastenburg, and Goering summoned his courage to tell Hitler what
had been decided. Perhaps he felt now as he had once told Schmidt
he always felt in the past when he had to tell Hitler something unpleasant: "I often make up my mind to say something to him, but
then when I come face to face with him my heart sinks into my
boots." Now he had to convince Hitler that the traditional strategy
was wrong; the Luftwaffe's sole remaining task was to defend the
Reich. All that mattered now was the fighter plane. They waited,
Galland, Milch and Korten, Jeschonnek's successor as Chief of
Staff. Then Goering emerged. He did not look at them, but walked
past them into an adjoining room. Then he called in Galland and
Peltz, the general of bombers. What Galland saw came as a terrible
shock to him. Goering, his head buried in his arms as he leaned
over the table, was weeping. He moaned, scarcely able to speak
clearly. Eventually he managed to tell them this was a moment of
terrible despair. Hitler had lost faith in him, had rejected everything he had proposed, and had commanded the Luftwaffe to
bomb England on a large scale, smashing Allied terror with German counterterror. Goering had been forced to agree that Hitler,
as always, was right, and he rose now to his feet and told Peltz
he was to be the assault leader against England. This, the Führer
had said, was the Luftwaffe's last chance to redeem its honor.

The result was a series of raids the losses from which soon became intolerable. When Galland expressed his dissatisfaction, at
a conference with Goering held in the autumn at Veldenstein to
discuss a wholly impracticable long-distance cannon which was
to be fitted to the Messerschmitt-410, Goering merely shouted at
him. Galland, equally angry, asked to be relieved of his command.
Goering agreed to this, but later refused to release him. The pattern
of the Luftwaffe staff in any case changed overnight like that of a
kaleidoscope. On one occasion Goering had even tried himself from

the confines of Carinhall to direct an attack on an invading American bomber force, only to send his fighters in a totally wrong direction. During the first ten months of 1943 the American Air Force claimed that it had destroyed over three thousand German fighter planes, a figure Galland accepts. Goering was forever complaining, and at one staff conference Galland tore off his Knight's Cross and banged it on the table, silencing him and staring him out.

According to Goebbels, Goering was at Hitler's headquarters on September 9, "furious about the treachery of Italy" and pressing Hitler to make some form of public statement. The collapse on the eastern front called for this, but, strangely enough, according to Goebbels, "Goering is now somewhat more optimistic about air warfare than he was; in fact, in my opinion somewhat too optimistic." Such sustained optimism, however, could be achieved only by his turning his face from the truth. Speer recollected at Nuremberg a fantastic incident at Hitler's headquarters when Goering forbade Galland to make any further reports on the matter after he claimed that enemy long-range fighters were penetrating as far as Liège. Goering refused to accept the solid evidence that some of these fighters had in fact been shot down as deep in European territory as this.[5]

On November 2 Goering visited the Messerschmitt works to discuss the possible adaptation of the new jet fighter into a fighter-bomber. As early as May, Galland had flown the prototype ME 262 at 520 m.p.h.—the Germans now had the fastest plane in the world. He had flown it straight to Veldenstein and roused Goering with his own enthusiasm. But Hitler had refused to sanction production and had in fact insulted both Goering and the Luftwaffe chiefs by holding a conference of the aircraft designers and engineers without inviting any of them to be present. The result of this was that Hitler, without even consulting Goering, had ordered Messerschmitt to produce some more prototypes. It was not until six months later that he permitted Goering to authorize the mass production of the jet fighter, and then only in the form of a fighter-bomber. Goering was therefore able at a special demonstration of the jet plane at Rastenburg in December to assure Hitler that the aircraft could carry at least one bomb of a thousand pounds. He gave this assurance to Hitler without any final technical confirmation that it would indeed be possible to adapt the plane as a bomber; he was solely concerned, as Galland realized while he stood by listening, to tell Hitler what he wanted to hear, that at last he had a blitzbomber that would strike fear and terror into the hearts of the armies assembled for his destruction both in the west and the east.[6]

By the winter, Goering was evidently to some extent recovered from his decline, and Goebbels remarks in his diary on November 14 that he is showing himself more in public and has "recovered from his recent period of stagnation," with the result that "his authority is gradually being strengthened." On November 8 he had in fact given a lengthy address of two and a half hours on aerial warfare to an assembly of Reichleiters and gauleiters—not as effectively as he should have done, thought Goebbels, because Goering had tried to make the point that he had already launched his reprisal raids against Britain in 1940! Afterward he had had dinner with Goebbels and even managed to charm that icy heart. "Personally he is an exceptionally lovable character," wrote Goebbels.

On November 30 Goering made what was to be his final broadcast. In it he reminded the German people of how the gallant band of Spartans defended the pass of Thermopylae against the Persian hordes; this, he said, was the spirit in which Germans should defend their Fatherland. He did not attempt to minimize the Allied air raids. "Even if every German city is razed to the ground," he cried, "the German people would still survive. . . . The German people existed before there were any cities, and we may even have to live in holes in the ground. . . . If Berlin vanished from the face of the earth it would be dreadful but not fatal. The German people has existed in the past without Berlin. But if the Russians reach Berlin the German people will have ceased to exist."[7]

After the large-scale raids on Berlin had begun, at Hitler's command Goering went to the western front personally to supervise a retaliatory blow against London from the air, but he found the Luftwaffe no longer capable of developing such raids on any scale. Galland claims that only 275 tons of bombs were dropped on London during January and February. The Luftwaffe was forced to concentrate on defense, and its losses were very heavy.

According to evidence given by Bodenschatz at Nuremberg, Goering was now trying in every way he could to regain his position with Hitler, who was gradually excluding him from his conferences and private discussions concerning the war. He proved, as in the case of the dispute over the use of the jet fighter, quite unable to stand up to Hitler, and the brunt of the Führer's anger with the Luftwaffe seems to have been left to fall on Bodenschatz, who remained his principal representative at Hitler's headquarters, and on Milch and Galland. Milch recollects a further scene in February 1944 between Goering and Hitler on the Obersalzberg, after both Milch and Galland had urged yet again that the new jet fighter be kept free from the wholly unsuitable adaptation for bombing on which Hitler continued to insist. Hitler raged, "I want bombers, bombers, bombers. Your fighters are no damned good, anyway," and Goering once again gave way before the Führer's anger.[8]

Speer's revised and centralized program for the mass production of a few selected types of aircraft, and those mainly fighters, was presented to Goering at an important conference on the Obersalzberg in April 1944.[9] Goering spoke with the voice of Hitler. His "final shattering decision," as Galland put it, was that "the heavy bomber remains the kernel of the armament in the air." Accordingly, Speer's plan had to be modified. In the end, as Galland puts it, the bombers never left the assembly line; they were destroyed in the course of construction. Had they been completed they would have lacked the fuel to fly. With a fighter strength which Galland assessed as only one to seven against the Allies, he formed the close-combat storm-fighter wings with men prepared to approach the bomber formations and attack at point-blank range, even ramming the aircraft in a desperate attempt to destroy them, the pilot bailing out just before impact.

At the end of March and the beginning of April 1944, there occurred the case of the shooting of fifty of the eighty British and Commonwealth Air Force officers who, as prisoners of war at Stalag Luft III, had attempted a mass escape on the night of March 24–25 but had been recaptured.[10] Stalag Luft III, which was situated at Sagan, was technically a Luftwaffe camp and therefore under Goering's supervision. The circumstances that led to the murder of the men (for that is what it was, since their death on recapture violated international agreements concerning the treatment of prisoners of war) were subject to constant examination during the Nuremberg trial, and it was during the course of giving his particular evidence that Milch, who appeared as a witness on behalf of Goering, admitted the disintegration of the high command's administration in 1944. He spoke of "the great confusion existing in the highest orders at that time." All through, he said, "there was terrible con-

fusion. . . . Hitler interfered in all matters and himself gave orders
. . . [and] during that time I hardly ever saw Goering." As for the
shooting itself, it appeared to result from an order by Hitler issued
in March that all prisoners of war (other than British and American) who were recaptured after attempting escapes should be secretly shot by the police. How far Goering could personally be held
responsible for the error in his own camp remained in some doubt
at Nuremberg. He claimed to have been on leave throughout
March and only to have heard of the shootings on his return to
Berchtesgaden, where Hitler had his headquarters at that time.
Goering claimed that he made the strongest protest he could, first
to Himmler and then to Hitler, saying how harmful the repercussions of this would be on Luftwaffe air crews who had to bail out
over enemy territory. In Goering's own words: "The Führer—our
relations were already extremely bad and strained—answered rather
violently that the airmen who were flying against Russia would also
have to reckon with the possibility of being immediately beaten
to death in case of an emergency landing, and that the airmen going to the west should not want to claim any special privilege in
this regard. I told him thereupon that these two things had no connection with each other."

Statements made under interrogation by officers both inside
and outside the Luftwaffe implied that it would have been virtually impossible for Goering, who on his own admission had returned from leave by March 29 at the latest, to know nothing of
the shootings, which were taking place from March 25 to April 13
on Hitler's orders. He could, therefore, have countermanded these
instructions and stopped them. Goering insisted that he was ignorant of what was happening, and it is true that there was no one to
testify that he had been given the exact information; Milch also
denied having the knowledge until it was too late. As Goering put
it, "I was not present at the time when the command was given by
the Führer. When I heard about it, I vehemently opposed it. But
at the time when I did hear of it, it was already too late. . . . I myself considered it the most serious incident of the whole war."

During the night of June 5–6 Goering received the phone call
that all the Nazi high command dreaded: Bernd von Brauchitsch
telephoned him at Veldenstein to say that the invasion of France
had started. Early in the morning Goering left his retreat to attend
a conference on the situation created by the Allied landings. This

was held at Klessheim, a castle near Salzburg, during the afternoon
of June 6, and both Ribbentrop and Himmler were present. The
Luftwaffe's situation at the time of the Allied landings in Normandy made it impossible, as we have seen, for effective opposition
to be made to the vast flying fleets of Allied fighters and bombers.
The Luftwaffe's air crews were hopelessly outnumbered from the
start, concentrating as they were on the defense of the Reich itself
from the ceaseless raids on armament works and synthetic-fuel
plants that were accessible from the air.

According to Galland, the Luftwaffe on D Day had less than a
hundred fighters ready to oppose the Allied landings. "On the day
of the invasion, not more than 319 aircraft could meet the enemy,"
he wrote later. The key order for the transfer of the fighter strength
in Germany to the new front in France was not given till the second day of the invasion, and communications were so disrupted
that news of the invasion itself did not reach Flying Corps II at
Compiègne until eight o'clock in the morning. The whole transfer
plan had, in any case, to be changed owing to damage and disruption on the airfields and to opposition in the air itself. Morale was
at the lowest among the pilots and air crews. "The Allies have total
air supremacy. . . . The feeling of being powerless against the
enemy's aircraft . . . has a paralyzing effect," reported the commander of one of the panzer divisions.

On the night of June 12–13, the famous secret weapon of Peenemünde, the Luftwaffe's V-1 robot bomb (V for *Vergeltung*, vengeance) was first launched against London. The mysterious ramps
along the Channel coast had been heavily and continuously
bombed at low level by the Allies; replicas of these sloping platforms had been built in Florida for practice in the most effective
methods of destroying them. The flying bomb was a form of pilot-
less aircraft built not only at Peenemünde but at Friedrichshafen
and other centers, and about nine thousand were launched, principally against London, during the three months following the initial
launching in June. The V-1 carried a ton of high explosive, had
a range of up to 150 miles and flew at about 2,500 feet at a speed
that at its greatest approached 400 m.p.h. Barely a third of the
bombs launched reached their targets; they either were exploded
in flight by the Allied fighters and the ground defenses or failed to
explode at all. The V-1 proved a propaganda weapon that helped
to maintain German morale; after the initial surprise caused by it

in London, the British accepted it as an additional danger of war, but less hazardous in the end than the fearful raids of the blitz period. The damage from blast was widespread, and the East End of London, particularly Stepney and Poplar, suffered badly. By the end of 1944, three quarters of a million homes in Greater London were added to the already heavy total of damaged property. Hitler and Goering miscalculated again when they thought, after trials with a captured Spitfire, that the V-1 was invulnerable from the air and would bombard Britain into submission from a hundred launching sites along the Channel. By the time the V-1 was ready for launching, many of the ramps had been damaged and enough was known of the weapon for an increasingly effective defense to be organized when the launchings finally began. On July 5 Churchill was able to reveal in the House of Commons that the first 2,754 bombs had killed only 2,752 people. The bomb ceased to be a major tactical weapon.

Meanwhile the Allied invasion, which by July was fully established, was paralleled by Russian penetration of Poland and the threat this meant to East Prussia. According to Galland, Goering was inaccessible and he kept away from the Luftwaffe command. During July, the carrying out of a plot to kill Hitler at his daily staff conference, inspired mainly by a group of generals who wanted to eliminate Goering and Himmler in a single act of assassination along with the Führer, had to be postponed twice. On July 11 Goering was present at the staff conference but not Himmler, and the attempt planned for that day was abandoned. The second time, on July 15, Hitler himself left before the bomb, which was hidden in a briefcase, could be placed. Then it was decided to concentrate the plot on Hitler alone. The conferences, which Goering attended when he was available, took place either at the Berghof in the south or at the Wolf's Lair in Rastenburg, according to Hitler's movements. On the third attempt, on July 20 at Rastenburg, the bomb exploded in Hitler's presence, but Count Klaus von Stauffenberg's briefcase holding it had been moved away from the Führer, to the far side of the support of the heavy table, by a Colonel Brandt as he leaned over to get a better view of Hitler's maps. Brandt was among those killed, but Hitler was only lightly injured by burns and bruises. He suffered, however, considerable shock and a temporary paralysis of the right arm. Bodenschatz, who was representing Goering, was severely injured. Himmler, who was at headquarters but not at the conference, immediately took charge of the investigations, while Goebbels, acting with considerable initiative, seized the chance offered him to take control of Berlin.

Goering was at his headquarters some fifty miles away when the news came of the attempt on Hitler's life and of its failure. Later he was to boast, "If the attempt had succeeded, I should have had to handle it," though Himmler had other views on this. Goering went straight to Rastenburg and arrived in time to join in another of those strange tea parties which so often seemed to occur at moments of crisis. For on July 20 Mussolini, dictator of Lombardy, if he was still dictator anywhere, was visiting Hitler; his train was delayed and he arrived, accompanied by Marshal Graziani, to be greeted by a Hitler who was pale and shaking and carried his arm in a sling.

All the hierarchy except Goebbels were now present: Goering, Ribbentrop, Himmler and Grand Admiral Doenitz, the new naval Commander in Chief, as well as Keitel and Jodl. After inspecting the debris, the dictators and their colleagues sat down to tea angry and unnerved. They knew by this time that the conspiracy had been planned on a considerable scale and involved many highly placed Army officers, for, thinking Hitler dead, the conspirators had already attempted to take over the administrative center of Berlin and had been prevented from completing its encirclement by the action of Goebbels, who knew that Hitler had survived. Recriminations broke out in a savage display of ill-manners which took little account of the presence of the guests from Italy. Hitler at first listened, chewing pills of varied colors, while his commanders, their voices raised, began to shout at each other; Doenitz blamed the disasters of the war on the Army; Goering agreed, only to be attacked at once by the Grand Admiral for the failure of the Luftwaffe. Goering, flushed and angry, defended his service and then turned to Ribbentrop and attacked him for the futility of his foreign policy. The quarrel reached a stage where he actually threatened Ribbentrop with his field marshal's baton. "You dirty little champagne salesman," he yelled, "shut your damned mouth!" He called him Ribbentrop, and this more than anything nettled the other, who had secured his titular "von" only through his adoption by an aunt. Ribbentrop demanded to be treated with respect, shouting, "I am still the Foreign Minister, and my name is *von* Ribbentrop!" Only when the Roehm plot was mentioned did Hit-

ler's concentrated fury at the ingrates who had tried to take away
his life break out in a sudden scream for vengeance—not only
against all the men implicated, but against their wives and their
children as well. He was as good as his word. Mussolini, troubled
and embarrassed by the scene he had witnessed, withdrew from the
tea party. He never saw Hitler again.

The generals who were found guilty after a disgraceful form of
trial were hanged by the neck on ropes hauled up over meathooks—
all except Rommel, who, as the favorite soldier of the German
people, was told on October 14 to commit suicide, after which he
would be accorded a state funeral to save his face and that of
Hitler. Rommel, having informed his wife of his fate, was taken
away in a car and given a few minutes in which to shoot himself.
His wife was then notified, as he had told her she would be, that
he had died of a cerebral embolism, and the messages of sympathy
poured in. Among them was one from Goering.

Even Goering, Hitler's paladin, was not above suspicion. When
the postwar trials uncovered to some extent the maneuvers of
power among the Nazis, it was revealed that the Gestapo had been
ordered by Himmler to investigate Goering's connections with the
revolt; and Himmler was heard to remark to Doenitz that, if Hitler
had been killed, "it is absolutely certain, Herr Grossadmiral, that
under no circumstances would the Reich Marshal have become his
successor."[11]

The map of Europe, which in 1940 had been unrolled for Hitler
to trample on, now recoiled against him. By August the Russians
were on the borders of East Prussia and in the suburbs of Warsaw.
Rumania and her oil had gone and Bulgaria had withdrawn from
the fight, while France had been liberated from both north and
south, and Belgium and Holland penetrated. The Allies in the west
pushed forward until their supplies of fuel and ammunition ran
short; by September the forces of Germany were all but pressed
back inside their natural frontier.

During August Galland, finding Goering still inaccessible and
indeed "not well," appealed finally to Speer to help him persuade
Hitler not to use the last reserves from the Luftwaffe's training
schools to help fill the great void gaping in the German Army.
Speer, who had first taken over air armament as well as ground
armament production, went to see Hitler with Galland, only to be
turned out and told to look after his war industry. "If the Reich

Marshal does not act, then it is my duty to act," Speer had said, but he must have regretted his well-meant attempts to help when he met the angry and overwrought Führer. This was followed by a summons to a conference the next day in which Hitler said he would dissolve the useless fighter arm. He ordered Speer to set about transforming the aircraft production industry into a plant to manufacture heavy armament. Speer left the meeting in despair.

In his decision to strip down the Luftwaffe's remaining strength Hitler was no doubt influenced by the existence of Count Werner von Braun's pioneer rocket, the V-2. The first of these prophetic weapons was launched against Britain just as the victory against the V-1 had been finally achieved. Against the V-2 there was no defense at all except to destroy it before it was launched or to destroy its center of production. By September 1944 the V-2 was ready for action. There was a stockpile of some two thousand of these highly mobile rockets that could be launched from woodlands and forests with comparative ease, and the monthly production rate was to average five hundred right up to the end of the war. Its range was some two hundred miles, its speed 3,500 m.p.h., its weight two and a half tons at take-off (including its warhead of one ton of high explosive), and it reached a height of some seventy miles. Between September and December over four thousand of these bombs were launched by the German Army against London and Antwerp. It was the Army and not the Air Force that had charge of the V-2, but Goering transformed some of his Heinkel bombers so that they could launch V-1 bombs from the air. This form of raiding on London and Antwerp continued with decreasing effect until the end of the war. Hitler and Goering could, however, claim that they had managed to return to their old policy of aggression from the air during the final months of the war.

In October Hitler at last consented to the formation of a jet-fighter unit to operate the ME 262, though it was humiliating that the suggestion had to come initially from Himmler to the Führer, and not from Goering himself. The previous month, at a conference in Rastenburg on September 23, Goering, against Galland's wishes, had supported the mass production of a new and inferior jet plane, the HE 162, the Volks fighter, which it was hoped would be manned by thousands of schoolboys trained in gliders. After a miracle of production, the Volks fighter prototype was ready for demonstration in December, but it disintegrated in the air. The war was over before it was ready for mass production.

There was a certain revival of strength in the Luftwaffe in preparation for Hitler's final counteroffensive in the Ardennes. Goering, however, was so ineffective by now that at a conference on November 6 Hitler accused him of not knowing what was going on; as for the Luftwaffe, the Führer had come to a "devastating conclusion" concerning its ineffectiveness. Goering was foolish enough to attempt to regain his lost prestige by calling a conference of all the leaders of the day and the night fighter units at the headquarters of the Reich Air Fleet at Wannsee and attacking them, losing his self-control and insulting them in so aggressive a manner that he caused, as Galland puts it, "bitterness and revolt." Goering did worse than this; he had his words recorded and ordered that "the record be played at intervals to the pilots at action stations." The Luftwaffe men had their own views about both Goering and his speech which they did not bother to keep to themselves.

The offensive in the Ardennes, after some initial success, failed. In the new year Hitler was faced with the final converging of the great armies of the East and the West which pressed simultaneously on the borders of Germany. By the end of January, East and West Prussia were severed from the Reich. Zhukov was a hundred miles from Berlin. The Russians had taken Silesia, with all its essential raw materials. Goering had evacuated Rominten, the first of his properties to fall into the hands of the enemy.[12] Hitler last used the Wolf's Lair on November 20, and then it was abandoned to the enemy.

Goering's own description of the disposal of forces at this time by Hitler shows that strategy was reduced to what he himself described as a fire station. "The troops were sent wherever there was a fire," he said. "For instance, if the Eastern Command wanted troops for an anticipated action and the Western desired troops to check an attack already in progress, the troops were usually sent west. But it was the same principle as a fire department. Hitler, of course, made the final decision."[13]

At the close of the year Goering decided to promote General Karl Koller as Chief of Staff of the Luftwaffe. Koller was unwilling, but went to Carinhall, where Goering had called him for interview. He asked permission to speak frankly, which Goering granted;

Koller immediately criticized him for not visiting the operations headquarters for a year, for his habit of sending his adjutant to the phone when his senior officers wanted to consult him, and for neglecting so often to make necessary decisions on points that had been put to him. Koller said he had often been forced to protect himself by taking action on Goering's behalf and filing in the War Diary his unanswered telegrams requesting guidance. Goering simply pleaded with him to forget and forgive, gave him a free hand in everything and, with a show of boyish despair, promised to be "good" in future.

He was less boyish with Galland, whose criticism, either spoken or implied, he could not so readily accept. In January Galland was dismissed and sent on leave; no successor was appointed. Goering afterward considered him to be the driving force behind a delegation of fighter pilots that had talked to him at the Haus der Flieger and presented the pilots' case, which was that their general, Galland, had been removed, that the bomber command had precedence over the fighter command and received the ME 262 over their heads, that they were expected to achieve impossibilities in bad weather, and, finally, that Goering had insulted them and openly doubted their fighting spirit. Goering flew into a rage and threatened to court-martial their spokesman, Lützow, who was sent to Italy and told he must not communicate again with either Galland or the fighter pilots. As for the dismissal of Galland, Hitler himself intervened. Goering recalled him to Carinhall, made some show of magnanimity and told him Hitler had given permission for him to fly again in action. The mutineers and he were permitted to form their own unit of jet fighters. Galland, without loss of rank, ended the war as he began it, the captain of a squadron of fighters, but this time with jets.

The sheer garrulous futility of certain debates at the daily conferences at Hitler's headquarters, now removed to the Chancellery in Berlin, is shown by the transcripts of certain discussions which have survived.[14] On January 27 Hitler and Goering discussed endlessly General Student's character and manner of utterance, while some twenty-five senior officers, including Koller, stood by and listened. Goering gave imitations of Student's slowness of speech and said that, though he appeared half-witted, he was both staunch and intelligent. He said he would gladly take him back into the

Luftwaffe. After several minutes of reminiscence, this exchange took place:

GOERING: Well, I'll be glad to take him, because I know that when there comes a crisis you'll be enraged and call him back. I'm looking forward to that day.

HITLER: I am not looking forward to that day.

GOERING: No, but you'll take him back. Why should I expose such a superior man to all this jabber? You know him; he always spoke that slowly.

HITLER: The time I explained that business in the west, he developed the same slowness, but in the end he accomplished it just the same. The same thing applied to the liberation of the Duce.

GOERING: He did his work well in Italy on the whole, too. . . . I need him urgently; I want him to put some backbone into the parachute army and to reorganize the divisions. Then you will always have someone at your disposal when things get tough. He won't wiggle and wobble. It may be he might speak still more slowly, that is possible, but he would also retreat all the more slowly.

HITLER: He reminds me of Fehrs, my new servant from Holstein. Every time I tell him to do something, he takes minutes to think it over . . . but he does his work splendidly. It's just that he's terribly slow.

GOERING: And then Student is a man who thinks up the cleverest things.

HITLER: You can't deny that he thinks of things by himself.

They went on at inordinate length, gossiping about the characters and personalities of the generals in the front line, reminiscing about the First World War and worrying about the rank of retired officers brought back to serve in subordinate positions. "Only a complete bastard would stand for a demotion," remarked Goering. On this subject alone they talked for half an hour. At one point in the discussion Goering mentioned his hope that the British would not like to see a Soviet invasion of Germany. "They certainly didn't plan that we hold them off while the Russians conquer Germany," he said to Hitler. "If this goes on we'll get a telegram in a few days."

Hitler said he had deliberately set out to scare the British and the Americans with rumors that the Russians were conspiring to take over the whole of Germany. A kind of unholy glee entered into the discussion at the thought of the discomfiture this would cause in the minds of the conquerors in the west.

HITLER: . . . That will make them feel as if someone had stuck a needle into them.

GOERING: They entered the war to prevent us from going into the south, but not to have the East come to the Atlantic.

HITLER: That is evident. It is something abnormal. . . .

The evacuation of Carinhall came as the bitterest blow to Goering; he was deeply depressed. On Hitler's special order Emmy and the womenfolk left in January. It took the household staff weeks to pack the seemingly endless crates of treasures which, as we have seen, were sent south for storage at Berchtesgaden and elsewhere. Goering himself did not finally leave until April, though he traveled to the south on occasion; he had to remain in touch with Hitler in Berlin. He ordered Carinhall to be mined and destroyed after he had left it forever. He couldn't tolerate the idea of others living in the mansion that had been the symbol of his power and personality. Some while after the last vans had departed, leaving Carinhall an empty shell, the mines were detonated by German soldiers and the buildings split and fell in ruins.[15]

During the last weeks before Hitler's defeat and his suicide in the bunker of the Chancellery, the strange drama of intrigue within the Nazi leadership reached its final stage of adjustment. In this Bormann and Goebbels played the leading parts, contriving to share between them the lurid limelight in which Hitler chose to end his life, while in the shadows of the north Himmler in his sanatorium skirted round the possibilities of concluding a separate peace with the help of another Swedish peacemaker, Count Folke Bernadotte.

Goebbels made no secret now of his desperate contempt for Goering as the bombs blasted Germany's helpless cities into ruins that matched those of Warsaw and Rotterdam and Coventry. In February, Semmler says, he was in a state of tears at the disasters that had befallen Dresden, claiming that Goering should be court-martialed: "What a burden of guilt this parasite has brought on his head by his slackness and interest in his own comfort." He shook with anger at a story he had heard from Terboven of Goering shooting in the Schorfheide while the cities were being bombed. Goebbels had been Reich Trustee for Total War since July of the previous year and had brought in the most stringent mobilization decrees in August. On January 30 he was made Defender of Berlin, and he decided to stay in Berlin with his wife and children if the Führer should decide that this was the center from which to conduct the last stages in the total war of self-destruction.

Bormann had never associated with Goering in the way that Hitler had done. His comments on him are preserved in a few remarks that survive, mostly in the letters he wrote to his wife. Bormann was a secret man who concealed his power, preferring to keep close to Hitler and guide his master's will; he had none of the independence of Goebbels and nothing of his flamboyant personality. He had crept to power in the empty shoes that Hess had left behind, rising in four years from a trusted but minor party official to the position of Hitler's personal secretary, the man through whom everyone else was forced to go. In the final weeks, while Goering and Speer became the advocates of negotiation, Bormann shared with Hitler and Goebbels (though the latter feared and resented Bormann) the desire to see Germany utterly destroyed rather than survive the Nazi regime. Himmler shared the view of Speer and Goering, but he had no desire to associate with either of them.

Bormann knew that Goering had always tried to separate him from Hitler; he hated the Reich Marshal and delighted in his disgrace. As early as September 1944 he wrote to his wife: "The general grumbling about Goering's setup . . . is reaching quite unparliamentary forms of expression." And in October: "The Reich Marshal's style of living had transmitted itself, quite naturally, to the Air Force." In November he comments on the association that is growing up between Speer and Goering ("Neither of them can stand Goebbels—far less me"), and the following February he is sneering at Goering's greed because an adjutant at the Obersalzberg has asked for five kilos of honey for the Reich Marshal's household.[16] Bormann stood ready to deliver the final, subtle blow onee Goering should leave, but even he knew that it was necessary to wait for the appropriate opportunity. When Lammers asked him in January whether he thought the moment had been reached when Goering could be displaced as Hitler's acknowledged successor, he replied, "If the question had not already been settled, I do not think the Führer would now nominate the Reich Marshal; but I do not think he will change the appointment he has once made. Let us drop the matter."

At the conference on January 27, Hitler and Goering, as we have seen, indulged in the false hope that fear of the Russians would lead the Western Allies to conclude a separate peace with Germany. But in the event that peace could not be secured on terms that were favorable to Hitler, a desperate plan was worked out to create a mountain fortress in the south from which a last guerilla stand could be made; this plan was "mostly nonsense," said Kesselring after the war, but with the ministries evacuated south along with the works of art, it was expected that Hitler would agree to leave Berlin on April 20, which was his fifty-sixth birthday. There was another wild burst of hope when Roosevelt died on April 12, and the astrologers were hastily consulted. Conferences went on at all hours, for life in the bunker was as artificial as its perpetual lights. Goering, his heart already set on the south, is described by an officer who was present as ostentatiously bored—"He put his elbow on the table and sank his huge head into the folds of the soft leather of his briefcase." He even for a moment obscured one of Hitler's maps.[17]

Galland had a last meeting with Goering around April 10 on the Obersalzberg. On reflection he believes that Goering summoned him south in order to give some sort of official cover to his own visit, for he found the Reich Marshal busy supervising the disposal of his art treasures. Goering was at least civil to the officer he had degraded, and told him he thought Galland had been right after all. He seemed deeply depressed, and when they parted he said, "I envy you, Galland, for going into action. I wish I were a few years younger and less bulky." He pointed to his belly with an ironic smile. "If I were, I would gladly put myself under your command. It would be marvelous to have nothing to worry about but a good fight, as it was in the old days."[18] Galland was then dismissed to continue operations as best he could, and Goering returned to Berlin.

General Koller, Goering's representative along with General Christian in the *Führerbunker,* was now vainly trying to resolve or evade the nonsensical orders Hitler was giving for the reorganization of the jet-fighter squadrons. Koller, who kept a diary which is of the greatest importance for tracing the events of these last chaotic days in both Berlin and Berchtesgaden, wrote on April 17: "Hitler lashes out at the Luftwaffe every day. My refutations of his illogical arguments are simply brushed away. His fury is constantly kept alive by lying statements made by his own personal staff." All Hitler would say to Koller was, "You are responsible for seeing my orders fulfilled."

April 20, Hitler's birthday, was the occasion for a ceremony and a conference held belowground. Before the conference the distinguished gathering, which included Himmler, Ribbentrop, Goebbels, Goering, Keitel, Doenitz and Jodl, with Bormann hovering in the background, lined up for the macabre formality of handshaking and congratulations. Messages arrived that the Russians were already immediately south of Berlin, and Koller told Goering that if Hitler and everyone who intended to go south did not leave at once, he could not guarantee sufficient fuel for evacuation by air at some later time.

Goering's own fleet of cars was waiting already loaded. At the conference Goering asked Hitler who should go to Berchtesgaden, himself or Koller. Hitler replied, "You go. Koller stays here." Goering took his last leave of Hitler.

Koller meanwhile had left for the Luftwaffe's headquarters, which were now west of Berlin, near Potsdam. Christian, who had remained with Goering, telephoned Koller to break the bad news that he was required to remain with the Führer. The raids on Berlin disorganized Goering's departure, and for a while he lost touch with the fleet of cars, which was in the charge of Bernd von Brauchitsch. It was not till two-twenty on the morning of April 21 that Goering's cavalcade eventually reached the Luftwaffe headquarters; the long delay in traveling this short distance had been due to the time Goering had been forced to spend in air-raid shelters, where he managed to laugh and joke with whomever he found. Although Koller had sent word that he urgently wanted to see the Reich Marshal, Goering made no attempt to find him. Koller was angry when he heard Goering's cars rush off on their journey south at about three in the morning.

Koller had been left to deal alone with Hitler's constant, nagging phone calls, demanding that he put his planes in the sky for the defense of Berlin, which was by now under artillery fire. When Koller explained that planes could not leave the damaged airfields, Hitler shouted that the Luftwaffe was useless and its leaders should be hanged. Later that night he insisted that Goering had left a private army to defend Carinhall, and he refused to listen to Koller's explanation that this simply was not so; he ordered the private army to be thrown into the defense of Berlin and banged down the receiver. Then Koller's telephone rang again; Hitler ordered the men of the Luftwaffe to resist the attack northeast and rang off before Koller could speak. By ten-thirty Koller was being threatened with death for sabotage because he had not sent his men to join a nonexistent army.

The Luftwaffe by now was without supplies of fuel for its planes. The following day, April 22, in spite of Hitler's declaration over the telephone, "Mark my word, at the gates of Berlin the Russians will suffer the bloodiest defeat of their history," the confusion became worse and Hitler, according to Koller, was "behaving like a madman." Christian arrived and told Koller that the Führer had suffered a breakdown and was determined to die in the bunker. Koller decided later in the evening that he should report this to Goering.

The line to Berchtesgaden was poor, but Koller managed to reach Bernd von Brauchitsch. "The one we used to go to," said Koller warily, referring to Hitler, "won't leave where he is. But I've got to get away from here." "Goering wants you to come here," replied Brauchitsch, and the line went dead. Koller made contact with Jodl and confirmed the report that Hitler was to stay in Berlin. Jodl passed on to Koller what Hitler had said earlier in the day in his presence and that of Keitel. Jodl had challenged him that nothing could be done without the leadership staff, who had all gone south. "Well, then," Hitler had replied, "Goering can take over the leadership down there." But no one would fight for the Reich Marshal, they had said. "What do you mean, fight?" Hitler had sneered. "There's precious little fighting to be done! When it comes to negotiating for peace, Goering can do that better than I. Goering is much better at those things. He can deal much better with the other side." On hearing this, Koller at once flew south in a Heinkel, reaching Berchtesgaden eventually at noon on April 23.

The report that he brought from Berlin alarmed Goering. He was open in his criticism of Hitler's decision to stay in Berlin. But he did not know now what to do for the best. The military situation seemed hopeless. "Is Hitler still alive?" he asked Koller. He was worried in case Bormann might have supplanted him as Hitler's successor. Koller said he thought Berlin could hold out a week. "But the responsibility is now yours, Herr Reich Marshal. Hitler's decision yesterday made him the commandant of Berlin and excludes him from the leadership of the State and the supreme leadership of the Army."

Philipp Bouhler, a party official who was a close friend of Goering, was also there, and he agreed with Koller. But Goering remained full of misgivings, convinced that, because of the bad relations he had with Hitler, Bormann, his greatest enemy, would have become Hitler's successor. He was sure that if he attempted to take supreme command, Bormann would have him killed as a traitor. "He is merely waiting for his chance to liquidate me," said Goering. "If I act now, they'll call me a traitor. And if I don't act, I'll be reproached for having failed Germany in the decisive hour."

Goering had Hitler's decree of June 29, 1941, there in a steel box, and together they studied it, wondering what best to do. The wording was quite clear: "Should I have my freedom of action curtailed or be somehow removed, Reich Marshal Hermann Goering is to be my deputy or my successor in all my offices of State, Party and Army." This seemed decisive to Koller, Bouhler and Brauchitsch. But Goering was still uncertain, in case Hitler had meanwhile acted differently. He decided to consult Lammers, who was also in Berchtesgaden. Lammers' view was the same as that of the others. "The decree is valid and legal," he said. "The Führer has made no alternative edicts. Had he done so, I should have had to know of it. He couldn't have done it legally without my knowledge."

"If you want to make absolutely sure," said Koller, "why not send Hitler a message that puts the matter quite clearly?" Goering at once agreed.

They sat down to draft a message. Goering's attempt was long and full of legal protestations. Koller eventually drafted something briefer and more suitable:

My Fuhrer!

Since you are determined to remain at your post in Fortress Berlin, do you agree that I, as your deputy, in accordance with your decree of June 29, 1941, assume immediately the total leadership of the Reich with complete freedom of action at home and abroad?

If by 10 P.M. no answer is forthcoming, I shall assume you have been deprived of your freedom of action. I will then consider the terms of your decree to have come into force and act accordingly for the good of the people and the Fatherland.

You must realize what I feel for you in these most difficult hours of my life, and I am quite unable to find words to express it.

God bless you and grant that you may come here after all as soon as possible.

Your most loyal
HERMANN GOERING

The final, rather inconclusive sentence was added by Goering because he felt the message sounded too cold and formal without it.[19]

Before sending the message, Goering ordered the wireless posts to be taken over by staff officers for the sake of security. He also gave instructions for Colonel von Below in the *Führerbunker* to see that the Führer not only received the message but had every chance of leaving Berlin if he wanted to do so. He sent instructions to Ribbentrop and Keitel to report to him, unless the order was countermanded by Hitler himself, and he had Bormann informed that he had sent a message to the Führer and that he also should do his best to get Hitler away from Berlin. He even went so far, in spite of warnings from the others, as to consult Müller, Bormann's representative at Berchtesgaden. Müller did not like the proposal and said so.

Goering, Bouhler and Koller then had lunch and discussed the next step. Goering decided he would fly to see General Eisenhower the following day, April 24, and talk it out "man to man." He pondered over the draft of a proclamation to the Army and the German people. "The proclamation," he said to Koller, "should make the Russians believe that we are continuing the struggle on both sides, but the Americans and the British should infer from it that we want to fight only against the East and not against the West. As for our own soldiers, they should understand that although the war is going on, there is to be an end to it somehow, and on more favorable terms than we could have dared to assume recently." Koller remarked that to draft so involved and contradictory a proclamation was quite beyond his powers, but Goering persisted that he must try. Then there was the new Cabinet. Ribbentrop must go, of course. He, Goering, would probably have to take on the Foreign Ministry as well as all his other duties. He became exuberant and excited. To have sent the message to Hitler took a load off his mind, and he was looking forward to his contact with the British and the Americans. Goering began to dream of his new historic role.

Koller then left, going down the mountain road to the Villa Geiger, the Luftwaffe headquarters. He needed sleep, but he went into his office at five o'clock. Shortly after five and again at eight he received telephone calls from Goering. But between eight and nine o'clock attempts by himself and other staff officers to reach Goering's chalet by telephone failed. Something definitely seemed to be wrong.

When Goering's message was being transmitted to the bunker, Berlin was already surrounded by the Russians and could be reached only by air. Aboveground the sky thundered with planes, and the earth trembled with bombardments. Speer had flown in for his last meeting with Hitler—at which he confessed he had disobeyed his master's orders to destroy all of Germany's resources, but was immediately forgiven; Hitler did not know that Speer had planned to poison him in the bunker by injecting gas. Speer found him surrounded by the remainder of those who still clung to him —Goebbels and his wife Magda; Eva Braun, Hitler's mistress; Bormann; and even Ribbentrop, who was about to slip away and forsake this catacomb of madness and self-destruction. The endless discussion of Hitler's decision to stay and die was repeated, and Speer agreed with Goebbels that it was more dignified for him to do so than to seek to escape south. Then the radio message from Goering was put into Hitler's hands.

Bormann at once seized the opportunity to damn Goering in Hitler's eyes. The messages Goering had sent to Keitel, Ribbentrop and Colonel von Below requesting them to protect the interests of both Hitler and himself in this most difficult matter either were never received or were made ineffective by Bormann, who immediately set to work to interpret Goering's carefully worded statement in such a way as to discredit him still further, making it out to be an ultimatum to the Führer with a time limit. A radio reply was dispatched: "Decree of June 29, 1941, is rescinded by my special instruction. My freedom of action undisputed. I forbid any move by you in the direction indicated. Adolf Hitler."[20]

In the presence of Speer, Hitler gave way to his anger and said he "had known for some time that Goering had failed him, that he was corrupt, and that he was a drug addict." All Goering was fit for was to negotiate the capitulation. It did not matter, said Hitler with supreme contempt, who did that; the country that had failed him was worthless.

Then, in spite of the words he had said in Jodl's presence only a short while before, he set about avenging himself against the man who Bormann said was betraying him. He ordered Bormann to send a second message to Goering depriving him of his offices and his liberty. The text of this message is not recorded, but it was seen by two of the surviving officers on duty in the bunker, and they clearly recall its contents. Goering was informed that he was guilty of high treason both to National Socialism and to the Führer, that he was to be spared the death penalty only because of his earlier service to the party, but that he must voluntarily resign all his offices and the right of succession forthwith. To this he was re-quired to send an immediate answer, yes or no.

At the same time this message was dispatched, Bormann sent orders to S.S. officers Frank and Bredow, who were stationed on the Obersalzberg, ordering them to arrest Goering for high treason and also to confine his staff, including Koller, as well as Lammers. "You will answer for this with your lives," added Bormann to these local S.S. men in case they should feel intimidated by so grave a duty. The following day Bormann announced by radio to the German people on Hitler's behalf that Goering had resigned for reasons of health.

So when Koller failed to make contact with Goering by tele-phone between eight and nine o'clock on the evening of April 23, the reason was that the Reich Marshal was already under arrest. As soon as Goering had received Hitler's first radio message, he had countermanded his original messages to Ribbentrop and Keitel and informed them he had heard from the Führer. But it was too late; according to Bernd von Brauchitsch, the chalet had already been surrounded by seven o'clock. Robert Kropp opened the door to the S.S. officers, who entered with their revolvers drawn and took im-mediate charge of the Reich Marshal, confining him to his room. He was not allowed to see his wife or daughter or to communicate with his staff. The house was turned into a miniature prison, with everyone kept in his room.

Meanwhile Koller was becoming increasingly worried. He had seen a copy of Hitler's reply and this naturally disturbed him. His wife had joined him, and as they were eating late at night his bat-

man announced that an S.S. officer had arrived and wanted to see
him. It was Bredow, who came in and saluted just as the batman
was trying to persuade Koller to try to escape. Bredow apologized.
"Herr General," he said, "I have to arrest you by order of the
Führer."

"Do you know why?" asked Koller in astonishment.

"No, sir."

"Where is the Reich Marshal?" asked Koller.

"Under arrest."

"And Brauchitsch and the staff?"

"All under arrest."

"Do you realize," Koller protested, "that this is madness? The
Reich Marshal has acted quite correctly. He merely put a question
to the Führer."

Bredow apologized again. This, he hastened to explain, was
Ehrenhaft, honorable custody. Koller was invited to choose the
room in which he preferred to be placed under guard together with
his wife. He was forbidden to communicate with anyone. He had,
however, managed to conceal the draft he had been making of
Goering's proclamation, and he flushed these incriminating papers
down the lavatory at the first opportunity.

At five o'clock in the morning Brauchitsch was brought in to
Koller under guard with an order from Goering. Koller was to fly
to Berlin at once and explain matters to Hitler. "This is not really
Goering's order," said Bredow to Koller. "It is Hitler's order." Koller refused to fly before nightfall, and then only without an S.S.
guard. Later he was released by Hitler's special command. When
Koller heard that Hitler had summoned General Ritter von Greim
from Munich to give him command of the Luftwaffe, he sent
Greim a telephone message explaining all the facts in Goering's
favor. But Greim expressed no sympathy at all for Goering; in his
view the Reich Marshal should have stayed with Hitler in the
bunker.

Greim, who was impatient to leave, had trouble finding an aircraft to take him to Berlin; the constant air raids had damaged
every machine in the neighborhood. Eventually he arrived at the
Führerbunker badly wounded, accompanied by the famous air-
woman Hanna Reitsch, after hedge-hopping with a fighter escort
as far as Gatow Airport outside Berlin and completing the journey
to the bunker in a small training plane through fierce Russian fire.

With Hanna Reitsch's assistance he had landed in an avenue near the Chancellery; his right foot had been shattered.

Hitler welcomed the visitors and, according to Hanna Reitsch's hysterical account of their emotional meeting, immediately started to attack Goering.[21] He said that he had summoned Greim to Berlin "because Hermann Goering has betrayed and deserted both me and his Fatherland. Behind my back he has established connections with the enemy . . . and against my orders he has gone to save himself at Berchtesgaden. From there," added Hitler, "he sent me a disgraceful telegram." The Führer had tears in his eyes, according to Hanna Reitsch; his head sagged, his face was pale, and his hand was shaking uncontrollably as he showed them Goering's telegram. "An ultimatum!" he shouted. "A crass ultimatum." Greim and Hanna Reitsch grasped Hitler's hands and swore to atone with their lives for the wrong Goering had done their beloved Führer.

While Hitler was cursing the name of Goering on the evening of April 26, the former Reich Marshal, his staff, his family and his guards were facing the ordeal of life in an air-raid shelter without adequate sanitary equipment. Early in the morning there had been a heavy raid on Berchtesgaden during which considerable damage had been done to Hitler's and Goering's chalets; captives and captors alike only just reached the shelter in time.[22]

By dawn the following day, April 27, Koller, in response to Hitler's summons, managed to fly north as far as Rechlin. There he found it impossible to continue his journey, and he spent an unhappy day with Jodl, Keitel, Doenitz and Himmler, who avoided any mention of Goering in case they might seem to share in his disgrace. "Why, yes," said Himmler. "That affair of the Reich Marshal. Most unfortunate." He said he would talk about it later, but had far too much to do at present. Jodl and Keitel also feigned such pressure of work that they could not possibly spare time to listen to Koller's loyal attempts to re-establish Goering's name. "No doubt Goering meant well," said Doenitz noncommitally. "We'll talk about it after lunch." Eventually Greim spoke to Koller on the telephone and told him that there were after all no orders for him to come to Berlin (Bormann was seeing to it that any further thought of Goering should be banished from Hitler's mind), and that he had better go back to Berchtesgaden. Much relieved, he left at three-ten on the morning of April 28, but he was delayed on his journey and did not reach the Obersalzberg until April 29. There he learned that Goering had been removed, no one knew where.

Goering had in fact been taken to his castle of Mauterndorf at his own request.[23] The shelter was plainly an impossible place for a prolonged stay, and the S.S. had been persuaded to transport Goering, together with his family and certain members of his staff, on the icy mountain roads between Berchtesgaden and Mauterndorf.

Meanwhile in Berlin, Hitler had gone through the macabre celebration of his underground marriage to Eva Braun preparatory to his suicide, and then left his bride while he dictated his last will and testament during the small hours of the night. In it he referred directly to his suicide in the same sentence in which he formally rid himself of his oldest surviving comrade. "Before my death," he dictated to his secretary, "I expel former Reich Marshal Hermann Goering from the party and withdraw from him all rights that were conferred on him by the decree of June 29, 1941 . . . In his place I appoint Admiral Doenitz as President of the Reich and Supreme Commander of the Armed Forces. . . . Goering and Himmler, by their secret negotiations with the enemy without my knowledge or approval, and by their illegal attempts to seize power in the State, quite apart from their treachery to my person, have brought irreparable shame on the country and the whole people." Later that day he added a postscript to this formidable document of revenge on the German people; this postscript was addressed to Keitel on behalf of the armed forces. It does not survive, but was seen by Colonel von Below, who was a witness of Hitler's personal will. In it he uttered his final denunciation of Goering, praised the Luftwaffe for its bravery and blamed Goering for its failure. The next day, after formal handshakes, Hitler went to his room and shot himself through the mouth. This was at half past three on the afternoon of April 30. His body and that of his Eva, who had poisoned herself, were burned outside in the Chancellery garden in the late afternoon. Hitler's death destroyed the Third Reich and ended the martyrdom of Europe.

That same day two messengers in civilian clothes slipped into Berchtesgaden and visited Koller. They came, it seemed, from Goering in order to tell Koller how angry he was at what he termed Koller's "betrayal." This oral message was followed by one even more insulting. Koller's secretary received a telephone message from Mauterndorf in which Goering said, "If Koller isn't a swine, if he has a spark of decency left, he will come to see me tomorrow morning." This, naturally enough, angered Koller, more especially as it would mean spending many hours on the treacherous roads between Berchtesgaden and Mauterndorf.

The following day, May 1, was the first on which the world was free from the shadow of Hitler. But in the south they knew nothing yet of this. All Koller knew during the morning was that the road to Mauterndorf was almost impassable owing to military traffic and the icy conditions. But at noon a senior officer of the S.S. arrived with a sinister message signed by Bormann: "The situation in Berlin is more tense. If Berlin and we should fall, the traitors of April 23 must be exterminated. Men, do your duty! Your life and honor depend on it!" Koller, nervous that he might be considered one of these traitors, was relieved to find that the officer had come to him to explain that the S.S. hated Bormann and would never obey this order.

Later that evening another S.S. officer, Standartenführer Brause, arrived from Mauterndorf after taking some thirty-six hours to complete a journey that normally took less than three. Brause was quite open about the matter; he had made friends with Goering, but could not liberate him without proper authorization. "Herr General," he said, "you have more troops than I have. Why don't you liberate Goering by force?" Everyone by now needed an alibi. Koller felt he should get Goering liberated by order of Kesselring, the commander in the south. Kesselring, whom he telephoned, felt the order should come through Doenitz. All of them by now had heard officially of Hitler's death and knew of Doenitz' new position of authority. It had been announced by the Hamburg radio at ten o'clock that night.

The following day, May 2, Koller, who still felt it was useless for him to respond to Goering's continual commands and travel personally to Mauterndorf, attempted in vain to press Kesselring to give the order for his release. Meanwhile he sent what Luftwaffe men he could to Mauterndorf to give Goering as large a personal entourage as possible.

The situation was so uncertain and the communications so poor that no one seemed to know how best to fulfill what might be thought his duty. Both the Russians and the Americans were advancing closer each day, and everyone was anxious to fall into the hands of the Americans if possible. For this reason Koller began to worry about Goering, since Mauterndorf was east and therefore nearer to the Russians. It seemed plain from what he had heard that Goering had regained the initiative and, short of actual freedom, was having things much his own way. Koller, who very sensibly insisted on staying where he was and sending what help and messages he could to Goering, heard on May 4 that the Americans were advancing toward Berchtesgaden. On May 5 a certain General Pickert, who had passed through Mauterndorf the previous day, told Koller he had seen Goering standing at the entrance to the castle and had spoken to him in the presence of Brause. Goering wanted more men to protect him. "Koller must act now," he had said. He believed he was the most popular member of the Nazi leadership abroad, and that but for Bormann's intrigues he would now be Hitler's lawful successor. "Everyone knew my first move would have been to liquidate Bormann," he said. Asrit was, he still wanted to meet Eisenhower and talk things out "man to man."[24]

According to an account he gave subsequently, Goering in fact brought about his own release. During an interrogation he explained that he had seen men from a Luftwaffe signals unit passing by the castle; he had shouted to them, ordering them to come and rescue him. This was precisely what the S.S. wanted in any case, and no resistance was offered. Goering was delighted with this piece of strategy. "It was one of the most beautiful moments in my life," he said, "to stand there in front of my troops and see them present arms to their Commander in Chief." On May 5 Kesselring formally notified Koller of Goering's release and that he was sending a signal to Doenitz stating that Goering was ready to go and talk to Eisenhower.

Once he was released, Goering himself sent a message to Doenitz, dated May 6.

Are you, Admiral, familiar with the intrigues, dangerous to the security of the State, which Reich Leader Bormann has carried on to eliminate me? All steps taken against me arose out of the request sent by me in all loyalty to the Führer, asking whether he wished that his order concerning his succession should come into force. . . . The steps taken against me were carried out on the authority of a radiogram signed "Bormann." I have not been interrogated by anybody in spite of my requests and no attempt of mine to justify my position has been accepted. Reich-führer-S.S. Himmler can confirm the immense extent of these intrigues.

I have just learned that you intend to send Jodl to Eisenhower with a view to negotiating. I think it important in the interests of our people that, besides the official negotiations of Jodl, I should officially approach Eisenhower, as one marshal to another. My success in all the important negotiations abroad with which the Führer always entrusted me before the war is sufficient guarantee that I can hope to create the personal atmosphere appropriate for Jodl's negotiations. Moreover, both Great Britain and America have proved through their press and their radio, and in the declarations of their statesmen during the last few years, that their attitude toward me is more favorable than toward other political leaders in Germany. I think that at this most difficult hour all should collaborate and that nothing should be neglected which might assure as far as possible the future of Germany.

GOERING, MARSHAL OF THE REICH[25]

Doenitz did not bother to reply; he merely filed the message. After a momentary flourish of despairing resistance, he was now seeking the final means of capitulation. On April 29, unknown to Hitler, the German armies in Italy had surrendered unconditionally. On May 4, the surrender in northwest Germany to Montgomery had already taken place. Kesselring had capitulated in the south on May 5, and on May 7, the day after Goering's grandiloquent but unanswered message had been put away and forgotten, Doenitz authorized an unconditional surrender of all Germany to General Eisenhower.

But in the south Koller was still busying himself on Goering's behalf. On May 6 he had confiscated a castle at Fischhorn, Austria, on the southern shore of the Zell am See (the owner had refused to accommodate "the traitor" Goering), and then made arrangements for Goering to be transported there, ostensibly to meet the Americans, as he had desired. The following day Bernd von Brauchitsch arrived with two open letters from Goering, the first addressed to the nearest American divisional commander and the second to General Eisenhower. In the first he asked for personal protection, since he was "still feeling menaced," and for the safe delivery of his other letter to the Supreme Allied Commander; in the second he asked Eisenhower for an immediate personal conversation "man to man," as he continued to put it. Brauchitsch, provided with transport by Koller, set off to deliver the letters to the Americans.

On May 8, Greim and Hanna Reitsch suddenly arrived to complicate the situation. They were still full of heroics, still vituperating against Goering and praising Hitler. Greim was too ill from his wounds to remain longer out of hospital, and Koller, desperate to be rid of these unwelcome visitors (Greim was technically his commanding officer), arranged for him to be transported to hospital. Hanna Reitsch up to the last hysterically attacked Goering as the enemy of the two men to whom she was devoted, Hitler and Greim.

Then a telephone message came from Fischhorn during the morning to report that a detachment of Americans in jeeps had arrived for the safe custody of the Reich Marshal. The officer in charge, who had been detailed to receive Goering, was very angry indeed to find that he was not there. Koller, the resourceful organizer, gave orders that the Americans were to be provided with a good lunch; meanwhile he would try to find out where Goering had gone. He telephoned Mauterndorf, to find that Goering had, after all, felt that it was preferable for him to stay in his own castle, but he had failed to let Koller know of this. Koller at last lost his patience. The Americans were at Fischhorn waiting, he said, and Goering must undertake to go there at once.

After more trouble with Greim, who in the course of his journey to hospital had ordered the car to be stopped and had tried to change into civilian clothes in a field, Koller telephoned Mauterndorf again to see whether Goering was on the way. The housekeeper replied that he had left at about noon. Yet at four o'clock he still had not arrived at Fischhorn, and the Americans, tired of waiting, but determined not to return without their prize, had set out in search of him. He was finally discovered in a traffic jam near Radstadt and was taken on to Fischhorn. There, Koller learned over his telephone, Goering and his entourage had arrived "much relieved, everybody in splendid humor. . . . Goering is cracking jokes with the American soldiers."[26]

Koller now felt that he should meet the man for whom he had tried to do so much during the past weeks, but Goering curtly refused to receive him. He was changing for dinner, which he was to have with the American general in charge of the reception party.

If Koller telephoned tomorrow no doubt a convenient time could be arranged. Koller then had to turn his attention again to Greim, who was now asking to be shot as a deserter. The young officer in charge of him wanted to know what he should do. Koller gave his last order before the Americans, who were occupying Berchtesgaden, took full charge: the Commander in Chief of the Luftwaffe must go to hospital properly, accompanied by his officer.

The following day, May 9, Koller was still free to try to see Goering, but found that he had gone away with the Americans. He had, however, had the grace to leave a friendly message with Bouhler for Koller: "Goering wants to thank you for everything you have done. He now sees you were quite right and he very much regrets not to have recognized it earlier. He has expressly instructed me to tell you that you are the only person he really confides in. You were the only one who always stuck to his opinion. As for him, he has backed far too many wrong horses!" Goering would return, Bouhler thought, in about a week after seeing Eisenhower; Koller was skeptical about this. He saw Emmy Goering at a window high up in the castle, wearing a white dress and a sun hat. After this, Koller had no further contact with Goering; he was taken to England and kept there in captivity for two and a half years.

Goering was taken first to Zell am See, Austria, the headquarters of Robert J. Stack, commander of the Thirty-sixth Infantry Division, and later to Kitzbühel, about thirty miles away, where the American Seventh Army was based. Stack made Goering welcome —apparently too welcome to please Eisenhower. Even Koller heard a report that Goering was seen standing on the balcony of the hotel in Kitzbühel held by the Army, champagne glass in hand, laughing with the American officers, and he was photographed standing beside the flag of the Texas division to which he had surrendered. The handsome reception given him by the Americans received a bad press, and orders were given from Allied headquarters that he was to be treated in future as a normal prisoner of war. As he waited in vain for some message to come from Eisenhower his spirits sank, and he even discussed suicide with Brauchitsch, who was still with him.

He was flown to the Augsburg prison camp, where he was treated more strictly as a prisoner of war and accommodated in a two-room flat commandeered by the Americans.[27] Goering had his bed in one room; Brauchitsch and his adjutant slept as best they could in the other, which they shared with Robert Kropp. They lived on Army rations which they prepared for themselves in the kitchen. Major Paul, the officer in charge of them, was obviously under orders to establish a proper distance between himself and his prisoners. But even so the natural hospitality of the Americans could not be entirely suppressed—nor their curiosity about their famous prisoner. During the brief period Goering and Brauchitsch were at Augsburg, they were again entertained in the officers' mess; on these occasions Goering roused himself from his gloom and put on all his charm. The drinking, according to Brauchitsch, was heavy.

At Augsburg on May 11 Goering was photographed and interviewed by the press, and the attention of the world pleased him. He spoke of the failure of the German generals to convince Hitler that the war was lost by the middle of 1944. "Hitler," he said to the audience in front of him with their notebooks poised, "refused to accept this point of view. He ordered that it never be referred to again."

Augsburg was to prove a brief transition before Goering was put into a more permanent form of captivity. By now he realized that Eisenhower had no intention of communicating with him. He was told to make himself ready to leave on May 21, when he was flown from Augsburg to the prison center at Mondorf, near Luxembourg. He was allowed to take one officer with him. He chose rather to take Robert Kropp, his faithful servant.

X

Nuremberg

W HEN GOERING CAME to see me at Mondorf, he was a simpering slob with two suitcases full of paracodeine pills. I thought he was a drug salesman. But we took him off his dope and made a man of him." This was the view expressed by Colonel B. C. Andrus, the American commandant at the Bad Mondorf prison, where Goering was taken on May 21 from the airfield in a military truck by two soldiers, the rhythmic movement of whose jaws he was not to forget. They were the sign of an indifference to his status which was the one thing he feared might follow Eisenhower's complete disregard of his most distinguished prisoner.

His new prison was the Palace Hotel, gutted of all luxury and organized for hard living. The Americans renamed it "Ashcan." Goering was deprived of his pills and put on strict regimen designed to reduce his drug addiction and strip down some of the unhealthy load of flesh, which was affecting his heart. He weighed 280 pounds. One of the German doctors familiar with Hitler's circle, Dr. Brandt, had told the Americans that Goering was used to absorbing daily twenty times the normal dose of paracodeine tablets. They allowed him now eighteen tablets a day, reducing the quantity still further over a period of time until he was freed of the drug habit altogether. He was to be kept at Mondorf until his transfer to Nuremberg jail in September, after some four months' investigation by interrogation officers. By that time his weight had been reduced by sixty pounds, and he was fit and ready to take the stage at Nuremberg.

Robert Kropp had been flown to Mondorf with his master, and for a while he was put in charge of a small staff of German servants working at the prison. He did his best to look after Goering, who was beginning to realize that he was himself little more than an ordinary prisoner of war. Though deprived of his treasury of pills, Goering had managed, he told Kropp, to keep one of the capsules of poison that all the Nazi leaders were supposed to carry on their persons by order of their Führer. Kropp's last service for him was to steal a pillow, which was at once confiscated. Early in June Kropp saw the last of him; they said goodbye, and Goering, who was near to tears, thanked him. He told Kropp that his constant worry was the welfare of Emmy and the child. After Kropp had gone, a German prisoner of war became his batman.

It was in June that Sir Ivone Kirkpatrick renewed his acquaintance with Goering. Kirkpatrick visited Mondorf as British political adviser to General Eisenhower and spent two hours with Goering, who had a touch of bronchitis and was lying on an iron bedstead in his cell, wrapped in a flowered dressing gown. Goering received his visitor warmly and responded easily and readily to the questions about the war that Kirkpatrick put to him. He claimed that Hitler had launched into war at the moment most favorable to Germany, but that he had made a grave mistake in not taking the advice Goering had himself given him in 1940, to go through Spain with or without Franco's consent and capture Gibraltar and North Africa. Hitler, he said, thought he could win the war without Franco, but had he gained control of North Africa he could with safety have attacked Russia and America. As for the war in the air, the Battle of Britain was the turning point, even though, in Goering's view, it was a draw; nonetheless, it had been a grave disappointment to him. Later on, the strategic bombing of Germany had come just in time to save Britain from destruction by rockets and flying bombs. Goering evidently enjoyed the talk, and he begged Kirkpatrick to come again; he appeared to realize that he was doomed, but "he viewed his future with fortitude and made no effort to explain or excuse." The contrast between him and Ribbentrop, who was in a state of moral collapse, was very marked.[1]

Dr. Douglas M. Kelley, the psychiatrist in charge of the prisoners, found Goering most co-operative. The doctor had been given some account of Goering's drug addiction at the time he was taken prisoner. Goering told him he had resorted to paracodeine, which is a mild derivative of morphine, to help him bear toothache in 1937, and had used it ever since. Apparently no mention was made of the periodic cures administered by Kahle. His average daily dose of the very mild tablets that were specially prepared for him was about one hundred. This, Dr. Kelley claims, amounted in all to only three or four grains of morphine, which is not a substantial dose; his mind would remain unaffected by it. Goering took these tablets as an active habit, like chain-smoking, keeping a bottle of a hundred by him and consuming its contents every day. There was no secret about this; he would put them in his mouth during conferences and chew them like gum. They did not stimulate him, but they eased any pain there was in his body. Dr. Kelley found no great difficulty in breaking him of the habit; he simply challenged him to give it up as a strong man who should be ready to bear pain in the cause of good health.

He also found him unbelievably narcissistic about his body. Goering knew precisely the length and width of his scars, and he was meticulous in the care of his skin. He had a fine leather toilet case containing a multitude of preparations, including face lotions and powders for his body. According to Dr. Kelley, Goering thought his physique the finest in Germany. His underclothes were of the softest silk. He brought into captivity his three celebrated rings set with huge stones, one a ruby, one an emerald and one a blue diamond; he chose each day the ring with the stone that seemed best to suit his mood. His cigar and cigarette cases, his pens and his pencils, were all of gold, and he had four jeweled watches with him. He also carried an enormous unset emerald, about one inch by half an inch in dimension, which he claimed to be the largest he could procure. Yet although Goering was so conscious of his worth and his importance, he was among the easiest of the prisoners to handle. He was readily adaptable and accepted his misfortune with comparatively good grace. His sole concern, apart from his acute anxiety about his family, was to maintain the mystique of his authority and a recognition of his high place in the history of his country. He never once thought of himself as a criminal. He boasted to Dr. Kelley, "Yes, I know I shall hang. You know I shall hang. I am ready. But I am determined to go down in German history as a great man. If I cannot convince the court, I shall at least convince the German people that all I did was done for the

Greater German Reich. In fifty or sixty years there will be statues of Hermann Goering all over Germany."

The admiring form of interrogation which Goering had so much enjoyed ended at Augsburg. At Mondorf he was subject to rigorous investigation by officers with code names, who probed into the details of his personal affairs. As his health improved—and his cure was not altogether easy for him, for he twice suffered from withdrawal symptoms during the period when his paracodeine was being reduced—he became increasingly co-operative. But the range of the questioning to which he was subjected began to make him realize the enormous weight of criminal responsibility that the Allies considered he should bear. He gathered that some kind of public charge was to be preferred against him together with the other Nazi leaders and military chiefs.

The constitution of the International Military Tribunal, which was to begin its work at Nuremberg in November, was first laid down at a conference of the prosecutors appointed by the principal Allies, Britain, America, France and the U.S.S.R. Sir David Maxwell-Fyfe, Attorney-General of the United Kingdom, presided. On August 8, 1945, an agreement proclaiming the trial was signed at London, and a charter was appended establishing the tribunal and determining its procedure, which was based broadly on British and American practice in the courts of law. A copy of the London agreement was read to Goering at Mondorf.

After his transfer to the prison of the Palace of Justice at Nuremberg in September, he was confined in cell number 5, which was nine by thirteen feet. Here he had a bed, a chair, a table, a water closet and a washbowl. He was visible in every act except excretion, and his food was supplied to him in his cell through a trap door. He was permitted a shower once a week, and when his cell was periodically searched he had to stand by, stripped naked. During their confinement the prisoners were exercised each morning separately and shaved by a German barber. Only during the period of the trial, which began on Tuesday, November 20, were they permitted some degree of social life together while taking their meals. Throughout they were guarded by the tough and often truculent soldiers of the American First Division; the prison commandant remained Colonel Andrus, who had brought the prisoners from Bad Mondorf.

It was now that Goering at last received some news of his wife. He was deeply concerned to hear that Emmy was in prison at Straubing, together with her sister Else; here she was constantly interrogated. Edda joined her in prison at her mother's request, and they were not released until March 1946, when the trial had already run five months at Nuremberg. Goering and Emmy were eventually allowed to correspond with each other.

The International Military Tribunal at Nuremberg was one of the most extraordinary events in history. Dr. Stahmer, Goering's counsel, described it in court as "of significance in shaping new laws" and "of dimensions such as have never before been known in the history of law." [XXIII, p. 104]* As a technical feat, with its intricate system of multilingual translation through headphones (a system used here for the first time in any trial) and its recordings for world audiences by means of film and radio, it could have been organized only in our own century.

It is important to realize that it was the Americans who bore the cost of the trial and were responsible for its administration. They held and guarded the defendants; they looked after the courtroom and maintained its equipment. The great mass of German official documents were retained in American hands after they had been discovered and confiscated in the south following the evacuation of the government departments from Berlin. The huge task of reading and preparing these documents against time for use by the prosecution was one of the great contributions of America to the trial. Britain, Russia and France were responsible only for meeting the cost of their own judges and teams of prosecutors, all of whom were engaged in their work for well over a year.

Nevertheless, the trial was presided over by an Englishman, Lord Justice Lawrence (now Lord Oaksey). He conducted the proceedings with patience, courtesy and firmness, and with an impartiality that won tribute even from the defendants. It was a supremely difficult task to control such a formidable gathering of counsel representing five nationalities with widely differing traditions in court procedure.

Like all great spectacles of its kind, the trial had its dangers for

* The volume and page numbers following the excerpts in this chapter refer to the 22-volume British edition of the court testimony in the major trial at Nuremberg: *Trial of the German War Criminals. Proceedings of the International Military Tribunal* (London: His Majesty's Stationery Office).

those who promoted it, since the finer points of legal argument could easily become obscured by other factors which would more readily catch the candid eye of the camera or of the popular press. With the outcome of the trial a foregone conclusion, the human drama lay in how these men whose unlimited power had become a scourge to so many nations would behave under the duress of public investigation and cross-questioning by highly skilled legal minds representing collectively an act of justice by hundreds of millions of people. On the other hand, the state of tension existing in the courtroom at supreme moments of conflict in the trial resulted in an atmosphere of sympathy for any sign of sincerity, courage or ability to fight back that the men in the dock might show. But this has always been the case in trials which attract an unusual degree of public attention.

Goering knew that he was the star of the court drama, and that the trial would be his final and greatest opportunity to win back some regard for himself and for the regime of which he was now the principal surviving figure. He knew that the whole world would watch him with unique curiosity, that his behavior could make headlines in the world press and that his every gesture could be recorded for history. In spite of the humiliations and the tensions of the past months of captivity, in spite of his knowledge that his captors would most certainly execute him, he prepared himself to give the star performance of his life. He had everything to gain by this, and nothing to lose. He marshaled all the resources of his famous personality—his bluffness, his cynicism, his shrewdness, his humor, his phenomenal memory. He was determined to proclaim his leadership over the rest of the defendants. His captors had helped him by restoring his health and his self-confidence. The "simpering slob" was now an alert and intelligent man ready to do battle.

He was defeated by factors over which, in the end, he had no effective control. Many of the defendants broke away from his influence, and some displayed forms of abject penitence that made a degraded setting for Goering's last adventure in power. Of the senior defendants, men who had ranked close to the Reich Marshal, Ribbentrop was in a state of collapse, Hess was mentally unbalanced, and Schacht, Neurath and Papen were anxious only to disassociate themselves as much as possible from the proceedings, while Speer was a clear-minded penitent who became a most valuable ally for the prosecution. Frick, former Governor General of occupied Poland, retired into a form of religious hysteria, weeping and praying in his cell. Robert Ley had managed to commit suicide in October after a period of desperation and depression. The service chiefs, Keitel, Jodl, Raeder and Doenitz, deserted the cause under the plea that to a soldier orders are orders; they had done what they were told to do and had had no share in formulating the disastrous policy of Hitler. One by one they deserted "the fat one," and he was left the sole protestant of Hitler's greatness, facing alone the overwhelming odds of the evidence amassed against him and the regime he represented.

The final defeat for Goering was the sheer length of the trial itself. It lasted 218 days; the verbatim record of its proceedings published at Nuremberg was to fill twenty-three large volumes. Goering himself was eventually buried under the terrible weight of documents and the endless array of argument. The public became bored by the trial, and everyone concerned in it grew tired and irritated. This, quite as much as his ultimate failure to establish a credible defense, destroyed the publicity Goering sought to achieve. He was no longer news; all that could be said for him was that he stuck it out to the last bitter day, sitting with his head in his hands or with his chin resting on his chest, deep in thought or lost in depression.

Behind the scenes, another drama was being staged under the watchful eyes of the American prison psychologists. As soon as the actors left the stage of the courtroom, this second group of investigators took over the examination. Sitting with the prisoners at meals, visiting them like father confessors in their cells, reporting on them, recording their attitudes of mind, their behavior alone and with each other, their shifts of temperament and slides of fortune, the professional psychologists added their particular voices to the story of the trial. Dr. G. M. Gilbert was the psychologist responsible for the observation of Goering. The prisoners were also kept busy interviewing their lawyers and, except for those who chose to be as uninterested as possible, concentrating on the trial and the conduct of their defense.

The trial itself has been the subject of considerable debate. There were those who maintained that the tribunal, though unprecedented, was correctly conducted according to international law. And there were those who considered that the court had no actual legal basis and was solely a grave indictment by the victor of the vanquished, a solemn record for history of the overwhelming evidence that the principles for which the Nazis stood were vile and inhuman. Each country, as we have seen, had its team of prosecutors; that for the United States was led by Associate Justice Robert H. Jackson of the Supreme Court, that for Great Britain by Sir Hartley Shawcross and Sir David Maxwell-Fyfe, that for France by Auguste Champetier de Ribes, Charles Dubost and Edgar Faure, and that for the U.S.S.R. by General Rudenko and Colonel Pokrovsky. The case was made to rest primarily on recaptured German documents, the authenticity of which was never in doubt, and the nineteen defendants were given ample opportunity to defend themselves against the charges, which summarized in legal terms the extent of their crimes. Their regime had been responsible in one way or another for the death of some thirty million people, and the history of a quarter of a century of agitation, violence and oppression had to be traced and proved and argued during the nine months of the trial. Outside the Palace of Justice lay the ruins of Nuremberg, the once beautiful medieval city which had been chosen as the center for the greatest spectacles of the Nazis' power and national pride, and which was now to become the center for their exposure and degradation. Inside the Palace, Goering, Jodl and Keitel wore drab uniforms without insignia of rank, while the rest of the defendants appeared in civilian clothes; by the charter of the tribunal they had been deprived of their position as heads of state or superior orders. Apart from Goering, they looked weary and insignificant, and he too succumbed as the months of examination wore on.

Thirty days before the trial began, each defendant received in his cell a copy of the indictment, a bulky document of some 24,000 words, translated into German. Goering was served with his copy by a British officer, Major A.M.S. Neave, who was later to become a London barrister, but whose recent experiences had included a daring escape from a German prison camp, during which he had passed through Nuremberg itself; his present function was to deal with the legal rights and arrangements for the defendants, including their selection of counsel for the defense. Major Neave found Goering polite, nervous and strained; his mouth was twitching and he appeared to be on the verge of tears. He was most anxious to establish the correct action to take. A list of eligible counsel was given him from which he might choose the man to be responsible for his defense. He selected the one man in the list whose name he recognized, Dr. Otto Stahmer of Kiel, a very good barrister although he was seventy years of age.

As the guards in the prison at the Palace of Justice peered through the trap door of cell number 5, they saw Goering poring over the document which summarized the record of the Nazi regime under the four headings which constituted the charges against him: the common plan or conspiracy, crimes against peace, war crimes, and crimes against humanity. It had been signed in October in Berlin by the chief prosecutors and had become the official indictment of a great international assembly of nations, since by then eighteen countries had adhered to the charter setting up the tribunal. The defendants were accused not only individually under these four main charges, but also as key members of one or more of the organizations through which the Nazi regime had operated: the Reich Cabinet, the Leadership Corps of the Nazi Party, the S.S. and the S.D., the Gestapo, the S.A., the High Command of the Army (O.K.H.) and the High Command of the Armed Forces (O.K.W.). These organizations were themselves placed on trial as criminal groups.

The charge of common plan or conspiracy was of a general nature and included breaking treaties, planning and waging wars of aggression, the ill-treatment, murder and use as slave labor of the civilian population of occupied countries, the murder and ill-treatment of prisoners of war, the murder and persecution of people on racial and religious grounds, and the wanton destruction of cities, towns and villages, all on a scale unwarranted by any military necessity. "Of the 9,600,000 Jews who lived in the parts of Europe under Nazi domination," read the indictment, "it is conservatively estimated that 5,700,000 have disappeared, most of them deliberately put to death by the Nazi conspirators." [I, p. 6]

The other three charges detailed certain aspects of this general conspiracy, the evolution of the Nazi aggression as country after country passed into their power, the plunder of every kind of property and its removal to Germany, the appalling statistics of murder and torture in the concentration camps and the prisons, the horror of the *Nacht und Nebel* (Night and Fog) decree under which countless numbers of people disappeared without trace. Then followed the unending record of mass killings and the practice of the newly formulated crime of genocide, or racial extermination. In-numerable cases were cited of the torture and vicious ill-treatment of prisoners of war, more especially those from the eastern territories, who were regarded as subhuman and fit only for starvation, slavery and death.

The whole of the first day of the trial was spent in reading aloud this document, the prosecutors of each nation taking it in turn to recite a section of the charges and the details attached to them. On the second day, the defendants were asked to state whether they were guilty or not guilty. Goering, who was called upon first to put forward his plea, twice attempted with a brusque assertion of authority to make a lengthier statement, and was firmly stopped by the president. He had to be content with a single roundabout sentence: "I declare myself in the sense of the indictment not guilty." Lord Justice Lawrence, with his formidable courtesy, established his control from the start.

The trial was to last from the winter of 1945 to the summer of 1946. The whole of the winter, from November until March, was occupied in presenting the case for the prosecution, the lengthiest and most terrible indictment in the whole history of law. On the defense side the case for Goering, as the principal defendant, was put first, and this itself lasted from March 8 to March 22. The defense of the remainder of the men in the dock took the trial on to the summer, concluding on July 4. The final speeches of the defense and the prosecution lasted till the end of July; between that time and the end of August the secondary trial, that of the indicted organizations, followed. A brief supplementary submission in the defense of Goering was heard on August 30. On August 31 each defendant was permitted to make his final statement before judgment was pronounced after an interval lasting one month. On September 30 Lord Justice Lawrence commenced the reading of the judgment, followed in turn by the other judges, and then each prisoner was summoned individually to the courtroom to hear the pronouncement of sentence. The trial concluded on the afternoon of October 1, 1946.

The specific case against Goering was presented on January 8 by the American attorney Ralph G. Albrecht on behalf of the prosecution. He began by describing the well-known public character of Goering, which had even been seen in the early days of the trial itself—his show of "benevolence, his ever ready smile and ingratiat-

ing manner . . . his ready affirmation, by a pleasant nod for all
to see, of the correctness of statements . . . his chiding shake of
the head when he disagreed."

Counsel was concerned first to implicate Goering under counts
one and two of the indictment, the charges relating to the Nazi
conspiracy and aggression against other countries. He began with
a summary of Goering's career in association with Hitler, his rise
to personal power after 1933, the warlike character of many of his
utterances during the years preceding the war, and his energetic
pursuit of rearmament. "Goering," he said, "was in fact the central
figure in German preparation for military aggression." He showed
how Goering was involved in the *Anschluss*, in "the rape of Czechoslovakia," in the preparation for violence against Poland, in the
"ruthless exploitation" of occupied Soviet territory, and in the slave
labor program, beginning with the arrangement for a million Poles,
primarily agricultural workers, to be forcibly brought to the Reich,
and finally the approval of the deportation of several million men
and women from the occupied territories and some two million
prisoners of war, all to serve in German industry and agriculture.

The American prosecutor referred to document after document
signed by Goering or authorized by his acknowledged agents, ordering the seizure of property in the occupied territories (including
especially works of art), the spoliation of raw materials and machinery that Germany might be said to want, and the theft of
foodstuffs, leaving the local population on a diet that was carefully
calculated to keep it marginally on the right side of actual starvation. Documents were produced to show that Goering had been
entrusted with the economic exploitation of the Soviet territories
almost two months prior to the invasion.

Finally came proof of Goering's crimes against humanity: of his
continued connection with the concentration camps after these
had passed under the control of Himmler, especially in the exploitation of the labor force created from the inmates of the camps; of
his having helped to lead the campaign against the Jews, especially
in the form of economic oppression and the sequestration of property following the pogrom in 1938, and in the later extension to
the conquered territories of decrees originally designed to eliminate
Jews from German economic life. Nor was he free from implication in the final crime against the Jews, that of genocide. Albrecht

ended: "The presentation made to the tribunal on the individual responsibility of the defendant Goering has been intended to be merely illustrative of the mass of documentary evidence which reveals the leading part played by this conspirator in every phase of the Nazi conspiracy." This was said during the afternoon of January 8. Goering had to wait another two months before he could reply.

His long-enforced silence at the trial, in all from November 20 to March 8, told hard on a man of Goering's temperament. But he did everything he could to attract attention to himself both in court and out of it. In court, if he could not speak out loud, he could always make gestures. He knew he was the principal subject of curiosity; he was being filmed and photographed, and his behavior at first led to considerable comment in the press. When, at ten o'clock on the morning of November 20, the judges, robed in black, took their seats, every eye turned to look at the prisoners coming up from the cells. The emotion, half repulsion and half curiosity, which had accumulated over the years against the Nazis was concentrated now on this little gathering of men, shabby in appearance and disconcerted in manner, as they filed into place. But Goering lost little time in showing off his self-confidence. He displayed his contempt for what the advocates or his fellow prisoners were saying; time and again he turned to make gestures or whisper remarks. He shook his head when he disagreed, or squirmed in his seat. He scowled. He grinned. He laughed. Sometimes he swore and muttered to himself, and when Hess, who sat beside him throughout the trial, made a fool of himself, he constantly attempted to silence him. All the while he was alert to score what points he could in his favor. In the film record of the trial he can be seen scribbling notes, fingering his earphones, turning to the other defendants, checking points of fact, advising everyone around him with nods and asides as to what he should think and say. At one point Hess, goaded too far, turned on him and snapped, "Don't interrupt me!" All Goering could do then was to shrug his shoulders at the foolishness of this poor madman beside him.

During these five months of silence in public, Goering could unburden himself freely only to Dr. Gilbert, the prison psychologist, for he refused the services of the chaplain. Here at last he found the chance to talk, though he was, of course, able also to discuss his case with his counsel, Dr. Stahmer, and, once the trial had begun, with the rest of the defendants during the lunch interval, which was initially spent in the courtroom itself.

Goering at first seemed to be in his element and put on his initial act of the jovial realist and amusing cynic. He expressed contempt for the trial. "The victor will always be the judge and the vanquished the accused," he had said on first receiving the indictment. He regarded it as "a cut-and-dried political affair" and said, "I just wish we could all have the courage to confine our defense to three simple words: Lick my arse!" He went round among the defendants repeating this crudity with gusto during one of the lunch intervals, trying to make them all laugh with him. Just before entering upon his own defense he said, "Bringing the heads of a sovereign state before a foreign court is a piece of presumption which is unique in history!" He refused, in fact, to recognize the authority of the court.

As far as Germany was concerned he was completely cynical. When Gilbert pointed out that the German people were disillusioned now about the Nazi leadership, he replied, "Never mind what the people say *now*. That's the one thing that doesn't interest me a damn bit. I know what they said *before*. I know how they cheered and praised us when things were going well. I know too much about people." Later he said, "Democracy just won't work with the German people. . . . I'm glad I don't have to live out there any more—each trying to save his face and his neck by denouncing the party, now that we've lost."

He enjoyed his own particular sense of humor. "Of course we wanted to dissolve the Russian colossus!" he said to Dr. Gilbert and a group of the defendants during one of the lunch breaks. "Now you'll have to do it. . . . It will amuse me to see how you handle it. Of course, it's immaterial to me whether I'm watching from heaven or from the other place—the more interesting place." He enjoyed equally telling Dr. Gilbert how he came to join the Nazis. "I had a date to join the Freemasons in 1919. While waiting for them, I saw a pretty blonde pass by, and I picked her up. Well, I never did join the Freemasons. If I hadn't picked up that blonde that day, it would have been impossible for me to get into the party, and I wouldn't be here today." But he still relished the position he had held in the party: "They don't have to show films and read documents to prove that we rearmed for war. Why, I rearmed

Germany until we bristled! I'm only sorry we didn't rearm still more. Of course, just between us, I considered your treaties so much crap. I joined the party precisely because it was revolutionary, not because of the ideological stuff. Other parties had made revolutions, so I figured I could get in on one too. And the thing that pleased me was that the Nazi Party was the only one that had the guts to say 'To hell with Versailles!' while the others were crawling and appeasing."

He obstinately maintained his belief in Hitler. He was thankful, he said, the Führer was not alive to stand trial at Nuremberg. "It would be intolerable for me to have him standing before a foreign court. You men knew the Führer," he said to the other defendants over the lunch table. "He would be the first to stand up and say, 'I have given the orders, and I take full responsibility.' " Yet he also revealed his resentment at the way Hitler had treated him. "You know," he said to Gilbert, "it is not my purpose to exaggerate my love for the Führer, because you know how he treated me at the end. But I don't know what to say—I think maybe in the last year and a half or so, he just left things to Himmler . . ." His continued support of Hitler seemed due largely to self-interest and his sense of his own position in history. "You do not understand the people as I do. If I were to back down now after the way I supported him, they would only have contempt for me. Who knows how things will develop in fifty to a hundred years? . . . The death sentence? That doesn't mean a thing to me—but my reputation in history means a lot."

On another occasion he said to Gilbert, "If I can have the chance to die as a martyr, why, so much the better. Do you think everybody has that chance? If I can have my bones put in a marble casket, that, after all, is a lot more than most people can achieve."

He attempted throughout the trial to rule the other defendants. Although he rejected the ministrations of the chaplain, he agreed to attend the chapel services "because, as ranking man of the group, if I attend the others will follow suit." At least, that is what he said to the chaplain; to Dr. Gilbert he said, "Prayers, hell! It's just a chance to get out of this damn cell for half an hour." At the lunch intervals he would attempt to dominate the others, telling them what they should say, advice which was rarely taken well. The rest of the group became less and less impressed by Goering's mixture of bravado and cynicism. Speer, the most intelligent and

convinced anti-Nazi among the prisoners, said in January when
Gilbert visited him in his cell, "You know, Goering still thinks he's
the big shot and is running the show even as a war criminal." Later
he said again, "Goering knows his goose is cooked, and needs a retinue of at least twenty lesser heroes for his grand entrance into
Valhalla. . . . It's amazing what a tyranny he exercises over the
rest."

Because of this, solitary confinement was re-established by Colonel Andrus during the hours in prison. This angered all the defendants, but the effect on Goering was remarkable. He is described
by Gilbert as "dejected and tremulous like a rejected child." He
guessed that it was his aggressive and cynical influence that was
the cause of the punishment. He burst out, "Don't you see that all
this joking and horseplay is only comic relief? Do you think I enjoy
sitting there and hearing accusations heaped on our heads from all
sides? We've got to let off steam somehow. If I didn't pep them
up, a couple of them would simply collapse. . . . Don't you think
I reproach myself enough in the loneliness of this cell, wishing that
I had taken a different road and lived my life differently, instead of
ending up like this?" He was, for once, quite subdued, even
apologetic.

At the request of Colonel Andrus, on February 17 Gilbert drew
up lists dividing the prisoners into special small groups for lunch,
in which those who were convinced of Nazi wrongdoing could
neutralize those less inclined to accept the justice of the charges
against them. Goering was forced to eat alone, and he bitterly
resented the fact. Speer admitted afterward that Goering had been
exercising a kind of moral terror over the weaker defendants and
had actually been bargaining in terms of the testimony they should
give: he would say this if they would say that. Goering's own reaction was typical: "Just because I'm the Number One Nazi in this
group, it doesn't mean I'm the most dangerous. Anyway, the colonel ought to bear in mind that he's dealing with historical figures
here. Right or wrong, we are historical personalities here, and he's
nobody." He then compared himself, not for the first time, to
Napoleon in captivity.

On several occasions the prosecution darkened the courtroom for
the projection of films offered in evidence. These included the
scenes of atrocity recorded by service cameramen in the concentration camps and other places of suffering. The effect of these films

on the defendants was carefully noted by Gilbert. Some, like Funk and Frank, wept; some, like Speer and Hans Fritzsche of the Propaganda Ministry, were near to tears; Ribbentrop, Neurath, Schacht and Papen refused to look; others, such as Seyss-Inquart and Streicher, watched stolidly. Goering began by leaning forward, not watching; he looked dejected and he coughed. After the film, when Hess muttered, "I don't believe it," he told him to be quiet. The whole court was overcome by the sight of the film, and the prisoners filed out in complete silence. Afterward, in their cells, they were mainly incredulous; several, however, were still in tears of shame or completely unnerved by what they had seen. Goering's reaction was an odd one: "It was such a good afternoon, too, until they showed that film. They were reading my telephone conversations on the Austrian affair, and everyone was laughing with me. And then they showed that awful film, and it just spoiled everything."

Goering was well aware that the atrocity films represented crimes which were the single most serious charge he was likely to face as the senior defendant. Round much of the rest he could argue, using his authority and strength of personality to work his way through the cross-examination. But this exhibition in the darkened courtroom, with the unbearable images thrust upon the screen without compromise until neither the court nor the defendants themselves could stomach more, made it impossible for him, the man second to Hitler in the State, to maintain his offhand bravado. "That awful film" had indeed spoiled everything, as he had said. Soon, however, he discovered what seemed some sort of way out of this dilemma. "I still can't grasp all those things," he said to Gilbert. "Do you suppose I'd have believed it if somebody came to me and said they were making freezing experiments on human guinea pigs, or that people were being forced to dig their own graves and be mowed down by the thousands? I would just have said, 'Get the hell out of here with that fantastic nonsense. . . .' I just shrugged it off as enemy propaganda." When the Russians showed their atrocity films in mid-February he adopted precisely this attitude. "Anybody can make an atrocity film," he said to the others, "if they take corpses out of their graves and then show a tractor shoving them back in again." But it was evident that he was unable to convince even himself, let alone the others. When the Russians continued with their films, he laughed when the first shot appeared upside down (the film had not been rewound), and he refused to look at the scenes that were eventually shown. Afterward he said they were mainly the Russians' own atrocities on the Germans. In any case, he was a soldier and used to the sight of death. "I don't have to see a film to be horrified," he said. Later, during the testimony of a woman who had been a prisoner in Auschwitz, he took off his earphones and refused to listen. In the end he claimed he had no knowledge of such things. "You know how it is even in a battalion," he said to one of the defense attorneys, who had asked if anyone in authority knew anything of what was happening. "A battalion commander doesn't know anything that goes on in the line. The higher you stand, the less you see of what is going on below."

The thirteen-day hearing of Goering's defense opened on the morning of March 8 with the summoning of the first witness to appear on his behalf. This was Bodenschatz, testifying as the principal liaison officer between Goering's and Hitler's headquarters. What was soon to become a familiar round of questioning began when Stahmer tried to show how uninvolved Goering was in the more cruel or sordid of the Nazis' activities. When did Goering become out of favor with Hitler? Goering's constant work for peace and his endeavors with Dahlerus were described. What did he do to try to prevent war? Did he have any foreknowledge of the 1938 pogrom? None at all, said Bodenschatz. What did he do to try to extricate people from the concentration camps? He was constantly helping individual cases. What did the witness or Goering know about conditions in these camps? Nothing at all.

When Stahmer had finished, Jackson took over and cross-examined Bodenschatz with a view to making him implicate himself and Goering in the very matters which Stahmer had introduced in order to allow Bodenschatz to display their lack of implication. This narrowed down to the case of the concentration camps. Bodenschatz was careful to side-step, and this became the general technique of the trial. No, I was quite unaware of these matters. No, it never did to ask questions. No, I was on leave at the time. No, I cannot make any definite statement on this matter. The question of the efficiency of the Air Force and of the increasingly bad relations between Hitler and Goering after 1943 were continually revived.

Bodenschatz was succeeded on the stand by Milch, and Stahmer led him to testify to the effect that the German Air Force was built up for defensive reasons only, that Goering was always on the side of peace through strength. Milch also testified that Goering agreed with him that they should avoid having anything to do with Himmler's use of criminals for air-pressure and temperature tests. Neither he nor Goering had any knowledge of the nature of these experiments. In the matter of the treatment of prisoners of war, what Goering had said was, "Once they have been shot down, they are our comrades." As far as the corpses were concerned, Milch took the same line as Bodenschatz: "The people who knew about these conditions did not talk about them, and presumably were not allowed to talk about them." No one could know that there were over two hundred concentration camps, though everyone knew there were some; and no one knew what went on inside. Nor did anyone know about the extermination camps for the Jews. To have tried to interfere would have meant certain death for oneself and one's family; Milch said this in one of the most revealing moments during the trial.

Jackson had no difficulty in eliciting from Milch that it had been impossible for Goering or anyone else actively to oppose Hitler. "The Reich Marshal never strongly opposed the Führer in public, nor before any large group of his officers, because Hitler would not have tolerated such opposition." In the matter of trying to prevent Hitler's going to war with Russia, Milch said he had the impression that Goering "had previously discussed the subject with Hitler, but without any degree of success, because with Hitler that was impossible." This too became a recurrent theme at the trial. Every act, good or bad, stemmed from Hitler and could not be opposed, even by the most senior member of the leadership. With some irony, Jackson made Milch reveal point by point the weaknesses of an authoritarian state where no one could put forward proposals that he believed to be right or justifiable if they were critical even of the most ill-considered views of the Führer. Over all hung the fear of the Gestapo.

MILCH: It was not easy for any of us. We were all convinced that we were being constantly watched, no matter how high our rank. There was probably not a single person concerning whom a dossier was not kept, and many people were subsequently brought to trial as a result of these records. The ensuing difficulties did not affect only these people . . . or me personally; they included everybody right up to the Reich Marshal, who also was affected by them.

JACKSON: So you mean that from the Reich Marshal right down to the humblest citizen, there was fear of Heinrich Himmler and his organization?

MILCH: Well, the degree of fear may have varied. It was perhaps not so great in the highest and in the lowest ranks. [VIII, p. 280]

Jackson also tried to make Milch comment further on a statement he had made under interrogation that Hitler after March 1943 was no longer normal. How, Jackson asked, could Goering consent to serve under an abnormal man? Again Milch sidestepped.

MILCH: The abnormality was not such that one could say, "This man is out of his senses." . . . I believe that a doctor would be better able to give information on that subject. I talked to medical men about it at the time.

JACKSON: And it was their opinion that he was abnormal?

MILCH: That there was a possibility of abnormality was admitted by a doctor whom I knew well personally. [VIII, p. 281]

Further questions were put to the witness to try to implicate Goering and Milch directly in the use of forced labor recruited from prisoners of war and from the populations that either were developing a partisan movement or were likely to do so once the Allies had landed in France.

The British prosecutor G. D. Roberts brought up the recurrent question of the R.A.F. officers who had escaped from Stalag Luft III at Sagan in March 1944 and had subsequently been shot and their bodies cremated. Milch claimed to have had no knowledge of this matter at the time it happened. So did the next witness, Bernd von Brauchitsch, testifying as Goering's military adjutant.

The next principal witness for Goering's defense was Paul Koerner. Stahmer used his testimony to show that Goering in 1933 dissolved any unauthorized concentration camps that came to his notice, that he stopped the ill-treatment of the Communist leader Thaelmann and that in any case he ceased to control the Gestapo and the camps when Himmler took over in the spring of 1934. Koerner was further questioned on the Roehm purge, the 1938 pogrom and the Four-Year Plan. As before, all this was designed to show Goering's essentially moderate and pacific attitude. Jackson then returned to the attack, but Koerner stuck to his defense of Goering until Jackson suddenly interposed.

JACKSON: You were interrogated at Obersalzberg, the interrogation center, on October 4 of last year by Dr. Kempner of our staff, were you not?

KOERNER: Yes.

JACKSON: You stated, in the beginning of your interrogation, that you would not give any testimony against your former superior, Reich Marshal Goering, and that you regarded Goering as the last big man of the Renaissance, the last great example of a man from the Renaissance period; that he had given you the biggest job of your life and it would be unfaithful and disloyal to give any testimony against him. Is that what you said?

KOERNER: Yes, that is more or less what I said.

JACKSON: And that is still your answer?

KOERNER: Yes.

JACKSON: No further questions. [IX, pp. 19–20]

General Rudenko, who followed Jackson, was scathing about Koerner's negative replies to his questions on the plundering of the occupied territories. Koerner too claimed to know nothing about the concentration camps, as did Kesselring, who followed him into the box. Kesselring was called on to testify to the correctness of the raids on Warsaw, Rotterdam and Coventry as military targets and to the pattern of responsibility within the Luftwaffe, and to give his views about the conduct of the war. Kesselring was of the opinion that Hitler was ready to consider the advice of his generals. Maxwell-Fyfe's cross-examination was in the highest degree damaging to Kesselring, who had been commanding in Italy when the German forces committed atrocities against the Italians.

Goering took his stand in the witness box on the afternoon of March 13. In his cell he had been nervous with anticipation, his hands trembling and the expression on his face strained. He had told Gilbert again that he felt it wrong for him, as one of the heads of a sovereign state, to be brought before a foreign court. However, making careful use of Stahmer's prepared questions, he gave a detailed account of his association with Hitler and the party and of his own contribution, as he saw it, to the seizure of power and the subsequent moves in its consolidation. He made everything sound as plausible and as reasonable as he could, and he spoke ably and with great consciousness of his past authority. He was frank about his belief in the party and showed the pride he felt in the success of his personal efforts to bring it to power.

I wish to say it is correct that I—and I can speak only for myself—did everything which was at all within my personal power to strengthen the National Socialist movement, and to increase it, and have worked unceasingly to bring it to power in all circumstances as the one and only power. I did everything in order to secure the Führer the place as Reich Chancellor which rightfully belonged to him. [IX, p. 75]

He spoke at great length about the need to eliminate the hostile political parties, to establish a state secret police, and to found detention camps for those who were planning to overthrow the regime in its earliest days. He admitted that there were acts of brutality in these camps, and that unauthorized camps were set up by Karpfenstein, Gauleiter of Pomerania, and by Heines and Ernst, both of whom were associates of Roehm. He dissolved these camps, he claimed, and investigated any acts of brutality which came to his notice in the camps under his direct control.

That evening when he was back in his cell, Goering, like an overwrought actor, was unable to eat; he sat smoking his Bavarian pipe. He was very excited, and worried that he could not keep his hand from shaking. He refused to have the light on, and his mood turned somber as he talked to Gilbert of man as the worst of the beasts of prey, and how war would in future become more and more destructive. The following morning he heard of the death of Blomberg. "A man of honor," said Goering, turning aside for a moment from a discussion with Stahmer.

When the next session opened, in response to a further question from Stahmer he explained what he meant by the "leadership principle" and the particular need for it in Germany.

I upheld this principle and I still uphold it positively and consciously. One must not make the mistake of forgetting that the political structure in different countries has different origins, dif-

ferent developments. Something which suits one country extremely
well would, perhaps, fail completely in another. Germany, through
the long centuries of the monarchy, has always had a leadership
principle. . . . I am of the opinion that for Germany, particularly
at that moment of its lowest existence when it was necessary that
all forces be welded together in a positive fashion, the leadership
principle, that is, authority from above and responsibility from below, was the only possibility. [*IX, p. 82*]

The leadership principle, he added, is the basis of both the
Catholic Church and the government of the U.S.S.R.

He then went on to explain why the trade-unions had been dissolved as centers of political disaffection, and that the Roehm faction had been destroyed because it had wanted to use illegal methods of gaining power, whereas Hitler had been determined to use
methods that were legal. Men such as Roehm, Heines and Ernst,
he said, were plotting to overthrow the Führer.

I knew Roehm very well. I had him brought to me. I put to him
openly the things which I had heard. I reminded him of our mutual
fight and I asked him unconditionally to keep faith with the
Führer. He raised the same arguments as I have just mentioned,
but he assured me that of course he was not thinking of undertaking anything against the Führer. Shortly afterward I received
further news to the effect that he had close connections with those
circles that were strongly opposed to us. [*IX, p. 84*]

When the purge that followed led to more deaths than seemed
proper, Goering claimed, he interceded with Hitler and urged that
the killings be stopped immediately.

In the course of that evening I heard that other people had been
shot as well, even some people who had nothing at all to do with
this Roehm revolt. The Führer came to Berlin that same evening.
I learned this later that evening or night, and went to him at noon
the next day and asked him to issue an order immediately that any
further execution was, under any circumstances, forbidden by him,
although two other people who were very much involved and who
had been ordered to be executed were still alive. These people were,
in fact, left alive. I asked him to do that because I was worried that

the matter would get out of hand, as, in fact, it had already done to some extent, and I told the Führer that under no circumstances should there be any further bloodshed. [IX, p. 85]

However, he added,

. . . as my final remark on the Roehm putsch I should like to emphasize that I assume full responsibility for the actions taken against those people—Ernst, Heidebrecht and several others—by the order of the Führer, which I executed or passed on, and that, even today, I am of the opinion that I acted absolutely correctly and from a sense of duty. That was confirmed by the Reich President, but no such confirmation was necessary to convince me that here I had averted what was a great danger for the State. [IX, p. 85]

The examination then turned to his attitude toward the church, where Goering's extraordinary views showed his uncontrolled vanity.

Constitutionally, as Prussian Premier, I was, to be sure, in a certain sense the highest dignitary of the Prussian Church, but I did not concern myself with these matters very much. . . . I am not what you might call a churchgoer, but I have . . . always consciously belonged to the church and have always had these functions over which the church presides—marriage, christening, burial—carried out in my house by the church. My intention thereby was to show those weak-willed persons who, in the midst of this fight of opinions, did not know what they should do that if the second man in the State goes to church . . . then they can do the same. . . . On the whole I should like to say that the Führer himself was not opposed to the church. . . . He said that he did not consider himself to be a church reformer and that he did not wish that any of his political leaders should win laurels in this field. [IX, pp. 25–27]

What Hitler and he were concerned with was to keep church and politics separate, and he opposed in principle the arrest of clergy unless they were violently critical of the regime and took part in political affairs outside the church.

He then turned to the question of the Jews. He made a specious plea that Jewish influence was altogether out of proportion in German cultural and economic life, that the situation was unhealthy and could not be tolerated by patriots. However, he was violently opposed to the pogrom in 1938 and did his best to have this wasteful persecution stopped. He agreed, however, with the fine of one billion marks settled on the Jewish community and accepted full responsibility for promulgating the Nuremberg Laws.

I should like to emphasize that although I received oral and written orders and commands from the Führer to issue and carry out these laws, I assume full responsibility for them. They bear my signature, I issued them, and consequently I am responsible and do not propose to hide in any way behind the Führer's order. [IX, p. 92]

In the same way, he proudly accepted full responsibility for rebuilding the German Air Force and, although he was not an economic expert, for rebuilding the German economy. Of the Air Force he said, "I alone was responsible and am responsible, for I was Commander in Chief of the Air Force and Air Minister. I was responsible for the rearmament and building up of the Air Force and its spirit." [IX, p. 94] Of his work initially as Commissioner of Raw Materials and Foreign Exchange, he added, "It was decided that in this sphere I, though not an expert, should be the driving power and use my energy. . . . Thus I entered the field of economic leadership." [IX, p. 95]

At lunch during the recess, Goering said to Gilbert, "Well, how was it? You cannot say I was cowardly." He was aware that he had created a good impression among his fellow prisoners. Later that evening in his cell he was relaxed and self-satisfied. "Yes, it is quite a strain," he said. "And it's all out of memory. You would be surprised how few cue words I have jotted down to guide me." Once more the cell became the actor's dressing room.

During the afternoon session, Stahmer took him phase by phase through the history and development of his panoramic responsibilities, all of which he naturally presented in a positive light, as part of his unique service to his country. The examination, in spite of Lord Justice Lawrence's pleas for brevity, lasted some four days, including questions put by other defense counsel; the record of it amounts in the transcript of the trial to some 80,000 words, the length of a substantial book. The topics seemed to be presented in no particular order, questions concerning the occupation of the

Rhineland being followed by others about the Reich Defense Council and the Research Bureau (which was later to cause Goering difficulties because as a body it was directly associated with grossly inhuman experiments on living people). The cavalier way in which an authoritarian state can be run was revealed in statement after statement in which Goering enjoyed the recollection of his power. Typical of these statements was one in which he described how he and Hitler attempted to save Neurath's face (or, in effect, their own faces) after he had been retired from the Foreign Ministry.

In order to avoid lowering Herr von Neurath's prestige I myself was the one to make a proposal to the Führer. I told him that in order to make it appear abroad as if Neurath had not been entirely removed from foreign policy, I would propose to appoint him chairman of the Secret Cabinet Council. There was, to be sure, no such Cabinet in existence, but the expression would sound quite nice, and everyone would imagine that it meant something. The Führer said we could not make him chairman if we did not have a council. Thereupon I said, "Then we will make one," and offhand I marked down the names of several persons. How little importance I attached to this council can be seen in the fact that I myself was, I think, one of the last on that list. [IX, p. 99]

He was ironic about suggestions that Hitler should have taken more notice of the opinions of his generals on matters of policy as distinct from strategy. It was not Hitler's way to ask for such opinions, said Goering.

How does one imagine that a State can be led if, during a war or before a war which the political leaders have decided upon, whether wrongly or rightly, the individual general could vote whether he was going to fight or not, whether his army corps was going to stay at home or not, or could say, "I must first ask my division"; perhaps one of them would go along and the other stay at home. That privilege in this case would have to be afforded the ordinary soldier too. Perhaps this would be the way to avoid wars in future, if one asks every soldier whether he wants to go home or not. Possibly, but not in a "Führer" State. [IX, pp. 113–14]

Much time was spent going over the details of the *Anschluss*, the Munich Pact, the events leading up to the occupation of Czechoslovakia and the invasion of Poland, and Goering's appointment as Hitler's successor, which, according to him, the Führer had had in mind as early as 1934. Even when Hitler had acknowledged him to be the second man of the State, Goering said, the Führer did not at all times keep him informed as to what he was going to do, as in the case of the occupation of Czechoslovakia. Later he said of his prewar relations with Hitler:

Of course he informed me of all important political and military problems. He acquainted me with these problems for the most part in very many long discussions, which would take place for many hours, day after day. Many times, to be sure, I was surprised in regard to foreign political questions, but whenever possible I would include myself, and on one occasion he said, in fact, that I had a decided opinion of my own in foreign political matters and that he did not always find it easy to agree with me. But I want to emphasize that in all important political questions I was, of course, included. [IX, *p.* 111]

Goering's answers seemed to grow longer and longer. His extraordinary memory came into full play as each phase of the questioning gave him a fresh chance to deliver the burden of his case. There could be no doubt that here was the real Nazi authority as he poured out his version of the German penetration into the surrounding countries, his version of the bartering and pillaging of foreign art treasures, his version of the behavior of the German soldiers against the resistance movement in France—until in the end Jackson could stand it no longer and demanded of the president how far all this wordy commentary was relevant to the issues of the trial. Afterward, Goering adopted a man-of-the-world air of candor: "I do not in any way deny that things happened which may be hotly debatable as far as international law is concerned. Also, other things occurred which under any circumstances must be considered as excesses." What could you expect, he implied, when the German soldiers were threatened on every side by a nation supposed to be conquered? With the same air of authoritative reasonableness he defended the bombing of Rotterdam and

Coventry and stated his regret that Hitler turned down his advice against launching any attack on Russia while Germany was still in conflict with Britain.

As far as the acquisition of works of art from abroad was concerned, he explained the extraordinary competition that existed between himself and Hitler, both of whom wanted to establish their personal collections, which were, he said, destined for the nation. He claimed that he was willing to pay for the works of art he wanted from the collection at the Salle du Jeu de Paume, representing confiscated Jewish property.

From the beginning, however, I wanted to have a clear distinction made, inasmuch as I meant to pay for these objects which I wanted to have for the gallery I was going to build. Therefore, I ordered that an art expert, and, indeed, not a German but a Frenchman— it was some professor, whose name I do not recall and to whom I never have talked—appraise those things. I would then determine whether the price was too high for me, whether I was no longer interested or whether I was willing to pay the price. One part, the first part, was settled that way, but then the whole thing stopped because some of these objects were sent back and forth—that is, they went back to the Führer and they did not remain with me— and not until the matter was clarified could the payment be made. [*IX, p. 125*]

He answered the attacks made on him for taking food from the occupied countries ("We did not dismantle and transport the entire Russian economy down to the last bolt and screw, as is being done here. These are measures that result from the conduct of war. I naturally take complete responsibility for this.") and using forced labor from the prisoner-of-war and concentration camps ("At that time everyone had to work in Germany."). As for the charge that he had connived at the shooting of the R.A.F. prisoners in Stalag Luft III, this he resented most keenly, for, at the height of his unpopularity with the Führer, he had risked further displeasure by opposing in his presence any form of reprisals against flyers who were prisoners of war.

The examination by Stahmer turned next to Nazi administration and the responsibilities of the high command and of the various ministries with which Goering was connected. Then the story of the *Anschluss* was reviewed. In the course of this long series of statements on the morning of Saturday, March 16, Goering made a revealing aside about Hitler's conservatism, in a remark which has a curious relevance to himself in his later relations with the Führer:

I assume that . . . despite all tension, the decisive factor for the Führer was that it was extremely hard for him to get used to new faces, and that he did not like to make any changes in his entourage. He preferred to continue working with men . . . whom he did not like, rather than change them. [*IX, p. 166*]

Later he said of Hitler and himself during the period immediately before and after the start of the war, "There was no one who could even approach working as closely with the Führer and who was as essentially familiar with his thoughts and who had the same influence as I." [*IX, p. 175*]

During the weekend recess that followed, Goering rested. Gilbert records that he grumbled at the arguments for humanitarianism to which he was being subjected. The British Empire, he said, had not been acquired through humanitarianism, and America had "hacked its way to a rich *Lebensraum* by revolution, massacre and war." He felt it unjust that he should be chosen as history's scapegoat among the masters of conquest.

During the morning of Monday, March 18, the question turned on Goering's relations with the S.A. and the Gestapo; his reply to the question whether ill-treatment of prisoners took place during the period he was in control of the Gestapo is characteristic of his attitude to one of the most damaging of the charges he had to face. He said:

At the time when I was still directly connected with the Gestapo such excesses did, as I have openly stated, take place. In order to punish them, one naturally had to find out about them. Punishments were administered. The officials knew that if they did such things they ran the risk of being punished. A large number of them were punished. I cannot say what the practice was later. [*IX, p. 184*]

When the time came for Jackson to begin the cross-examination, there was an atmosphere of curiosity and expectation in the court. He began with a curious question: "You are perhaps aware that you are the only living man who can expound to us the true purposes of the Nazi Party and the inner workings of the leadership." This only served to please Goering, who replied, "I am perfectly aware of that." Both question and answer seemed to establish the relationship between these two men who were to argue and counter-argue for the best part of two days. The cross-examination had to be interrupted, however, while Dahlerus' evidence was taken, since he wanted to return to Stockholm and could not wait on indefinitely until Goering's long harangues were over.

Jackson's questions were too frequently of a kind that encouraged Goering to generalize about his actions and the patriotic emotion that inspired them. Compared with Goering's vast knowledge and experience in German politics and administration, Jackson's grasp of Nazi history was too scanty and ill-prepared to enable him to counter with facts Goering's skillful evasions and carefully calculated affronts. There were even occasions when Goering had to put him right on matters of fact. Goering's self-confidence rose as the sense of his growing success gradually spread through the courtroom. Everyone had expected to see his pride and effrontery laid low as question followed question in damaging sequence. It was known there was a wealth of documentary evidence against the Nazi leadership among the archives captured by the Americans. But evidently Jackson had not prepared himself sufficiently to break through Goering's guard and press his attack home to the point of drawing blood.

JACKSON: You established the leadership principle, which you have described as a system under which authority exists only at the top and is passed downward and is imposed on the people below, is that correct?

GOERING: In order to avoid any misunderstanding, I should like once more to explain the idea briefly, as I understand it. In German parliamentary procedure in the past the responsibility rested with the highest officials, who were responsible for carrying out the anonymous wishes of the majorities, and it was they who exercised the authority. In the leadership principle we sought to reverse the direction; that is, the authority existed at the top and passed downward, while the responsibility began at the bottom and passed upward.

JACKSON: In other words, you did not believe in and did not permit government, as we call it, by consent of the governed, in which the people, through their representatives, were the source of power and authority?

GOERING: That is not entirely correct. We repeatedly called on the people to express unequivocally and clearly what they thought of our system, only it was in a different way from that previously adopted and from the system in practice in other countries. We chose the way of a so-called plebiscite. We also took the point of view that, of course, even a government founded on the leadership principle could maintain itself only if it was based in some way on the confidence of the people. If it no longer had such confidence, then it would have to rule with bayonets, and the Führer was always of the opinion that that was impossible in the long run—to rule against the will of the people. . . . I consider the leadership principle necessary because the system which previously existed, and which we called parliamentary or democratic, had brought Germany to the verge of ruin. I might perhaps in this connection remind you that your own President Roosevelt, as far as I can recall—I do not want to quote it word for word—declared, "Certain people in Europe have forsaken democracy not because they did not wish for democracy, but because democracy had brought forth men who were too weak to give their people work and bread and to satisfy them. For this reason the peoples have abandoned this system and the men belonging to it." There is much truth in that statement. This system had brought ruin by mismanagement, and according to my opinion only an organization made up of a strong, clearly defined leadership hierarchy could restore order again. But, let it be understood, not against the will of the people, but only when the people, having in the course of time and by means of a series of elections grown stronger and stronger, had expressed their wish to entrust their destiny to the National Socialist leadership.

JACKSON: The principles of the authoritarian government which you set up required, as I understand you, that there be tolerated no opposition by political parties which might defeat the policy of the Nazi Party?

GOERING: You have understood this quite correctly. By that time we had lived long enough with opposition and we had had enough of it. Through opposition we had been completely ruined. It was now time to have done with it and to start building up. [IX, pp. 185–86]

Time and again, Goering used the questions as cues for lecturing the court on Nazi principles in such a way as to put them in what appeared to be a reasonable light. He admitted establishing the concentration camps to eliminate opposition.

JACKSON: Was it also necessary, in operating this system, to deprive persons of the right to public trials in independent courts? And you immediately issued an order that your political police would not be subject to court review or to court orders, did you not?

GOERING: You must differentiate between the two categories. Those who had committed some act of treason against the new State were naturally turned over to the courts. The others, however, of whom one might expect such acts, but who had not yet committed them, were taken into protective custody, and these were the people who were taken to concentration camps. I am now speaking of what happened at the beginning. Later, things changed a great deal. . . . [IX, p. 187]

JACKSON: But when it was State necessity to kill somebody, you had to have somebody to do it, did you not?

GOERING: Yes, just as in other states; whether it is called Secret Service or something else, I do not know. . . .

JACKSON: And there was nothing secret about the establishment of a Gestapo as a political police, about the fact that people were taken into protective custody, about the fact that there were concentration camps? Nothing secret about those things, was there?

GOERING: There was at first nothing secret about it at all. [IX, p. 189]

Irritation began to show itself in both men; Jackson felt that Goering was purposely avoiding the direct answer he was supposed to give, Goering that he was not being given the trial of strength he deserved.

JACKSON: I can only repeat my question, which I submit you have not answered: Did you at that time see any military necessity for an attack by Germany on Soviet Russia?

GOERING: I personally believed that at that time this danger had not yet reached its climax, and therefore the attack might not yet be necessary. But that was my personal view.

JACKSON: And you were the Number Two man at that time in all Germany?

GOERING: It has nothing to do with my being second in importance. There were two conflicting points of view as regards strategy. The Führer, the Number One man, saw one danger, and I, as the Number Two man, if you wish to express it so, wanted to put through another strategic measure. If I had imposed my will every time, then I would have probably become the Number One man. But since the Number One man was of a different opinion, and I was only the Number Two man, his opinion naturally prevailed. [*IX, p. 191*]

Goering's main line of defense was to broaden his shoulders and take full responsibility for his loyalty to the Führer, to whom he had taken his oath of allegiance, and for his part in establishing a system of authoritarian government in which he believed wholeheartedly and which he knew was necessary in order to restore Germany to health and strength as Europe's first nation. What angered him was any attempt to implicate him personally in acts of inhumanity. The concentration camps were Himmler's affair, and he knew nothing of the atrocities conducted there in secret; he was on leave during the period when the R.A.F. prisoners were shot for escaping from Stalag Luft III; he was concerned with breaking the stranglehold of the Jews on the German economy and not with breaking their bodies. When regrettable things happened, as of course they must in times of violent change or of war, he always punished the wrongdoers—provided the matter was within his jurisdiction and was brought to his notice. So the arguments went on, interminably, hour after hour, in the fifth month of the court's session. Jackson labored on, often, it seemed, following Goering with his questions rather than leading him. For instance, the question of why Goering had not sought to warn the German people of the dangers involved in going to war with the Soviet Union:

JACKSON: And yet, because of the Führer system, as I understand you, you could give no warning to the German people; you could bring no pressure of any kind to bear to prevent that step, and you could not even resign to protect your own place in history.

GOERING: There are quite a few questions here. I should like to answer the first one.

JACKSON: Separate them if you wish.

GOERING: The first question was, I believe, whether I took the opportunity to tell the German people about this danger. I had no occasion to do this. We were at war, and such differences of opinion, as far as strategy was concerned, could not be brought into the public forum during the war. I believe that has never happened in world history. Secondly, as far as my resignation is concerned, I do not wish even to discuss that, for during the war I was an officer, a soldier, and I was not concerned with whether I shared an opinion or not. I had merely to serve my country as a soldier. Thirdly, I was not the man to forsake a man to whom I had given my oath of loyalty, every time he was not of my way of thinking. If that had been the case there was no need to bind myself to him from the beginning. It never occurred to me to leave the Führer.

JACKSON: Insofar as you know, the German people were led into the war, attacking Soviet Russia, under the belief that you favored it?

GOERING: The German people did not know about the declaration of war against Russia until after the war with Russia had started. The German people, therefore, had nothing to do with this. The German people were not asked; they were told of the fact and of the necessity for it. [IX, p. 192]

Goering sometimes talked as if he were a teacher explaining obvious points of principle to students whom he considered dull and unperceptive:

Of course, a successful termination of a war can be considered successful only if I either conquer the enemy or, through negotiations with the enemy, come to a conclusion which guarantees success. That is what I call a successful termination. I call it a draw when I come to terms with the enemy. This does not bring me the success which victory would have brought, but, on the other hand, it precludes defeat. This is a conclusion without victors or vanquished. [IX, p. 193]

Jackson, and occasionally the president himself, tried to force Goering to answer just yes or no, not adding his points of explanation until afterward. This went entirely against Goering's nature and led to frequent abortive interchanges:

JACKSON: By the time of January 1945, you also knew that you were unable to defend the German cities against the air attacks of the Allies, did you not?

GOERING: Concerning the defense of German cities against Allied air attacks, I should like to describe the possibility of doing this as follows: Of itself—

JACKSON: Can you answer my question? Time may not mean quite so much to you as it does to the rest of us. Can you not answer yes or no? Did you then know, at the same time that you knew the war was lost, that the German cities could not successfully be defended against air attack by the enemy? Can you not tell us yes or no?

GOERING: I can say that I knew that, at that time, it was not possible. [IX, p. 193] . . .

JACKSON: I ask you just a few questions about Austria. You said that you and Hitler had felt deep regret about the death of Dollfuss, and I ask you if it is not a fact that Hitler put up a plaque in Vienna in honor of the men who murdered Dollfuss, and went and put a wreath on their graves when he was there. Is that a fact? Can you not answer that with "yes" or "no"?

GOERING: No, I cannot answer it with either "yes" or "no" if I am to speak the truth according to my oath. I cannot say, "Yes, he did it," because I do not know; I cannot say, "No, he did not do it," because I do not know that either. I want to say that I heard about this event here for the first time. [IX, p. 208]

On the question of his loyalty to Hitler he remained adamant.

JACKSON: And there was no way to prevent the war from going on as long as Hitler was the head of the German government, was there?

GOERING: As long as Hitler was the Führer of the German people, he alone decided whether the war was to go on. As long as my enemy threatens me and demands absolutely unconditional surrender, I fight to my last breath, because there is nothing left for me except perhaps a chance that in some way fate may change, even though it seems hopeless.

JACKSON: Well, the people of Germany who thought it was time that the slaughter stopped had no means to stop it except revolution or assassination of Hitler, had they?

GOERING: A revolution always changes a situation if it succeeds. That is a foregone conclusion. The murder of Hitler at this time, say January 1945, would have brought about my succession. If the enemy had given me the same answer, that is, unconditional surrender, and had held out those terrible conditions which had been intimated, I would have continued fighting whatever the circumstances. [IX, p. 194]

He denied that he had made any attempt to oust Hitler during the last days of the war.

GOERING: I can answer only for myself; what Himmler did I do not know. I neither betrayed the Führer nor at that time negotiated with a single foreign soldier. This will, or this final act, of the Führer is based on an extremely regrettable mistake, and one which grieves me deeply—that the Führer could believe in his last hours that I could ever be disloyal to him. It was all due to an error in the transmission of a radio report and perhaps to a misrepresentation which Bormann gave the Führer. I myself never thought for a minute of taking over power illegally, or of acting against the Führer in any way. [IX, p. 194]

Goering's spirits soon rose to the point where he felt he could afford to joke with the court. The opportunity came when he was asked whether he was responsible or not for the Reichstag fire.

GOERING: That accusation that I had set fire to the Reichstag came from a certain foreign press. That could not bother me, because it was not consistent with the facts. I had no reason or motive for setting fire to the Reichstag. From the artistic point of view, I did not at all regret that the assembly chamber was burned; I hoped to build a better one. But I did regret very much that I was forced to find a new meeting place for the Reichstag, and, not being able to find one, I had to give up my Kroll Opera House, that is, the second State opera house, for that purpose. The opera seemed to me much more important than the Reichstag.

JACKSON: Have you ever boasted of burning the Reichstag building, even by way of joking?

GOERING: No. I made a joke, if that is the one you are referring to, when I said that after this I would be competing with Nero and that probably people would soon be saying that, dressed in a red toga and holding a lyre in my hand, I looked on at the fire and played while the Reichstag was burning. That was the joke. But the fact was that I almost perished in the flames, which would have been very unfortunate for the German people, but very fortunate for their enemies. [IX, p. 196]

At other times he answered with asperity, for example when he was pressed on the question of German acquisition of Austria and the Sudetenland.

JACKSON: You still have not answered my question although you answered everything else. They were not taken from you by the Treaty of Versailles, were they?

GOERING: Of course Austria was taken away by the Versailles Treaty and likewise the Sudetenland, for both territories, had it not been for the Treaty of Versailles and the Treaty of St. Germain, would have become German territories through the right of the people to self-determination. To this extent they have to do with it. [IX, p. 202]

In the private notes he kept during the trial, Sir Norman Birkett (later Lord Birkett), Lawrence's alternate as president of the tribunal, made this most significant comment on Goering on March 18:

Goering reveals himself as a very able man who perceives the intention of every question almost as soon as it is framed and uttered. He has considerable knowledge, too, and has an advantage over the Prosecution in this respect, for he is always on familiar ground. He has knowledge which many others belonging to the Prosecution and the Tribunal have not. He has therefore quite maintained his ground and the Prosecution has not really advanced its case at all. Certainly there has been no dramatic destruction of Goering as had been anticipated or prophesied.

The following day he added, "Goering has now taken complete control and dominates the whole proceedings . . . and unless he is controlled the Trial will get more and more out of hand." Goering, he thought, had in fact made the occasion a "free platform . . . to explain and expand his ideas and beliefs for future generations of Germans," and "he was able to present at least a plausible case on about every aspect of the matter."

As Birkett considered it from the judges' bench, the cross-examination of Goering was a very critical moment, and, if unsuccessful, could only too easily threaten the fundamental value of the whole trial. The prestige of the tribunal as a solemn indictment of the Nazis and as a precedent in the administration of international justice was at stake. After the weary months spent in stating the elaborate case for the prosecution, with its inevitable overlaps, repetitions and expressions of national feeling, the fact that Goering was taking the stand had filled the courtroom once more and concentrated the attention of the world on this most prominent witness from the dark and defeated world of the Nazis. His counsel had given him every chance to place his actions and those of Hitler in a favorable light. Now was the chance to demolish the specious structure of his case while the world watched the valiant reassertion of humane and civilized values.

Goering presented the tribunal with a grave problem. His lengthy answers were for the most part just relevant enough to make it difficult for the president to intervene and stop him, except from time to time in a general way. As Birkett noted at the time, "This was where the cleverness of Goering was fully shown." He held the stage for two days with "cleverly constructed statements which were not strictly answers to the questions at all."

The result was that he proved more than a match for Jackson, who gradually began to show a certain lack of self-confidence. The parry and thrust of the cross-examination, the series of leading questions that carried the witness forward to some carefully prepared trap in which he would suddenly find himself placed in a difficult and unanswerable position, never occurred. Goering knew his documents, knew his answers, always was ready with his explanations and plausible excuses which only became more plausible as his confidence grew at the expense of the prosecution.

Birkett became deeply concerned at this threat to the dignity of the trial which meant so much as a demonstration by the Allies of justice for the defeated as distinct from vengeance upon them. He wrote in his notes:

The first factor creating this situation was the extraordinary personality of Goering himself. Throughout this trial the dead Hitler has been present at every session, a dreadful, sinister and in some respects an inexplicable figure; but Goering is the man who has really dominated the proceedings, and that, remarkably enough, without ever uttering a word in public up to the moment he went into the witness box. That in itself is a very remarkable achievement and illuminates much that was obscure in the history of the past few years. He has followed the evidence with great intentness when the evidence required attention, and has slept like a child when it did not; and it has been obvious that a personality of outstanding, though possibly evil, qualities was seated there in the dock.

Nobody appears to have been quite prepared for this immense ability and knowledge, and his thorough mastery and understanding of the detail of the captured documents. He had obviously studied them with the greatest care and appreciated the matters which might assume the deadliest form. . . .

Suave, shrewd, adroit, capable, resourceful, he quickly saw the elements of the situation, and as his confidence grew, his mastery became more apparent. His self-control, too, was remarkable, and to all the other qualities manifested in his evidence he added the resonant tones of his speaking voice, and the eloquent but restrained use of gesture.

By the time the cross-examination was interrupted in order that Dahlerus could be called to the witness stand, Goering seemed to have emerged at any rate as partial victor. He had been questioned on many matters—the leadership principle and his relations with Hitler, the concentration camps, the S.S., the attack on Russia, the Reichstag fire, the Roehm purge, German territorial expansion, his relations with Schacht, German rearmament and his personal attitude to war. His weakness had been his recurrent evasion, his strength his uninhibited acceptance of responsibility for his part in what he regarded as the most positive aspect of Nazi policy and practice in government. His first major defeat in the trial came from certain admissions drawn from Dahlerus himself, who had come specially from Stockholm to act as a witness on his behalf.

Examined first by Stahmer, Dahlerus was taken point by point through the complicated succession of negotiations which he had undertaken in the belief that they might serve to prevent war between Germany and Britain. The intention, obviously, was to show the trouble to which Goering had gone to encourage these negotiations, all of which, claimed the defense, revealed his personal opposition to the war. It was Maxwell-Fyfe, however, who during the cross-examination first began to question Goering's motives in his dealings with Dahlerus. Was the German intention to avoid war as a means of resolving the Polish question, which Hitler had himself raised, or to keep Britain out of an armed aggression which was already predetermined? Was Goering, in other words, the conscious instrument of Hitler to calm the fears of Britain and prevent her from committing herself to armed intervention in support of Poland? Maxwell-Fyfe pressed several damaging admissions from Dahlerus:

MAXWELL-FYFE: Now, you remember that day that you had the conversation with him, and later on he rang you up at eleven-thirty before your departure?

DAHLERUS: Yes.

MAXWELL-FYFE: I just want you to tell the tribunal one or two of the things that he did not tell you on that day. He did not tell you, did he, that two days before, on August 22, at Obersalzberg, Hitler had told him and other German leaders that he, Hitler, had decided in the spring that a conflict with Poland was bound to come? He did not tell you that, did he?

DAHLERUS: I never had any indication or disclosure on the declared policy on April 11, or May 23, or August 22.

MAXWELL-FYFE: . . . He never told you that Hitler had said to him on that day [May 23] that "Danzig is not the subject of the dispute at all, it is a question of expanding our living space in the east." And I think he also did not tell you that Hitler had said on that day, "Our task is to isolate Poland, the success of the isolation will be decisive." He never spoke to you about isolating Poland?

DAHLERUS: He never indicated anything in that direction at all. . . .

MAXWELL-FYFE: Goering never told you at the time you were being sent to London [that] all that was wanted was to eliminate British intervention.

DAHLERUS: Not at all. [IX, pp. 223–24]

Maxwell-Fyfe quoted damaging sections describing Hitler, Goering and Ribbentrop from Dahlerus' book The Last Attempt, and gradually maneuvered him into the position of becoming in effect a witness for the prosecution:

MAXWELL-FYFE: So that, of the three principal people in Germany, the Chancellor was abnormal, the Reich Marshal, or the Field Marshal as he was then, was in a crazy state of intoxication, and, according to the defendant Goering, the Foreign Minister was a would-be murderer who wanted to sabotage your plane?

[*The witness nodded.*] [*IX, p. 226*]

Finally Dahlerus admitted, "At the time, I thought I could contribute something to preventing a new war, I could definitely prove that nothing was left undone by the British, by His Majesty's Government, to prevent war. But had I known what I know today, I would have realized that my efforts could not possibly succeed." [*IX, p. 230*]

Goering, back once more under direct examination by Stahmer in connection with Dahlerus' evidence, did his best to retrieve the situation. But the damage was done, and Goering seemed now to be floundering:

GOERING: During all these negotiations it was not a question, as far as I was concerned, of isolating Poland and keeping England out of the matter, but rather it was a question, since the problem of the Corridor and Danzig had come up, of solving it peacefully, as far as possible along the lines of the Munich solution. That was my endeavor until the last moment. If it had been a question only of eliminating England from the matter, then, firstly, English diplomacy would surely have recognized that immediately—it certainly has enough training for that. However, it did enter into these negotiations. And, secondly, I probably would have used entirely different tactics. [*IX, p. 234*]

He dismissed the personal impression of himself, Hitler and Ribbentrop in the latter section of *The Last Attempt* as purely subjective, and the ambiguity of his own position as that of a soldier who was also acting as a diplomat.

It was my firm determination to do everything to settle in a peaceful way this problem that had come up. I did not want the war; consequently I did everything I possibly could to avoid it. That has nothing to do with the preparations which I, as a matter of duty in my capacity as a high-ranking soldier, carried out. [*IX, p. 236*]

After this interlude, Jackson resumed his cross-examination in the later afternoon with some questions relating to the Reich Defense Council and the occupation of the Rhineland. Again he complained of Goering's attempt to avoid answering questions directly by entering at once into lengthy explanations which obscured the issues involved by adding new ones. Then followed the incident which became world news overnight: Goering made Jackson openly lose his temper in court.

JACKSON: Well, those preparations were preparations for armed occupation of the Rhineland, were they not?

GOERING: No, that is altogether wrong. If Germany had become involved in a war, no matter from which side, let us assume from the east, then mobilization measures would have had to be carried out for security reasons throughout the Reich in this event, even in the demilitarized Rhineland; but not for the purpose of occupation, of liberating the Rhineland.

JACKSON: You mean the preparations were not military preparations?

GOERING: Those were general preparations for mobilization, such as every country makes, and not for the purpose of the occupation of the Rhineland.

JACKSON: But were of a character which had to be kept entirely secret from foreign powers?

GOERING: I do not think I can recall reading beforehand the publication of the mobilization preparations of the United States.

JACKSON: Well, I respectfully submit to the tribunal that this witness is not being responsive, and has not been in his examination, and that it is—[*The witness interposes a few words here.*] it is perfectly futile to spend our time if we cannot have responsive answers to our questions. [*The witness interposes slightly here.*] We can strike these things out. I do not want to spend time doing that, but this witness, it seems to me, is adopting, and has adopted, in the witness box and in the dock, an arrogant and contemptuous attitude toward the tribunal which is giving him the trial which he never gave a living soul, or dead ones either. [*IX, pp. 242–43*]

Jackson had flung down his earphones in a rage, and there was a moment of acute tension and embarrassment. This loss of temper destroyed for the moment the dignity of the prosecution, and

the president felt obliged to announce an adjournment. Goering was highly pleased with himself and said to the other defendants, "If you all handle yourselves half as well as I did, you will
do all right." The following day Jackson continued his complaints
at length about Goering's reference to the United States, until
eventually the president suggested that though it was, of course,
wrong for Goering to have made this remark, "it is a matter which
I think you might well ignore."

The principal phase of the cross-examination that followed this
diversion was concerned with Goering's actions against the Jews.
Here evasion became more difficult; he was too directly involved
in the documents offered in evidence against him. It was now that
the minutes of the notorious Cabinet meeting on the Jewish problem following the pogrom of November 1938 were quoted at
length, with every callous remark by Goering read aloud in court.
Goering tried to explain away his crudity by saying that it was an
expression of his ill-temper with Goebbels. But Jackson continued
to read the minutes of this meeting, pressing home every point at
which Goering was openly conspiring to use the machinery of state
to rob the Jews of their property, including even the insurance on
the goods which had been looted from Jewish stores. He read the
statement Goering had made at the meeting in which his exaspera-
tion at the thought of the huge losses involved in the pogrom was
expressed in the remark to Heydrich that he wished two hundred
Jews had been killed rather than so many valuable things lost.

JACKSON: Do I read that correctly?
GOERING: Yes, this was said in a moment of bad temper and
excitement.
JACKSON: Spontaneously sincere, was it not?
GOERING: As I said, it was not meant seriously. It was the expression of spontaneous excitement caused by the events, and by
the destruction of valuables and the difficulties which arose. Of
course, if you are going to bring up every word I said in the course
of twenty-five years in these circles, I myself could give you instances of even stronger remarks. [IX, p. 262]

Goering now had to face further damning records of his persecution of the Jews, in particular his decrees designed to eliminate
Jewish trade in Austria and the confiscation of art treasures for-

merly owned by Jews. He had to answer for his requisitioning of labor from among prisoners of war and Russian civilians in the occupied areas, and his anger rose when he was held to account for an order in his name which seemed to imply that German commando forces to hunt partisans should be recruited from among "those with a passion for hunting, who have poached for love of the sport," and that they could "murder, burn and ravish." Goering objected strongly to the suggestion of rape.

GOERING: No, it is not correct. I say this because it is a most significant concept which has always particularly contradicted my sense of justice, for shortly after the assumption of power I instigated a sharpening of the German punitive laws on this matter. I want to show, in the light of this word and this concept, that this entire latter part could not have been uttered by me and I deny having said it. I will absolutely and gladly take responsibility for even the most serious things which I have done, but I deny that this statement, in view of my opinions, could ever have been uttered by me. [IX, p. 279]

Later he said that he never ordered villages to be burned or hostages to be shot, and that he violently opposed the suggestion toward the end of the war that the Geneva Convention should be abandoned so that prisoners of war or flyers descending in parachutes could be shot.

When Maxwell-Fyfe followed, he used methods of cross-examination very different from those of Jackson; his aim was to show that the defendant was lying or evading evidence incriminating to him. He tried to drive Goering into a trap over his knowledge of the shooting of the R.A.F. prisoners who had escaped from Stalag Luft III on the night of March 24, 1944. The shooting went on from March 25 to April 13; Goering claimed that he was on leave when the shootings began, that he was not informed of them at the time, and that he protested violently when at length he learned what had happened.

GOERING: Insofar as escaped prisoners of war committed any offenses or crimes, they were of course turned over to the police, I believe. But I wish to testify before the tribunal that I never gave any order that they should be handed over to the police or

sent to concentration camps merely because they had attempted
to break out or to escape, nor did I ever know that such measures
were taken. [*IX, p. 288*]

Maxwell-Fyfe surrounded him with documents which seemed to
make it impossible for Goering, as Commander in Chief of the
Luftwaffe, not to have known about the matter in time to take
action to prevent it.

MAXWELL-FYFE: You understand that what I am suggesting to
you is that here was a matter which was not only known in the
O.K.W., not only known in the Gestapo and the Kripo, but was
known to your own director of operations, General Forster, who
told General Grosch that he had informed Field Marshal Milch.
I am suggesting to you that it is absolutely impossible and untrue
that in these circumstances you knew nothing about it. . . . What
I am suggesting is that both you and Field Marshal Milch are saying that you knew nothing about it when you did, and are leaving
the responsibility on the shoulders of your junior officers. That is
what I am suggesting, and I want you to realize it.

GOERING: No, I did not wish to push responsibility onto the
shoulders of my subordinates, and I want to make it clear—that is
the only thing that is important to me—that Field Marshal Milch
did not say that he reported this matter to me. And, secondly, that
the date when Forster told Milch about this is not established. It
is quite possible that, on the date when this actually happened, the
Chief of Staff of the Luftwaffe might already have conferred with
me about it. The important factor is—and I want to maintain it—
that I was not present at the time when the command was given
by the Führer. When I heard about it, I vehemently opposed it.
But at the time when I did hear of it, it was already too late. [*IX,
pp. 295–96*]

He was genuinely angry that he could be thought to be involved
in so dishonorable an act. "I myself," he repeated, "considered it the
most serious incident of the whole war." He went on:

I told Himmler plainly that it was his duty to telephone me before
the execution of this matter, to give me the possibility, even at this
time, to use my much diminished influence to prevent the Führer

from carrying out this decree. I did not mean to say that I would have been completely successful, but it was a matter of course that I, as Chief of the Luftwaffe, should make it clear to Himmler that it was his duty to ring me up first of all, because it was I who was most concerned with this matter. I told the Führer in very plain terms just how I felt, and I saw from his answers that, even if I had known of it before, I could not have prevented this decree.

MAXWELL-FYFE: Well, that may be your view, that you could not have got anywhere with the Führer, but I suggest to you that when all these officers that I mentioned knew about it, you knew about it, too, and that you did nothing to prevent these men from being shot, but co-operated in this foul series of murders.

Maxwell-Fyfe reopened the question of Goering's true motives in his dealings with Dahlerus, and his attitude concerning the violation of the neutrality of Belgium and Holland. In document after document, quoting Hitler's speeches and the memoranda of meetings at which Goering was present, the prosecutor exposed the opportunism of Hitler in the matter of aggression. He ended this phase of his cross-examination as follows:

MAXWELL-FYFE: Is it not quite clear from that that all along you knew, as Hitler stated on August 22, that England and France would not violate the neutrality of the Low Countries and you were prepared to violate them whenever it suited your strategical and tactical interests? Is not that quite clear?

GOERING: Not entirely. If the political situation made it necessary and if in the meantime the British view of the neutrality of Holland and Belgium had been obtained.

MAXWELL-FYFE: You say not entirely. That is as near agreement with me as you are probably prepared to go.

Goering next tried to fight back over the charge of German aggression in Yugoslavia, claiming that it was linked directly with hostile moves in Russia. Maxwell-Fyfe produced damaging evidence of Goering's ruthless attitude to the fight against the partisans, and then turned his attention to the concentration camps.

MAXWELL-FYFE: Are you telling the tribunal that you, who up to 1943 were the second man in the Reich, knew nothing about concentration camps?

GOERING: I did not know anything about what took place and the methods used in the concentration camps later, when I was no longer in charge.

MAXWELL-FYFE: Let me remind you of the evidence that has been given before this court, that as far as Auschwitz alone is concerned, four million people were exterminated. Do you remember that?

GOERING: This I have heard as a statement here, but I consider it in no way proved—that figure, I mean. . . .

MAXWELL-FYFE: . . . Assume that these figures—one is a Russian figure, the other a German—assume they are even fifty per cent correct, assume it was two million and one million, are you telling this tribunal that a minister with your power in the Reich could remain ignorant that that was going on?

GOERING: This I maintain, and the reason for this is that these things were kept secret from me. I might add that in my opinion not even the Führer knew the extent of what was going on. This is also explained by the fact that Himmler kept all these matters very secret. We were never given figures or any other details.

MAXWELL-FYFE: But, witness, had you not access to the foreign press, the press department in your ministry, to foreign broadcasts? You see, there is evidence that altogether, when you take the Jews and other people, something like ten million people have been done to death in cold blood, apart from those killed in battle. Something like ten million people. Do you say that you never saw or heard from the foreign press, in broadcasts, that this was going on?

GOERING: First of all, the figure ten million is not established in any way. Secondly, throughout the war I did not read the foreign press, because I considered it nothing but propaganda. Thirdly, though I had the right to listen to foreign broadcasts I never did so, simply because I did not want to listen to propaganda. Neither did I listen to home propaganda. Only during the last four days of the war did I—and this I could prove—listen to a foreign broadcasting station for the first time. [IX, p. 310]

Later Maxwell-Fyfe briefly challenged Goering's loyalty to Hitler in view of these facts.

MAXWELL-FYFE: Do you still seek to justify and glorify Hitler after he had ordered the murder of these fifty young flying officers at Stalag Luft III?

GOERING: I am here neither to justify the Führer Adolf Hitler nor to glorify him. I am here only to emphasize that I remained faithful to him, for I believe in keeping one's oath not in good times only, but also in bad times when it is much more difficult. As to your reference to the fifty airmen, I never opposed the Führer so clearly and strongly as in this matter, and I gave him my views. After that, no conversation between the Führer and myself took place for months.

MAXWELL-FYFE: The Führer, at any rate, must have had full knowledge of what was happening with regard to concentration camps, the treatment of the Jews, and the treatment of the work- ers, must he not?

GOERING: I already mentioned it as my opinion that the Führer did not know about details in concentration camps, about atrocities as described here. Insofar as I know him, I do not believe he was informed.

MAXWELL-FYFE: I am not asking about details; I am asking about the murder of four or five million people. Are you suggest- ing that nobody in power in Germany, except Himmler and per- haps Kaltenbrunner, knew about that?

GOERING: I am still of the opinion that the Führer did not know about these figures. [IX, p. 312]

Maxwell-Fyfe closed his cross-examination with a final scathing challenge to Goering's credibility under oath. He was using two documents, the second of which was the record of a conference in which Goering heard directly from Lohse, a Reich commissioner for the eastern occupied territories, that the Jews were being "dis- posed of" in Hungary.

MAXWELL-FYFE: I call your attention to the statement that "there are only a few Jews left alive, tens of thousands have been disposed of." Do you still say, in the face of these two documents, that neither Hitler nor yourself knew that the Jews were being exterminated?

GOERING: This should be understood: From this you cannot con- clude that they have been killed. It is not my remark, but the re- mark of Lohse. On that question I also answered. The Jews were only left in smaller numbers. From this remark you cannot conclude that they were killed. It could also mean that they were removed.

MAXWELL-FYFE: About the preceding remark, I suggest that you make quite clear what you meant by "there are only a few Jews left alive, whereas tens of thousands have been disposed of."

GOERING: They were still living there. That is how you should understand that.

MAXWELL-FYFE: You heard what I read to you about Hitler, what he said to Horthy and what Ribbentrop said, that the Jews must be exterminated or taken to concentration camps. Hitler said the Jews must either work or be shot. That was in April 1943. Do you still say that neither Hitler nor you knew of this policy to exterminate the Jews?

GOERING: For the correction of the document—

MAXWELL-FYFE: Will you please answer my question? Do you still say neither Hitler nor you knew of the policy to exterminate the Jews?

GOERING: As far as Hitler is concerned, I have said I do not believe it. As far as I am concerned, I have said that I did not know, even approximately, to what degree this thing took place.

MAXWELL-FYFE: You did not know to what degree, but you knew there was a policy that aimed at the extermination of the Jews?

GOERING: No, a policy for emigration, not liquidation, of the Jews. I only knew there had been isolated cases of such perpetrations. [IX, pp. 314–15]

MAXWELL-FYFE: Thank you.

After this, everyone knew that Goering, whatever he might try to say in retaliation, was utterly discredited. The minutes of the meeting on August 6, 1942, were read; they showed that Goering had expressed himself forcibly to the Reich Commissioners on the need to "extract everything possible out of the territories" and warned them they were "certainly not sent there to work for the welfare of the population." Goering was reminded that he had said, "I intend to plunder and to do it thoroughly." Faced with the document, he could not deny that he had spoken these words, or refute the references to the two million men and women taken to Germany for forced labor.

RUDENKO: But you do not deny the underlying meaning that you were speaking here of millions of people who were carried off forcibly to Germany for slave labor.

GOERING: I do not deny that I was speaking of two million workers who had been called up, but whether they were all brought to Germany I cannot say at the moment. At any rate, they were used for the German economy.

RUDENKO: You do not deny that this was forced labor, slavery.

GOERING: Slavery, that I deny. Forced labor did, of course, partly come into it, and the reason for that I have already stated.

RUDENKO: But they were forcibly taken out of their countries and sent to Germany?

GOERING: To a certain extent deported forcibly, and I have already explained why. [IX, p. 325]

The examination by General Rudenko which now followed was a formal one and was especially concerned with the invasion of the Soviet Union and Goering's participation in its planning. The documents cited showed that Goering was more concerned to anticipate obtaining food supplies for Germany from these territories than to preplan their political annexation.

RUDENKO: . . . You considered the annexation of these regions a step to come later. As you said yourself, after it was won you would have seized these provinces and annexed them.

GOERING: As an old hunter, I acted according to the principle of not dividing the bear's skin before the bear was shot.

RUDENKO: I understand. The bear's skin should be divided only when the territories were seized completely, is that correct?

GOERING: Just what to do with the skin could be decided definitely only after the bear was shot.

RUDENKO: Luckily, this did not happen.

GOERING: Luckily for you. [IX, p. 320]

With studied politeness the questioning went on to put on record Goering's part in pillorying the occupied territories and forcing them to supply the German nation.

Rudenko tried to obtain an admission from Goering, which he refused to give, that instructions issued to German officers ordering them to shoot civilians who resisted, and, later, to take the lives of fifty to a hundred Communists for every German killed, were known to him at the time. Nor would Goering admit to any detailed knowledge of the treatment given to Soviet prisoners of war, or to the validity of Himmler's assertions, made in a speech, that thirty million Slavs must be exterminated. Rudenko ended his cross-examination with a dramatic challenge to Goering on his fundamental responsibility. This developed into a fierce exchange.

RUDENKO: If you thought it possible to co-operate with Hitler, do you recognize that, as the second man in Germany, you were responsible for the organizing on a national scale of murders of millions of innocent people, independently of whether you knew about those facts or not? Tell me briefly, yes or no.

GOERING: No, because I did not know anything about them and did not cause them.

RUDENKO: I should like to underline again, "whether you knew about these facts or not."

GOERING: If I actually did not know them, then I cannot be held responsible for them.

RUDENKO: It was a duty to know about these facts.

GOERING: I shall go into that.

RUDENKO: I am questioning you. Answer me this question: Was it your duty to know about these facts?

GOERING: In what way my duty? Either I know the fact or I do not know it. You can only ask me if I was negligent in failing to obtain knowledge.

RUDENKO: You ought to know yourself better. Millions of Germans knew about the crimes which were being perpetrated, and you did not know about them?

GOERING: Neither did millions of Germans know about them. That is a statement which has in no way been proved.

RUDENKO: My last two questions: You stated to the tribunal that Hitler's government brought great prosperity to Germany. Are you still sure that that is so?

GOERING: Definitely, until the beginning of the war. The collapse was due only to the war being lost.

RUDENKO: As a result of which, you brought Germany—as a result of your politics—to military and political destruction. I have no more questions. [IX, p. 335]

Following this, the chief prosecutor for France did not feel it necessary to put further questions to the defendant. Goering was disappointed to find he was deprived of the chance of making some final speeches. Nevertheless, he was well pleased with himself and asked Gilbert whether the prosecution counsel had been impressed. "Rudenko was more nervous than I was," he said. On reflection, however, he admitted that the anti-Jewish measures had been a mistake; he certainly would never have supported them had he known the excesses to which they would lead. "I only thought we would eliminate Jews from positions in big business and government, and that was that," he said. He felt he had handled the difficult question of his loyalty to Hitler well.

The following day Gilbert visited Emmy Goering, who had just been released and was now living with Edda in some discomfort in an isolated house situated in the woodlands near Neuhaus. She spoke bitterly of Hitler's ingratitude to her husband; Goering's continued loyalty she regarded as the front he must show to the world, even to the man who had ordered his wife and child to be killed. Emmy was convinced of Hitler's insanity. "You know my husband," she added. "He is not a man obsessed by hatred. He only wanted to enjoy life and let other people enjoy it. . . . Oh, if I could only speak to him for five minutes! Just for five minutes!" She seemed quite helpless without her husband, and Gilbert had to arrange that her clothes, which had been impounded, should be given back to her. He consented to take Goering a letter from her, and a postcard from Edda. Goering took these with great emotion and kept them to read in private. Gilbert told him of the conversation he had had with Emmy and how shocked she was at her husband's persistent loyalty to Hitler. Goering merely smiled at this; such matters, he said, were "not a woman's affair." He could not show disloyalty before a foreign court.

"I don't believe any more that Hitler himself sent that order. That was the work of that dirty swine Bormann. I tell you, Herr Doktor, if I could have that pig alone in this cell I would strangle the bastard with my bare hands!" And although he laughed at his own fury, he unconsciously kept his fist clenched for several minutes after his outburst.

It was to be another five months before Goering stood again in the witness box and took center stage at the trial. For four months he had to listen to the cases of his companions in the dock and to the concluding speeches of the defense and the prosecution; then a further month was given up to the defense of the indicted Nazi organizations. All this while, Gilbert kept his careful records of the expression of Goering's views and of his behavior.

The biggest problem for him was to accept Hitler as a mass murderer. Gilbert impressed on him his lack of understanding of psychopathology. He made him agree that Himmler was a psychopath, but Goering put his head in his hands at the thought that Hitler was the same. He seemed inclined in the end to accept the suggestion that Hitler had left the problem of extermination to Himmler and turned his back on the consequences. Dr. Gilbert explained to him the technique of extermination which made the mass killings possible.

As the defendants began to give ground before the prosecution and even, as in the case of Frank, openly to admit their guilt, his disgust deepened. Frank admitted knowledge of the atrocities—"in contrast to those around the Führer who did not know anything about these things." In his cell afterward, Goering sweated and grumbled. If Frank had known, why had he not brought the knowledge to him so that the matter could have been dealt with?

Frick called Dr. Hans Gisevius as one of his witnesses, and this was to prove a considerable embarrassment to Goering. From the start of his testimony, Gisevius set out to attack Goering, implicating him in the murders and other excesses committed by the Gestapo in 1933. Above all, he involved him directly in the Reichstag fire: "I am prepared to refresh defendant Goering's memory concerning his complicity in and his joint knowledge of this first *coup d'état* and the murder of the accomplices." [*XII, p. 211*] He renamed the Roehm purge the Goering-Himmler purge. Gisevius had been on the staff of the Ministry of the Interior during this period and had seen the radiogram that Goering and Himmler had sent to the police headquarters, as well as Goering's final instruction that all documents relating to June 30 should be burned.

Then suddenly Gisevius, in the middle of answering a question, asked the court's permission to reveal an "incident." Goering, he said, had tried through his counsel, Dr. Stahmer, to exert pressure to keep evidence on the Blomberg case out of the trial. Jackson rose at once and demanded that this matter be made public. The various defense counsels involved were at once thrown into disorder, set each against the other. Dr. Stahmer's very confused version of the incident was as follows:

Goering told me that it was of no interest to him if the witness
Gisevius did incriminate him, but he did not wish that Blomberg,
who died recently—and I assumed it was only the question of
Blomberg's marriage—he, Goering, did not want these facts concerning the marriage of Blomberg to be discussed here in public. If
that could not be prevented, then of course Goering, for his part—
and it is only a question of Schacht, because Schacht, as he had
told me, wanted to speak about these things—would not spare
Schacht. [XII, p. 214]

Dr. Dix, counsel for Schacht, had a somewhat different version
of how Stahmer had put the matter:

He said to me, "Listen, Goering has an idea that Gisevius will
attack him as much as he can, but if he attacks the dead Blomberg,
then Goering will disclose everything against Schacht, and he
knows lots of things about Schacht which may not be pleasant for
him. He, Goering, had been very reticent in his testimony, but if
anything should be said against the dead Blomberg, then he would
reveal things against Schacht." [XII, p. 215]

Later in the examination, Gisevius gave his own version:

Dr. Stahmer approached, obviously very excited, and asked Dr.
Dix for an immediate interview. Dr. Dix refused, on the ground
that he was talking to me. Dr. Stahmer said in a loud voice that he
must speak to Dr. Dix immediately and urgently. Dr. Dix took
only two steps aside, and the conversation that followed was carried on by Dr. Stahmer in such a loud voice that I was bound to
hear most of it. I did hear it and said to attorney Dr. Kraus, who
was standing nearby, "Just listen how Dr. Stahmer is carrying on."
Dr. Dix then came over to me, very excited, and, after all this fuss,
in response to my questions as to what precisely was the demand
of the defendant Goering, he told me what I had already half
heard anyway. [XII, pp. 278–79]

Stahmer was deeply upset by this exposure to the court and
wanted to make a further statement to the tribunal, but Goering
persuaded him to let the matter drop. His blackmail had recoiled
upon himself.

Gisevius, who was more excited than anyone else, had interrupted so much that the president had been forced to silence him sternly. When eventually he was allowed to speak, he said, "To my thinking, it is the most rotten thing Goering ever did, and he is just using the cloak of chivalry by pretending that he wants to protect a dead man, whereas he really wants to prevent me from testifying in full on an important point, that is, the Fritsch crisis." [XII, p. 216]

Frick, whose witness Gisevius was, seemed the only person among those directly involved who remained unperturbed. In the brief recess that followed this scene, Goering called Gisevius a petty traitor, a minor official of whom he had·never previously heard.

Gisevius, back on the stand, continued his denunciations. He told how he advised Schacht in 1935 to avoid any connection with Goering, who Schacht still thought was the conservative influence among the Nazis:

I contradicted Schacht vehemently regarding his views about the defendant Goering. I warned him. I told him that in my opinion Goering was the worst of all, precisely because he was riding under the middle-class and conservative cloak. I implored him not to utilize the services of Goering in framing his economic policy, since this could only have bad results. [XII, p 223]

When the stormy session was over, Goering could barely be induced to enter the elevator that took him to the level of the cells. He was shouting at the other defendants and at their counsels.

The following day the story of Blomberg's fall in 1938 was recounted to Goering's discredit; it was followed immediately by evidence in the case of Fritsch. Later in the day, when the cross-examination of Gisevius began, the testimony against Goering was renewed. The Reichstag fire was the work of Goebbels, said the witness, but Goering was also actively involved. As for the Roehm purge:

We ascertained that Himmler, Heydrich and Goering had compiled exact lists of those to be murdered, because I myself heard in Goering's palace—and this was confirmed by Daluege, who was present, and also by Nebe, who was present from the very first second—that no one of those who were killed was mentioned by name; all that was said was, "Number so and so is now gone," or "Number so and so is still missing," or "It will soon be number so and so's turn." [*XII, p. 265*]

Gisevius even quoted Goering's cousin against him:

Herbert, as well as his brothers and sisters, had warned me years ago about the disaster which would overtake Germany if at any time a man like their cousin Hermann should get a position of even the smallest responsibility. They acquainted me with the many characteristics of the defendant, which all of us had come to know in the meantime, starting with his vanity and continuing with his love of ostentation, his lack of responsibility, his lack of scruples, even to the extent of making steppingstones of the dead. From all this I already had some idea what to expect of the defendant. [*XII, p. 271*]

With Gisevius gone, Goering gradually relaxed. He had watched carefully the response of the judges to this attack on him, and the other defendants had reacted strongly against him in the nervous shifts of favor that constantly affected the cliques in the prison cells.

When Schacht's turn came to take the stand, he testified in detail about his differences with Goering. Jackson quoted in court the famous statement about Goering's character which Schacht had made under interrogation:

I have called Hitler an amoral type of person, but can only regard Goering as immoral and criminal. Endowed by nature with a certain geniality which he managed to exploit for his own popularity, he was the most egocentric being imaginable. The assumption of political power was for him only a means to personal enrichment and personal good living. The success of others filled him with envy. His greed knew no bounds. His predilection for jewels, gold and finery was unimaginable. He knew no comradeship. Only so long as someone was useful to him was he a friend to him, but only on the surface.

Goering's knowledge in all fields in which a government member should be competent was nil, especially in the economic field. Of all the economic matters which Hitler entrusted to him in the autumn of 1936 he had not the faintest notion, though he created a large official machine and misused his powers as lord of all economy most outrageously. In his personal appearance he was so theatrical that you could only compare him with Nero. A lady who had tea with his second wife reported that he appeared at this tea in a sort of Roman toga and sandals studded with jewels, his fingers bedecked with innumerable jeweled rings and generally covered with ornaments, his face painted, his lips rouged. [*XIII, p. 53*]

The court was highly amused by this description, but Goering was naturally enough very angry and threatened to get even. In the dock he was heard saying, "This is no place to bring up a thing like that—even if it is true. It can't help him. I don't know why he brought that up." That night he retired to bed with a headache and asked for pills. "The way I behave in my own house is my affair," he said, looking sick and dejected. "Anyway, I didn't use lipstick!"

The next direct attack on Goering came once more from his own side. Raeder was suddenly faced, like Schacht, with statements he made many months previously under interrogation. He was embarrassed when questions he had answered while imprisoned in Russia concerning the Blomberg affair were read out in court by Maxwell-Fyfe: He had "lost confidence" in both Hitler and Goering, and he accused Goering of deliberately fostering the marriage so that Blomberg should be disgraced and the post of Commander in Chief of the Wehrmacht be given to him. The full statement, had it been read, would have been far worse; it included such sentences as "The person Goering had a disastrous effect on the fate of the German Reich," and it referred to his "unimaginable vanity," his untruthfulness, his greed and his "soft, unsoldierly manner."

By the following weekend Goering was ill and complaining, according to Gilbert, of both sciatica and treachery. He was absent from the court, where his prestige had suffered too severe a blow. He felt deserted now by the military caste from whom he had hoped to receive his principal support. As Jodl took the stand, he was heard to mutter, "Well, this is my last hope." But Jodl too denied his self-appointed master. Goering became cynical in his conversation with Gilbert: "What the devil do you mean, morality, word of honor? You can talk about word of honor when you promise to deliver goods in business; but when it is the question of the interests of a nation, then morality stops! . . . When a state has a chance to improve its position because of the weakness of a neighbor, do you think it will stop at any squeamish consideration of keeping a promise? It is a stateman's duty to take advantage of such a situation for the good of his country!"

The next defendant to testify against Goering was Speer. He was the most intelligent and clear-minded of all the principal Nazis; he understood the enormity of the Nazi system in which he had shared and which at the very end he had ceased to serve. He had even planned, he said, to kill Hitler by injecting poison gas into the bunker. Goering sat appalled and silent. Speer, back in his cell, damned Goering as a coward who had no moral right whatsoever to try to turn a "rotten business" into a heroic legend. In the court he revealed how Goering had forbidden Galland to reveal that the enemy's fighter planes were perfectly well able to penetrate deep into German territory.

In his cell Goering, still deeply disturbed by Speer's testimony, tried to adjust himself to his own values and sense of loyalty. As he said to Gilbert, "What a tragicomedy! I was hated and ordered shot by the Führer in the end. If there's to be any denunciation of the Führer, I was the one who had the right to do so. But I didn't do it because of the principle of the thing. Do you think I had any personal love for him? I swore my loyalty to him and I cannot go back on that. I had a hell of a time keeping it, too, I can tell you. Just try being Crown Prince for twelve years sometime—always loyal to the King, disapproving of many of his policies, and yet not being able to do anything about it. The only thing I could honorably have done was to make an open break. But I couldn't do that when we were in the middle of a four-front war. I am what I am—'the last Renaissance figure,' if you please." Meanwhile, he wanted something to read; he was trying to obtain a German translation of *Gone with the Wind*.

On Thursday and Friday, July 4 and 5, Stahmer made his final speech in defense of Goering. This speech was long and learned, and most people agreed that Stahmer made the best of what had become an impossible case. He described the historical background out of which the Nazi movement had grown, and he showed Goering always in the light of a patriot loyal to Hitler and to Germany. Goering had acted lawfully according to the law of his time; he could not be regarded as a conspirator, since he was serving the established Leader of the State and a leader, moreover, who shaped policy as he wanted it and not as his subordinates necessarily felt was right. As for being a conspirator in launching a war of aggression, Goering had been shown to be active in trying to prevent war. His belief in a strong German Army was based on the assumption that strength of arms prevented war. Stahmer then went on to prove that Goering was virtually without any prime authority in the State; his position, Stahmer declared, could not be used to incriminate him.

As second man in the State, Goering could neither rescind nor change nor supplement Hitler's orders. He could give no orders whatsoever to offices of which he was not directly in charge. He had no possibility of giving any binding orders to any other office, whether it was an office of the party, the police, the Army or the Navy, nor could he interfere in the authority of these offices which were not his own. [XVIII, p 117]

Dr. Stahmer justified Goering's economic exploitation of the occupied territories by stating that the Allies waged an illegal economic war on Germany, forcing her to supply herself from the areas open to her because of the blockade imposed on her from the sea. His acquisition of works of art through rightful confiscation was undertaken on behalf of the State.

As for the shooting of the R.A.F. prisoners of war, Goering played no direct part in this, and once he had heard of it he protested most strongly; neither was he involved in giving orders for the shooting of the "terror flyers." "Reich Marshal Goering until the end of the war maintained the old-airman standpoint," declared Stahmer.

He then dealt as best he could with what he knew were the most serious elements in the charges against Goering—that he established a reign of terror in 1933, founded the concentration camps and was a party to genocide. As to the reign of terror, Stahmer claimed that all Goering did was secure the State at a time of great crisis; while he had charge of the camps, his authority was on the side of humanity and discipline. He was as much concerned with the "education" of the political prisoners and with their release as he was with making legitimate use of the few recognized camps he had set up. He was acting as a "political trustee" of the German government. As for the extermination of the Jews, this idea "apparently originated in Heydrich's and Himmler's brains and was kept secret in a masterly manner." Goering "could never have approved of such a measure." "That the defendant was no race fanatic became generally known by his expression 'I decide who is a Jew.' "

In his peroration, Stahmer concluded by quoting the words of Nevile Henderson when he had said that Goering ascribed every achievement to Hitler and that "he himself was nothing." This judgment still applied today, concluded Stahmer, but "his loyalty became his disaster."

The concluding speeches for the prosecution came at the end of July and lasted four days. The heat in the courtroom was intense when Jackson rose to give one of the great speeches of the trial. After so many months weighed down by evasion, by the blinding mass of documents, the visual horrors of the films of genocide, the bickering over detail, the scenes of tension and excitement followed by the long boredom of minute legalities, suddenly came the full expression of the intense emotions that underlay the trial.

Words had to be found that in some memorable way gave these men whose deaths were drawing near the answer of civilization to their barbarism. Jackson read a prepared speech, closely documented, filled with brief quotations that thrust the crimes back into the faces of the guilty and tore aside their evasion of responsibility. "No other half century," he said, "ever witnessed slaughter on such a scale, such cruelties and inhumanities, such wholesale deportations of peoples into slavery, such annihilations of minorities." Point by point he detailed what had been demonstrated and proved in guilt. Goering's name was seldom long off his lips. He referred to the "strange mixture of wind and wisdom which makes up the testimony of Hermann Goering," a testimony unequaled in integrating "the crimes of Nazi oppression and terrorism within Germany . . . with the crime of war. . . . The large and varied role of Goering was half militarist and half gangster. He stuck his pudgy finger in every pie. . . . He was equally adept at massacring opponents and at framing scandals to get rid of stubborn generals. . . . He was in the forefront in harrying Jews out of the land. . . . He was, next to Hitler, the man who tied the activities of all the defendants together in a common effort."

Jackson was scathing in his denunciation of the attempts by the defendants to evade responsibility and even knowledge of what was being done in the name of a State of which they were "the very highest surviving authorities." The cumulative ignorance of what went on in their own administration was nothing short of ludicrous. There was Goering—"Number Two man who knew nothing of the excesses of the Gestapo which he created, and never suspected the Jewish extermination program although he was the signer of over a score of decrees which instituted the persecution of the race." He ended:

It is against such a background that these defendants now ask this tribunal to say that they are not guilty of planning, executing or conspiring to commit this long list of crimes and wrongs. They stand before the record of this trial as bloodstained Gloucester stood by the body of his slain King. He begged of the widow, as they beg of you, "Say I slew them not." And the Queen replied, "Then say they were not slain, but dead they are . . ." If you were to say of these men that they are not guilty, it would be as true to say that there has been no war, there are no slain, there has been no crime. [XIX, p. 406]

The court was moved to silence. Then the president called on Sir Hartley Shawcross, who was to deal more specifically with the "legal guilt" of the defendants. Once more Goering's name recurred as the historical development of Nazi administration both before and during the war was described in detail, in a speech which was closely reasoned rather than emotional in treatment and delivery. In dealing with specific charges, Shawcross referred to the shooting of the R.A.F. prisoners and claimed that "Goering's participation is a matter of inevitable inference," because the order was given by Hitler, because Goering had been proved present at the meeting when the order was decided upon, and, last, because his immediate subordinates certainly knew about it. During the second day of the speech, after detailing the fearful record of genocide and the mass extermination of prisoners and other unwanted people, he turned on Goering.

Goering's responsibility in all these matters is scarcely to be denied. Behind his spurious air of bonhomie, he was as great an architect as any in this satanic system. Who, apart from Hitler, had more knowledge of what was going on, or greater influence to affect its course? The conduct of government in the Nazi State, the gradual buildup of the organization for war, the calculated aggression, the atrocities—these things do not occur spontaneously or without the closest co-operation between the holders of the various offices of state. Men do not advance into foreign territory, pull the trigger, drop their bombs, build the gas chamber, collect the victims, unless they are organized and ordered to do it. Crimes on the national and systematic scale which occurred here must involve anyone who forms a part of the necessary chain, since without that participation, plans for aggression here, mass murder there, could become quite impossible. The Führer principle by which the Nazis placed their bodies and their very souls at the disposal of their Leader was the creation of the Nazi Party, and of their own. When I addressed you at the opening of this trial, I remarked that there comes a time when a man must choose between his conscience and his leader. No one who chose, as these men did, to abdicate their consciences in favor of this monster of their own creation can complain now if they are held responsible for complicity in what that monster did. [XIX, p. 641–42]

Jackson had ended by quoting Shakespeare; Shawcross quoted Goethe:

Years ago Goethe said of the German people that someday fate would strike them, "would strike them because they betrayed themselves and did not want to be what they are. It is sad that they do not know the charm of truth, detestable that mist, smoke and berserk immoderation are so dear to them, pathetic that they ingenuously submit to any mad scoundrel who appeals to their lowest instincts, who confirms them in their vices and teaches them to conceive nationalism as isolation and brutality." With what a voice of prophecy he spoke—for these are the mad scoundrels who did these very things. [XIX, p. 470]

These were the principal speeches for the prosecution. Those by the French and Russian prosecutors were corollaries reinforcing what had already been said. General Rudenko, in particular, listed the crimes of Goering in a catalogue of facts.

This concluded the first phase of the trial; there then followed the formal defense of the indicted organizations, which occupied the greater part of August.

On August 20, however, Goering had a further brief examination in the box, when Maxwell-Fyfe pressed hard to make him reveal some knowledge of the inhuman medical experiments carried out on helpless prisoners at Dachau and other camps in the name of the Reich Research Bureau, of which he was president. Goering protested violently that he knew nothing of these practices, and insisted, "The experiments with women, and so on, which were described here are so utterly in contradiction to my views as regards women that I would have resented such experiments most deeply, not only now, afterward, but then, at the time." However, certain of the experiments had even been filmed, and lectures on them had been given to members of the Air Force staff. Still Goering denied all knowledge of these experiments for which Himmler's staff were ultimately responsible.

On August 31, Goering made the brief final plea which was permitted to each of the defendants. He complained that the prosecution had pieced together statements he had made over the years, taken them out of context and misrepresented what he had really meant. He claimed that no absolute proof had been produced of his complicity in or even knowledge of the mass killings, the atrocities and the murder of individuals.

I condemn utterly these terrible mass murders, and so that there shall be no misunderstanding in this connection, I wish to state emphatically . . . before the high tribunal that I have never decreed the murder of a single individual at any time, nor decreed any other atrocities, nor tolerated them, while I had the power and the knowledge to prevent them. [XXII, p. 380]

The Allies, he said, were treating Germany now in just the same way as they had accused the Germans in this trial of treating the occupied territories. However, whatever might happen to their captured leaders, the German people as a whole should be held free of guilt; they had merely placed their trust in the Führer and, from then on, had no further influence on events. Then he ended:

I did not want a war, nor did I bring it about. I did everything to prevent it by negotiation. After it had broken out, I did everything to assure victory. . . . I stand behind the things that I have done, but I deny most emphatically that my actions were dictated by the desire to subjugate foreign peoples by wars, to murder them, to rob them or to enslave them, or to commit atrocities or crimes. The only motive which guided me was my ardent love for my people, and my desire for their happiness and freedom. And for this I call on the Almighty and my German people as witnesses. [*XXII, p.* 381]

At lunch the same day, Papen violently attacked Goering for refusing to acknowledge his responsibility; Goering merely laughed at him. The prisoners were left to brood in their cells for a further month while the judgments were being prepared and their sentences determined. It was a period of nervous tension and despondency during which even Goering admitted final defeat. "You don't have to worry about the Hitler legend any more," Gilbert reports him to have said. "When the German people learn all that has been revealed at this trial, it won't be necessary to condemn him; he has condemned himself."

From the middle of September, Emmy Goering was allowed, along with the wives of the other prisoners, to visit her husband for half an hour daily in prison during the last weeks of his life. When they met, there was always a grille between them and a guard on duty. They could not touch hands or kiss. The visits were naturally a great strain for both husband and wife, and were discontinued from September 30, when the court resumed its sessions. She saw him only once more by a special arrangement. Goering remained stolidly cheerful at these meetings with Emmy, breaking down and weeping only once, when Emmy took Edda with her to see him.

Previously they had been allowed to correspond, though the letters that passed between them were, naturally enough, censored. But Goering was not afraid to express his love for Emmy, as this extract from one of his letters shows:

To see your beloved handwriting, to know that your dear hands have rested on this very paper: all that and the contents themselves have moved me most deeply and yet made me most happy. Sometimes I think my heart will break with love and longing for you. That would be a beautiful death.

At another time he wrote:

My Dear Wife,

I am so sincerely thankful to you for all the happiness that you always gave me; for your love and for everything; never let Edda get away from you. I could tell you endlessly what you and Edda mean to me and how my thoughts keep centering on you. I hold you in passionate embrace and kiss your dear, sweet face in passionate love.

Forever,

Your Hermann[2]

On September 30 the court reassembled to hear the judgment. Lord Justice Lawrence, as president of the tribunal, was the first to read. He was followed by Justice Birkett; then the French, the American and the Russian judges each took turns to read until, finally, Lawrence took over once more to read the closing sections. So the voices and the languages changed about as the judgment was revealed, first tracing the history of Nazi government and demonstrating its record of aggression, its denial of human rights and liberties and its violation of pacts and agreements, and then repeating the details of cruelty and barbarism given in evidence.

On the following day, Tuesday, October 1, the president reached the judgment on the individual defendants. The first was Goering. His record was briefly summarized from the period he joined the party in 1922, and he was judged "the moving force for aggressive war, second only to Hitler." He had used and approved the use of forced labor; he had, on his own admission, despoiled the occupied countries. He had persecuted the Jews, primarily by driving them out of the economy of Germany and the occupied territories, but also by directing Himmler to—in his own words—"bring about a complete solution of the Jewish question."

Lawrence concluded:

There is nothing to be said in mitigation. For Goering was often, indeed almost always, the moving force, second only to his Leader. He was the leading war aggressor, both as political and as military leader; he was the director of the slave labor program and the creator of the oppressive program against the Jews and other races, at home and abroad. All these crimes he frankly admitted. On some specific cases there may be conflict of testimony, but in terms of the broad outline his own admissions are more than sufficiently wide to be conclusive of his guilt. His guilt is unique in its enormity. The record discloses no excuses for this man. [*XXII, p. 487*]

In the afternoon the defendants were held ready while the tribunal assembled for the last time. One by one they were to be led up to hear their sentences pronounced. In the hall the American guards tested the equipment: "One—two—three—O.K." The psychologists stayed below with the prisoners.

Goering was the first to be called. He was led into the court through the sliding door at the rear of the dock, and there he stood alone, adjusting his earphones for the translation of his sentence. The president began to speak. "Hermann Wilhelm Goering, on the counts of the indictment . . ." But he had to stop, because Goering was indicating a fault in the circuit; he was not receiving the translation. Judge and prisoner faced each other while the technicians restored the equipment.

The president spoke again. "Hermann Wilhelm Goering, on the counts of the indictment on which you have been convicted, the International Military Tribunal sentences you to death by hanging."

At last the German words came through the earphones: ". . . *Tod durch den Strang.*" Goering stood absolutely still, watched by everyone in silence. Then he dropped the earphones with a clatter, turned and went out.

Below in the cell, Gilbert was waiting for him, still watchful for reactions. Goering arrived, his face pale and fixed, his eyes staring. "Death," was all he said as he sat down on his bed. Then his hands began to tremble and he gripped a book in an effort to control himself. His eyes filled with tears and his breathing grew hard; he asked to be left alone. When Gilbert returned later, Goering said that he had known he would receive the death penalty and that it was better so; it was the only sentence possible for martyrs. But he was still worried, even in these last days of his life, about what the psychologists might write about him; the interpretation of an inkblot test taken long before, when he had attempted to brush away the red spots from the page, still worried him.

Goering's words to Papen when he learned that the latter had been acquitted were, "*Ich freue mich für Sie.* I'm glad for you."[3] The day after he was sentenced, he formally petitioned to "be spared the ignominy of hanging and be allowed to die as a soldier before a firing squad." This was refused, and he was left to live out the fourteen days before the executions, which were due to take place on October 15 on a gallows erected in the gymnasium of the prison. He was permitted to see Emmy once only after sentence had been passed; she came three days before his death.

On the night of October 15, two hours before his execution was due to take place, Goering asked for the last rites according to the Lutheran Church. He was refused, since he had made no sign of sorrow or repentance during the whole of his period in prison. Nor was repentance in his heart, for he had succeeded, no one knew how, in obtaining a phial of crystals which, when swallowed and dissolved in the acids of the stomach, brought him a slow and painful death.[4]

The guards were alert, watching the prisoners who had received the death sentence and who were soon to be taken down one by one to the gymnasium, led by Goering. Peering through the grille in the cell door, one of the guards saw Goering twisting in convulsions. The doctor was rushed to the cell, but within five minutes, at ten minutes to eleven, Goering lay dead.

Two hours later, in the small hours of the night, Ribbentrop took Goering's place as the first man to die by the rope. Then followed the others, Keitel, Kaltenbrunner, Rosenberg, Frank, Frick, Streicher, Sauckel, Jodl, Seyss-Inquart. Their dead bodies were burned and their ashes were scattered. Goering, who had cheated the scaffold, was thrown with the others into the fire.

APPENDIX

The Reichstag Fire

DURING 1960 the popular German journal *Der Spiegel* published a series of articles by Dr. Fritz Tobias, an official of the Social Democratic Party, challenging the assumption, which at that time was almost universally accepted, that the Reichstag fire on the night of February 27, 1933, was instigated by the Nazis; that Goering and Goebbels, if not Hitler himself, were implicated; that Goering's motive had been to hasten the mass arrest of the leading members of the Communist Party, who were represented as responsible for burning the Reichstag as part of a plot to overthrow the new Nazi regime during its first weeks in power; and that to this end the Nazis introduced the Dutch incendiary van der Lubbe into the Reichstag and then attempted to prove at the trial that he was a Communist agent. (Van der Lubbe, when he could be induced to speak at all, always boasted that he alone was responsible for the fire, yet it was shown at the trial that he could have been in the building for only a comparatively short while, in spite of which the fire he was said to have started spread with tremendous rapidity and caused great damage.)

The claim now made by Dr. Tobias in his articles in *Der Spiegel* was that van der Lubbe was wholly responsible for the fire, that he had set about the arson with great skill and efficiency, and that the Nazis could not in the end be proved to have had anything to do with it. The articles naturally caused a sensation, and the argument was taken up in Britain by A.J.P. Taylor in *History Today* (August 1960) and in the *Sunday Express* (January 22, 1961). Dr. Tobias subsequently elaborated his case in a book of considerable length, *Der Reichstagsbrand* (Grote Verlag, 1962).

Dr. Tobias originally undertook his investigation in order to prove that the Nazis were indeed implicated in the fire, and it was only during his researches that he came to believe the opposite. It did not prove difficult for him to refute the obvious falsifications contained in the notorious *Brown Book of the Hitler Terror*, originally published in Paris in 1934 under the auspices of the Communist Party in order to make Goering appear the central figure in the plot. He also disproved other groundless allegations, for example that van der Lubbe was a homosexual.

But he has allowed his refutations to carry him too far, as Heinrich Fraenkel has shown in an extensive review of Dr. Tobias' book in *Der Monat* (May 1962). In the course of Fraenkel's researches on Goering in Germany and Holland he found evidence that convinced him beyond any doubt of van der Lubbe's psychological maladjustment and his pathological desire for both publicity and martyrdom; of his physical inability to have fired the Reichstag entirely alone; and of his association with the Nazis immediately prior to the fire. Summarized, this evidence is as follows:

1. The testimony of Simon Harteveld of Leiden, the man who trained van der Lubbe when he was a mason's apprentice, that in his teens he became permanently almost blind as the result of a practical joke played on him while he was working on a building site. Everyone who had dealings with van der Lubbe acknowledges the poorness of his vision.

2. The testimony of Harteveld that he indoctrinated van der Lubbe with a particular brand of left-wing politics which was against the party line of the Communists and encouraged him to take individual action on behalf of the proletariat. Van der Lubbe suffered from the psychological maladjustment known as the Herostratus complex, named after the man who burned the temple at Ephesos in order to win fame. The effects of this complex took various forms in van der Lubbe's career before the period of the Reichstag fire. He attempted to gain publicity for himself by starting to swim the Channel without any training or preparation; he tried to claim leadership in a strike at the Tielemann factory with which he had had nothing to do, in order to win fame through his consequent victimization. At another factory he claimed to have smashed windows when the damage had been done by other work-

ers. He was, in fact, determined to be victimized for something.

3. The testimony of a trained nurse, Frau Mimi Storbeck, formerly a German and now a naturalized Dutch subject who is in charge of a children's home in Haarlem. A few days before the fire, when Frau Storbeck was a district nurse in Berlin, van der Lubbe was brought to her by two S.A. men who described him as a foreign vagrant in need of public assistance. The S.A. men did all the talking, and Frau Storbeck realized that van der Lubbe was nearly blind. Although he seemed to be in a state of starvation, he refused to eat the food she offered him.

4. The testimony of Dr. Stomps of Haarlem, the Dutch lawyer who was sent by a committee set up in Holland to investigate van der Lubbe's case in 1933, at the time of the trial. For a full hour he tried in vain to persuade the defendant in his cell to sign the official request which would have given him the right to have the help of a Dutch lawyer in a German court. Van der Lubbe refused to speak to him. Dr. Stomps's final words to him were, "Don't you want to be saved from execution?" Van der Lubbe turned on him with a grin and uttered one word, "No!"

The facts concerning the Reichstag fire are at present being officially investigated by the Institut für Zeitgeschichte in Munich. Meanwhile, no evidence has come to light so far which directly incriminates Goering. But it seems certain now that the Nazis were in some way involved with van der Lubbe, the "official" incendiary.

BIBLIOGRAPHY

The following bibliography contains only those books which are of special importance or interest in the study of Goering's career; it is not intended to represent the history of Germany or of the Third Reich, though certain general histories are included because of their many references to Goering. Readers are referred also to the introductory remarks to the Notes on each chapter, where the titles of books which proved to be of particular importance as sources are given.

Collections of Official Papers

CIANO'S DIPLOMATIC PAPERS, edited by Malcolm Muggeridge. London: Odhams, 1948.

DOCUMENTARY BACKGROUND TO WORLD WAR II, edited by James W. Gantenbein. New York: Columbia University Press, 1948.

DOCUMENTS ON BRITISH FOREIGN POLICY, 1919-39. Second Series, Vols. I-VIII; Third Series, Vols. I-IX. London: His Majesty's Stationery Office, 1946 onward.

DOCUMENTS ON GERMAN FOREIGN POLICY, 1918-45. Series C, Vols. I-III; Series D, Vols. I-IX. London: H.M.S.O., 1949 onward.

DOCUMENTS CONCERNING GERMAN-POLISH RELATIONS AND THE OUTBREAK OF HOSTILITIES BETWEEN GREAT BRITAIN AND GERMANY. London: H.M.S.O., 1939.

DOCUMENTS AND MATERIALS RELATING TO THE EVE OF THE SECOND WORLD WAR, Vols. I and II. Moscow: Foreign Languages Publishing House, 1948.

FRENCH YELLOW BOOK. DIPLOMATIC DOCUMENTS, 1938-39. London: Hutchinson, 1939.

HITLER DIRECTS HIS WAR, edited by Felix Gilbert. New York: Oxford University Press, 1951.

NAZI CONSPIRACY AND AGGRESSION, Vols. I-X. Washington: U.S. Government Printing Office, 1946. English translations of documents collected for the major Nuremberg trial.

POLISH WHITE BOOK. OFFICIAL DOCUMENTS CONCERNING POLISH-GERMAN AND POLISH-SOVIET RELATIONS, 1933-39. London: Hutchinson, 1939.

TRIAL OF THE GERMAN WAR CRIMINALS: PROCEEDINGS OF THE INTERNATIONAL MILITARY TRIBUNAL, Vols. I-XXII. London: H.M.S.O. This is the edition of the Nuremberg trial record that is quoted herein; it is referred to in the notes as I.M.T. A 23-volume edition of the proceedings was published at Nuremberg as *Trial of the Major War Criminals*.

TRIAL OF THE MAJOR WAR CRIMINALS BEFORE THE INTERNATIONAL MILITARY TRIBUNAL. DOCUMENTS IN EVIDENCE, Vols. XXIV-XLII. Nuremberg. The text of the documents accepted in evidence at the chief Nuremberg trial, in their original language.

Historical Studies

Ansel, Walter. HITLER CONFRONTS BRITAIN. Durham, N.C.: Duke University Press, 1960.

Churchill, Winston. THE SECOND WORLD WAR, Vols. I-V. London: Cassell, 1948 onward.

Cooper, R. W. THE NUREMBERG TRIAL. London: Penguin Books, 1947.

Craig, Gordon A. and Gilbert, Felix, editors. THE DIPLOMATS. Princeton, N.J.: Princeton University Press, 1953.

Crankshaw, Edward. GESTAPO. London: Putnam, 1956.

Dulles, Allen Welsh. GERMANY'S UNDERGROUND. New York: Macmillan, 1947.

Fitz Gibbon, Constantine. THE BLITZ. London: Wingate and Ace Books, 1959.

Flanner, Janet. MEN AND MONUMENTS. New York: Harper, 1947.

Jarman, T. L. THE RISE AND FALL OF NAZI GERMANY. London: Cresset, 1955.

Knight-Patterson, W. M. GERMANY FROM DEFEAT TO CONQUEST. London: Allen and Unwin, 1945.

Lee, Asher. THE GERMAN AIR FORCE. London: Duckworth, 1946.

Liddell Hart, B. H. THE OTHER SIDE OF THE HILL: THE GERMAN GENERALS TALK. London: Cassell, 1948.

Namier, L. B. DIPLOMATIC PRELUDE. London: Macmillan, 1948.

———. EUROPE IN DECAY. London: Macmillan, 1950.

———. IN THE NAZI ERA. London: Macmillan, 1952.

Neumann, Franz. BEHEMOTH. London: Gollancz, 1942.

Reed, Douglas. THE BURNING OF THE REICHSTAG. London: Gollancz, 1934.

Reitlinger, Gerald. THE FINAL SOLUTION. London: Valentine Mitchell, 1953.

————. THE SS, ALIBI OF A NATION. London: Heinemann, 1956.

Richards, Denis, and Saunders, Hilary St. George, R.A.F., 1939-45. London: H.M.S.O., 1953-54.

Rieckhoff, H. J. TRIUMPH ODER BLUFF? Geneva: Interavia, 1945.

Rossi, A. THE RUSSO-GERMAN ALLIANCE. London: Chapman and Hall, 1950.

Shirer, William L. THE RISE AND FALL OF THE THIRD REICH. New York: Simon and Schuster, 1960.

Shulman, Milton. DEFEAT IN THE WEST. London: Secker and Warburg, 1949.

SURVEY OF INTERNATIONAL AFFAIRS. Annual surveys for period 1920 to 1938. London: Oxford University Press for the Royal Institute of International Affairs, 1925 onward. Subsequent volumes: THE WORLD IN MARCH, 1939 and HITLER'S EUROPE (2 vols.).

Taylor, A. J. P. THE ORIGINS OF THE SECOND WORLD WAR. London: Hamish Hamilton, 1961.

Wheatley, Ronald. OPERATION SEA LION. New York: Oxford University Press, 1958.

Wheeler-Bennett, J. W. MUNICH, PROLOGUE TO TRAGEDY. London: Macmillan, 1948.

————. NEMESIS OF POWER. London: Macmillan, 1953.

Wiskemann, Elizabeth. THE ROME-BERLIN AXIS. New York: Oxford University Press, 1949.

Memoirs, Diaries and Biographies

Alfieri, Dino. DICTATORS FACE TO FACE. London: Elek, 1954.

Bernadotte, Folke. THE CURTAIN FALLS. New York: Knopf, 1945.

Blood-Ryan, A. W. GOERING, THE IRON MAN OF GERMANY. London: Long, 1938.

Bodenschatz, Karl. JAGD IN FLANDERS HIMMEL. Munich: Verlag Knorrund Hirth, 1935.

Boldt, Gerhardt. IN THE SHELTER WITH HITLER. London: Citadel Press, 1948.

Bormann, Martin. THE BORMANN LETTERS. London: Weidenfeld and Nicolson, 1954.

Bross, Werner. GESPRÄCHE MIT HERMANN GÖRING. Flensburg: Verlag Christian Wolff, 1950.

Bullock, Alan. HITLER. London: Odhams Press, 1952.

Butler, Ewan and Young, Gordon. MARSHAL WITHOUT GLORY. London: Hodder and Stoughton, 1951.

Ciano, Galeazzo. CIANO'S DIARY, 1937-38. London: Methuen, 1952.

————. CIANO'S DIARY, 1939-43. London: Heinemann, 1947.

Coulondre, Robert. DE STALINE À HITLER. Paris: Hachette, 1950.

Dahlerus, Birger. THE LAST ATTEMPT. London: Hutchinson, 1948.

Diels, Rudolf. LUCIFER ANTE PORTAS. Zurich: Zwischen Severing und Heydrich Interverlag, 1949.

Dodd, Martha. THROUGH EMBASSY EYES. New York: Harcourt, Brace & Co., 1939.

Dodd, William E. AMBASSADOR DODD'S DIARY, 1933-38. London: Gollancz, 1948.

Fromm, Bella. BLOOD AND BANQUETS. London: Bles, 1943.

François-Poncet, André. SOUVENIRS D'UNE AMBASSADE À BERLIN. Paris: Flammarion, 1946.

Frischauer, W. GOERING. London: Odhams, 1951.

Galland, Adolf. THE FIRST AND THE LAST. London: Methuen, 1955.

Gilbert, G. M. NUREMBERG DIARY. New York: Farrar, Straus, 1947.

Gisevius, Hans Bernd. PSYCHOLOGY OF DICTATORSHIP. New York: Ronald Press, 1950.

————. TO THE BITTER END. London: Cape, 1948.

Goebbels, Joseph. THE GOEBBELS DIARIES. London: Hamish Hamilton, 1948.

————. MY PART IN GERMANY'S FIGHT. London: Paternoster Library, 1938.

Goering, Hermann. REDEN UND AUFSÄTZE. Munich: Eher, 1935.

————. GERMANY REBORN. London: Elkin Matthews, 1934.

Gritzbach, Erich. HERMANN GOERING: THE MAN AND HIS WORK. London: Hurst and Blackett, 1939.

Guderian, Heinz, PANZER LEADER. London: Michael Joseph, 1952.

Halder, Franz. HITLER AS WARLORD. London: Putnam, 1950.

Halifax, Lord. THE FULNESS OF DAYS. London: Collins, 1957.

Hanfstaengl, Ernst. HITLER: THE MISSING YEARS. London: Eyre and Spottiswoode, 1957.

Hassell, Ulrich von. THE VON HASSELL DIARIES, 1938-44. London: Hamish Hamilton, 1948.

Heiden, Konrad. DER FÜHRER. London: Gollancz, 1944.

Henderson, Sir Nevile. FAILURE OF A MISSION. London: Hodder and Stoughton, 1940.

Hermann, Hauptmann. THE LUFTWAFFE, ITS RISE AND FALL. New York: Putnam, 1943.

Hibbert, Christopher. MUSSOLINI. London: Longmans, 1962.

HITLER'S TABLE TALK. London: Weidenfeld and Nicolson, 1953.

Howe, Thomas C. SALT MINES AND CASTLES. New York: Bobbs Merrill, 1946.

Hossbach, Friedrich. ZWISCHEN WEHRMACHT UND HITLER. Wolfenbütteler Verlagsanstalt, 1949.

Kelley, Douglas M. TWENTY-TWO CELLS IN NUREMBERG. New York: Greenberg, 1947.

Kesselring, Albert. SOLDAT BIS ZUM LETZTEN TAG. Stuttgart: Athenäum Verlag, 1950.

Koller, Karl. DER LETZTE MONAT. Mannheim: Norbert Wohlgemuth Verlag, 1949.

Kirkpatrick, Sir Ivone. THE INNER CIRCLE. London: Macmillan, 1959.

Lochner, Louis. WHAT ABOUT GERMANY? New York: Dodd, Mead, 1942.

———. TYCOONS AND TYRANT. Chicago: Regnery, 1954.

Ludecke, Kurt G. W. I KNEW HITLER. London: Jarrolds, 1938.

Manvell, Roger and Fraenkel, Heinrich. DR. GOEBBELS. New York: Simon and Schuster, 1960.

Papen, Franz von. MEMOIRS. London: Deutsch, 1952.

Rommel, Erwin. THE ROMMEL PAPERS. London: Collins, 1953.

Schacht, Hjalmar. ACCOUNT SETTLED. London: Weidenfeld and Nicolson, 1948.

———. MY FIRST SEVENTY-SIX YEARS. London: Wingate, 1955.

Schellenberg, Walter. THE SCHELLENBERG MEMOIRS. London: Deutsch, 1956.

Schmidt, Paul. HITLER'S INTERPRETER. London: Heinemann, 1951.

Semmler, Rudolf. GOEBBELS, THE MAN NEXT TO HITLER. London: Westhouse, 1947.

Shirer, William L. BERLIN DIARY. New York: Knopf, 1941.

———. END OF A BERLIN DIARY. New York: Knopf, 1947.

Trevor-Roper, H. R. THE LAST DAYS OF HITLER. London: Macmillan, 1947.

Thyssen, Fritz. I PAID HITLER. London: Hodder and Stoughton, 1941.

Valland, Rose. LE FRONT DE L'ART. Paris: Plon, 1961.

Weizsaecker, Ernst von. THE WEIZSAECKER MEMOIRS. London: Gollancz, 1951.

Welles, Sumner. THE TIME FOR DECISION. New York: Harper, 1944.

Wheeler-Bennett, J. W. HINDENBURG: THE WOODEN TITAN. London: Macmillan, 1936.

Wilamowitz-Moellendorff, Fanny von. CARIN GÖRING. Berlin: Verlag von Martin Warneck, 1934.

Young, Desmond. ROMMEL. London: Collins, 1950.

NOTES

CHAPTER 1

The principal sources for this chapter, in addition to the past biographies of Goering which we have consulted, are the personal recollections of Fräulein Erna and Fräulein Fanny Graf of Munich and of Professor Hans Thirring, the eminent physicist, all of whom knew Goering intimately when they were children together. It is Professor Thirring who vouches for the intimate relationship that existed between Frau Franziska Goering and von Epenstein. Any doubt as to Epenstein's Jewish origin is dispelled by the inclusion of his name in the "Semi-Gotha." The legendary or semilegendary feats of Goering's youth are recorded in the official biography written by Erich Gritzbach, *Hermann Goering: The Man and His Work*, the text of which Goering edited himself—and he later insisted on drawing the greater part of the royalties for doing so! Goering's career during the latter part of the First World War is described by Karl Bodenschatz in his book *Jagd in Flanders Himmel*, from which the quotations from Goering's war reports are taken.

We have been able to supplement this book by obtaining additional information from Bodenschatz and from Hermann Dahlmann (see note 4 below). The story of Goering's meeting with Carin von Kantzow is told with great sentiment by her sister, the late Fanny von Wilamowitz-Moellendorff, in her book *Carin Göring*.

1. Goering himself told this story to Dr. Gilbert, the prison psychologist at Nuremberg. See the article by Gilbert in the *Journal of Abnormal and Social Psychology*, Vol. 43, No. 2 (April 1948).

2. The principal stories of Goering's exploits given here originate from Gritzbach's biography, which, it should be remembered, Goering himself edited.

3. A story of some psychological significance was told to Heinrich Fraenkel (whose name will in future be indicated in these notes by the initials H.F.) by Professor Thirring: When Goering was about fifteen years old and already overproud of his exceptional skill and daring as a climber, he arranged to join a team made up of the Thirring brothers and an

Englishman called Bob Dunlop, all much older than himself, who were to make the difficult ascent of the south face of the Gurpetschek. Goering, however, was still at an age when he had to ask his godfather's permission before making such a climb, and, conditions at dawn being just right one morning, the older climbers felt they must go ahead without him, as he was not free to leave at once. When Goering learned that they had gone on he was so furious that he followed them and watched the climb through binoculars. When the others returned in the evening he made a hysterical scene and, almost in tears, accused them of "dishonorable conduct" and a "breach of faith." Then he sneered at their abilities as climbers, calling them mere amateurs.

4. Hermann Dahlmann, a former *General der Flieger* in the Luftwaffe, in conversation with H.F. was more dubious than Bodenschatz of Goering's qualities both as flyer and as officer. He had known Goering well since 1914, and he claims that it was Loerzer who brought pressure to bear on the authorities to get Goering awarded the Pour le Mérite before he had in fact shot down the required twenty-five enemy planes, a score he never achieved. He received the decoration as a "veteran" pilot and was inordinately delighted with it. When later on he was put in command of the Richthofen squadron, he had, according to Dahlmann, more difficulty in maintaining discipline than Bodenschatz makes out, and he became very unpopular with his men on account of his arrogance, an unpopularity that stayed with him long after the war was over—and, indeed, lasted until he came to power and the men who had formerly served under him thought better of trying to avoid him.

5. This account of Captain (later Air Commodore) Beaumont's encounters with Goering appears in Butler and Young, *Marshal without Glory*. When H.F. spoke to him about this he claimed the authors were inaccurate. He did not, however, explain in what way the account was inexact.

6. Quoted in Gritzbach, *op. cit.*, p. 173.

7. This story was told to Roger Manvell (who will in future be indicated in these notes by the initials R.M.) in Stockholm by the Swedish journalist Miss Inger Reimers, who knows the lady concerned and vouches for the truth of the story, which has an amusing corollary. In 1933, when Goering came to power, he sent the lady a signed photograph of himself with his private telephone number. Later this photograph proved to be very useful. During the occupation of Denmark she wrote for an anti-Nazi journal and was visited in the night by the Gestapo. As soon as they found the photograph among her papers they immediately became respectful and withdrew.

8. For Count von Rosen the swastika meant nothing but a

badge that he and some friends had adopted at school and which he came to use as a family symbol. He was to introduce the swastika into the design for his bookplate, and it can still be seen at Rockelstad and in the memorial window to the Rosen family in the House of the Nobility in Stockholm. When the Count presented a plane to Finland during the war against Russia, it too had a swastika painted on it for good luck, and Finland later adopted the symbol for all military planes. This information was given to R.M. in Stockholm by Uno Lindgren, a friend of the Rosen family.

9. A copy of this rare book, printed in German, was shown to R. M. by Uno Lindgren in Stockholm.

10. *Trial of the German War Criminals: Proceedings of the International Military Tribunal* (British edition), IX, pp. 64–65. The volumes of the Nuremberg trial proceedings will in future be indicated by the initials I.M.T.

CHAPTER 2

From the date when this chapter begins, Goering's story for the most part coincides with that of Hitler and the Nazi movement. For general historical background our two principal sources have been William L. Shirer's *The Rise and Fall of the Third Reich* and Alan Bullock's *Hitler—A Study in Tyranny*. For personal information about Goering during this period we are indebted to Ernst Hanfstaengl. The letters written to her parents by Carin Goering are taken from Fanny von Wilamowitz-Moellendorff's biography of her sister. The details of Goering's confinement in Langbro sanatorium are taken principally from Butler and Young, *Marshal without Glory*. The principal psychiatrist at Langbro at the time of Goering's treatment, Professor Olaf Kinberg, died in 1960. R.M., however, interviewed a psychiatrist in Stockholm who had observed Goering during the period immediately preceding his confinement in Langbro, when he was still being treated in private hospitals. He was very violent and had to be put in a strait-jacket. The psychiatrist emphasized, however, that he was not insane; his instability came wholly from the influence of the morphine in his system. During the period of Goering's illness, all reports on individuals made by doctors in Sweden were public documents. This is no longer the case, but when Goering came to power the Communists were able at first to get hold of Goering's medical reports and certificates. The certificate ordering his confinement at Langbro was reproduced in *The Brown Book* in 1933.

1. I.M.T., IX, p. 65.

2. *Hitler's Table Talk*, p. 168.

3. Hanfstaengl, *The Missing Years*, p. 71. See also p. 111.

4. Goering was concerned to keep the story of his rescue from the streets as obscure as possible. This is the account given H.F. by Hanfstaengl: "He told me how he

had managed to crawl up behind one of the monumental lions in front of the Residenz palace after he had been hit. Some of the Brownshirts had then carried him to the first doctor in the Residenzstrasse, who happened to be a Jew; for many years afterward Goering spoke warmly of his kindness and skill." A fuller account was given to H.F. by Dr. T. Eitel, who knew Frau Ballin well, since she was his patient at the Oberstdorf sanatorium. The Ballins were distantly related to the well-known Albert Ballin, the friend of the Kaiser and chief of the Hamburg-America Line. They lived at the Odeonsplatz, according to H.F.'s informant, and Goering was brought to them by some storm troopers, who, unaware that they were Jews, knocked on their door and asked if they were prepared to take in "a wounded man, a knight of the Pour le Mérite." Herr Ballin answered that he was prepared to take in anybody in distress regardless of his decorations. Later, according to the Hanfstaengls, Goering enabled the Ballins to emigrate to South America without too much trouble, taking some of their money with them, a most unusual privilege.

5. Goering was in fact taken across the border to Innsbruck by a Dutchman, a wealthy supporter of the party named Schuler. This information was given to H.F. by Hanfstaengl. The Goerings had a friend in Innsbruck, a specialist in children's ailments called Dr. Sopelsa, to whose house the fugitives were taken. Dr. Sopelsa's widow now lives in Salzburg and is a friend of the Thirrings. She told H.F. how her husband examined Goering's wound and saw that it was necessary to get him to hospital immediately.

6. See Frischauer, *Goering*, p. 64.

7. See Butler and Young, *Marshal without Glory*, pp. 84–87.

CHAPTER 3

Goering's return to Germany brings him back into the history of the Nazi movement as a whole. In addition to the principal sources already mentioned, we have received personal information about Goering during this period from Ernst Hanfstaengl, Hans Streck and Karl Bodenschatz, among others noted in their place. Carin's letters, as before, come from her sister's biographical study, which is also the principal source for the facts concerning her last years with Goering. Goering's own account of his services to the Nazi movement were given in some detail before the International Military Tribunal in Nuremberg.

1. Information concerning Goering's financial situation at this time and his various business commitments was given H.F. by Dr. Justus Koch, Ernst Hanfstaengl and Erhard Milch.

2. Heiden, *Der Führer*, pp. 238–39.

3. During this critical time Goering stayed in Munich at the

house of Hans Streck, whom H.F. interviewed. Streck, a musician, had taken part in the putsch of 1923. It was Roehm who asked the Strecks if they would accommodate Goering, as he had no money for a hotel. He slept on their sofa overnight, leaving the living room when the servant arrived to clean in the morning. He was at first very depressed and even told them of an attempt at suicide, but he was determined to reinstate himself with the party, though this was not easy in view of the criticism of Hitler that, according to Streck, he was known to have made while he was in exile. It was essential to his business career for him to secure from Hitler assurances that he would be allocated one of the seats in the Reichstag won by the Nazi vote at the next election. Only after three meetings with Hitler did he get the promise he needed. He came back happy from this final meeting. In spite of his poverty, Frau Streck remembers his silk pajamas, his black silk kimono embroidered with gold dragons, his signet ring and his well-manicured hands. When he left he inscribed a flowery message of thanks in the Strecks' visitors' book. It is also of interest that Streck was singing tutor to Hitler's overfavorite niece, Geli Raubal. Hanfstaengl also believes Goering's indiscreet attitude to Hitler during his period of exile to be the cause of Hitler's coldness; according to Hanfstaengl, Goering more or less blackmailed Hitler into taking him back after their four and

a half years of separation. After he had succeeded, he rushed in great excitement to Hanfstaengl's house shouting that he was going to be a Reichstag deputy; he told Hanfstaengl that he had challenged Hitler to take him back on grounds of both sentiment and expediency. Hanfstaengl believes that Hitler must have calculated during his meetings with Goering whether it was better for the party to have this excitable man as a friend or as an enemy, and that he decided in the end that he could be a powerful ally, given the opportunity. A few weeks later at a private meeting he announced, "I have decided that Party Comrade Goering is to have a safe seat." See also Hanfstaengl, *Hitler: The Missing Years*, p. 143.

4. See Manvell and Fraenkel, *Dr. Goebbels*, p. 84.

5. Thyssen, *I Paid Hitler*, p. 131.

6. Quotations from Goering's speeches here and below are taken from Gritzbach, *op. cit.*, pp. 128, 74–76.

7. Thyssen, *op. cit.* (p. 142), claims that Goering spent a week with the ex-Kaiser at Doorn in the autumn of 1932.

8. Quoted in Bullock, *Hitler*, p. 146.

9. See Knight-Patterson, *Germany from Defeat to Conquest*, p. 483.

10. Schacht, *My First Seventy-six Years*, p. 279.

11. Opinions seem to vary as to Goering's abilities as a driver. Hitler's opinion is recorded in *Hitler's*

Table Talk, p. 311. Milch agrees that Goering was a dangerous driver. On the other hand, Birger Dahlerus praises Goering's stylishness on the road when he drove him from Carinhall to Berlin. Frau Emmy Goering claims he was a marvelous driver, though in 1934 they both had a near-fatal accident when Goering's car collided with a truck near Rosenheim.

12. See Blood-Ryan, *Goering, the Iron Man of Germany*, pp. 136–37. When Frau von Papen complained to Goering, around the year 1932, about the Nazis' attitude to the Catholics, he replied, "That could soon be changed. Why doesn't the Catholic Church disown the Old Testament?" He pointed out to her that all that mattered was to get rid of the Jewish origins of Christianity. Papen told this to H.F., adding that Goering was probably half joking.

13. Quoted in Blood-Ryan, *op. cit.*, p. 151. Goebbels' comments during this period come from his published diary, *My Part in Germany's Fight*.

14. Quoted in Butler and Young, *Marshal without Glory*, p. 113.

15. Quoted in Blood-Ryan, *op. cit.*, pp. 155–56.

16. I.M.T., IX, p. 69.

17. These tributes to Hitler appear in Goering's book *Germany Reborn*, pp. 77–98.

18. According to Knight-Patterson, *op. cit.* (p. 542), Goering received 367 votes, against 135 for the Socialist candidate and 80 for the Communist candidate.

19. Quoted in Gritzbach, *op. cit.*, p. 142.

20. Papen told H.F. that there were no permanent ill-feelings between himself and Goering as a result of this trick. Papen accepted it as a clever piece of political maneuvering. The quotation from his *Memoirs* appears at p. 208, that from *Germany Reborn* at p. 101, and that from I.M.T. in IX, p. 69.

21. Papen, *op. cit.*, p. 242.

22. Goering, *Germany Reborn*, p. 111. The quotation that follows is from Wheeler-Bennett's life of Hindenburg, *The Wooden Titan*, p. 434.

CHAPTER 4

In addition to the principal sources on the history of Nazi Germany and Goering's evidence at Nuremberg, we have drawn on both the published memoirs and the personal recollection of Papen, Schacht, Hanfstaengl, Schwerin von Krosigk and Hans Bernd Gisevius in obtaining further information for this chapter. We have consulted, among many other sources on the Reichstag fire, the excellent contemporary account written by Douglas Reed, but have supplemented this published material by investigations more particularly concerning the connections between the Dutch incendiary van der Lubbe and the Nazis, which may now be considered incontrovertible. There is still no positive evidence that Goering either initiated or was concerned in initiating the fire. Subsequently he enjoyed maintaining a mystery about whether or not he had known anything about it; it became one of his recurrent jokes. H.F. was present at the legal inquiry into the origins of the fire held in London in 1933, at which such evidence as was brought together (not all of it by any means genuine) was certainly aimed at implicating Goering. At the Nuremberg trial, however, Gisevius made Goebbels the principal instigator of the arson. See also the Appendix to this book, "The Reichstag Fire." For Goering's connection with the Gestapo and the S.S. we have consulted principally Gerald Reitlinger's book on the S.S. Special information was given us by Frau Goering, Karl Bodenschatz and Willy Schade, the expert on forestry who was manager of Goering's shoot. There are innumerable published descriptions of Carinhall written by visitors whom Goering took on conducted tours of his mansion and his estate; their descriptions vary only because the mansion was in a constant state of development. The best description of the estate itself remains that given by Gritzbach in his official biography of Goering.

1. Gritzbach, *op. cit.*, p. 22.

2. Gritzbach to H.F.

3. Papen, *Memoirs*, p. 256.

4. *Documents on British Foreign Policy*, Second Series, IV, pp. 230–31.

5. Quoted in Blood-Ryan, *op. cit.*, pp. 187–88.

6. Quoted in Heiden, *op. cit.* p. 430.

7. Goering, *Germany Reborn*, pp. 126–27.

8. See *Documents on German Foreign Policy*, Series C, I, pp. 93–94.

9. Goering, *Germany Reborn*, p. 134. The quotation that follows is from Frischauer, *op. cit.*, p. 101. Shirer, *op. cit.*, p. 193, quotes the story by Halder. Goering's statement to General Donovan is quoted by Papen in his *Memoirs*, p. 271. Schwerin von Krosigk and Papen both told H.F. about Goering's remarks made during his captivity at Mondorf.

10. *Documents on British Foreign Policy*, Second Series, IV, p. 431.

11. Information given to H.F. by Bertus Smith of The Hague.

12. The first of these two contradictory statements by Diels can be found in Shirer, *op. cit.*, p. 193, the second in Papen's *Memoirs*, p. 271.

13. Martha Dodd's interesting if melodramatic account of the behavior of both Diels and Goering during the trial can be found in her book *Through Embassy Eyes*, pp. 58–62. In spite of Goering's threats, Dimitroff managed to leave Germany after the trial. When Ambassador Dodd published his diary in 1941, he claimed that Diels (who was already hostile to Goering and in danger because of certain knowledge he possessed about the Reichstag fire) appealed to an unnamed American journalist to do what he could to save Dimitroff from assassination. The story was then carefully

leaked to the foreign press and thus elicited a denial from Goebbels, who admitted that Goering, who was away at the time, had spoken indiscreetly. When Hanfstaengl's book appeared in 1957, he recalled that Martha Dodd told him what her father had learned and that, together with Louis Lochner, he arranged for Goering's press officer, Sommerfeldt, to lunch with a new and inexperienced representative of Reuter's agency who could brashly blurt out the rumor he had heard and ask for a statement on Goering's behalf. Sommerfeldt was then forced to vouch for Dimitroff's right to quit Germany unmolested, which he did. Unfortunately for Hanfstaengl, Goering subsequently found out his part in this affair. Martha Dodd makes no mention of this matter in her book.

14. A legal inquiry into the causes of the Reichstag fire was organized privately in London during the autumn of 1933 on the premises of the Law Society in Carey Street. The chairman was Lord Marley, and Sir Stafford Cripps headed a group of prominent lawyers who sifted the evidence presented by many witnesses who had recently fled from Germany; H.F. was present. The inquiry has frequently been regarded as Communist-inspired; though many prominent Communists took part, those conducting the inquiry were by no means entirely from the left. For instance, the well-known American lawyer Arthur Garfield Hays took part and subsequently attended the trial at Leipzig; he describes his experiences in his book *City Lawyer* (1942). Lawyers from several countries were observers at the inquiry.

15. Quoted in Shirer, *op. cit.*, p. 195.

16. The text of Hitler's telegram is given in Blood-Ryan, *op. cit.*, p. 211; Goering's account appears in his *Germany Reborn*, p. 136.

17. Kropp gave this account to H.F.

18. Frau Goering gave H.F. the following details of her first acquaintance and subsequent friendship with Goering: Her first meeting was casual only, during a party rally in Weimar at which a private performance of scenes from the German classics in which she appeared had been arranged. The meeting that finally led to their friendship took place some months later in 1932, also at Weimar, when they were introduced to each other by a mutual woman friend. They walked and talked about Carin, whose death was still much on Goering's mind. By the time he was made president of the Reichstag they were living together in his flat on the Kaiserdamm, where Emmy had her own room which Goering took pride in furnishing as well as he could afford.

19. A possible affair with Margarete von Schirach is mentioned in Blood-Ryan, *op. cit.*, p. 262. That with Käthe Dorsch belonged to his youth, and she remained a friend of the family after the mar-

riage of Goering and Emmy, though Goering remained strictly faithful to Emmy.

20. For these statements see Alan Bullock's *Hitler*, p. 235, and Heiden, *Der Führer*, p. 462.

21. Thyssen, *op. cit.*, pp. 68, 168.

22. Rieckhoff in *Triumph oder Bluff?* (p. 37) infers that Goering forced Hindenburg's hand in the matter of his promotion by announcing to the press in advance that he had been made a general. Milch told H.F. that this story was untrue. He was himself sent to Blomberg to discuss a number of promotions, including his own and Goering's. He told Blomberg that Goering expected to be created a full general and certainly not a major general as Blomberg had intended, since Goering was at that time only a captain. Blomberg finally agreed and on October 19, 1933, Goering was made a general, and the promotion was backdated to October 1, 1931, in order to give him seniority. Goering was delighted.

23. The principal source for Goering's private habits is the information given by Robert Kropp to H.F. Details provided by the cutter, Cap, which follow, were also given in conversation with H.F.

24. A number of the particulars that follow come from Blood-Ryan, *op. cit.*, pp. 216–25.

25. Hanfstaengl, *op. cit.*, p. 212.

26. Galland, *The First and the Last*, p. 17.

27. See *Documents on British Foreign Policy*, Second Series, VI, pp. 749–51.

28. Details of this ceremony of interment were given H.F. by Bodenschatz, who played a prominent part in bringing the body to Carinhall. Bodenschatz also examined Himmler's car; there were holes in the windshield, but they could just as likely have been made by flying stones as by bullets.

CHAPTER 5

Special sources for this and the next chapter, in both of which Goering's life is closely bound to the history of the regime as a whole, include Papen, Bodenschatz and Schacht; of considerable interest and importance are the published memoirs of ambassadors, ministers and diplomats, such as Nevile Henderson, Lord Halifax, François-Poncet, Coulondre, Kirkpatrick and, to a lesser extent, Ambassador Dodd. The comments of Ciano and Hassell are useful, and we have drawn considerably on the published *Documents on German Foreign Policy* and the *Documents on British Foreign Policy*, together with the diplomatic papers published in the *Polish War Book*, the *French Yellow Book* and other collections as indicated below. Namier's studies of diplomacy were of particular use—*Diplomatic Prelude*, *In the Nazi Era* and *Europe in Decay*; so also were the studies published annually up to 1938 for the Royal Institute of International Affairs, the *Survey of International Affairs* and the subsequent volumes, *Hitler's Europe*. Elizabeth Wiskemann's *Rome-Berlin Axis* is helpful on Goering's relations with the Italians. Goering's own evidence at Nuremberg and the account of his activities that he gave in *Germany Reborn*, a book written specially for publication in England in 1934, have been drawn on, and so have the published reminiscences of Paul Schmidt, Hitler's official interpreter, who also worked for Goering. Information concerning the nature of the periodic cures for drug addiction which Goering underwent were obtained from the Kahle sanatorium in Cologne and from Robert Kropp. Dahlerus, of course, published his own recollections of his discussions with Goering in his book *The Last Attempt*.

1. See I.M.T., IX, p. 79.

2. The entire German police were united under one department in June 1936. Writing in 1937, Gritzbach, Goering's official biographer, says (p. 42) that his "direct and intimate connection with the German police remains as direct and intimate today as it was when he placed Himmler over them." He then speaks of the "mutual trust and comradeship" between Goering and Himmler "in the pursuit of their common task."

3. Papen confirmed in conversation with H.F. that Goering undoubtedly saved his life by placing him under house arrest.

4. See Wheeler-Bennett, *Nemesis of Power*, p. 323.

5. This account of the cere-

mony was confirmed by Milch in conversation with H.F.

6. Goering was echoing a remark once made by Dr. Lueger, mayor of Vienna and a notorious anti-Semite. There is ample evidence that Goering helped many Jews whom he favored for one reason or another, such as the Ballins, whose story has already been told. Frau Goering assiduously brought to his attention cases she thought deserving and interceded for the men and women involved; so also did Käthe Dorsch and Gustaf Gründgens, the famous actor, who was another family friend.

7. Kropp told H.F. about Frau Goering's first knowledge that Goering wanted to marry her: "I was to drive her somewhere where the Chief was to join her for the weekend—I think it was Weimar. The Chief had given me a sealed envelope which I was to hand to Frau Sonnemann with strict instructions she was not to open it until we had arrived. She took the envelope, but, being a woman, she opened it at once. I saw her beam with delight; she jumped straight out of the car before we started, rushed back into the house, where she had just left Goering, and threw her arms round him. Only later did I learn what was in the letter—just two words in the Chief's handwriting: 'Wir heiraten' [We're getting married]."

8. Schmidt, *Hitler's Interpreter*, pp. 30, 32.

9. See Namier, *Diplomatic Prelude*, pp. 220–21; the *Polish War Book*, pp. 25–26; *Survey of Inter-*

national Affairs, 1935, I, pp. 205–6. For the April mission below, see Schmidt, *op. cit.*, pp. 27–30.

10. See Bullock, *Hitler*, p. 328.

11. See I.M.T., IV, p. 66.

12. Schacht's account of his battle with Goering over economic policy can be found in his memoirs, *My First Seventy-six Years*, Chapter 49. See also *Account Settled*, pp. 98–100. On the matter of Goering's ability as a minister handling economic affairs, Winkler, one of Hitler's principal advisers on such matters, subsequently told H.F. that Goering could assess a balance sheet by intuition. When H.F. repeated this to Schacht he merely laughed and said, "Goering as an economist was a bloody fool." But in many respects Goering was a good executive who knew how to delegate authority.

13. For these various meetings in Italy see Wiskemann, *Rome-Berlin Axis*, pp. 72–74; Schmidt, *op. cit.*, pp. 62–64; the *Ciano Papers*, pp. 80–81, and *Documents on German Foreign Policy*, Series D, I, Nos. 199, 208.

14. See Hibbert, *Mussolini*, p. 83.

15. See *Survey of International Affairs*, 1937, I, pp. 325-26, 409, 471n.

16. Ellen Wilkinson gave her own account of this episode to H.F.

17. For the visits of Lord Londonderry to Goering see Schmidt, *op. cit.*, p. 52, and Papen's *Memoirs*, p. 399; for the visit of the Windsors, Schmidt, p. 74.

18. See François-Poncet, *Souvenirs d'une ambassade à Berlin*, pp. 10, 272, and Coulondre, *De Stalin à Hitler*, pp. 272-77.

19. *Polish White Book*, pp. 36-39.

20. Henderson, *Failure of a Mission*, p. 80. The quotations that follow are from p. 84.

CHAPTER 6

The principal sources for background have already been outlined in the introductory note to Chapter 5. Special evidence as to Goering's income and financial resources was given us by Dr. Justus Koch, Frau Goering's legal adviser, from whom we obtained a copy of an affidavit on the subject sworn after the war by Herr Gerch, the senior administrative officer in charge of Goering's personal affairs from 1937 to 1945.

1. *Hassell Diaries*, pp. 23-24. Milch in conversation with H.F. considered that Goering knew something at any rate of the record of Blomberg's wife before he married her. Milch was present when Hitler was confronted with the homosexual boy who was prepared to become Fritsch's accuser. See also Wheeler-Bennett, *Nemesis of Power*, Gerald Reitlinger's *SS*, and Schellenberg's *Memoirs*, p. 32.

2. A complete copy of the transcriptions is held at the Wiener Library in London, and it is from this that our quotations are taken.

3. Goering's activities during the night of the *Anschluss* and the

following day receive particular attention in *Survey of International Affairs*, 1938, II, pp. 62-64; Namier, *Europe in Decay*, pp. 174-76; Wheeler-Bennett's *Munich*; and Henderson's *Failure of a Mission*. See also *Documents on German Foreign Policy*, Series D, II, pp. 157, 164, 168, 183, and *Documents* on British Foreign Policy, Series III, I, pp. 32, 36, 40, 44.

4. Transcript of Goering's telephone call to Ribbentrop held at the Wiener Library.

5. See *Documents on British Foreign Policy*, Third Series, I, Nos. 152, 241, 439.

6. For the statements made by Goering in this paragraph see I.M.T., IV, 67; Trial Documents R-140 and USA 160; *Survey of International Affairs*, 1938, III, pp. 43-44, 530-32; and Shirer, *Rise and Fall of the Third Reich*, pp. 476-77.

7. See *Survey of International Affairs*, 1938, II, pp. 302-3.

8. This famous document was quoted endlessly at Nuremberg. Our transcription is taken from the copy held by the Wiener Library.

9. Trial Document PS 710. Quoted in Reitlinger, *Final Solution*, p. 21.

10. Goering's methods of work were described to H.F. by Milch, Bodenschatz, Brauchitsch, Wohltat and Schwerin von Krosigk and supported in an interrogation of Diels that took place on October 22, 1945. Kesselring's quotation comes from his *Soldat bis zum Letzten*, p. 160. Speer's statements

come from a series of interrogations conducted during August and September 1945.

11. Bernd von Brauchitsch described this conversation to H.F.

12. See *Documents on German Foreign Policy*, Series D, II, Nos. 248 and 284; *Documents and Materials relating to the Eve of the Second World War* (U.S.S.R. Ministry of Foreign Affairs), I, pp. 149-50.

13. Richthofen's request is recorded in *Documents on German Foreign Policy*, Series D, III, No. 695.

14. *Ibid.*, II, No. 816.

15. *Ibid.*, IV, Nos. 68, 69 and 112. Also Bullock, *op. cit.*, p. 440, and Shirer, *Rise and Fall of the Third Reich*, p. 433.

16. Goering also admitted this at the time to Henderson. See *British Blue Book*, pp. 18-19. And see Wheeler-Bennett, *Munich*, p. 344.

17. Goering, of course, carried such instruments for other purposes. Milch told H.F. about this point of detail.

18. See Alfieri, *Dictators Face to Face*, p. 25.

19. See *Documents on British Foreign Policy*, Series III, V, Nos. 377 and 510.

20. See *German-Polish Relations*, May 28, 1939, and *Documents on German Foreign Policy*, Series III, V, Nos. 658-659. Also Henderson, *Failure of a Mission*, pp. 225-27.

21. See *Nazi Conspiracy and Aggression*, VI, pp. 718-31.

22. For reference to these meetings of the Council, see I.M.T.,

XVIII, p. 67; for the British ambassador's report see *German-Polish Relations*, p. 119, and *Documents on British Foreign Policy*,
Series III, VII, No. 263; for reference to the Vogler report, see
Louis P. Lochner, *Tycoons and
Tyrants*, p. 58.

23. Goering had for some time
been pressing for an increase in the
importation of raw materials from
Russia; see Shirer, *Rise and Fall
of the Third Reich*, pp. 476-77.
For Bodenschatz's visit to the embassies, see Namier, *Diplomatic
Prelude*, p. 189.

24. There can be little doubt
as to Goering's sincerity in not
wanting war; this attitude is not
at variance with his opportunism.
That war was probably inevitable
at some distant date in the future
he obviously accepted, but he
hoped that hostilities would be
postponed as long as possible for
his own comfort as well as for the
good of Germany. This attitude
coincided with that of Hitler's
generals and led them to consider
replacing Hitler by Goering when
the Führer forced the war on them
sooner than they wanted it.

25. For a fuller consideration of
Goering's dealings in art see Chapter 8.

26. The names of the seven
businessmen were given at the
Nuremberg trial; see I.M.T., IX,
p. 230. The names as they are reproduced are misspelled in a number of instances. They should read:
Charles McLaren and C. F. Spen-
cer, who were directors of John
Brown and Co.; S. W. Rawson, a

Sheffield manufacturer; Sir Robert
Renwick; Brian Mountain; A. Hol-
den; and T. Mensforth, a member
of a large electrical firm.

27. Apparently Goering made
his famous boast on a number of
occasions. See Shirer, *Rise and Fall
of the Third Reich*, p. 517n.;
Semmler, *Goebbels*, p. 97n. Meier
is the most common of all German names.

28. See Halifax, *Fulness of
Days*, p. 209.

29. See above page.

30. See Namier, *Diplomatic
Prelude*, p. 331. Goering seems to
have been the last person Hitler
informed of this cancellation.
Compare the situation later when
he was not consulted by Hitler
over the reply sent to the British
ultimatum. See also the quotation
from an interrogation of Goering
after the war given in Shirer, *op.
cit.*, p. 557.

31. At Nuremberg Goering
strenuously denied behaving to
Hitler in this manner.

32. See the *Hassell Diaries*, pp.
69-72. On the same day, August
31, Thyssen claims he sent a telegram to Goering urging him to
secure a period of truce "to gain
time for negotiation"; later, on
September 22, he sent him a memorandum from his place of exile in
France demanding, among other
things, that the German public be
told that he, Thyssen, was against
war. Goering, according to Thyssen, demanded that he come back
and recant, in which event he
would suffer no recrimination for
what he had done and said. Thys-

sen refused. See his *I Paid Hitler*, pp. 33, 36, 39-43 and 45.

33. The text Goering gave Dahlerus is fuller than that which was subsequently published. See Dahlerus, *The Last Attempt*, and Namier, *Diplomatic Prelude*, pp. 430-31.

34. See Henderson, *Failure of a Mission*, pp. 275, 282. Also Namier, *Diplomatic Prelude*, p. 377n. It would seem that Goering gave Henderson a copy of the note withheld from him by Ribbentrop.

CHAPTER 7

In addition to our principal background sources, information for this chapter was gathered from Telford Taylor, *March of Conquest*; Elizabeth Wiskemann, *Rome-Berlin Axis*; Asher Lee, *The German Air Force* and *Blitz on Britain*; Adolf Galland, *The First and the Last*; Constantine Fitzgibbon, *The Blitz*; Reitlinger, *The Final Solution* and *SS*; Walter Ansel, *Hitler Confronts England*; H. J. Rieckhoff, *Triumph oder Bluff?*; and B. H. Liddell Hart, *The Other Side of the Hill*. We have also drawn on the diaries of Hassell, Ciano and Semmler and the memoirs and papers of Sumner Welles, Alfieri, Paul Schmidt, Schacht, Schellenberg, Goebbels and Rommel. The I.M.T. *Trial Proceedings* and the associated documents published in *Nazi Conspiracy and Aggression* are of great importance for the period of the war, and we are specially grateful for the personal help and advice we have received for this period from Galland, Milch, Schacht, Semmler, Schwerin von Krosigk, Brauchitsch and Bodenschatz.

1. The strategy of blitzkrieg was expounded as early as 1921 by the Italian General Douhet in his book *The Command of the Air* (see Fitzgibbon, *The Blitz*, Chapters 1 and 2). Goering knew Douhet's book and admired it.

2. Taylor, *March of Conquest*, p. 25.

3. This significant statement by Goering was reported to H.F. by Bodenschatz. However, both Bodenschatz and Brauchitsch deny that Goering had secret intentions to join any conspiracy against Hitler.

4. See documents belonging to this period in *Documents on German Foreign Policy*, Series D, V.

5. See I.M.T., II, p. 421 *et seq.*, and IV, p. 71.

6. Galland quotes the following monthly figures for the production of fighter, as distinct from bomber, aircraft: 1940, 125; 1941 (under Udet), 375; beginning 1942, 250; 1943 (under Milch), 1,000; autumn 1944 (under Speer), 2,500. The ratio of fighters to bombers in 1939 was about 1 to 3; in 1940, only 1 to 4. Official American surveys conducted after the war emphasize the astonishingly low level of the German output of armaments during the period 1940–42; British production was in fact higher than that of Germany, which still seemed to be thinking in terms of a short war. British production figures for fighter planes during the middle months of

1940 reached almost 500 a month. Himmler's intelligence service was far more accurate in these matters than Goering's, but Goering naturally preferred to gather comfort from the lower figures given him by his own men. See Schellenberg, *op. cit.*, p. 125.

7. See Rossi, *The Russo-German Alliance*, p. 109.

8. *Ciano's Diary*, 1939–43, p. 210. See also Wiskemann, *op. cit.*, p. 180, and Rossi, *op. cit.*, p. 54.

9. Shirer, *Berlin Diary*, p. 299.

10. Trial Document EC 606.

11. General Student reported this to Liddell Hart. See the latter's *The Other Side of the Hill*, p. 149.

12. During 1938 General Felmy had been told to prepare a plan for the annihilation of British resistance by air attack. The plan he produced was intended to prove that the Luftwaffe could not achieve this; the operation would be beyond its likely strength. Goering scrawled his wrath on the plan: "I did not ask for a study that sets forth the possibilities and establishes our weaknesses—these I alone know best of all." Jeschonnek sent the plan back to Felmy with an oral message that if Goering "commits the Luftwaffe against England in a concentration of all squadrons, then will the heavens over London grow dark." Felmy foresaw such awkward problems as the need for an exceptionally strong fighter cover for Goering's bombers and the lack of any training in navigation in flight over the sea. See Ansel, p. 191, and Rieckhoff, pp. 16–17 and 110.

13. Goering refused Raeder's request that the Luftwaffe should mine Scapa Flow and the estuaries to hamper the British fleet during the movement of German ships to Norway.

14. Rieckhoff in *Triumph oder Bluff?* gives an extraordinary picture of the Luftwaffe command, with the technical men at loggerheads with the designers and manufacturers, and many of the senior officers, promoted too rapidly, anxious to cover up deficiencies and save face before Goering and Hitler, who soon had a totally false impression of the forces at their disposal. The ground organization was given a tremendously luxurious look in order that the morale of the young flyers, as the elite of the master race, should be kept as head-in-cloud as possible.

15. A copy of Halder's diary is deposited with the Wiener Library. Jodl's diary can be found in *Nazi Conspiracy and Aggression*, IV, pp. 377–411.

16. Shirer, *Rise and Fall of the Third Reich*, p. 733. Halder in his pamphlet *Hitler as Warlord* (published first in German in 1949) anticipated the accusation against Goering expressed in his letter to Shirer. There he wrote (p. 30): "The encirclement of the French and British forces, which was the aim of the whole occupation, had been on the point of being achieved, when Goering warned Hitler against leaving such a success to the generals, suggesting that if he did they might win a

prestige with the German people which would threaten his own position. Goering offered the services of his Air Force to complete the destruction of the almost encircled enemy, without any help from the Army." This accusation was based, according to Halder, on statements made in 1946 by two senior Air Force officers. Other factors in the decision were Hitler's desire to conserve the armored divisions for the conquest of France, and the fact that the territory round Dunkirk was unsuitable for tanks. Also, the almost miraculous evacuation from the harbor and the beaches was certainly not foreseen as possible.

17. Milch gave this information to H.F.

18. According to Butler and Young in *Marshal without Glory* (p. 202), Goering even tried, in vain as it happened, to take over the British embassy as a private residence.

19. Shirer, *Berlin Diary*, p. 435. During July Goering again met Dahlerus and suggested that the King of Sweden might attempt to set up a peace conference between the Germans and the British. See I.M.T., IX, pp. 220–21.

20. On July 22, 1938, Goering had spent a day on the new German destroyer *Hermann Schumann*. He showed his contempt for the Navy by saying, "From the summer of 1939, Germany will possess air formations that present such a threat to the British fleet that utilization of its home bases will be rendered impossible." He was fond of saying, "I will need the Navy only as submarine weather-reporting stations in the Atlantic." (Ansel, *op. cit.*, p. 111.)

21. At the start of the Battle of Britain the R.A.F., it is estimated by Ronald Wheatley in his book *Operation Sea Lion*, had some 600 to 700 fighters in service; the Luftwaffe had some 950 fighters, 1,000 level bombers and 300 dive bombers. Denis Richards, official historian of the R.A.F., puts the number of German aircraft on active service, including units available from both Scandinavia and France, as 250 dive bombers, 1,000 level bombers and 1,000 fighters, whereas the British had only some 700 fighters with which to oppose them. Rieckhoff, however, makes (*op. cit.*, p. 82) a sobering comment on Luftwaffe statistics, proving that a unit supposed to have forty-five planes available could have, say, twenty in operation one day and literally none the next through damage, nondelivery, overhaul, engine maintenance, mechanical alteration, radio repair. Hence Goering was often deploying paper aircraft and cursing their nonappearance over Britain.

22. The German losses in the fortnight August 23 to September 6 were 378 aircraft; the British losses were 277. In the following fortnight, during the London blitz, Germany lost a further 262 planes, to the British loss of 144. When the day raids ended in October Galland put the losses at about one third of the bombers and one quarter of the fighters.

Meanwhile in aircraft production Britain outpointed Germany by constructing 9,924 planes during 1940 to Germany's 8,070 (see Shirer, *Rise and Fall of the Third Reich*, p. 781).

23. See Koller's statement to Frischauer in *Goering*, p. 213. Milch gave his opinion to H.F. that Hitler had by no means given up the idea of invading Britain at some time in the future, and that it is unlikely that the thought of invading Russia had taken definite shape in his mind as early as this.

24. See Rossi, *The Russo-German Alliance*, p. 121.

25. See I.M.T., IX, p. 136; Shulman, *Defeat in the West*, quoting an interrogation of Goering by the Americans, pp. 56–57; and Student's statement to Liddell Hart, *op. cit.*, pp. 231–33.

26. Milch in conversation with H.F. For the background to Goering and Student's visit to Hitler see Liddell Hart, *op. cit.*, pp. 228–31.

27. Trial Document PS 2718.

28. I.M.T., III, p. 6; *Nazi Conspiracy and Aggression*, V, p. 378. See also I.M.T., III, pp. 4–7; IV, pp. 75–76; VI, pp. 151–54; and Trial Documents PS 2718 and 1743 and USSR 10.

29. For the full text in translation of this conference, see *Hitler's Europe*, II, pp. 230–36. For Goering's excuses about this conference see I.M.T., IX, p. 317 *et seq.*

30. I.M.T., IV, p. 75, and VII, pp. 231–32.

31. See I.M.T., IV, p. 79, and IX, p. 250. See also Shirer, *Rise*

and Fall of the Third Reich, p. 964. On May 20, 1941, Goering had banned all voluntary emigration by the Jews from France and Belgium on the grounds that this cut across the main evacuation scheme and so anticipated the "final solution" which was now so close at hand. See Reitlinger, *Final Solution*, p. 82.

32. See I.M.T., IV, pp. 71-72.

33. It has been suggested that Goering was directly responsible for driving Udet to suicide. Bernd von Brauchitsch denies this; in conversation with H.F. he claimed that Udet was literally worried to death by work for which he was unsuited and because of trouble with a woman.

34. *Ciano's Diplomatic Papers*, pp. 464–65.

35. See I.M.T., IV, pp. 71–73, and XV, p. 183 (Documents PS 1666 and 1183). See also *Nazi Conspiracy and Aggression*, IV, p. 183.

36. I.M.T., VII, p. 167 *et seq.*; IX, p. 322 *et seq.*; and XV, p. 203. Documents USSR 170.

37. See Schellenberg, *op. cit.*, pp. 216–17, 300–301, 344.

38. For these initial meetings with Goebbels see his *Diaries*, pp. 96 *et seq.* and 142–43.

39. Papers relating to the Pieper case are preserved in the Wiener Library.

40. See Schacht, *My First Seventy-six Years*, pp. 418–19.

41. For the relations of Goering and the Rommels, see Young, *Rommel*, pp. 179–80, and *The Rommel Papers*, pp. 366–69.

42. See *Ciano's Diary*, 1939–43, pp. 529–32.

43. Halder, *Hitler as Warlord*, p. 6.

44. The generals in giving their opinion of Goering had little love to spare. See Liddell Hart, *op. cit.*, pp. 130, 456, and Shulman, *op. cit.*, pp. 85–86.

45. Schwerin von Krosigk gave this information to H.F.

46. Semmler, *Goebbels*, p. 60.

47. I.M.T., IX, p. 200.

SPECIAL NOTE:

In testimony made by Goering during interrogation by a British investigator at Nuremberg (April 6, 1946), he claimed to have been responsible for the entire air war against Britain. The pause that followed the collapse of France was due, he said, partly to the need to reorganize and strengthen the Luftwaffe, and partly to uncertainty in his own mind whether the invasion of England or the conquest of the Mediterranean should come first. He also explained that the diversion of his bombing attacks from the strategic centers of the R.A.F. to London in order to fulfill Hitler's demand for retribution prevented him from destroying the principal defense in Britain against the invasion, namely the R.A.F. and the Navy, though he also admitted that the Germans were very short of shipping space. Both the Air Force and the Navy would have had to be crippled from the air before any landing could have been successful. He told Hitler that Britain's morale would never be broken by the raids on London; Bath was attacked, he said, because on one occasion he had mentioned to Hitler that government offices had been evacuated there from London. In reply to a direct question on the fact of the matter, he admitted with a broad grin that he never himself flew on any mission over Britain in wartime, and this was recently confirmed to the authors by Brauchitsch.

We are very grateful to Mr. McLouis Jacketts, head of the Air Ministry Historical Branch, and to Mr. Denis Richards, co-author of *R.A.F., 1939–45*, the officially sponsored history of the R.A.F. during the Second World War, for supplying details of the above interrogation of Goering. Mr. Richards has also made for us the following assessment of Goering as Commander in Chief of the Luftwaffe:

"That the Luftwaffe was beaten and broken long before the German land forces tasted defeat in the west was in no small measure the fault of its own corpulent chief. The swashbuckling, the bonhomie and the easy charm had served well enough in the years of the prewar buildup, and up to the point where the German military machine cut its all-too-easy way across the Low Countries and France. But as soon as the Channel was reached and a new and unrehearsed phase of the war opened up, his imperfections as commander became clear. At the very beginning of the Battle of

Britain he called off, almost as soon as they had started, the German attacks on our coastal radar stations—attacks which, had they been continued, might well have decided the whole issue. A few weeks later he threw away his second great chance. He abandoned his very successful onslaught against our fighter sector stations and turned instead to bombing London. This he did on direct orders from Hitler, and here we have one of the keys to his weakness as a commander: he presented to Hitler no considered or consistent plan either for the development or for the strategic employment of the German Air Force, but simply bowed to the Führer's erratic bidding. This he did even when he knew the Führer's bidding to be nonsense.

"Above all, although the Luftwaffe in 1940 possessed radio aids to night attack far beyond anything then in service with the R.A.F., Goering had given no serious thought to air operations outside the two spheres of direct military support and simple terrorization. He proved unable either to mount an effective strategic attack or to repel one. Typical of his limitations was his later mishandling of the Me 262—the first jet aircraft to see service.

"Long before the end of the war, Goering's inadequacy as head of the Luftwaffe was almost notorious. He was receiving the fruits of German scientific invention, but failing to organize or employ them effectively. Unable to repel the Anglo-American attacks, he was also without means of mounting any comparable offensive of his own; at a time when the Allied bombing was becoming increasingly accurate and successful, the Luftwaffe could retaliate on the British homeland only with their vexatious but indiscriminate and, in the circumstances, ineffective V weapons. But by then the once brilliant figure of the Reich Marshal had long ceased to dominate any scene beyond the confines of his own Carinhall. Immured on his private estate remote from the storm centers, he had become more and more a cipher—a vehicle for the transmission of unsound orders from Hitler, and a figure increasingly ignored by his able subordinates who were actually fighting the war."

CHAPTER 8

There are a number of books which deal either wholly or partially with the Nazi despoilation of the art collections of Europe. The principal of these are *Salt Mines and Castles*, by Thomas C. Howe, and Rose Valland's *Le Front de l'art*. The matter was much discussed at the Nuremberg trial, and the principal documents connected with the Rosenberg Task Force are included in the documents published in connection with the trial. H.F., however, made special investigation in Germany, Holland and France, and received invaluable help from the Rijksinstituut voor Oorlog Documentatie in Amsterdam, where considerable material exists concerning Goering's art deals during the war, and from Dr. Bruno Lohse, Goering's art adviser and agent in Paris. He also met Andreas Hofer and Mlle. Valland. The well-known but still "classified" Report on Art Looting compiled for the Office of Strategic Services in 1945 also provided us with valuable information.

1. Gretl Afzelius (nee Thirring, sister of Professor Hans Thirring) told H.F. how proudly Goering would refer to the family castles. When she was first introduced to his Swedish relatives, Goering said airily of her, "She was brought up at one of our castles!"

2. Frau Emmy Goering told this story to H.F.

3. See Thomas C. Howe, *Salt Mines and Castles*, p. 210; also I.M.T., IX, p. 125.

4. The Art Looting Investigation Report, known as the Rousseau Document after Theodore Rousseau, one of the principal investigators along with Thomas C. Howe, reveals that Goering's art collection before the war only amounted to some 200 pictures.

5. See I.M.T., III, pp. 62–65; IV, p. 72; IX, p. 115. The principal Trial Documents involved are PS 136, 138, 141, 3042.

6. See I.M.T., III, pp. 69–71. Among the more famous collections stolen by Rosenberg in collaboration with the Vichy government were those of the Rothschild family and the Katz, Kahn, Weill, Seligmann and Schloss collections.

These and many other collections were seized on the specious excuse that they might be smuggled out of France into Spain. Goering insisted that the French authorities should have first call on whatever they required for the Louvre, and the works sent to Germany were sometimes paid for, though at a very low valuation. The money earned this way was paid to the Vichy Commission for Jewish Affairs, never to the original owners.

7. Trial Document PS 1985. See also I.M.T., VII, p. 180.

8. Dr. Lohse told H.F. of the case of the eighty-year-old Jewish art expert Professor Friedlaender. He had left Germany for Holland, and after the occupation Goering did what he could to protect him. When eventually the Gestapo arrested him, Lohse flew to Berlin to intercede with Goering, who told him Hitler had forbidden him to act any further on behalf of deserving Jews. "You know how I admire the old man," said Goering. "But I can't do a thing." Then he grinned at Lohse. "But why don't you do something yourself? Use your initiative!" Lohse, without using Goering's name, bluffed the Gestapo into releasing Friedlaender, who survived the war, staying in Amsterdam. Shortly before his death he gave Lohse a signed photograph to commemorate his intervention.

9. Document in Rijksinstituut, Amsterdam.

10. *Ibid.*

11. *Ibid.*

12. See Janet Flanner, *Men and*

Monuments, p. 248. Also documents held at the Rijksinstituut, Amsterdam.

13. De Boer in conversation with H.F.

14. Goering paid nearly two million guilders for his bogus Vermeer, partly in cash and partly by exchanging against the price of the picture some thirty works whose combined valuation still fell short of the total for the "Vermeer." The Vermeers themselves emerged in a carefully contrived atmosphere of secrecy; Hofer only managed to see the first of them with difficulty in case he might be wanting to acquire it for Goering. This was the Christ in the House of Mary and Martha. It had been brought to the dealer de Boer, nailed to the bottom of a wooden box, by its owner, who insisted on remaining anonymous. When Hofer did eventually see it, he accepted it as genuine, as did his wife, who was an expert cleaner and restorer of pictures, and he wrote to Goering on July 7, 1943, describing the picture as "the latest sensation" but advising against paying for it the enormous sum the anonymous owner demanded. De Boer, however, had heard there was a second "Vermeer" that had been discovered and he said that he would try to find it for Goering. But in September 1943 Alois Miedl, the German art dealer who had taken over the Goudstikker Gallery, telephoned Hofer from Amsterdam to report that he was coming to Berlin with a very important picture. This proved to be the Christ and the Woman Taken in Adultery; this was also nailed to the bottom of a wooden box and had an anonymous owner who was demanding two million guilders for the work. Goering managed to forestall an attempt to acquire this picture for Hitler, and after much bartering he finally agreed to pay in the manner described above the price of 1,650,-000 guilders. The anonymous owner was van Meegeren himself.

15. Held in the Deutsches Zentralarchiv, Potsdam.

16. Information provided by the Rijksinstituut, Amsterdam.

17. The giving and receiving of presents became part of the Renaissance ritual of Goering's life. He received far more than he gave, but he was not ungenerous in providing innumerable presents for his staff on such formal occasions as Christmas. Hundreds of presents were packed and sent out, and many more were given personally at the gatherings assembled at Carinhall to exchange good wishes with the Reich Marshal and his wife. Vanity as much as goodwill prompted these attentions; silver pencils, for example, would be given out, or even, as a special favor, a fine gun for a sportsman. But once Christmas was over, January would become the season for receiving gifts, and those who wanted to keep his favor sent him the expensive birthday presents which they had either discovered or been told that he wanted. Hundreds of presents arrived, some of great value, making each year sub-

stantial additions to Goering's collection of art. Examples were a Dutch river landscape by Salomon van Ruysdael given by Dr. Friedrich Frick, an industrialist, and valued at 80,000 marks; a sixteenth-century French tapestry given by Dr. Planck of Cologne and valued at 45,000 marks; a winter landscape by Jan van Goyen presented by Alois Miedl, an art dealer who had handled many works for Goering but gave him this painting, valued at 80,000 marks. A case which particularly angered Goebbels in the midst of his personal campaign for total war was the request for advice from the mayor of Berlin in January 1944 as to what the city should give Goering that year; in previous years, according to Semmler's record of Goebbels' angry comments, Goering's adjutant would telephone the city authorities early in the month and advise on the right present to buy for Goering—perhaps a Vandyke costing 250,000 marks. Goebbels felt that 25,000 marks was more correct, but it is interesting to note that even he accepted the fact that the city should give Goering a present of some sort. The records in fact show that in 1942 the city gave Goering a painting by Tintoretto valued at 220,000 marks, but that in 1944 the authorities took Goebbels' advice and gave him a painting of the school of Antonio Moro valued at only 25,000 marks.

18. Gisela Limberger told H.F. that Goering once took her to Paris so that she could see for herself the origin of the works that caused her so much labor.

19. See Janet Flanner, *Men and Monuments*, p. 243.

20. According to Louis P. Lochner (*The Goebbels Diaries*, p. 197) the Americans found some 25,000 bottles of champagne in Goering's Alpine chalet.

CHAPTER 9

In addition to the principal sources, information for this chapter was taken from Professor Trevor-Roper's *The Last Days of Hitler*; Karl Koller's *Der Letzte Monat*; Asher Lee's *The German Air Force*; Adolf Galland's *The First and the Last*; Milton Shulman's *Defeat in the West*; *The Goebbels Diaries*; and Felix Gilbert's *Hitler Directs His War*. Of exceptional value have been the personal recollections of Bernd von Brauchitsch, who accompanied Goering south after he parted from Hitler. Of importance also are the accounts given us by Frau Goering, Karl Bodenschatz, Adolf Galland, Erhard Milch and Robert Kropp.

1. See Gilbert, *Hitler Directs His War*, pp. 40, 44.

2. See Frischauer, *Goering*, pp. 246–47. The authority of Kropp and Koller is given for the statement that Goering was deeply depressed at this time and resorting to drugs. Frischauer's authority for the conversation between Goering and Jeschonnek before the suicide is given as "a close friend."

3. Schellenberg, *op. cit.*, p. 301.

4. See Chapter 6, note 27, and Semmler, *Goebbels*, p. 97.

5. See I.M.T., XVII, p. 58.

6. The initial fault for this incident in fact lay with Messerschmitt himself, who had responded to what he thought was an idle question by Hitler as to whether this new plane could carry a bomb. Messerschmitt without sufficient thought had said, "Yes, my Führer," whereupon Hitler affirmed that the plane was to be regarded primarily as a bomber. Goering was at first as upset by this decision as the others in the Luftwaffe, but he lacked the authority to assert this point of view with Hitler, who, tired of advice that went against his wishes, forbade anyone to mention the subject again in his presence. This decision shortened the war by a considerable period.

7. See Butler and Young, *Marshal without Glory*, pp. 233–34.

8. Milch in conversation with H.F.

9. See Galland, *op. cit.*, p. 262. The previous month Goering had recommended the increased allocation of prisoners of war to the armament works. See I.M.T., VIII, p. 287.

10. See I.M.T., IX, pp. 144–45 and 283 *et seq.*

11. See Reitlinger, *SS*, p. 334 and note.

12. Fifteen trucks took Goering's property from Rominten in October when it was threatened by the Russian advance. See Frischauer, *Goering*, p. 255.

13. See Shulman, *op. cit.*, p. 259. Goering's statement was made during interrogation.

14. See Gilbert, *Hitler Directs His War*, p. 111 *et seq.*

15. Accounts of the evacuation of Carinhall were given H.F. by Frau Emmy Goering, Bernd von Brauchitsch and Willy Schade. Brauchitsch last saw Carinhall on April 19. Rose Valland told H.F. that she went to Carinhall later, as soon as she could gain entry to Germany. She found the place in ruins, including the mausoleum. Here she found a skull among the rubble. It could only have been Carin's. "I dropped it and, being a Christian, offered a prayer to *le bon Dieu!*" she said.

16. See *The Bormann Letters*, pp. 112, 131, 146–47, 191. The remark made by Bormann to Lammers, which follows, is quoted by Trevor-Roper in *The Last Days of Hitler*, p. 100.

17. See Boldt, *In the Shelter with Hitler*, p. 27.

18. Galland in conversation with H.F.

19. Brauchitsch remembers well the lengthy discussion over the text of this message to Hitler. Goering was deeply worried. The final sentence was drafted by Goering himself to make the message seem more human and voice concern for Hitler, but its exact meaning was never very clear.

20. See Trevor-Roper, *The Last Days of Hitler*, p. 151 *et seq.* Also I.M.T., XVII, p. 57, and Frischauer, *Goering*, p. 265.

21. See Shirer, *End of a Berlin Diary*, p. 158, and *The Last Days of Hitler*, p. 164.

22. The famous raid on Bercht-

esgaden by the R.A.F. occurred at about 9 A.M. Hitler's Berghof was destroyed. The S.S. barracks were severely damaged. A bomb fell close to Goering's chalet, and a section of the structure caved in. The air-raid shelter could not contain everyone who crowded into it, and captors and captives (all suffering from various degrees of shock) moved into the safer *Stollen*, or mine shaft, in the mountain. Bernd von Brauchitsch has vivid memories of this period.

23. Brauchitsch told H.F. that everything was disorganized at this time and the morale of the S.S. guards was low. According to Kropp, Goering, together with his family and members of his staff, was taken to Mauterndorf three days after the air raid, traveling in a convoy of cars overnight. Kropp writes: "We could move around freely in Mauterndorf castle as well as in the courtyard. Goering treated the two commanding S.S. officers as if they were his guests; they attended his dinner table even though their orders were to shoot Goering, his family and his entire entourage as soon as Berlin fell into enemy hands. In Mauterndorf Goering was certainly not short of codein pills. He could take as many as he wished."

24. See Shulman, *op. cit.*, p. 296.

25. See Butler and Young, *op. cit.*, p. 259.

26. Brauchitsch was present at this lunch, which he reports to have been a good meal suitable for an officers' mess. The atmosphere was not without a certain excitement and relief after the long journeys they had all undertaken in bad road conditions. From the point of view of the Americans, to have captured Goering was a notable triumph. From Goering's point of view the meeting seemed the first step toward a new phase of prestige, since he would negotiate an honorable surrender. The lunch therefore had something of the air of a celebration in beautiful surroundings in the spring.

27. Goering was in Augsburg nearly a fortnight. Apart from interrogations, he and his companions had nothing to do but think, and the inactivity depressed Goering, who brooded in his room. The Americans undertook to protect his family. Brauchitsch recalls sharing with Kropp the task of destroying part of the enormous quantity of paracodeine tablets that Goering had brought with him. They flushed large numbers down the lavatory pan, since it did not seem right for the Americans to discover him in possession of so many thousands of these pills. Nevertheless, Goering retained a substantial reserve in his toilet case.

CHAPTER 10

The principal sources for this chapter, in addition to the official record of the trial itself, are the studies made of Goering by the American prison psychiatrists, Dr. Douglas M. Kelley and Dr. G. M. Gilbert, in their publications 22 *Cells in Nuremberg* (by Kelley) and *Hermann Goering, Amiable Psychopath* and *Nuremberg Diary* (by Gilbert); since the entries in *Nuremberg Diary* are dated, we have not given page references for our quotations in the text. The late Lord Birkett's notes on the behavior of Goering in the courtroom were kindly given to us by him shortly before his death. Other personal accounts relating to the period have been obtained from Frau Emmy Goering, Robert Kropp, Papen and Schwerin von Krosigk.

1. See Kirkpatrick, *The Inner Circle*, pp. 194–96.

2. Quoted in Kelley, *22 Cells in Nuremberg*, p. 62.

3. Confirmed by Papen to H.F.

4. The mystery of how Goering obtained the cyanide capsule with which he poisoned himself remains unsolved. Papen claims (*Memoirs*, p. 551) that on two occasions American guards offered him means of killing himself, one so insistently that Papen had to report him to the officer in charge. Milch claimed that it was not difficult to conceal the capsules that all the principal Nazis, including himself, carried in case of need, and he discounts completely the claims of Bach-Zelewski that it was he who smuggled the capsule to Goering in his cell; Goering had no regard whatsoever for this man. However, Frau Goering believes he did not have the capsule at the time of her last interviews with him a fortnight and then three days before his death. On both occasions she murmured a "Have you got––?," using a key word they both understood, and he shook his head. She believes that he finally obtained what he wanted from one of the guards. According to Frischauer, the small metal container found beside him was exactly similar to that found wedged in a cavity of Himmler's gums; Himmler had committed suicide in captivity after being stripped and searched. The official explanation given to the press by Major Frederick Teich, the prison operations officer, was that Goering had kept the capsule with him throughout his imprisonment and concealed it inside the rim of his lavatory in the cell; Teich discounted completely the theory that before captivity Goering had undergone a special operation which enabled him to hide the capsule in his flesh near the scar of his war wound, which, after his death, was found to have reopened.

INDEX

Beaumont, Captain Frank, 37
Bechstein, Carl, 73
Beck, Józef, 206
Beck, General Ludwig, 194, 196
Belgium, 209, 235, 240, 242, 305
Belgrade, Yugoslavia, 254
Below, Colonel von, 316, 317,
    321
Beneš, Eduard, 196, 198, 199,
    201
Berchtesgaden, 50, 117, 149,
    161, 164, 197, 216, 217,
    247, 276, 292, 293, 310,
    313, 320, 323
Berghof, the, 251
Berlin, Germany, 65, 278, 299,
    304, 311, 313, 315, 317,
    321, 322
Berliner Arbeiterzeitung, 70
Berlin Folklore Museum, 112
Berlin Sports Stadium, 79
Bessarabia, 250
Birkett, Sir Norman (Lord Birk-
    ett), 363–65, 391
Bismarck, Prince Otto von, 21,
    109
Black Front, the, 70
Black Reichswehr, 51
Bled, Yugoslavia, 154
Blitzkrieg, the, 229–30, 240,
    242–45, 248–50
Blomberg, Erna Grühn, 166,
    169
Blomberg, General Werner von,
    89, 91, 95, 124, 129, 147,
    155, 162, 166–67, 168,
    169, 348, 380, 381
Blood-Ryan, 116–17
Bock, Field Marshal Fedor von,
    252
Bodelschwingh, Friedrich von,
    138

Bodenschatz, General Karl, 33,
    34, 35, 117, 132, 201,
    211, 214, 216, 222, 227,
    232, 269, 275, 277, 288,
    299–300, 303, 344
Boris, King, of Bulgaria, 203
Bormann, Martin, 275, 276,
    278, 279, 310, 311, 313,
    314, 315, 316, 317, 318,
    320, 322, 323, 362, 378
Bose, Herbert von, 133
Bouhler, Philipp, 315, 316, 326
Brandt, Colonel, 303, 328
Bratwurstglöckle tavern, Mu-
    nich, 50–54
Brauchitsch, General Bernd von,
    302, 313, 314, 318, 319,
    326, 327, 346
Brauchitsch, General Walther
    von, 168, 192, 194, 229,
    231, 285
Braun, Eva, 317, 321
Braun, Count Wernher von, 306
Brause, Standartenführer, 322,
    323
Bredow, General Kurt von, 133,
    318
Brenner Pass, 144, 152, 172
Britain, Battle of, 248–50, 251–
    52, 329
Britain and the British, 188, 202,
    206, 207, 217, 218, 220–
    21, 222, 223, 226, 227,
    233, 234, 236, 240, 245,
    246, 247, 251, 252, 253,
    254, 257, 260, 263, 294,
    297, 303, 306, 309, 316,
    317, 329, 331, 332, 335
British Air Force, 34; *see also*
    Royal Air Force
*Brown Book of the Hitler Ter-
    ror,* 103, 395